Sewing Manual: Skirts *and* Trousers

From the PATTERN *to the* FINISHED GARMENT

PROMOPRESS[11]

CONTENTS

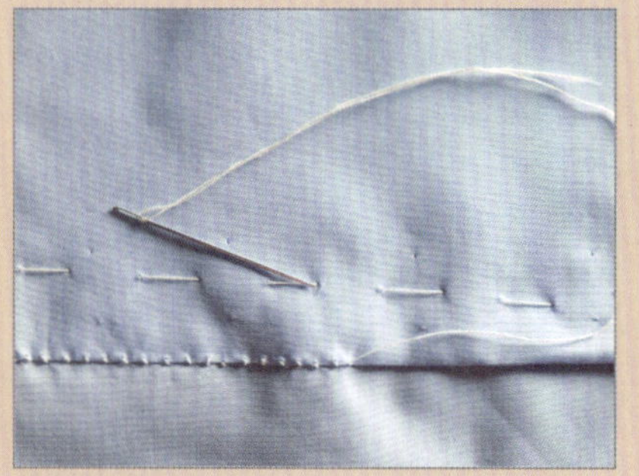

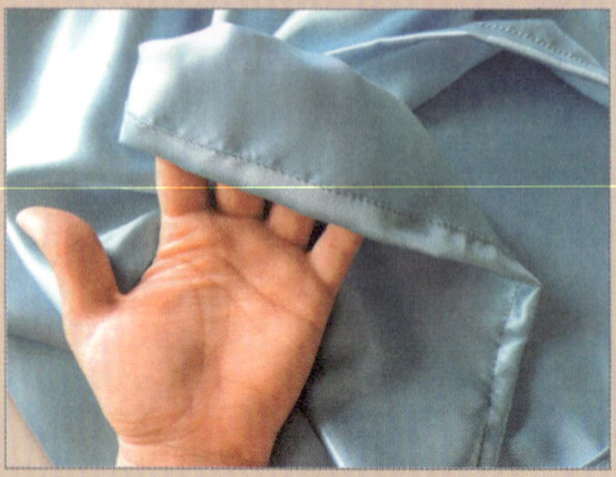

Sewing Manual: Skirts *and* Trousers

Hoaki Books, S.L.
C/ Ausiàs March, 128
08013 Barcelona, Spain
T. 0034 935 952 283
F. 0034 932 654 883
info@hoaki.com
www.hoaki.com

hoaki_books

All the photos in the book are by the author

Sewing Manual: Skirts and Trousers
From the Pattern to the Finished Garment

ISBN: 978-84-17412-81-4

Original title: *Gonne e pantaloni - Dal Cartamodello alla realizzazione pratica*

Author: Anna De Leo
English translation: Emma Sayers
Layout: Wendy Moreira
Editing: Martina Panarello
Cover design: spread

D.L.: B 19803-2020
Printed in China

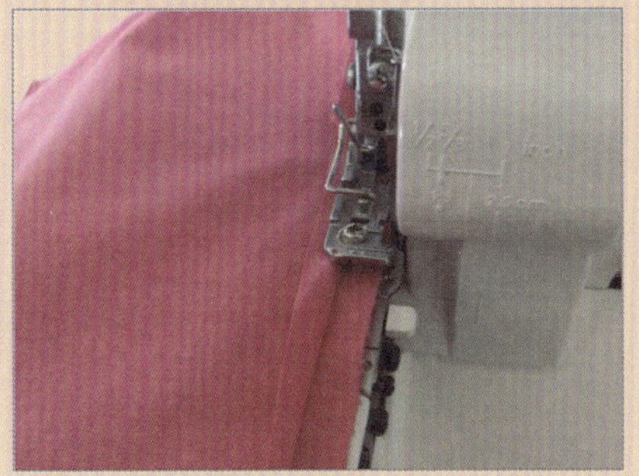

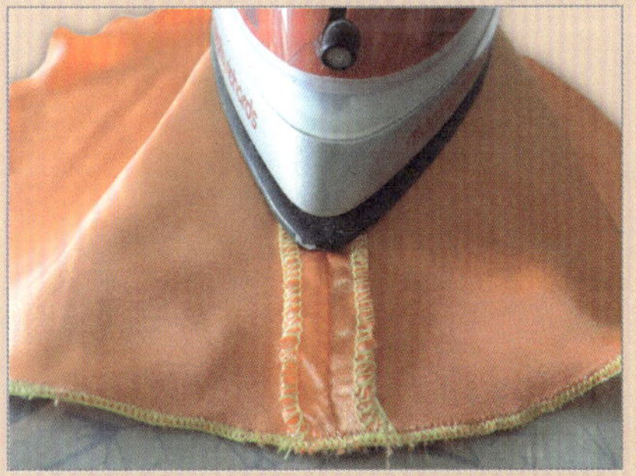

Anna De Leo was born in Cosenza in 1987. In 2014, she was awarded the title of "Dressmaker" for women's fashions, at a branch of the Euromode School Italia, in Bormio in the Valtellina valley. In 2015, she moved to Udine, where she attended the dressmaking course at the IRES (Institute of Economic and Social Research Friuli Venezia Giulia).

Later, she enrolled in the Fashion Design course at the Milan Fashion Campus in Milan and in an online course to become a Personal Shopper and Image Consultant. From 2015 to 2017, she worked for various tailors, refining the knowledge and skills that would allow her to turn her hand to making clothes and studying new design techniques. In 2017, she attended a course at the Udine Chamber of Commerce to become an entrepreneur. She was determined to set up her own company, but the unexpected success of her self-published book convinced her to combine her two great passions: writing and her love of fashion.

INTRODUCTION

I bet you have been keeping a dream locked away in a drawer for a long time: the dream of learning how to sew, to design a skirt, a pair of trousers, a dress, all by yourself, exactly as you imagine them, exactly as you want them. You probably find yourself looking at fabrics, thinking about how you could transform them into something unique, tailored to you, to your style. But the amount of time we are able to set aside to explore our aspirations is often short and it is not always easy to find the right opportunity to get started: worthwhile sewing courses and comprehensive online information are scarce. So the desire remains an idea of unexpressed creativity.

It may seem strange to you but, writing the pages of this book really made me think about you, because I too have kept my passion locked away in a drawer for a long time. When I left "a steady job" seven years ago and made the move to a less comfortable place, it was because I wanted to experience a new life that would finally bring my true aspirations to the fore. I knew that in order to realise my dream, I had to go back to school and begin a demanding journey, but the desire to learn has always been stronger in me than lethargy. I remember that, as I made the 140 km trip every day to the professional institute where I was studying, I thought only of the joy I would feel on entering the laboratory. But maintaining a high level of enthusiasm was not always easy, so I decided to dedicate this book to all the people out there who, just like me, feel a strong desire to follow their passion for sewing. With each chapter, I want to lead you into a special world, where you are alone with just a piece of fabric and your imagination. I will be there to guide you step by step, whenever you want to read me, whenever you feel inspired, whenever you want to escape while staying put, perhaps sitting on your sofa.

In this book, I will help you to draw patterns and create the simplest and most common skirt and trouser designs; it's a real one-theme course that you can follow with ease from home, starting from scratch. And don't worry if you've never even held a needle between your fingers before. I'll start by explaining the most common hand stitches, and guide you right up to using the sewing machine. Now that I have told you my story and we have got to know each other a little better, now that you have the right energy, the right inspiration... let's begin this journey together! I wish you the best of luck in achieving everything you want!

Anna

WHAT WE NEED TO MAKE A START

To start, you will need the following equipment (some of these items can be found in a haberdashery store):

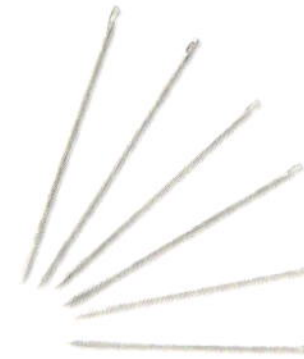

NEEDLES

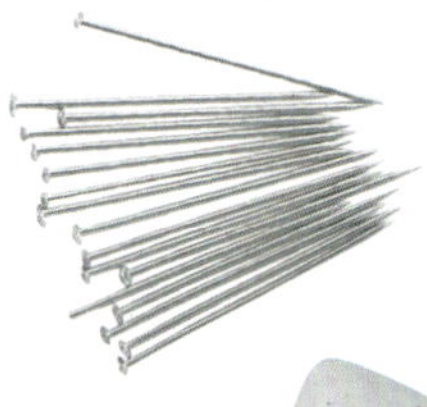

PINS

REELS OF THREAD IN VARIOUS COLOURS

DRESSMAKING CHALK

TAILOR'S TAPE MEASURE

THIMBLE

TACKING THREAD

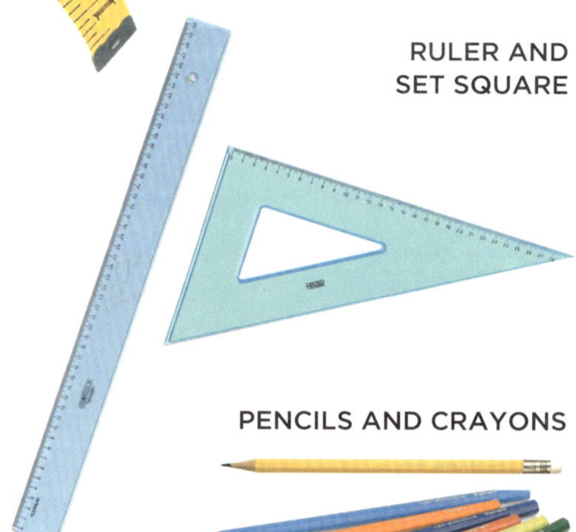

RULER AND SET SQUARE

IRONING BOARD AND IRON

PENCILS AND CRAYONS

SEWING MACHINE

SEWING SCISSORS

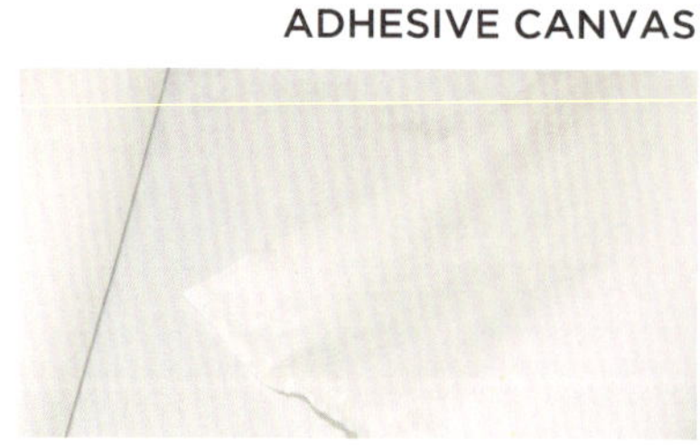

ADHESIVE CANVAS

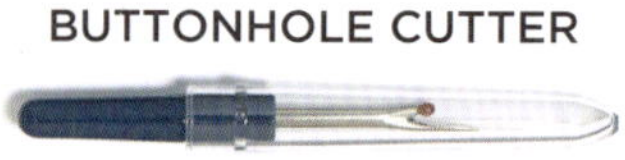

BUTTONHOLE CUTTER

SEWING BY HAND

To begin this journey, you have to know the main hand stitches and learn how to do them correctly. Before you start sewing by hand, make sure you are wearing a thimble. This is a protective device that will prevent you from hurting yourself and is used to push the needle through the fabric. It usually fits on the middle finger, but you can wear it on whichever finger seems best for you.

TACKING STITCHES

Tacking stitches are long and loose linear stitches that are easy to remove, and serve to join two pieces of fabric together before you sew them together with the machine. Special tacking thread is often used, but you can also use normal thread on particularly delicate fabrics. Tacking stitches are normally used to hold together parts that are difficult to stitch, so that the fabric does not slip under the machine and you get a perfect result. They are also used to assemble pieces of a tailored suit for the first fitting. For example, they are often used to sew a sleeve onto an armhole, or onto very stretchy fabrics, since it would be impossible to get the best result if only the sewing machine was used. To do this, thread the tacking thread through a medium-sized needle, then take two pieces of fabric to do a test, putting them on top of each other (1). Use the needle to pierce the right side of the fabric, pass it through to the wrong side, then pull it through to the right side at about 1 cm (0.39") away and repeat the action (2).

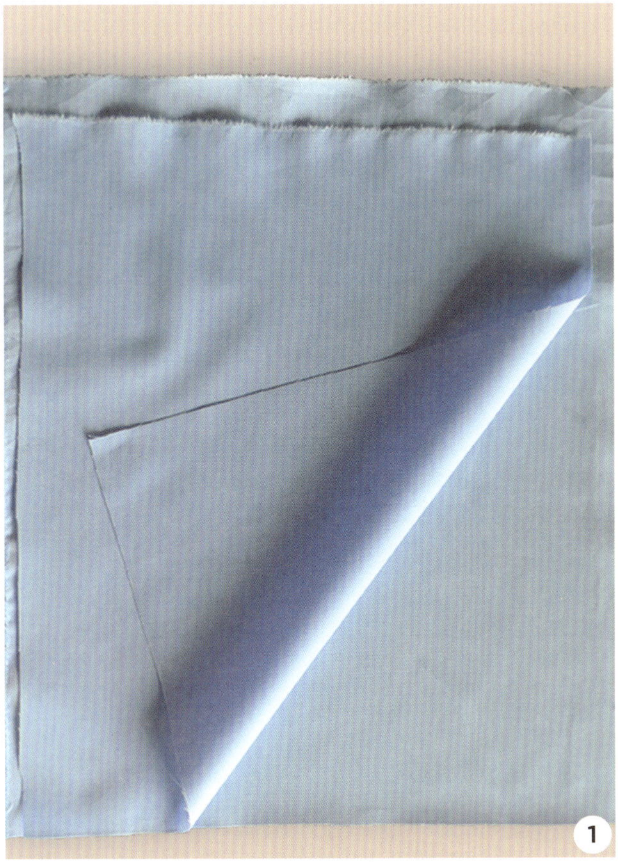

"LOOSE" OR GUIDE STITCHES

Also called "marks", these are "loose" stitches, as the name implies, which serve to leave marks on the fabric, but are otherwise invisible. In tailoring, they can be used to mark the seam allowances on the pieces of a garment that you are working on.

Do the same as you did for the tacking stitches, but thread the stitches very slowly (1), without pulling. Once you have completed the section to be marked, open out the two layers of fabric (2 - 3) and cut the stitches open (4), leaving a mark on both sides.

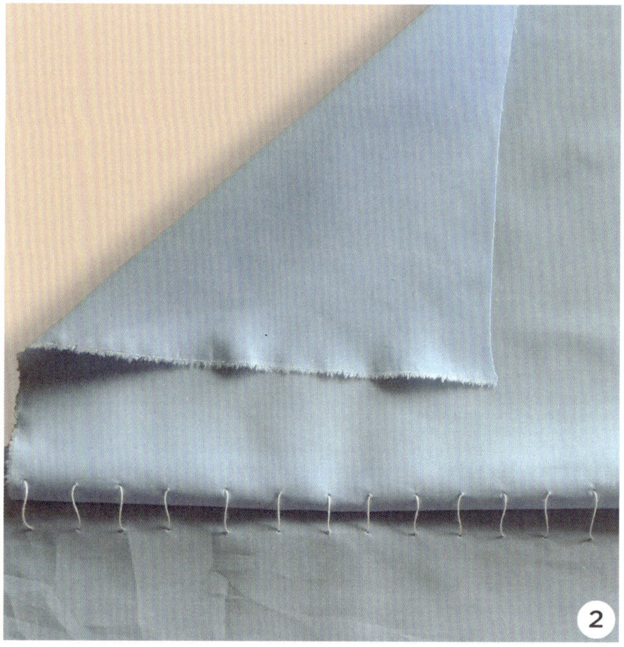

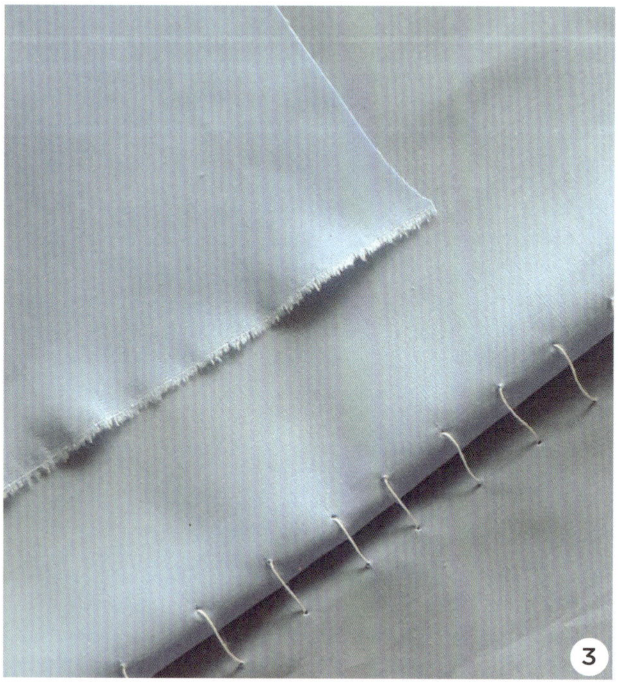

UNDERSTITCH

This is a type of loose stitch that is invisible on the front of the fabric. It is commonly used to make invisible hems on trousers or skirts. To do a test, take two pieces of fabric and place them one on top of the other (1); fold a border of about 2 cm (0.78") on the fabric that will be placed on top: it will be facing the fabric positioned below. Hold the two layers of fabric together with a tacking stitch. Sew from right to left, with a larger stitch on the fabric below and a micro stitch on the fold line of the border of the fabric positioned above (2); this stitch must be so small and delicate that it cannot be seen on the right side of the fabric. This should result in a triangle-shaped stitch of about 1 cm (0.39") (3).

INVISIBLE STITCH

As the name describes, this is a type of stitch that cannot be seen: the result is therefore imperceptible on both the wrong and right side of the fabric. This stitch is commonly used to attach a lining, but can also be used for other tasks; in any case, it should not be visible. To do a test, place two pieces of fabric one on top of the other, just like you did for the understitch. Sew from right to left, threading a micro-stitch on the fabric positioned below to a micro-stitch on the fold line along the border of the fabric positioned above (1); the stitches must be close together and very small (2). Use yarn that is the same colour as the fabric. Here, it is shown in a contrasting colour, so you can understand the process better.

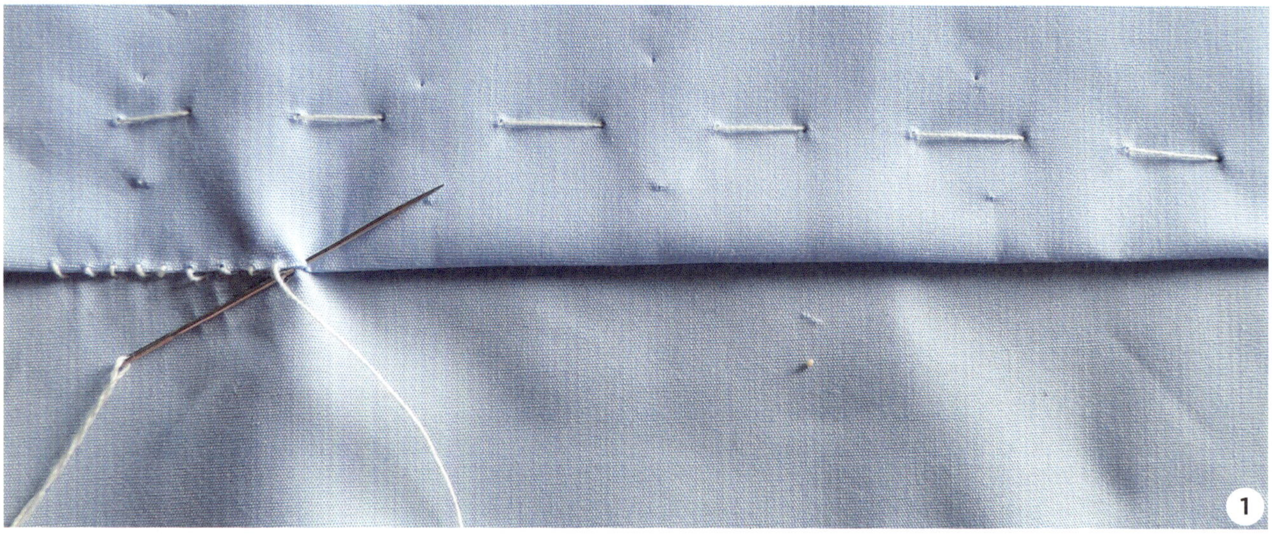

1

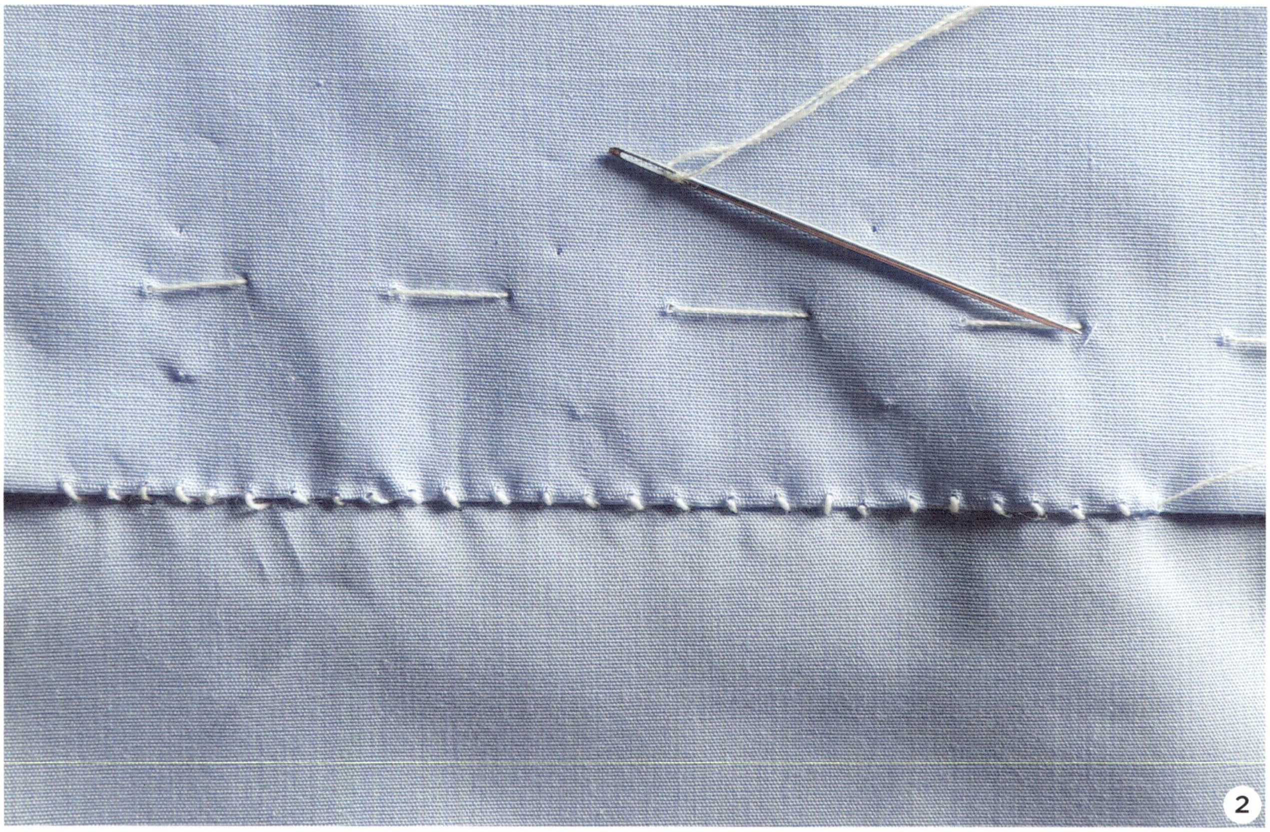

2

BACKSTITCH

The backstitch is similar to the classic linear stitch made by most sewing machines. It can be defined as an aesthetic, finishing or flat fell seam, which is meant to be visible on the garment. In tailoring, it can be used to sew patches onto sleeves or trousers by hand. To do a test, put two pieces of fabric one on top of the other, as you did previously for the other hand stitches. Do the same as you did for the tacking stitch, but once the needle has emerged on the right side of the fabric, thread it back to the same point from where it started, so that it goes back on itself, as the name suggests. Thread the needle through to the right side of the fabric again by jumping the space of two stitches and then go back again.

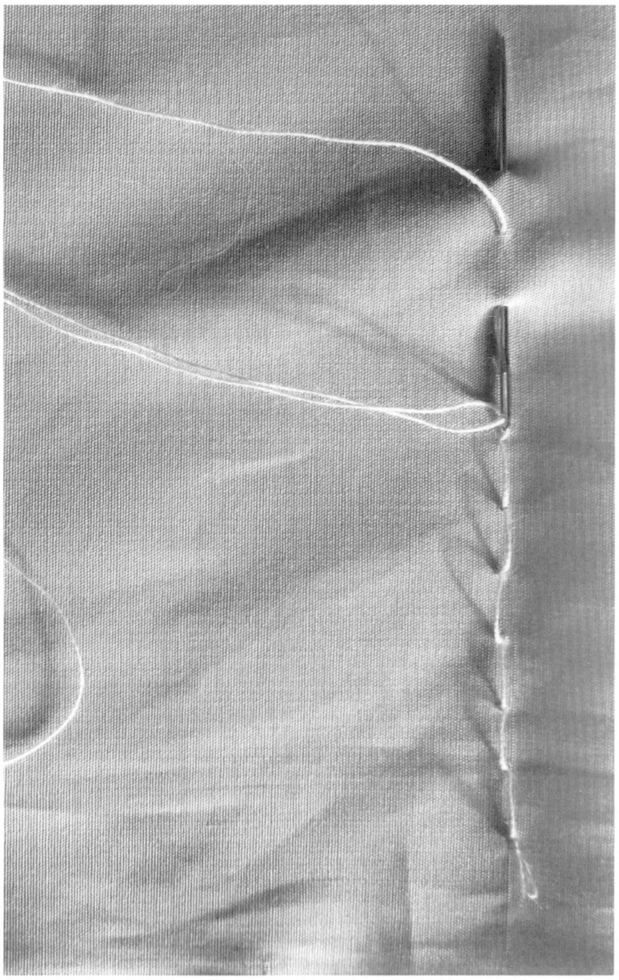

HALF BACK STITCH

The half back stitch is similar to the back stitch, in that it is also an aesthetic stitch that is sewn by hand to make a finishing or flat fell seam. In tailoring, it can be used to sew zips onto garments by hand. The half back stitch is done in the same way as the back stitch, except that the needle does not go back to the same point from where it initially started, but just goes back by half a stitch.

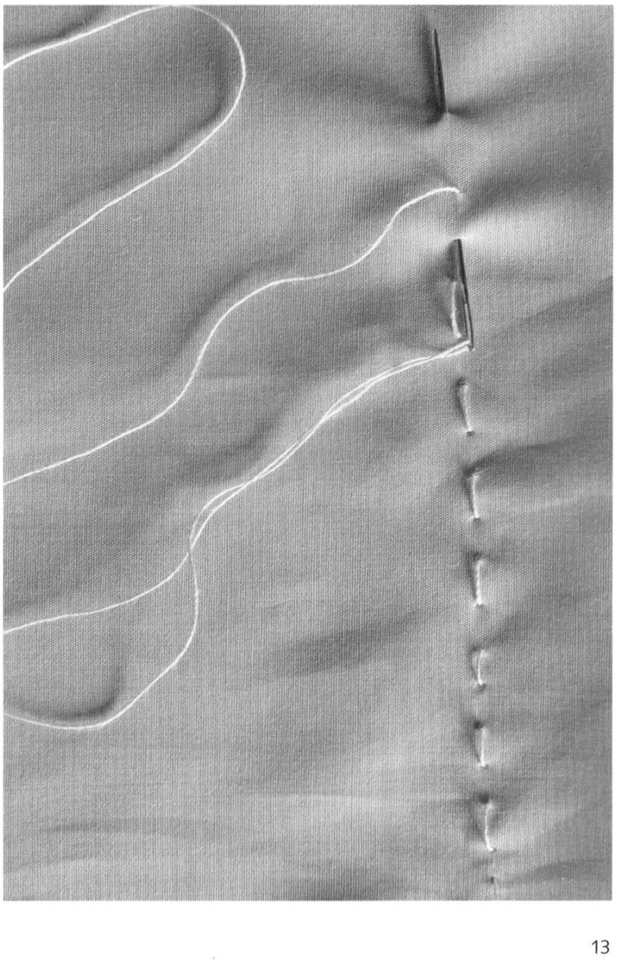

NEEDLES AND THREADS

The needle is the most important thing in sewing. The first known needles were made of bone or wood; in antiquity they were made of bronze, while modern ones are made of steel. They can be divided into needles for sewing by hand and needles for sewing on a machine. All needles, with their various characteristics related to their use, have some things in common, such as the eye (where the yarn is threaded through) and the point, (which serves to pierce the fabric or material for which the needle is being used). Each needle is categorised by what it will be used for, its size and the type of point it has. Universal needles can be used for most fabrics; for jersey or elasticated fabrics, stretch needles are used instead. There are also special needles for leather and denim. To avoid damaging the fabric, it is essential that you choose the right kind of needle. In addition to the right needle for a given fabric, it is equally important to choose the right size. In general, very thin needles are used for lightweight, delicate fabrics and medium-sized needles are used for medium-weight fabrics, while very thick needles are used for heavy and thick fabrics. Their size is ordered by specific numbers: for example, needles for sewing machines are categorised by a scale that ranges from 60 to 110, where 60 is the thinnest and 110 is the thickest. The same goes for hand sewing needles: they are categorised by a scale from 1 to 12, where number 1 is the thickest and number 12 is the thinnest. Once you have the right needles, choosing the right yarn is the second most important thing in sewing. There are many types of yarn and they differ according to their use, colour and thickness.

First of all, yarns are divided into natural and synthetic: among the natural ones are cotton, silk and wool threads. Cotton thread is the most commonly used for simple sewing, but it does not excel in elasticity: this limits its use, as it may easily break with some of the stretchier kinds of fabrics. Silk thread is

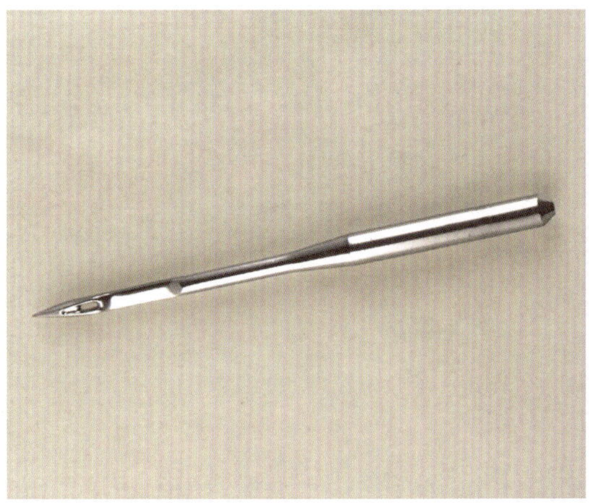

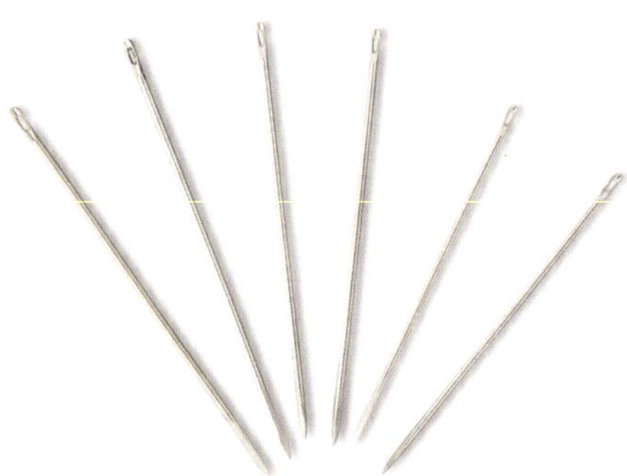

Above left: universal needles, sized 70 to 100.
Above centre: stretch needles, size 75.

Top right: sewing machine needle.
Right: hand sewing needles.

Yarns of various colours.

Polyester thread, thickness 50.

used in embroidery, but it is also sometimes used in tailoring when making buttonholes by hand. In tailoring, polyester thread is one of the most commonly used - and most appropriate - yarns for making repairs: this synthetic thread is known for its considerable elasticity and strength, which guarantees excellent final results.

Choosing the right yarn for your sewing project is very important: it is essential that you choose good quality products, think about the right thickness and select the colour that exactly matches the garment or fabric you are going to be working on. I find that the ideal thread is made of polyester, thickness: 50.

THE SEWING MACHINE

The sewing machine is used for joining fabrics or leathers together, by means of a seam. This is made possible by the up-and-down oscillation of a special needle, thereby threading one or more yarns back and forth through the materials that are being joined together. The invention patents of the very first sewing machines date back to the late 1700s and early 1800s. Despite multiple attempts to make this particular machine work perfectly, only Isaac Merrit Singer succeeded in the venture in 1851, patenting his first sewing machine, which would later achieve iconic status in history. The first sewing machines were operated by hand, using a special crank. With their right hand, tailors would action the movement of the needle and the bobbin, pulling the fabric through; their left hand would control the position and direction of the fabric.

Later on, sewing machines were operated with a treadle: connected by a belt, underneath the table on which the machine was affixed, the treadle would be pushed with the foot to achieve movement; both hands were therefore free to move the fabric around

as desired. Today, the movement is produced by an electric motor: the command to operate the sewing machine is given by a pedal that is pushed with the foot.

There are various types of sewing machines currently available on the market, from mechanical to electronic, from standard to industrial and of various price ranges.

If you are a beginner who is approaching the world of sewing for the first time, I recommend that you spend a very modest amount on your sewing machine. I myself started with a machine that cost €100, because this is more than enough to spend when learning how to sew, whether it is for a simple hobby or an introduction to your dream job.

INEXPENSIVE FAMILY SEWING MACHINE

It is important to learn about the sewing machine before starting to use it. All models are made in more or less the same way: that is, they have a space to insert the spool of thread at the top and a space to insert the spool of thread at the bottom.

Although the various machines on the market seem similar, in reality each one has its own peculiarities, so I advise you to read the instruction manual carefully before using it.

Below, I give a simple explanation of its various parts and how to start using it; I refer to an inexpensive mechanical machine, because it is simpler to understand and affordable for everyone.

This is an electric sewing machine that is plugged in to the power supply. Usually, the cable for the pedal that activates the machine with pressure from the foot is also connected by the same power cable.

An expensive sewing machine will have lots of functions, but with this one we can clearly see the ones that are essential for learning how to sew.

1. Connect the power cord and pedal to the sewing machine.
2. Connect the power cord to an electrical outlet.
3. Switch on the sewing machine, using the appropriate button.
4. Take an empty bobbin and place it in the space provided.
5. Put the bobbin in the space provided and thread the yarn along the indicated pathway, so that you will be able to wrap the yarn around the bobbin.
6. Apply pressure to the pedal with your foot, so that the bobbin collects the yarn and wraps it around itself, and stop when it has enough.
7. To be able to start sewing, remove the bobbin and place it in the space under the needle.

8. "Thread the machine", that is, pass the yarn on the bobbin along the appropriate pathway, as indicated on the machine itself or as illustrated in the instruction manual.
9. Use the appropriate wheel to adjust the stitch length (stitch #3 is commonly used, with shorter stitches being used on lightweight fabrics; the heavier the fabric, the longer the stitches).
10. Use the appropriate wheels to adjust the thread tension and vary the amount of pressure on the foot pedal, according to what sort of fabric you are using. This can vary from machine to machine, so it is best to consult the instruction manual first.

THE FEET

Each sewing machine is equipped with feet, which are suitable for different seams and different uses; the ones used throughout this manual are the standard presser foot for linear seams, the zipper foot and the invisible zipper foot. The feet can be different for each type of sewing machine.

MAIN PARTS OF THE SEWING MACHINE

1. Tension selector switch
2. Tension lever
3. Thread cutter
4. Foot
5. Needle plate
6. Free arm / accessory compartment
7. Reverse lever
8. Spool cap
9. Stitch length selector
10. Stitch selector
11. Horizontal spool pin and spool cap
12. Bobbin tension stud
13. Second spool pin housing
14. Hand wheel
15. Switch for the motor and light
16. Plug housing
17. Bobbin thread guide
18. Upper thread guide
19. Front cover
20. Handle
21. Foot lifter
22. Rheostat
23. Power cable
24. Standard foot
25. Zipper foot
26. Buttonhole foot
27. Button foot
28. Bobbins
29. Allen key
30. Quilt / seam guide
31. Buttonhole cutter/brush
32. Oil
33. Needles
34. Jaw cover plate
35. Spool cap

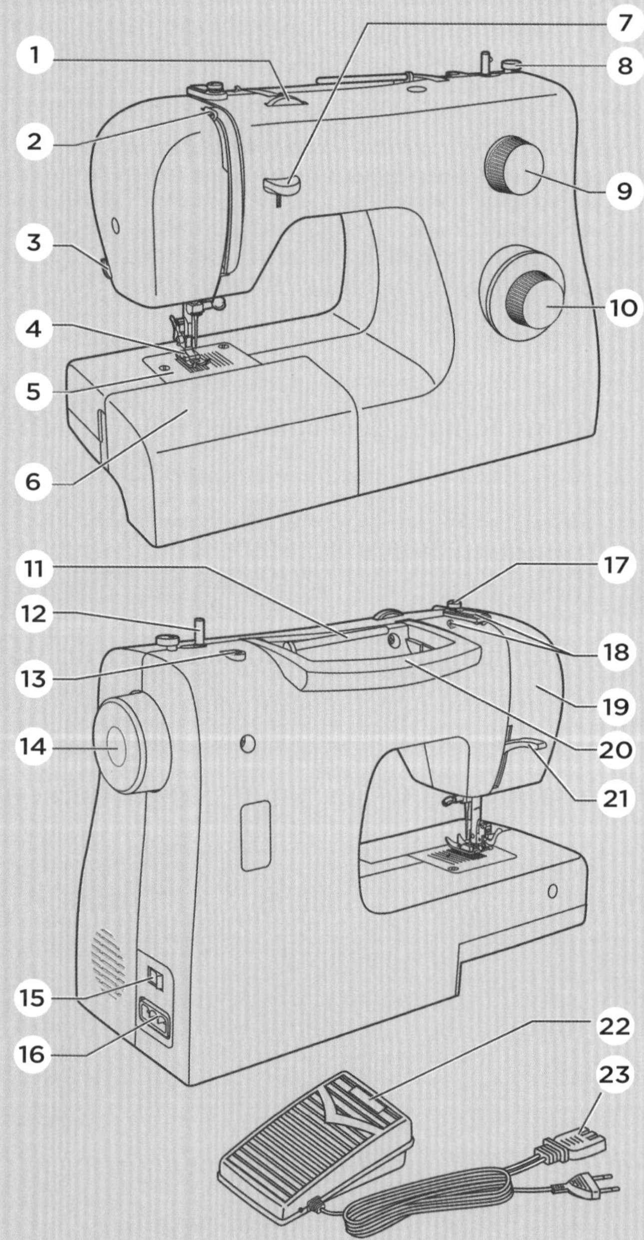

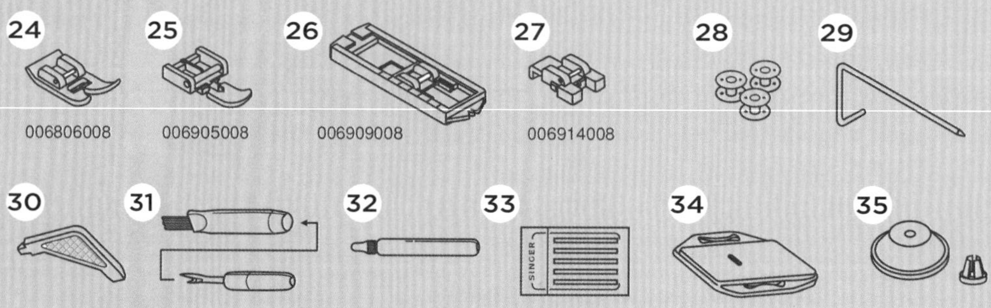

EXAMPLES OF FEET

For a straight stitch

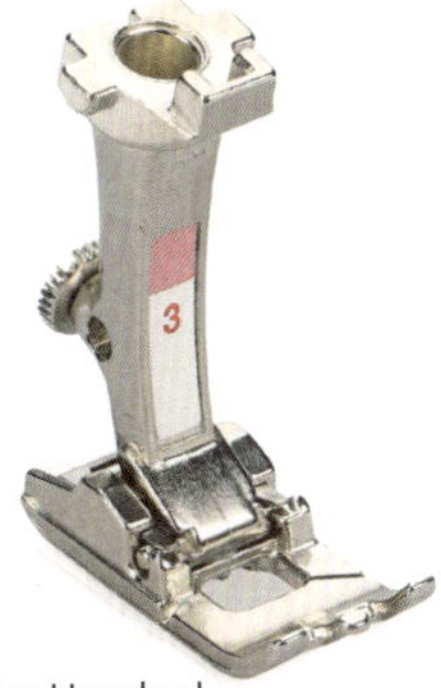

For buttonholes

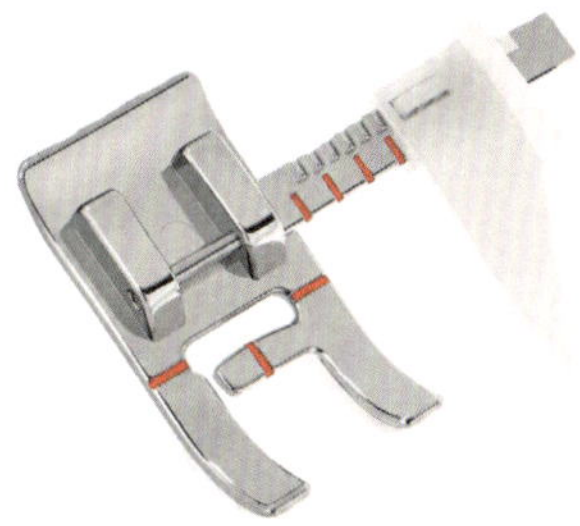
With adjustable guide

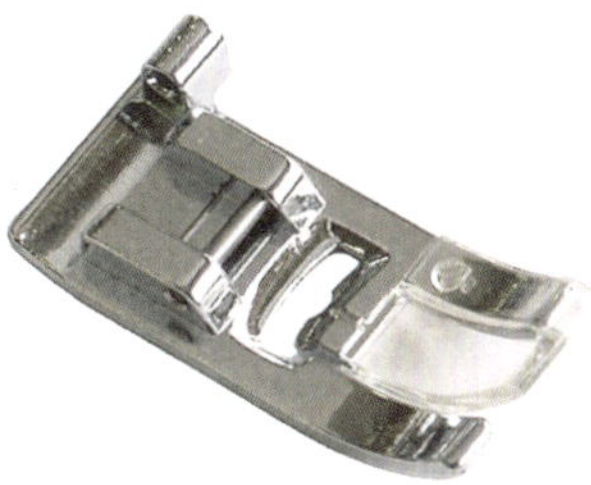
For zig-zags

Compensating foot

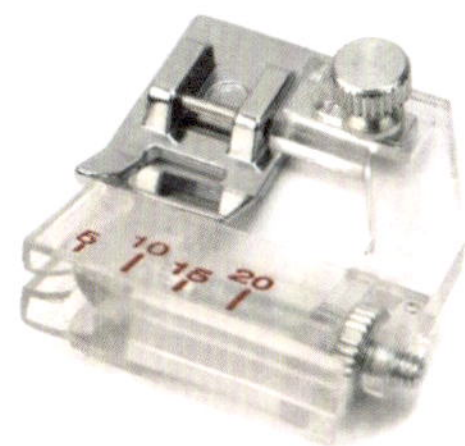

Adjustable trimmer

For a rolled hem

Curler

For invisible zips

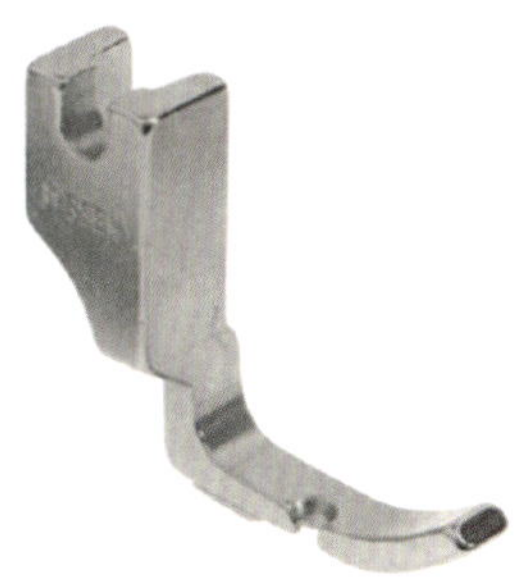
For zips

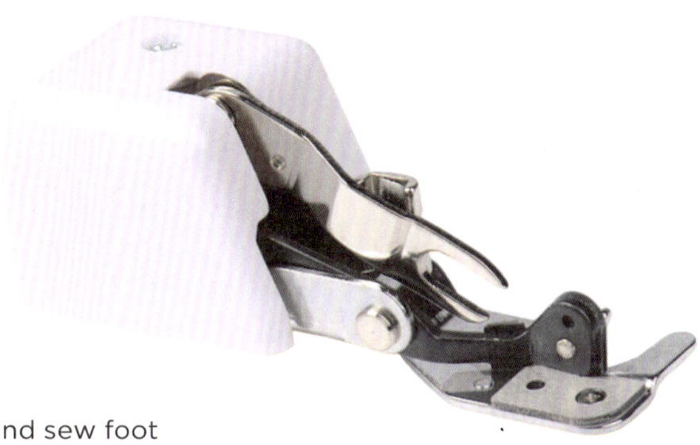
Cut and sew foot

MACHINE STITCHES

LINEAR STITCH AND ZIG-ZAG STITCH

The two stitches that we will use here are the "linear" stitch - the classic straight stitch that is used to join fabric together - and the "zig-zag" finishing stitch that stops the fabric from fraying. In mechanical machines, the type of stitch is regulated by a knob, where each type of stitch is labelled with a number (for example: 1. linear stitch, 2. zig-zag stitch). When you first start to use the sewing machine, I suggest you take a piece of fabric - preferably of medium thickness and in a light-coloured cotton - and sew the stitches in a contrasting colour, so you will be able to see them more easily. On a piece of fabric, draw straight lines, oblique lines and circles with a pencil, using a ruler to help you. Slip this piece of fabric under the machine foot and try to sew exactly

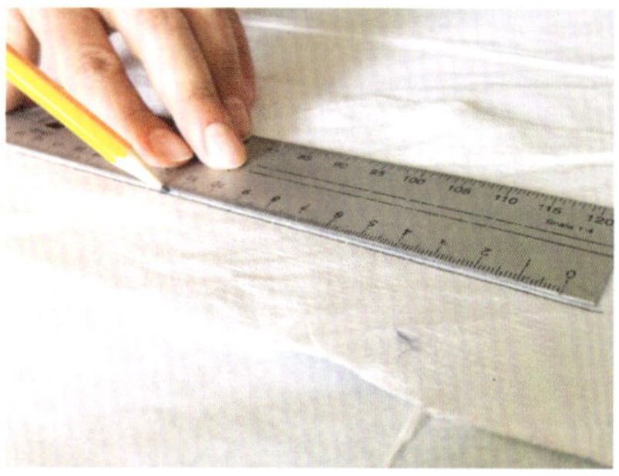

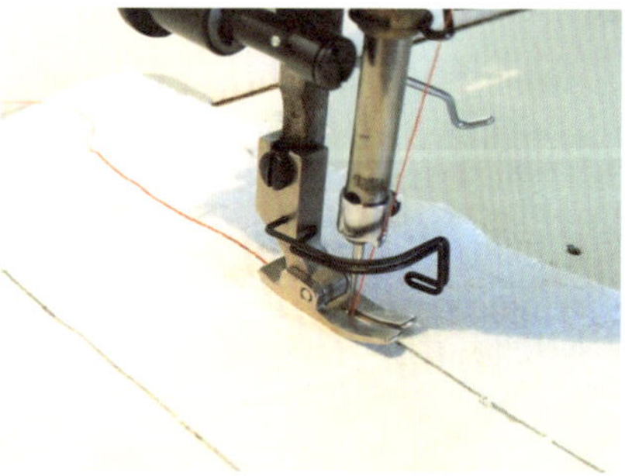

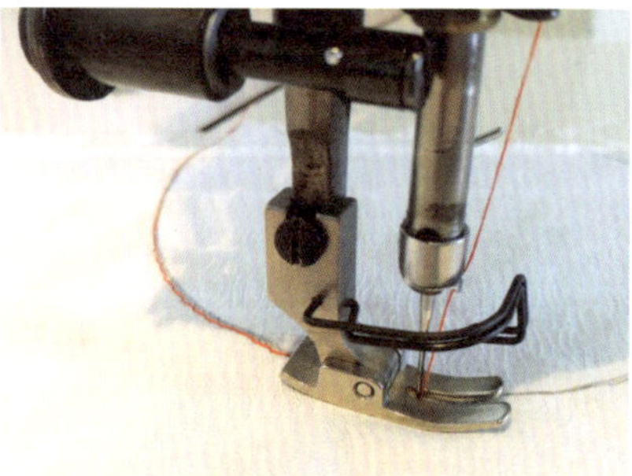

along the lines you have drawn on it. Repeat this until you are able to easily adjust the pressure of your foot on the pedal, to make perfectly straight and curved seams. This exercise will help you become familiar with the sewing machine and make you completely autonomous and confident in its use. Before tackling the not exactly simple task of making skirts and trousers, it is important that you master at least some of the hand and sewing machine stitches. In order for the stitches to remain firm and not come out, remember to "weld" the seams at the beginning and at the end, using a back stitch, which you can do using the special button or knob on your machine.

If you can manage the straight stitch, repeat the exercise with the zig-zag stitch, first on the lines drawn in pencil, then on the edges of the fabric, being careful not to go over the same stitch, creating a bump; it must be flat and constant. For the more experienced among you, or simply for those who want to achieve a more professional finish, there is a special machine called a "cut and sew": it is a professional tool that can be used in a home or industrial setting. It creates an excellent finish and can be used on stretchy fabrics, such as jersey.

THE CUT-AND-SEW-MACHINE

If you are not satisfied and would like a more professional finish, you can use the cut-and-sew-machine instead of a zig-zag stitch on the sewing machine.
The cut and sew is a machine that is predominantly used to finish off the edges of a garment. There are different types of cut-and-sew-machines on the market, with various functions and price ranges. This type of machine can be used in an industrial or household setting: the first model shown here is used in industrial or artisanal enterprises, while the second is generally used by people who love to sew for themselves or as a hobby, rather than for members of the public. The household cut-and-sew-machine can also be used in a company that serves the public, but generally the industrial type is preferred for that because it can support a greater workload and lasts longer over time.

For what we're interested in, ie the household kind of cut-and-sew-machine, there are several available on the market that hold four or five threads, but which can be used for only two or three threads at a time. But can you tell the difference? As already mentioned, this machine can have various functions: the main one being to finish off the edges of a garment; generally only three threads are required for this. Other functions of the cut-and-sew-machine are: the rolled, or "roulé", edge and the coverstitch.

A rolled hem is often used for finishing off the edges of stoles or any other sort of ceremonial garment that uses very light fabrics, such as chiffon, organza, voile, etc...

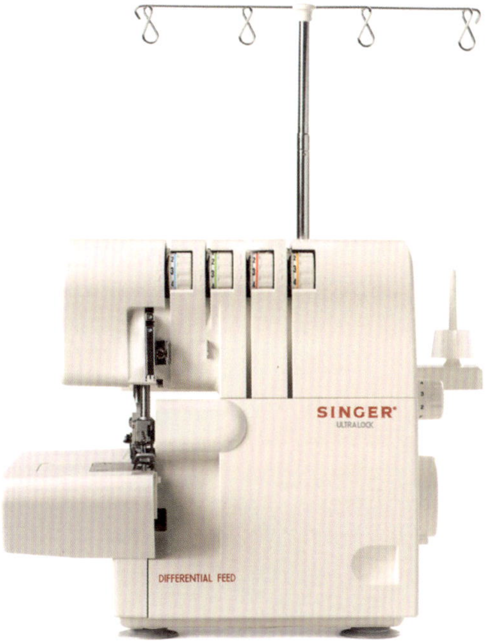

Cut and sew Singer 14SH654.

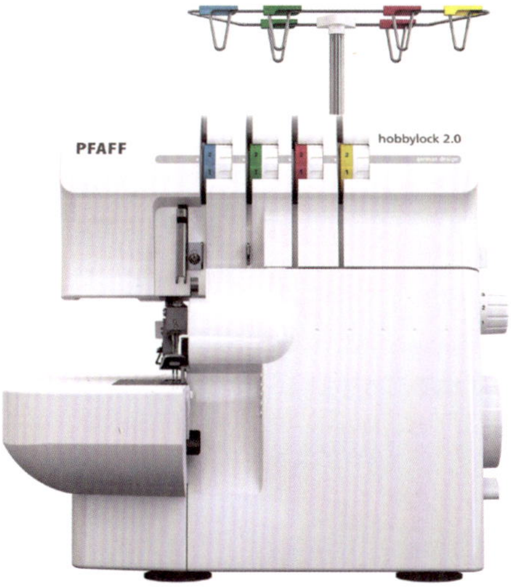

Cut and sew Pfaff HobbyLock 2.0

Example of a rolled hem

Example of the coverstitch

It can be created using either two or three threads; generally speaking, the lighter and more delicate the fabric, the more we tend to exclude the use of the third thread. To set the function to rolled hem on your machine, consult the instruction manual; usually it just requires pulling a small lever. As for the coverstitch, on the other hand, it is used for sewing fabric together as well as for adding a finishing touch. It is generally used for elasticated fabrics, such as jersey or a sweatshirt, and we usually notice it on the edges of ordinary T-shirts on the market.

Three threads are enough to make the coverstitch, and not all cut-and-sew-machines have this particular function. Before being used for this particular stitch, machines with the "coverlock" function must first be "converted".

That is, the plate underneath the foot and the foot itself need to be changed. The "blade" must also be removed. To carry out these operations, read your machine's instruction manual carefully. Some machines use one, two or even three needles to finish off with. Only one needle is used if you simply want to finish off; two needles are used if you want to sew a cover stitch at the same time; the third needle is generally used for the coverstitch. To change or insert a needle into the cut-and-sew-machine, use the Allen key, which can be found among the accessories compartment. The needles differ in size. Specific needles are chosen according to the fabric you will be using: for example, the lighter the fabric, the thinner the needle; the heavier the fabric, the stronger the needle needs to be.

HOW TO THREAD THE CUT-AND-SEW-MACHINE CORRECTLY

It is very important to understand how to thread the cut-and-sew-machine correctly, because it is easy to miss a few threads, meaning the stitch is not made properly and it cannot be used. Each cut-and-sew-machine may be different, but read on to find a few generic instructions below, so that you can proceed correctly with the help of the instruction manual. When threading a cut-and-sew-machine with three threads, in order to finish off correctly, just one needle is enough - you can use the one shown on the right.

1. First of all, open the flap door on the cut-and-sew-machine and lift the foot.
2. Here, you will usually find a colour guide on how to proceed correctly, in order to thread the cut and sew machine.
3. As you can see, the threading pathways are labelled with different numbers and colours.
4. Once all the threads have been loaded, lower the foot and check whether or not pressing the pedal causes the chain to form.
5. Do a test with a scrap piece of fabric.

If, on the other hand, you also want to sew as well as finish off, just follow the fourth pathway and add a second needle.

You can sew fabrics such as jersey, Lycra or elasticated fabrics in general, to create garments such as tracksuits, pyjamas, T-shirts, leggings, sweatshirts, etc directly on the cut-and-sew-machine (ie. without using the sewing machine first). The threading pathway will be the same for the coverstitch, just change the plate and the foot, and remove the blade before carrying out the procedure.

CAUTION! In order to thread the machine correctly, follow the pathway exactly as indicated. So if, for example, number one is blue, start with the blue pathway; if number two is yellow, continue with the yellow pathway after the blue and so on. The needle is usually the last part to be threaded. All the threads must be positioned under the foot and, using the tweezers, must be oriented in the opposite direction to you, slightly diagonally and to your left.

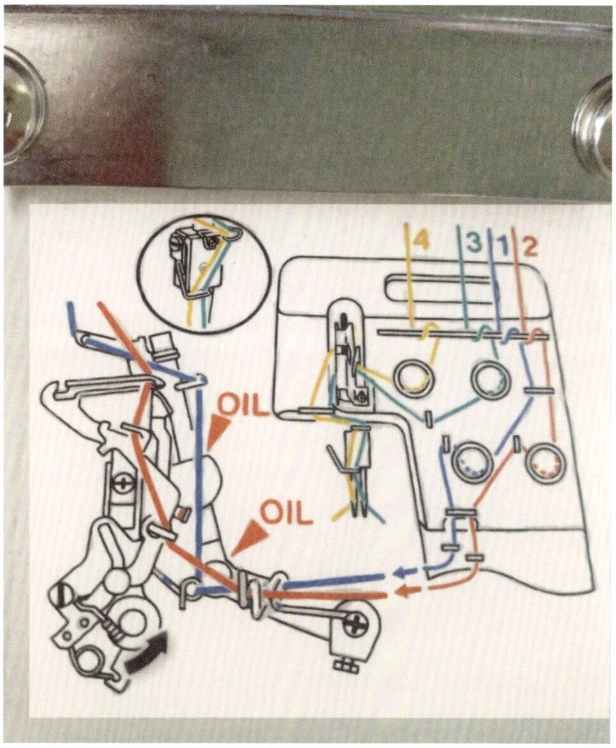

Coloured thread guide.

GETTING THE TENSION RIGHT ON THE CUT-AND-SEW-MACHINE

Another very important aspect for the correct use of the cut-and-sew-machine is getting the tension right. It is important to adjust it correctly to get a regular stitch size. The tension varies according to the fabric you use: for fabrics of medium thickness, such as cotton, the tension is usually set to number four on the adjustment wheels. My personal advice for beginners who want to understand how the different tensions work, is to thread the cut-and-sew-machine with different coloured threads. That way, not only can you evaluate the overall result of the threads as they are intertwined on the fabric, but you can also see the specific tension that each of them has. Use yarns that contrast with the scrap piece of fabric you are using to do a test. To carry out the test, place the fabric under the foot with the edge in line with the blade. The result must be regular on both sides of the fabric, and the meeting point of all the threads will be exactly along the edge. You are doing it correctly if the finishing stitch does not pull the fabric, nor is it too loose. By following my advice to use different coloured threads for the first tests, you will easily be able to solve any of the mishaps mentioned above. In general, then, adjust the tensions according to the fabric you are using and do a few tests until you get the result you want.

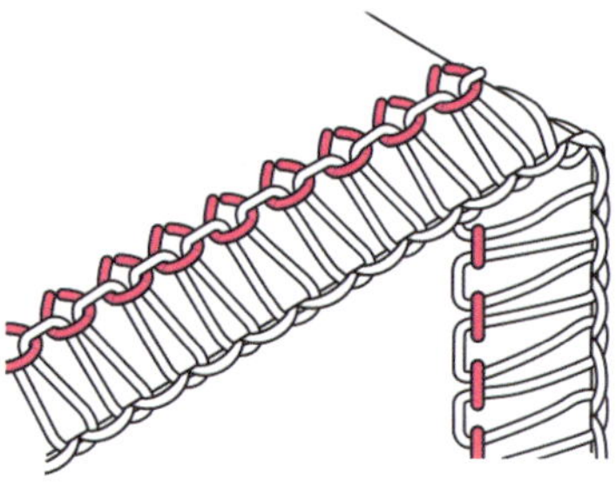

An example of a slow, loose thread.

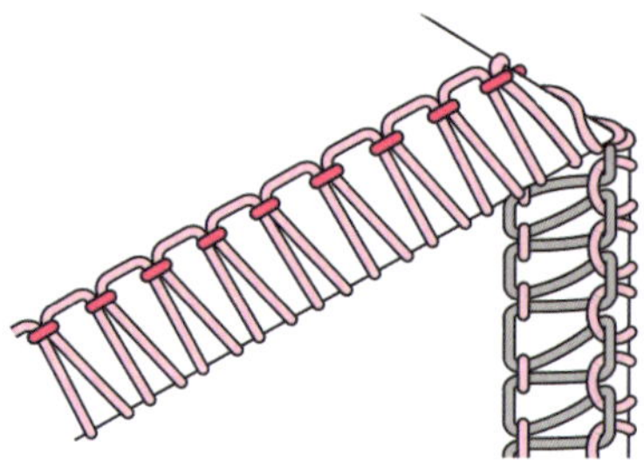

Here, the upper loop of thread is taut and the lower loop is loose. This creates a wrinkled effect on the fabric.

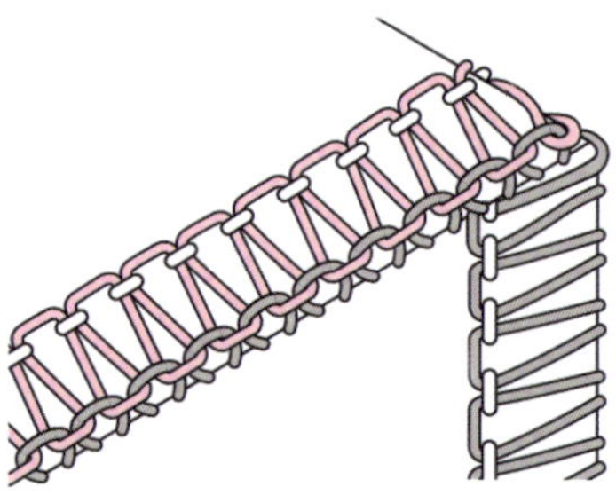

Here, the upper loop of thread is loose and the lower loop is taut.

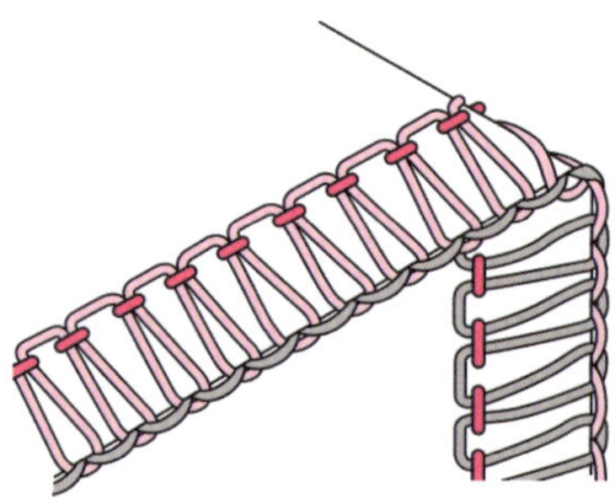

Correct final result.

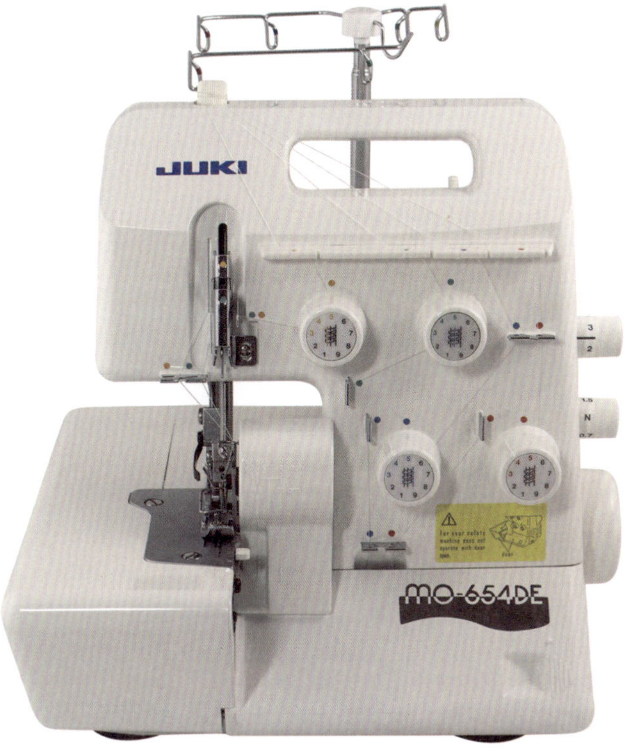

ADJUSTING STITCH LENGTH

As with sewing machines, the cut-and-sew-machine also has a knob to adjust the stitch length. This knob will be slightly different on each model, but it is generally located on the right of the machine. The stitch length is indicated by corresponding numbers: select #1 for a very short stitch and #4 for a very long stitch. The stitch length should be adjusted according to the fabric you are using: the lighter the fabric, the shorter the stitch; the heavier the fabric, the longer the stitch. For a rolled edge, select the stitch type according to the effect you want to achieve: small stitches for a thicker hem; longer stitches for a thinner hem.

DIFFERENTIAL FEED ADJUSTMENT

Having a differential feed is indispensable when sewing elasticated fabrics, such as jersey and wool; it makes sure that the fabric does not curl up or stretch out of shape, thereby guaranteeing a perfect stitch.

The differential feed must also be adjusted according to the type of fabric you are working on and it is therefore necessary to carry out tests, by moving the corresponding knob to the various settings. You only have to change the settings for elasticated fabrics; for non-stretchy fabrics, simply leave the knob on the middle setting.

TERMINOLOGY AND TRICKS OF THE TRADE

PATTERNS
These are technical drawings – drawn on paper or on the computer – of a given item of clothing; they can be standardised or made to measure. They provide the basis for making any item of clothing.

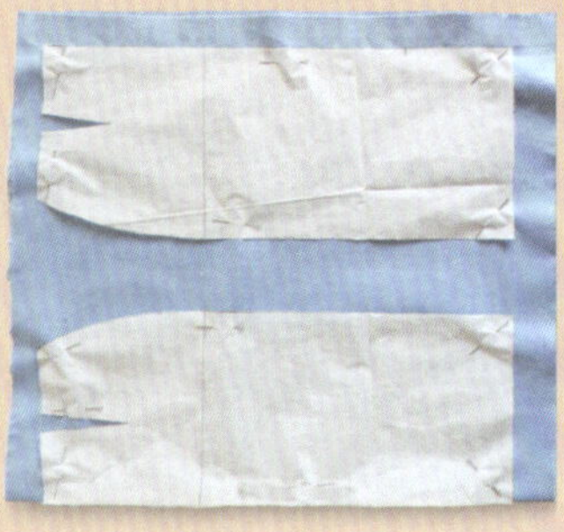

SELVEDGE
This is the border along the edge of a piece of fabric.

THE “RIGHT” AND “WRONG” SIDES OF THE FABRIC
By the “right” side of the fabric, we mean its best side: ie. the side that will be seen once it has been made into an item of clothing. The “wrong” side is the exact opposite and generally refers to the inside of the garment.

STRAIGHT GRAIN
The straight grain relates to how the fabric of a garment falls or what it looks like. If a piece of clothing has been made by cutting along the straight grain, it “falls” nicely and appears to be flawless. In order to cut a garment perfectly along the grain, the pattern is positioned on the fabric exactly parallel to the selvedge. The straight grain also relates to the webbing used to reinforce the seams.

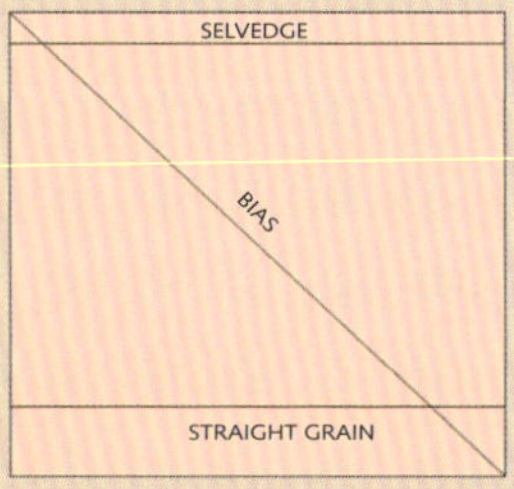

FOLD LINE
This is the exact line on which the new edge will be folded. Along this fold, the fabric will be turned towards the wrong side of the garment in order to make the hem.

SEAM ALLOWANCES
The seam allowance is the extra fabric at the edge of each of the pieces that make up the garment. They allow you to assemble them easily or give you extra room to make a hem.

PLACKET
Made of fabric, this part of a garment serves as a finishing touch and strengthens the seams. There are various types of placket: they can be found on the inside of the front of a jacket or coat, to which the lining is sewn; along the zip of a jacket; on the necklines and cuffs of dresses and sweaters.

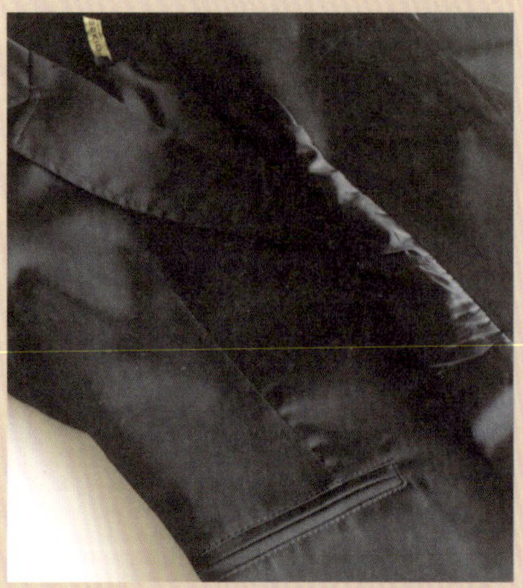

DARTS
These are the tailored pleats that serve to mould the garment around the narrowest points of our body (for example, the darts on a skirt or shirt serve to pull the garment in at the waist, so that they fit the shape of the wearer).

FLAT FELL SEAM OR TOPSTITCHING
The flat fell seam is a visible seam; it is often used to mark out the seam allowances, but it can also be added just for aesthetic reasons.

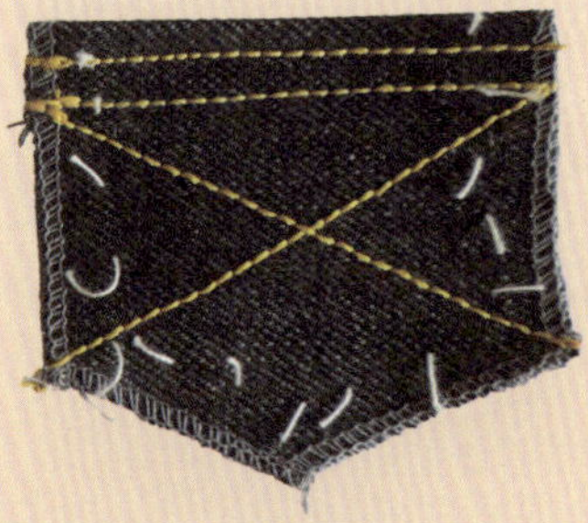

FINISHING TOUCHES
The finishing touches are added to a garment once it has been sewn together, in order to make it look nice and to remove any loose threads. Hand-stitching the hem and plackets on an item of clothing are considered finishing touches.

BEFORE YOU START

STUDYING THE PATTERN

In this manual, we will first show you how to study a pattern to build tailor-made clothes, and then go through the sewing techniques that will help you to obtain the finished product.

But what does it mean to study a pattern? Whether you are tailoring by hand or in an industrial setting, items of clothing are made using a pattern, which is a technical drawing that is drawn out onto a piece of paper or designed on a computer. It is used directly on the fabric, so you can cut it correctly into the shape of the garment you want to make.

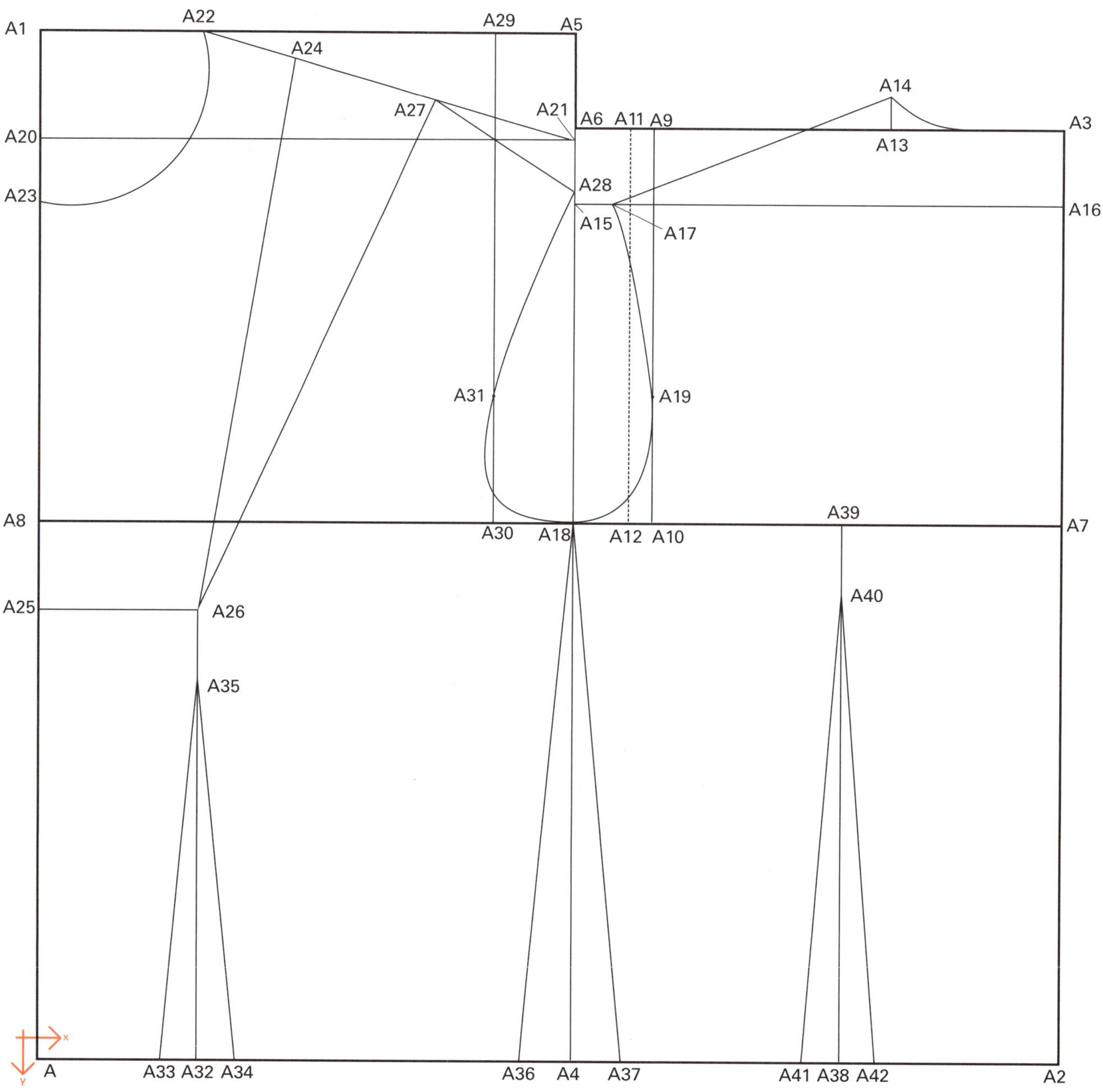

For example, making a pattern for a bodice using geometric methods.

Some types of clothes can be made without using a pattern, but often it is only by using a technical drawing that a perfect end result can be achieved.

However, for clothes that are made-to-measure, a technical drawing is not enough to make a garment that fits well. Once the pieces have been cut out, the tailor proceeds with the "tacking" phase, followed by an initial fitting, where any defects can be eliminated and adjustments can be made, so that the garment fits the wearer's figure perfectly. More than one fitting may be required to obtain an impeccable result. In some cases, especially for beginners or when making more complicated garments, it is a good idea to use a piece of "test fabric". This allows you to make mistakes without ruining expensive fabrics, so you will feel more confident when making the garment.

The test piece should just be an inexpensive piece of fabric that is similar in yield to the fabric you will be working on.

In this manual, I only refer to designs for artisanal tailoring, because that is how skirts and trousers are made.

When making clothes by hand, the most important points are:
1. Taking correct measurements.
2. Getting the fit right.
3. Technique.

TAKING CORRECT MEASUREMENTS

There are measures written on the bottom of each pattern and each pack; these can be personalised or standardised.

When making clothes by hand, only personal measurements are taken into consideration.

Measures vary according to the item of clothing being made; in this manual, we only refer to measurements for making skirts and trousers.

With the help of a measuring tape, take the measurements of the following points on the model:
1. Waist circumference.
2. Hip circumference.
3. Hip height.
4. Length of skirt or trousers, starting from the waist.
5. Knee height.
6. Thigh circumference.
7. Knee circumference.
8. Ankle circumference.

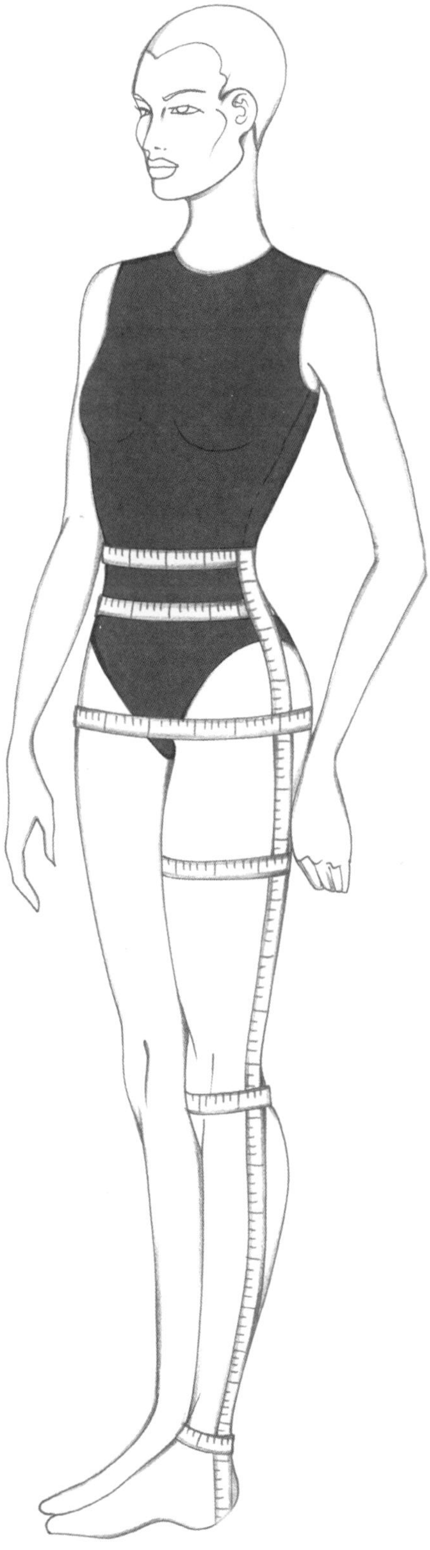

GETTING THE FIT RIGHT

Even when you do not need some of these to make a skirt or pair of trousers, it is good to know what they are, as these are fundamental points in made-to-measure tailoring.

When we talk about getting the "fit" right, we mean the item of clothing should be comfortable to wear, and this is expressed in centimetres.

It varies according to three different factors:

1. the garment's design: a tunic has a wider fit than a sheath dress;
2. the type of garment: a sheath dress adheres to the body more than a jacket or coat does;
3. the type of fabric: a better fit is required for heavier fabrics than for lighter fabrics.

There are several methods for calculating the right fit, one of which is called the "wearability scale", which is based on standard industrial tables.

According to this scale, the fit increases by degrees, and each degree is equivalent to a size:

- the first degree of wearability, equivalent to 4 cm (1.57"), is required for making a sheath dress;
- the second degree of wearability, equivalent to 8 cm (3.14"), is required for making a shirt;
- the third degree of wearability, equivalent to 12 cm (4.72"), is required for making a jacket;
- the fourth degree of wearability, equivalent to 16 cm (6.29"), is required for making a coat.

Along with other criteria, the fit is calculated "by sight": based on their experience, the tailor can guess the right fit. They base their assessment on the model's figure, the type of garment being made, the type of design and the type of fabric being used. This is a decidedly more difficult approach and requires a lot of experience.

TECHNIQUE

Technique can vary according to the type of school the tailor attended and the amount of experience they have gained over the years. Many design techniques are protected by an invention patent that belongs to whoever conceived them, which means that they can be used in private, but cannot be taught or publicised without authorisation.

Some tailors use pre-made patterns that have standardised sizing, while others play on geometric designs: the pattern is designed from scratch, using only a ruler, reference measurements and mathematical calculations. Regardless of the method used, the end result depends on the tailor's talent and the amount of experience they have acquired.

TAILORING

Tailoring is the process of making an item of clothing and consists of several stages: treatment of the fabric before cutting it; positioning the pattern on the fabric; inserting the seam allowances; cutting; guide stitches; tacking; test pieces; garment assembly; finishing touches and ironing.

BEFORE YOU CUT THE FABRIC

In industrial manufacturing, fabrics go through special treatments that prevent the eventual garments from shrinking once they are washed. With artisanal manufacture, however, tailors themselves have to make sure the various fabric treatments have been done, before the cutting process can start.

Cotton, linen and viscose, for example, must be washed before being cut, while wool should simply be ironed on the back.

In the case of silk, on the other hand, it is best not to carry out any treatments, to avoid ruining the fabric and removing its shine. However, since silk can shrink, it is a good idea to have it dry cleaned during the cleaning phase.

Synthetic or artificial fabrics do not require any treatment before cutting them, since they do not tend to shrink when washed.

POSITIONING THE PATTERN

The yield of the finished garment depends on this phase. First of all, it is essential that the pattern is positioned perfectly along the grain.

Before you get to grips with what is meant by cutting along the grain, it is important to understand the composition of the fabric, which consists of:

- Warp: the vertical threads that make up the weave in a piece of fabric.
- Weft: the horizontal threads that make up the weave in a piece of fabric.
- Selvedge: the border along the length of a piece of fabric that is parallel to the warp threads.
- Bias: the 45° angle, with respect to the direction of the warp and weft threads.

It is always best to cut along the straight grain. This is because the warp threads are generally stronger than the weft threads. It also stops the fabric from sagging or being pulled out of shape and guarantees an optimum yield of the finished garment.

To get the pattern in a perfect straight line, position it alongside the warp threads, exactly parallel to the selvedges of the fabric. When using a pattern, you can also cut in the direction of the weft or the bias if you want to obtain special effects, such as draperies, ruffles or flounces.

For this, position the pattern correctly and secure it with pins.

INSERTING SEAM ALLOWANCES

Once you have pinned the pattern to the fabric, insert the seam allowances: with chalk, mark out where you are going to cut. The seam allowances are the surplus of fabric required for the assembly process.

In general tailoring, unlike industrial manufacturing, a 2-cm (0.78") margin is left on all sides except for the ends, where there is usually a 5-cm (1.96") margin; this is to allow for later adjustments to the garment.

CUTTING AND GUIDE STITCHES

Using fabric scissors, cut along the marks you have just made in chalk (1 - 2). Then, with the tacking thread, sew guide stitches all the way around the edge of each pattern, which are still pinned to the fabric. This procedure makes sure you get clear markings on both sides of each piece of fabric, which is useful once you start to put the garment together (3 - 4). Using guide stitches also allows you to be precise throughout the process of making the garment.

TACKING AND YOUR FIRST FITTING

Detach the pattern from the fabric and divide up all the pieces of the garment by cutting open the guide stitches (see page 10) that you made previously (1 - 2 - 3). Using the tacking thread, start putting the pieces of the garment together, using the guide stitches as a reference (4 - 5).

Now you can have your first fitting, correcting it on the person you are making it for, using pins to help you.

You can modify any imperfections later, in the final assembly phase. As mentioned above, the first fitting can also be done with test fabric.

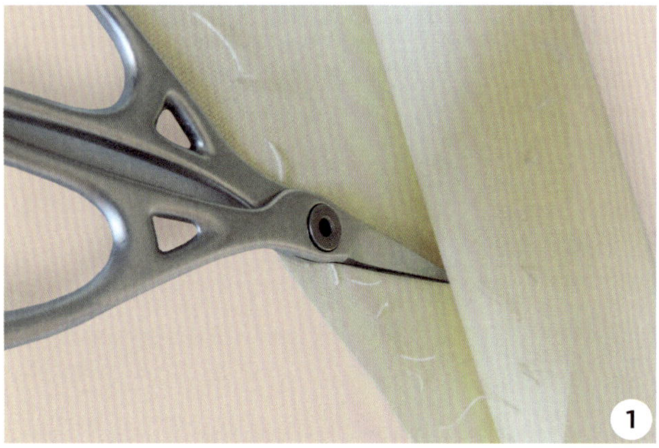

1

2

3

4

5

ASSEMBLING THE GARMENT

If there are any changes to be made during the first fitting, remember to make them on the garment before proceeding with the final assembly. "Assembly" is the process by which the parts are joined together with a linear machine stitch. In order to speed up the process, you can consider removing all the guide stitches from the garment, leaving only the tacking stitches. At this stage, you can sew over the tacking stitches with a linear stitch, then remove the tacking and finish off the edges with a zig-zag stitch or using the cut-and-sew-machine.

ADDING THE FINISHING TOUCHES AND IRONING

The finishing touches are all those final steps that are required to make the garment look nice. The most generic and well-known finishing touches are those made to the edges: zig-zag stitches or finishing off with the cut-and-sew-machine, to prevent the edges from fraying. The hem on a skirt, dress or pair of trousers, the placket of a jacket or collar, or the lining covering the seams can also be considered finishing touches.

It is important to iron the garment once it has been put together, since this makes it look better, but it is also an important stage in the assembly process. It is said that the iron is the tailor's best friend; I would add that if it is not used correctly, it could easily become our worst enemy! It is important to use a great deal of caution when ironing fabrics. This is because the more delicate ones can get a "shiny effect" or burn if you don't use a piece of protective cloth over the top.

VARIOUS FEATURES IN TAILORING

Before we begin our journey into the various designs of skirts and trousers, and dive into the complicated steps of making them, it is a good idea to first mention some very important points about the manufacturing process and some of its features.

WAISTBANDS AND FASTENERS

Every skirt or pair of trousers has a waistband - which is either visible or hidden inside - and a zip or fastener. In most cases, the type of waistband depends on the design of the garment. Skirts and trousers can be high-waisted or low-waisted. The choice of waistband depends on which of these designs it has.

For high-waisted designs, a "straight waistband" is used (1), while for low-waisted designs, a "curved waistband" is used (2). But what are the differences between the two? The straight waistband is nothing more than a rectangle folded over twice, since it must "embrace" only the waist and does not need to be shaped or adjusted. The curved waistband, on the other hand, is drawn directly onto the pattern paper, and takes the shape of the person who will be wearing the garment.

For elegant garments, such as a pencil skirt or a pair of classic office trousers, a high waist and corresponding straight waistband are usually recommended. For a more sporty or extravagant design, such as for a miniskirt or pair of jeans, the curved waistband is more suitable.

Fasteners can take the form of a zip, buttons, toggles, hooks, or any other kind of object that serves to fasten a garment together. Choosing the right sort of fastener also depends on the type of garment you are making.

For example, there are classic zips and invisible zips. While classic zips are visible on the garment, invis-

1

2

ible ones are completely imperceptible, which is why they are the most commonly used zips for chic items of clothing, such as elegant skirts, classic trousers or formal dresses.

Where to put the zip also depends on the kind of clothing it is for: on a pencil skirt, for example, it would be best to insert it in the middle at the back; on a pair of high-waisted classic trousers, place it along the hip on the left side; on a denim miniskirt, jeans or sports trousers, it is nice to see the zip in full view, front and centre. On a full skirt, however, a side zip rather than a rear fastener would be more appropriate, so as not to spoil the flow of the design. The same rule applies to certain skirts - such as those with an asymmetrical hem, or with a train or flounces attached - and trousers. In addition to zips, buttons are another type of garment fastener: they can be the normal kind (that need a buttonhole), or press studs. For greater convenience, especially for the beginners among you, I recommend using press studs for the skirts and trousers discussed in this book, since buttonholes are very difficult to make by hand, even when the method is explained well. Also,

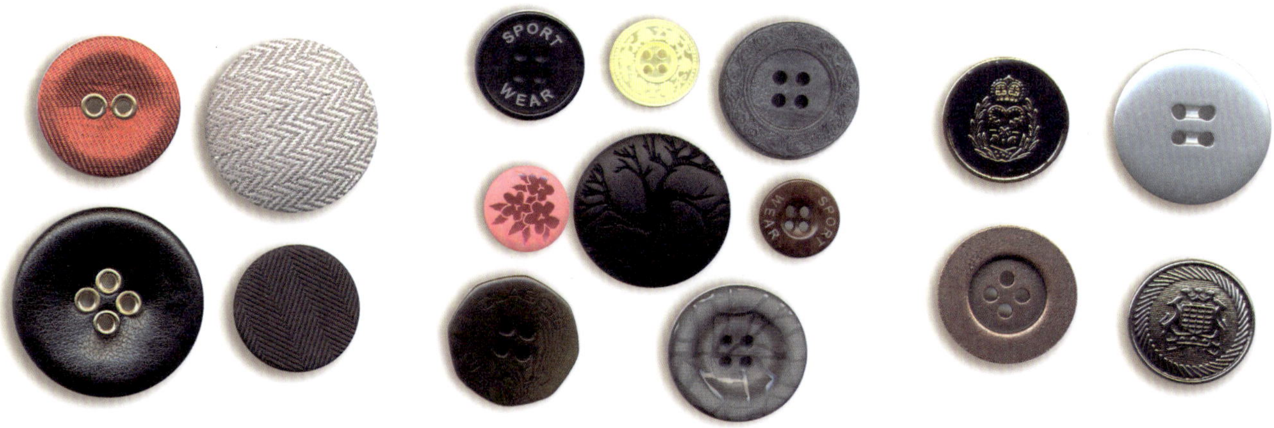

although many sewing machines are able to make buttonholes automatically, the result does not always meet expectations.

Since making waistbands and inserting zips is exactly the same for most of the skirts and trousers covered in this book, the following explanations are a good introduction. The instructional samples I made are all in 1:2 scale.

DESIGNING AND TAILORING A STRAIGHT WAISTBAND

Draw the straight waistband as a rectangle, which is as long as the waist circumference, plus 3 cm (1.18") as a useful overlap for buttonholes and buttons, and 2 cm (0.78") is enough for a good seam allowance.

Example: 70 cm (27.55") waist circumference + 3 cm (1.18") overlap + 2 cm (0.78") seam allowance = 75 cm (29.52") total length of the waistband.
Twice as wide as the final desired width + 2 cm (0.78") for the seam allowances.
Example: if you want the waistband to be 4 cm (1.57") wide, draw it 8 cm (3.14") wide + 2 cm (0.78") for seam allowances = 10 cm (3.93") total width.

Cut out the resulting rectangle and pin it to the fabric you are using. Then cut around the edges, since the seam allowances have already been added.

You will need to reinforce the waistband with a special canvas, called adhesive canvas, which you can buy at a haberdashery. Cut a piece of adhesive canvas the same size as the strap that will be used as the waistband, then position it with the section that will be glued facing the back of the strap and iron over it to make it stick to the fabric (1). Fold the strap in half, along its ends, on the right side of the fabric and then hold it in place with pins, followed by tacking stitches, and then sew it together (2).

Trim the fabric 0.5 cm (0.19") from the seam, cutting off the excess: this trick allows you to turn the strap more easily onto its right side (3). Turn the strap over onto the right side of the fabric and iron it (4).

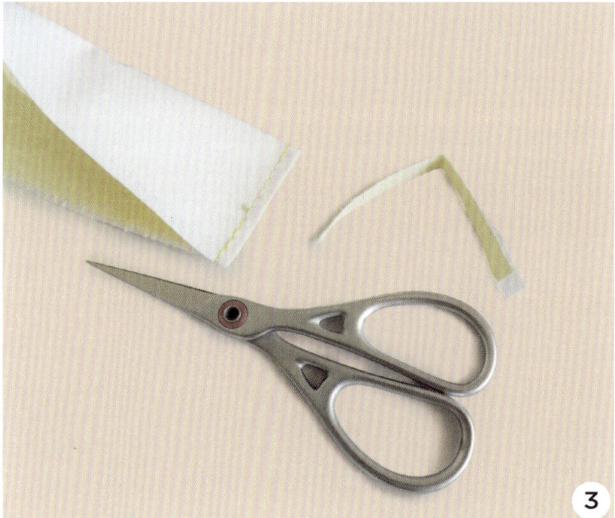

Lay the strap along the waist circumference of the skirt or pair of trousers, making sure that the right side of the fabric is facing up on the strap, just as it is on the rest of the garment. Fasten it with pins along one edge only, tack it and then sew it together.

The ends of the strap must line up with where the garment will join together, so that the section on the right fastens to the section on the left, while the overlap of the strap must be positioned to the right of the joining section and must not be visible (5 - 6 - 7 -8).

Now turn the strap back on itself towards the wrong side of the garment and attach it using pins and tacking stitches, so that it covers the seams. Finish it off with an invisible hand stitch (9).

The strap can also be finished off with a sewing machine, using a linear stitch on the right side of the fabric. Finally, sew press-studs onto the overlap to fasten the garment together.

8

9

DESIGNING AND TAILORING A CURVED WAISTBAND

First, establish the desired height of the waistband, then draw it directly onto the pattern of the skirt or trousers, just like in the following diagram:

- A1_A21 same as the height of the waistband.
- A10_A22 same as A1_A21.
- Draw a line between A21_A22 to represent the part of the waistband that will be at the front of the skirt or trousers.
- A2_A23 same as A1_A21.
- A11_A24 same as A2_A23.
- Draw a line between A23_A24 to represent the part of the waistband that will be at the back of the skirt or trousers.

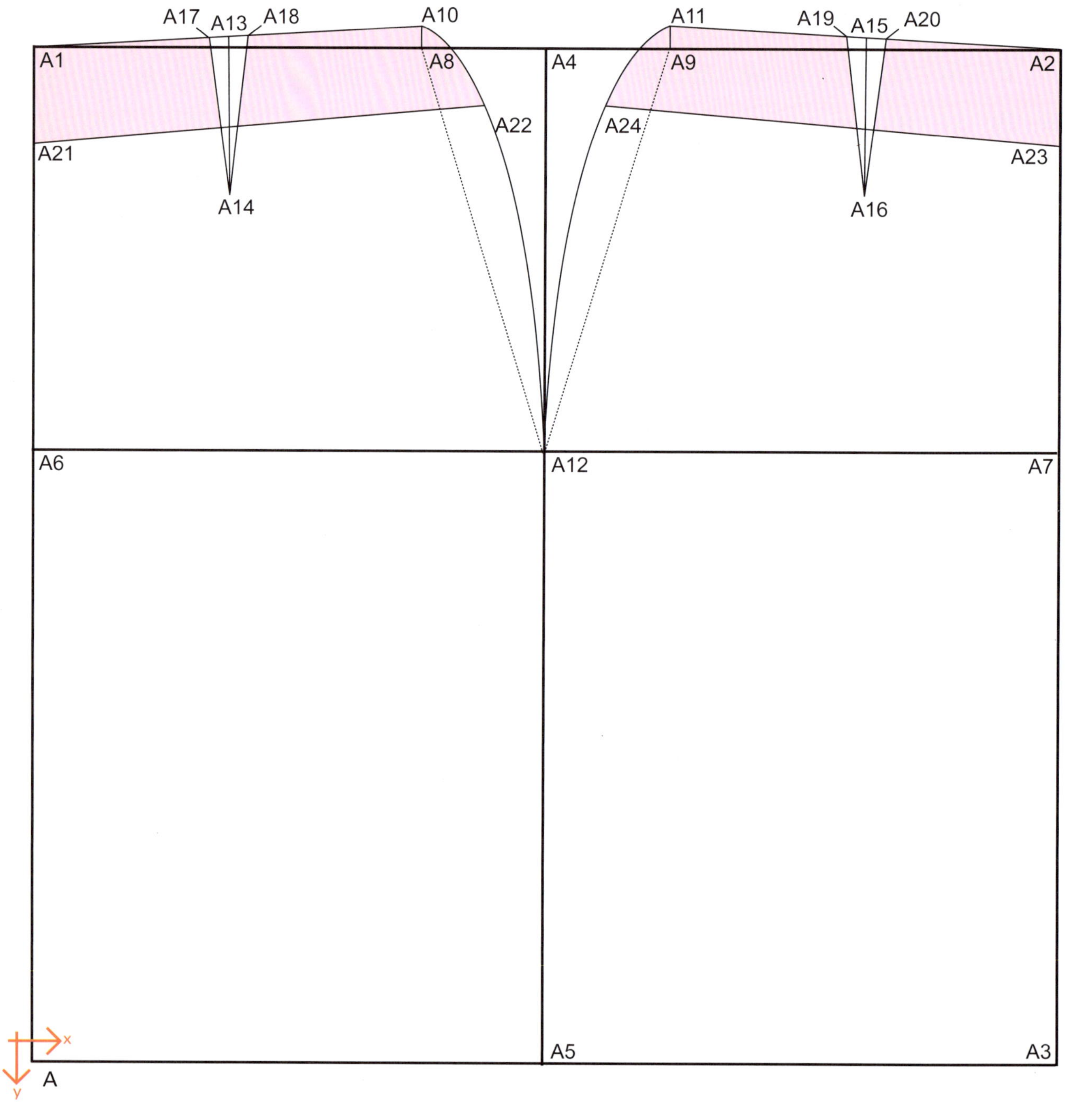

Cut out the resulting two straps, including the darts, and close the darts with adhesive tape (1).

Position the straps onto the double-folded fabric, so that the middle of the front lines up with the crease on the folded fabric. If you have decided to put the fastener in the middle on the back of the skirt or trousers, position the back of the strap - which is still folded in two - so that there is a seam allowance in the middle of the back. If, on the other hand, you have decided that the fastener of the garment should be on one side, also position the back of the waistband so that the middle lines up with the crease in the fabric that is folded in two (2).

Once you have pinned the straps to the fabric, mark out the seam allowances in chalk or a pencil (at least 1 cm / 0.39") along their entire perimeter), then cut along the lines you've drawn. Remember that the fabric must be folded by joining the two selvedges, with its right side on the inside. Both parts of the waistband should be cut twice, so that there is an inner strap and an outer strap.

Add guide stitches along the perimeter of the patterns (3), then detach the pattern from the fabric and cut the guide stitches on the inside, in order to get all the pieces you need to construct the waistband. That is: you should have two parts of the waistband strap for the front of the garment and two parts of the strap for the back of the garment. The strap at the back should be in 4 pieces if you plan to put a fastener in the back of the garment.

Reinforce all the pieces with adhesive canvas that is cut into the same shape, just like you did for the straight waistband (4). Join together the front and back parts, leaving the edges open where the fastener will be. Tack and sew with linear stitches (5).

Attach one of the straps along the waist circumference of the garment, so that the right side of its fabric lines up with the right side of the garment fabric – just like you did for the straight waistband. Then pin them together and sew tacking stitches (6). Next, use the sewing machine to sew along the tacking stitches with a linear stitch (7).

Sew the inner strap to the outer strap (which is already sewn onto the garment), making sure that the right side of its fabric lines up with that of the outer strap. Remember: all seams have to match up (8).

On the right side of the inner strap, use the sewing machine to make a visible flat fell seam, which will make it easier to fold the fabric over towards the wrong side of the garment (9 - 10).

5

6

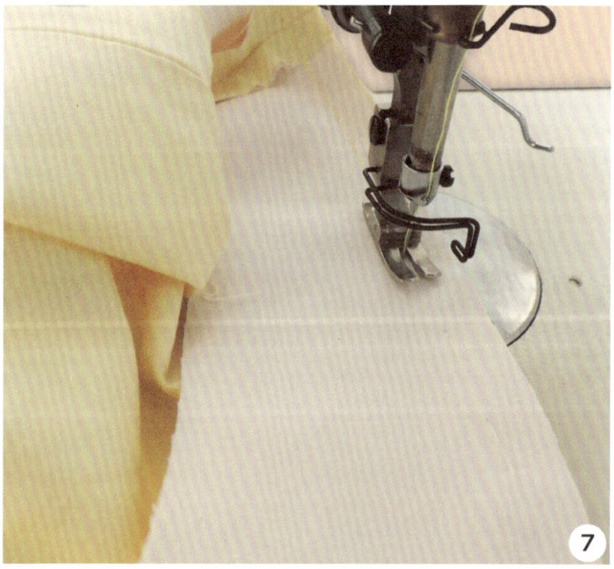
7

8

Now fold the inner strap towards the back of the garment and turn its edges towards the inside, so as to cover the seams. Finish off by sewing blind stitches by hand, or use the sewing machine to do a linear seam, a few millimetres away from the fold on the outer strap (11 - 12).

9

10

11

12

THE CLASSIC ZIP

The classic zip is mainly used for more sporty items of clothing. It is not particularly difficult to insert one into an item of clothing. To sew it in, you'll need to insert the special zip foot on the sewing machine, which often already supplied.

The zip must be exactly as long as the space you have left for it on the garment.

Fold the edges towards the wrong side of the garment and lay the zip down so that its teeth are resting alongside the fold of the fabric. Then attach it with pins (1). Sew tacking stitches along the entire length of both edges (2) to get the best result.

Use the special foot on the sewing machine to sew the zip onto the garment; the zip should be open (3).

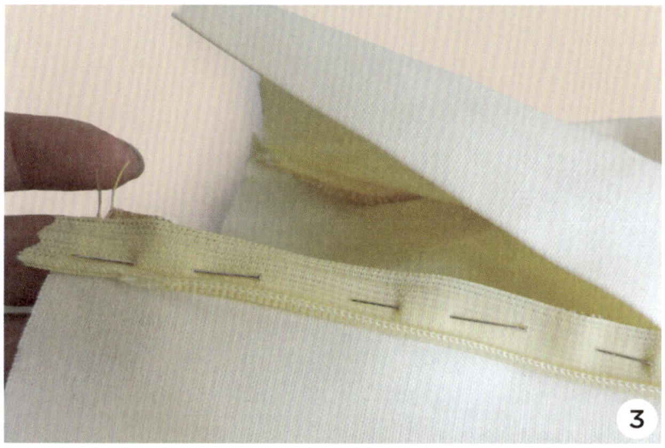

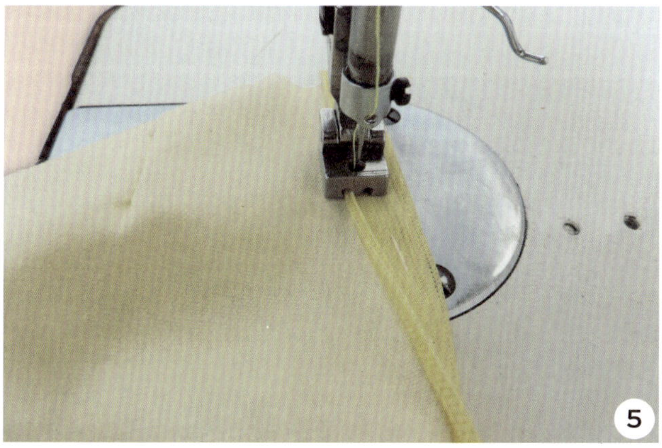

THE INVISIBLE ZIP

Unlike the classic one, the invisible zip is particularly used for elegant garments, precisely because it is imperceptible. In order to be able to sew it more easily, it is good to buy one that is slightly larger than the space available (1). For this, too, in order to be able to sew the invisible zip, you will need to attach a special foot, which is often supplied with the sewing machine. Unlike the classic zip, it should only be inserted along the edges. Turn the edges towards the wrong side of the garment and then, starting from the first edge, position the zip along it, so that the teeth touch the fold (2).

Fold the edges over and pin the zip in place (3). Then sew tacking stitches (4). No seams should be visible on the right side of the garment. Tack both sides of the zip, then use the special foot to machine sew along the edges, where you tacked it (5). Once you have sewn it on and zipped it up, it will be absolutely invisible!

DIFFERENT TYPES OF FINISHING TOUCHES

As explained previously, "finishing touches" means anything that complements a garment and makes it look nice, such as a hem, a placket, a strap or simply finishing off the edges so that they do not fray. In tailoring, the finishing touches are very important and deserve proper attention. A garment cannot be said to have been tailored if it does not have these finishing touches. This is why I cannot skip the explanation of this important and necessary point.

In tailoring, there are various types of finishing touches; the first ones of interest being those relating to the seam allowances. Even if they are not visible on the outside side of the garment, a tailored garment must also be perfect on the inside.

Seam allowances can be finished off either with a zig-zag stitch, which most sewing machines have among their functions, or - the more professional choice - using the cut-and-sew-machine (1).

Other finishing touches that you should pay particular attention to are those relating to waistbands. As we have seen, above, waistbands can either be finished off by hand or by machine. Of course, if it is a particularly elegant garment, it is best to do the finishing touches by hand rather than by machine.

When adding the finishing touches to waistbands by hand, sew invisible stitches onto the back of the garment (2); when using a sewing machine, simply sew a visible seam onto the right side of the waistband, obviously with the edges facing the wrong side of the garment (3).

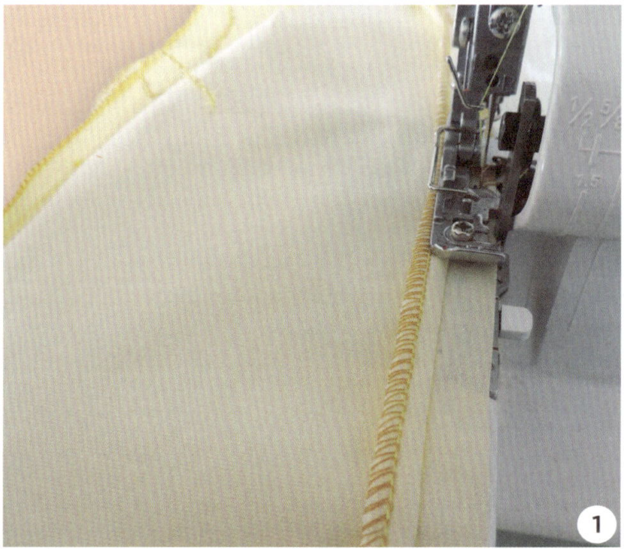

1

The last but not least of all the finishing touches - for both trousers and skirts - is the hem. You can do it by hand or with the sewing machine, but in some cases it is best to do it with a cut-and-sew-machine. It really depends on the type of garment. Just like with waistbands, finishing off hems makes items of clothing look more elegant and refined. Specifically, it is best to sew a hem by hand when making a classic or pencil skirt, or palazzo trousers, while a machine-sewn hem may be fine for a miniskirt, a wraparound skirt or jeans. For flared skirts, on the other hand, it is best to do the hem with a cut-and-sew-machine, especially in the case of very light fabrics such as chiffon.

2

3

MACHINE-STITCHED HEM

When making an item of clothing, with the pattern pinned onto the fabric (1), make a machine-sewn hem by leaving a 2-4 cm (0.78")-(1.57") allowance at the bottom, depending on how wide you want the final hem to be (if, for example, you want to make the final hem 1 cm / 0.39" wide, leave a 2 cm / 0.78" allowance at the bottom of the garment).

Fold the hem over twice, the same size, towards the wrong side of the garment (for example, fold 1 cm / 0.39" twice), then fasten it with pins and sew tacking stitches (2). Sew on the wrong side, a few millimetres away from the fold (3).

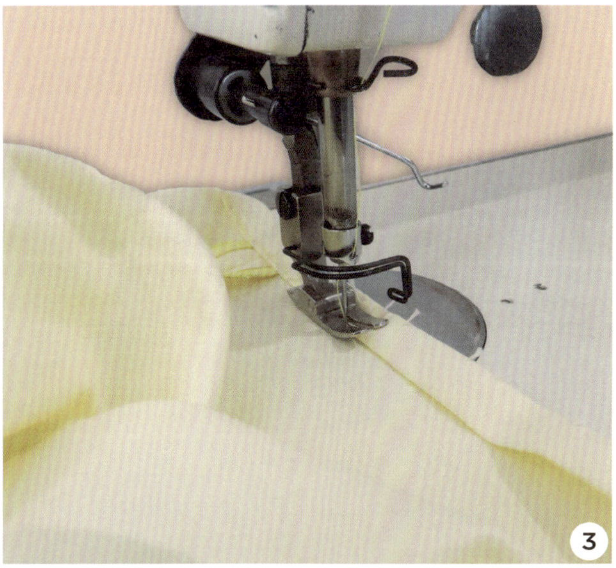

HAND-STITCHED HEM

When making an item of clothing by hand, with the pattern pinned onto the fabric, make a hem by leaving a minimum of 5 cm (1.96") at the bottom. Once you have assembled the garment and added the finishing touches, turn the bottom edge back on itself and fold it where you have sewn the guide stitches (1). Hand sew an understitch, so you can't see it on either side of the garment (2).

CUTTING AND SEWING A HEM

As already mentioned, it is sometimes best to make the hem with a cut-and-sew-machine, because of its special hemming function. This is especially true when a skirt is cut on the bias, ie. a full- or half-wheel skirt, or when adding flounces and ruffles. To find out how to activate the special function to sew this type of hem, consult the instruction manual for your cut-and-sew-machine.

LINING A SKIRT

Some skirts need to be lined, either to make them more comfortable to wear or for purely aesthetic reasons. The procedure for lining a skirt is very simple: in general, you would use the same pattern that you used to make the skirt itself - except for pleated or flounced skirts, for example. For the lining, just make a second, identical skirt, that is just a little bit shorter than the main skirt.

Once you have made the lining and added the finishing touches, insert it inside the main skirt. Make sure that the wrong side of the lining faces the wrong side of the main skirt fabric. Sew the lining and the skirt together at the waist and attach the waistband. If you are making a pleated skirt, or one with flounces attached to it, just make a classic skirt lining to insert inside.

VISIBLE BIAS BINDING

Bias binding is generally added as a finishing touch. If you want to add visible bias binding, it must first be folded in two and ironed, making sure that one part is slightly wider than the other (1-2). On the edge of the garment - on the right side of the fabric - sew the flap of the lower part of the bias binding onto the wrong side of the flap (exactly inside the fold), so that the right side of the bias binding touches the right side of the fabric and the edges of the flap and the garment line up perfectly (3 - 4).

Once you have sewn the flap on the lower part on the bias binding, line up the crease you made with the iron with the edge of the garment and fold the upper part of the bias binding onto the wrong side of the fabric (5). Still on the right side of the fabric, sew along the crease between the bias binding and the fabric, keeping the other part of the bias binding folded along the wrong side (6). This will give the garment a perfect, professional look.

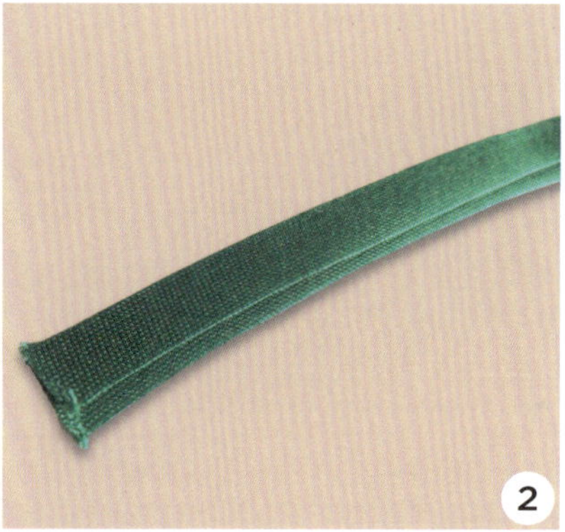

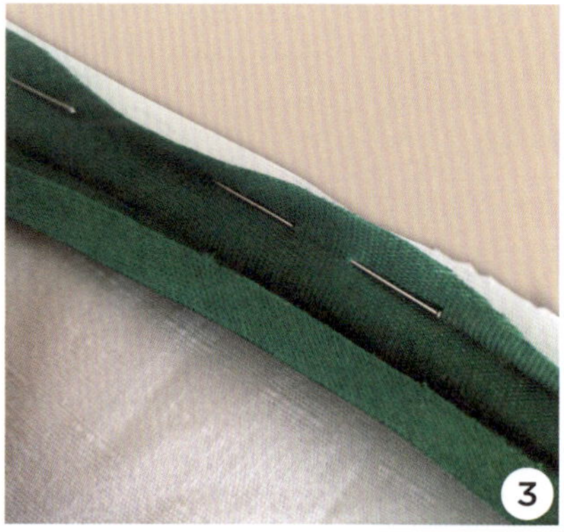

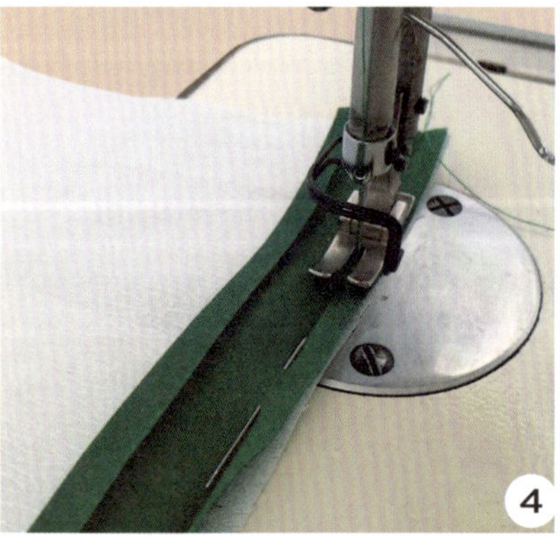

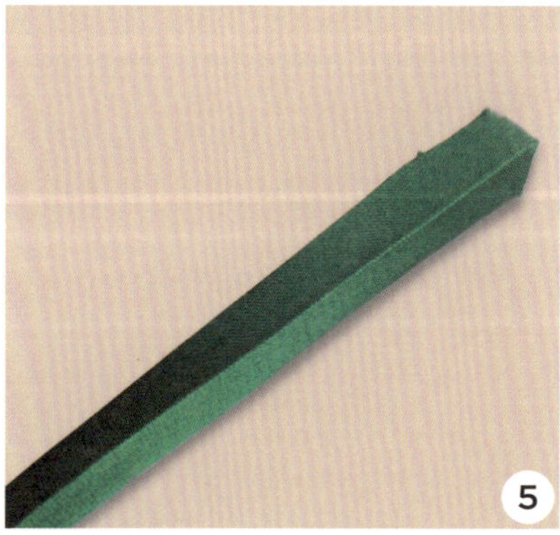

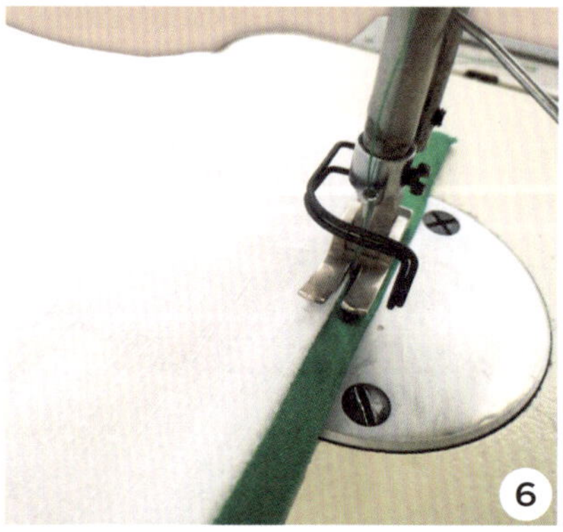

INVISIBLE BIAS BINDING

If, on the other hand, you want to insert "invisible" bias binding, you do not need to iron it; instead, sew along one of the flaps, on the edge of the right side of the fabric (1) and, once sewn, fold the whole bias binding towards the wrong side of the fabric and attach it either with a hand stitch or with the sewing machine again (2).

Fold the bias binding towards the wrong side of the fabric (3 - 4). Finish it by hand with invisible stitches (5).

1

2

3

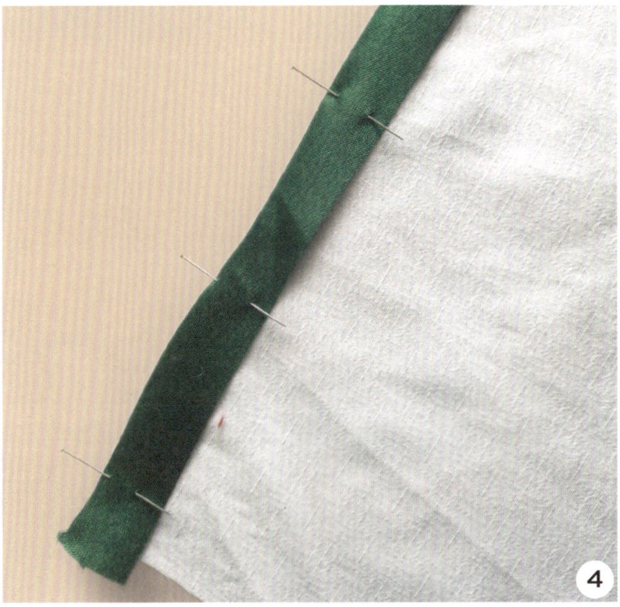

4

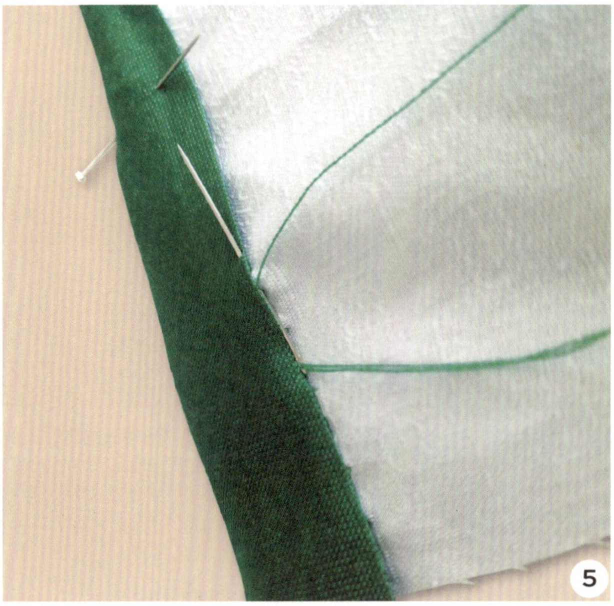

5

DESIGNING AND TAILORING A SKIRT

SKIRTS: HISTORY AND DESIGN

BRIEF HISTORY

The skirt was originally conceived in much the same way as the cape, which is a sleeveless overcoat with a hood - similar to a poncho - that was worn over other garments or armour, later becoming a simple cloak or a large robe with a hood. Later, it became a garment worn by men and women, as both an over and under garment.

The first evidence of skirts being worn dates back to the Mesopotamian period. In those times it was worn long, with flounces, and made of sheepskin. The Egyptians, on the other hand, called it a "cloth" and it was worn in various lengths. In the Middle Ages, it was replaced by the tunic. During the Renaissance, skirts started being worn again. Their shape and the workmanship put into them would differ according to social class.

It was only at the end of the 1600s that the skirt started to take the shapes we know today, becoming an exclusively feminine garment, except for the famous Scottish kilt, which is traditionally worn by men. 1900 saw the creation of the first modern suit. Later, inspired by female emancipation and freedom, the "Chanel Suit" - a two-piece suit consisting of jacket and skirt - made its mark in history.

During the Second World War, in order to face the difficulties of the era, culottes were introduced. Stylist Mary Quant introduces the mini-skirt in 1960, having been inspired by the anti-conformist atmosphere of the time.

Today, the skirt comes in many different styles and fabrics - more than any other garment - and seems to describe the essence of feminine elegance, with designs that suit any occasion.

BASIC DESIGNS

There are lots of different kinds of skirts: each one flattering the figure in its own way.

To make things easier for those of you who are new to the world of sewing and patterns, I have chosen to demonstrate only the most simple and well-known designs.

With the exception of a few styles, all skirts are made using the same basic design: a paper pattern that uses geometric methods, but based on your own measurements.

Once you have taken the measurements, as instructed in the previous chapter, equip yourself with tissue paper, a ruler, a set square, a pencil, rubber and sharpener, so you can draw the basic design of the skirt.

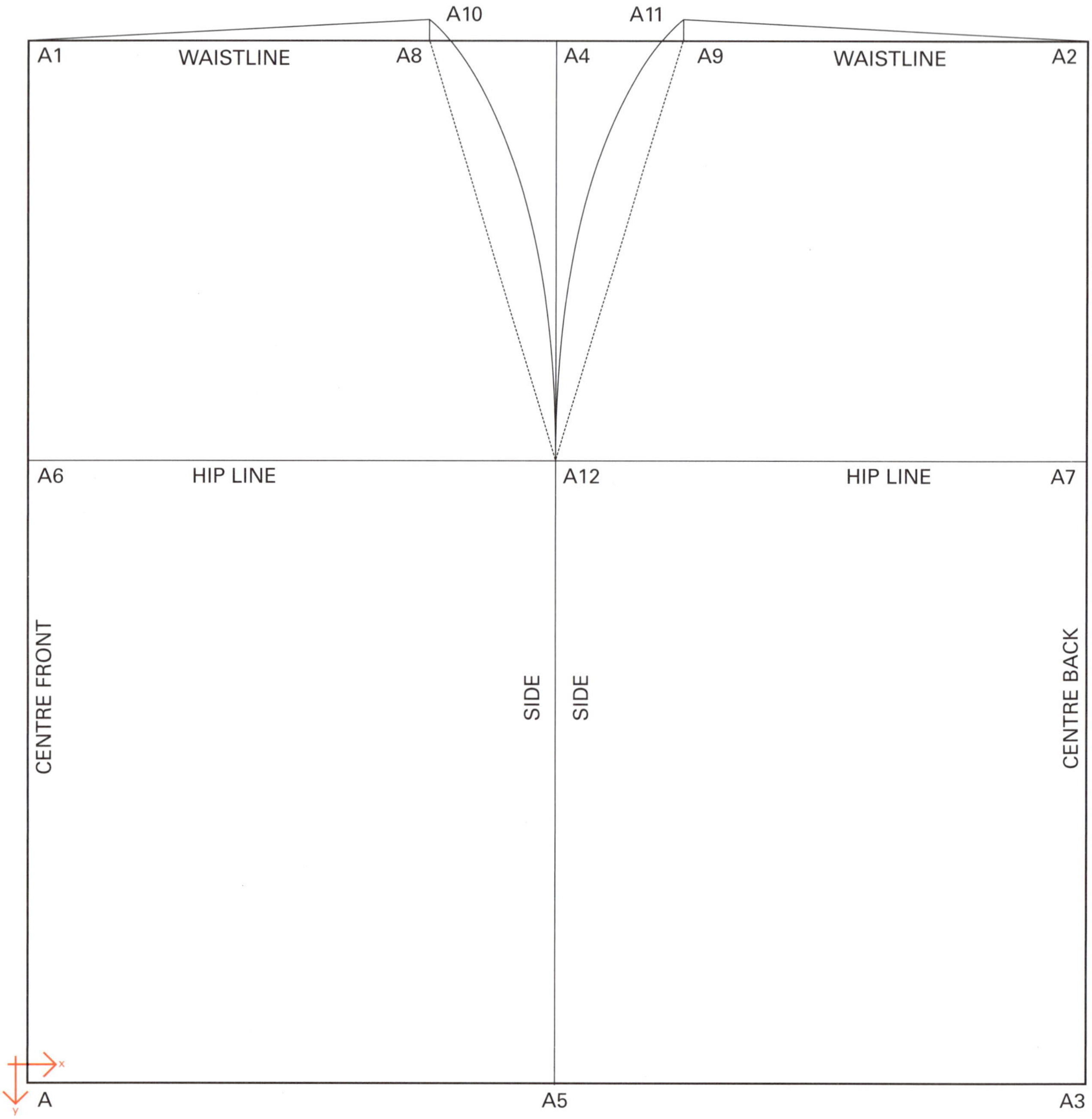

Once you have studied the diagram and carefully followed the explanation, draw your basic pattern.

- A1_A2 being half the circumference of the hip (for example, hip circumference 100 cm : 2 = 50 cm / 39.37" : 2 = 19.68").
- A1_A being the length of the skirt (for example, 50 cm / 19.68").
- A_A3 same as A1_A2.
- A2_A3 same as A1_A.
- Combine A1_A_A3_A2_A1 to get the quadrature.
- The line A1_A2 represents the waistline.
- A1_A6 is the height of the pelvis (for example, 20 cm / 7.88"). The pelvis height is the distance between the waist and the widest part of the hip, measured with the tape measure along the hip.
- A2_A7 same as A1_A6.
- Draw the hip line to join A6_A7 together.
- A1_A4 is half of A1_A2 (for example 50 cm : 2 = 25 cm / 19.68" : 2 = 9.84").
- A_A5 same as A1_A4.
- A4_A5 represents the line of the hips.
- A1_A represents the centre line at the front of the skirt, A2_A3 represents the centre line at the back of the skirt.
- A1_A8 same as 1/4 of waist circumference + 2 cm (0.78") (for example, 70 cm : 4 = 17.5 + 2 = 19.5 / 27.56" : 4 = 6.89 + 0.78" = 7.67").
- Draw a dotted line between A8_A12.
- A2_A9 same as A1_A8; draw a dotted line between A9_A12.

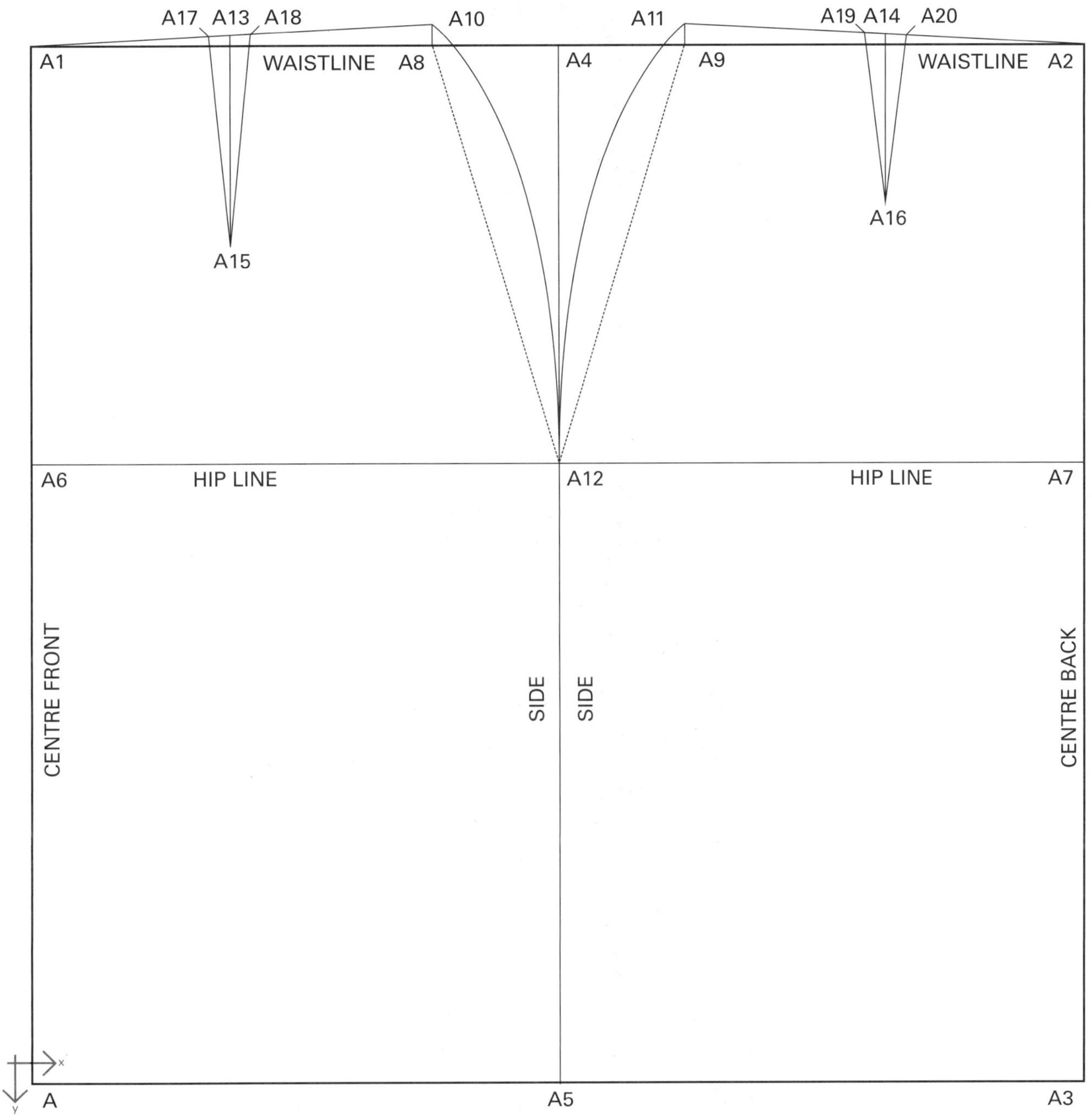

- A8_A10 = 1 cm (0.39") (this measurement can vary according to the width of the hip).
- A9_A11 same as A8_A10.
- Draw a line between A1_A10 and A2_A11.
- Draw a curved line between A10_A12 and A11_A12, like in the diagram.

These curved lines represent the roundness of the hips.

Once you have made the basic quadrature, you need to insert the darts. The darts make the skirt fit the figure:

- A1_A13 is half of A1_A8.
- A2_A14 is the same as A1_A13.
- A13_A15 = 10 cm / 3.93" (fixed size).
- A14_A16 = 8 cm / 3.14" (fixed size).
- A13_A17 = 1 cm / 0.39" (fixed size).
- A13_A18 same as A13_A17.
- Draw a line between A17_A15_A18 and draw the dart on the front of the skirt.
- A14_A19 = 1 cm / 0.39" (fixed size).
- A14_A20 same as A14_A19.
- Draw a line between A19_A16_A20 and draw the dart on the back of the skirt.

The skirt pattern is now ready and can be used to base most known skirt designs on.

To clarify, all the skirt patterns in this book are made to 1/2 scale, but the procedure is identical at full scale.

FLARED SKIRT WITH STRAIGHT WAISTBAND

You do not need a pattern to make this sort of skirt. First, choose some fabric; it is important to remember that in order to get the flared effect once the skirt is finished, it is better to choose a medium-weight fabric, rather than a very lightweight one.

Fold the fabric on a tabletop, with its right side facing inwards, and join the selvedges together. With the help of a tape measure, a ruler and a piece of chalk, draw a line on the fabric to determine which part will be the skirt and which part will be the waistband (1).

More specifically, the skirt must be no wider than the width of the fabric you have chosen and it can be as long as you want it to be, but leave at least 4 cm (1.57") for the hem and the seams.

The waistband should be as wide as the waist circumference, plus 2 cm (0.78") for seam allowances, plus 3 cm (1.18") for the button overlap; twice the length of the final length, plus a minimum 2 cm (0.78") seam allowance (for example, if the final waistband will be 4 cm / 1.57" wide, draw the width of the waistband as being equal to 8 cm / 3.14", ie. double the final width, plus 2 cm / 0.78" for seam allowances, making the total width 10 cm / 3.93").

Cut along the line you've just drawn with the chalk, to end up with two pieces: the skirt and its waistband (2). Take the part relating to the skirt as a reference and use pins to block the edges at the selvedges, then sew tacking stitches (3). Leave a gap (at least 20 cm / 7.87") to insert the zip.

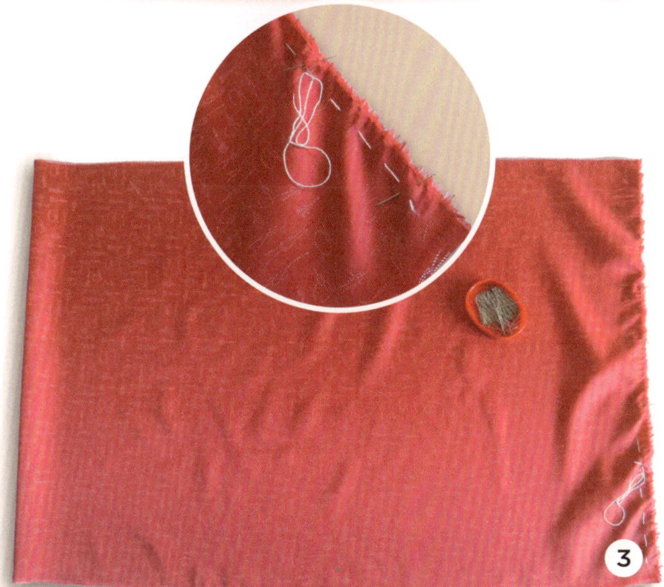

Sew along the tacking stitches with a linear machine stitch (4 - 5) and iron the edges open (6). Along the bottom of the skirt, on the sewn part and not where you've left space for the zip, prepare the hem to be machine-sewn. That is, fold 1 cm (0.39") over twice and hold it together with pins and tacking stitches (7). If you want a wider hem, fold 2 cm (0.78") over twice. Sew along the tacking stitches (8 - 9).

4

5

6

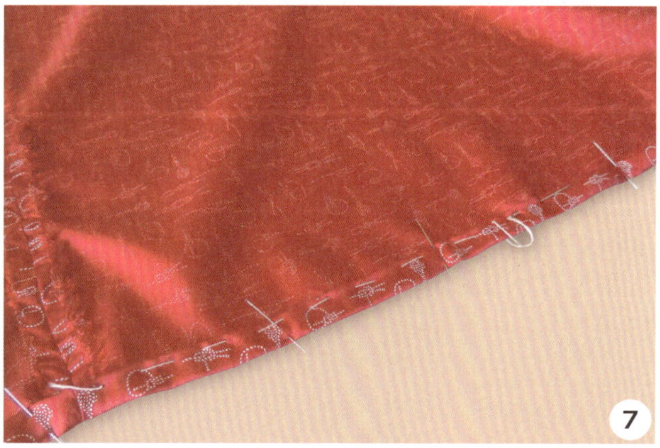
7

8

9

Along the circumference of the skirt, at 1 cm (0.39") from the edge, sew a linear seam with a very long stitch. Do not weld the seam at the beginning or at the end, but instead leave a "tail of thread" at both ends (10). This procedure will allow you to gather the skirt at the waist. Once you have sewn it, pull the "tails" so the fabric wrinkles up (11).

Insert the zip in the space you provided (12), then prepare the straight waistband and sew it on along the circumference of the skirt (13), as explained on page 39. When attaching the waistband, try to distribute the wrinkles evenly, leaving a 3-cm (1.18") overlap on the right side of the middle of the back so you can add a button.

10

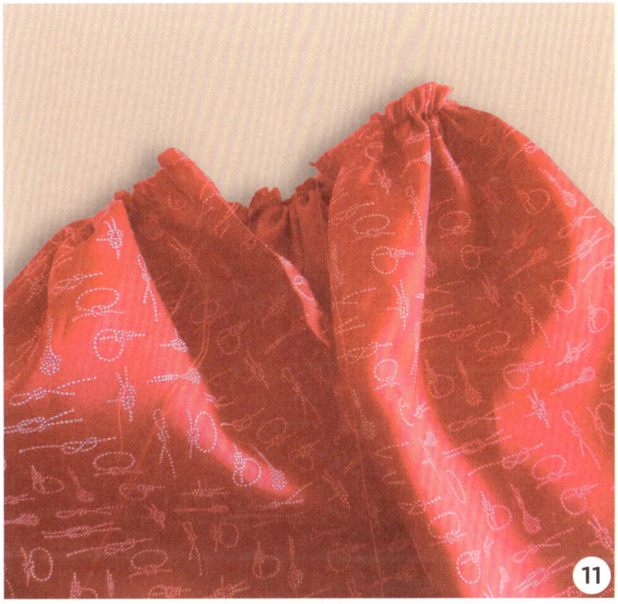
11

12

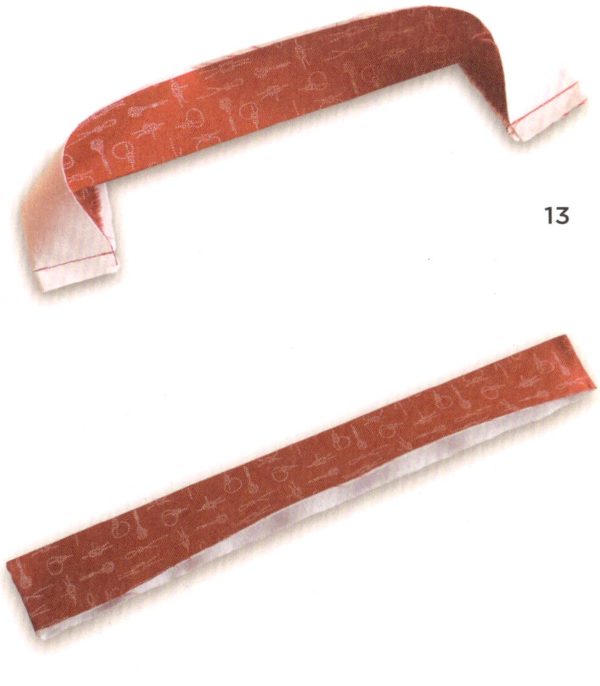
13

Finish off the edges with a zig-zag stitch using the cut-and-sew-machine (14) and add a press stud in the middle of the back of the skirt (15), or a normal button and buttonhole, if you prefer, and the skirt is ready to be worn!

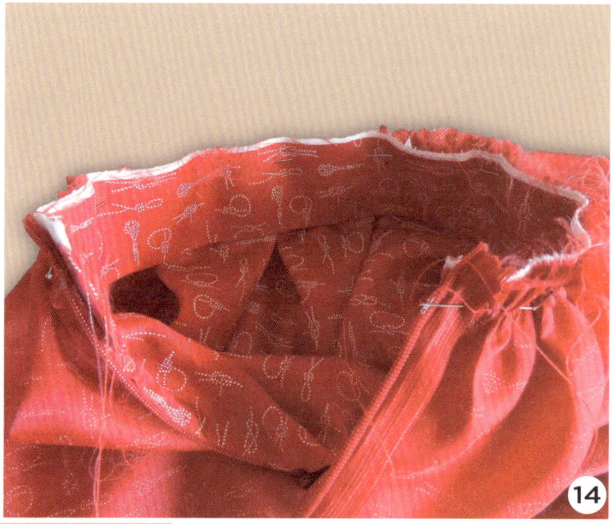

I made the mock-up skirt with a medium-thick polyester fabric. If you want to get a similar end result, I recommend you use the following fabrics:

- Satin
- Mikado
- Duchesse
- Khadi
- Cotton

To get a less "wide" effect, you can use fabrics that tend to "fall" more easily, like chenille, viscose or chiffon.

FLARED SKIRT WITH ELASTICATED WAISTBAND

This design looks wrinkled up at the waist, thanks to an elastic band inserted inside the waistband, and is usually mid-to-long in length.

Most skirt designs require a paper pattern to base them on. A skirt with an elasticated waistband, however, does not require any technical design and is therefore very simple to make.

The only measurement that needs to be taken is that of the waist circumference. To clarify, the patterns in this book are made to 1/2 scale, but the procedure is identical at full scale.

To proceed, choose a fabric and place it on a tabletop, then fold it in half with its selvedges touching. With the help of some chalk and a tape measure, draw out how long you would like the skirt to be, including seam allowances (for example, 50 cm / 19.68" for the length of the skirt plus 4 cm / 1.57" for seam allowances), while the width will be equal to the total width of the fabric used.

The same rule also applies to the waistband: that is, only draw out the width, which must be twice the width of the final waistband, plus the seam allowances (for example, if the final waistband will be 4 cm / 1.57" wide, draw it as 8 cm / 3.14" plus 2 cm / 0.78" for the seam allowance); the width of the waistband will be equal to that of the fabric (1). Cut along the lines drawn in chalk, thereby obtaining the skirt and the waistband (2).

On the wrong side of the fabric and at the selvedges - of the skirt and the waistband - keep everything in place with pins and use tacking stitches if you deem it necessary (3). Then use a sewing machine to sew a linear seam 1 cm (0.39") away from the edge (4 - 5). Iron the edges open and then fold the waistband over (6).

Once you have pinned it in place and added tacking stitches (7), sew the waistband onto the skirt with a linear seam on the right side of the fabric (8), leaving a small gap with no stitches (9). Use this gap to thread the elastic band into the waistband (9).

1

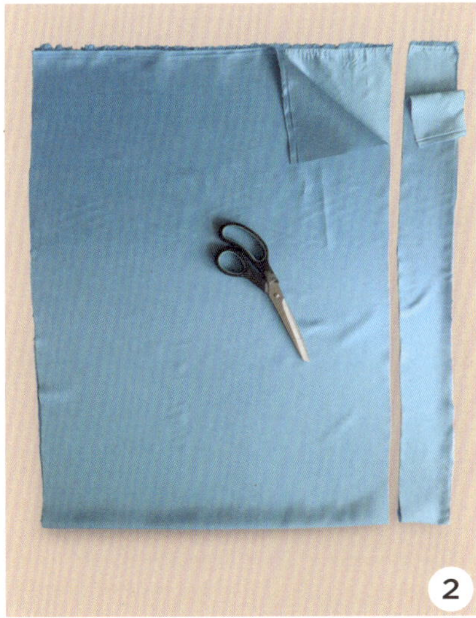
2

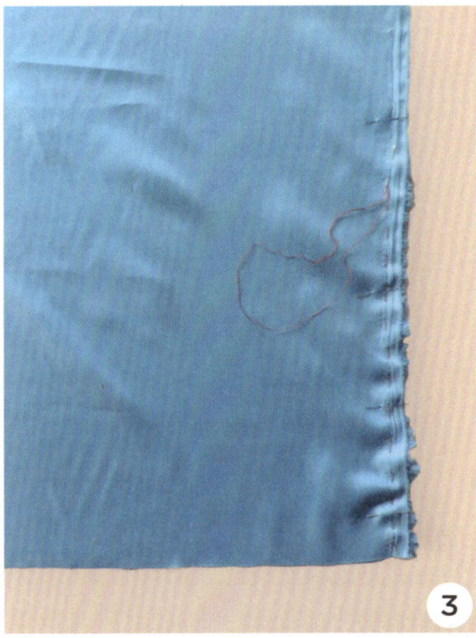
3

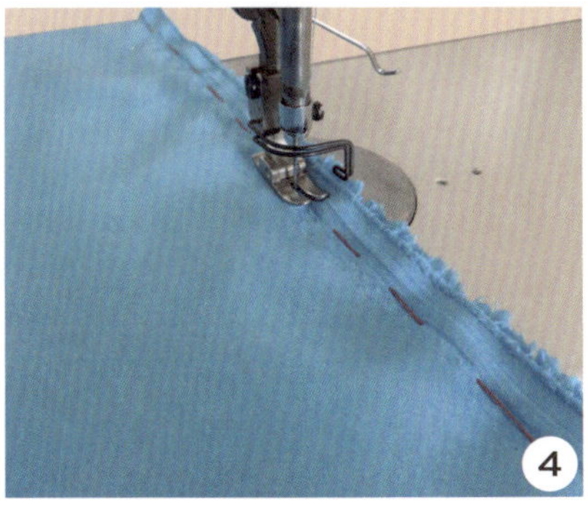
4

5

6

Now make the hem of the skirt by folding the edge over twice towards the wrong side of the fabric, to the desired size. For example, turn 1 cm (0.39") over backwards twice (10).

Hold the hem in place with pins, sew tacking stitches and then sew a linear seam a few millimetres away from the crease where you folded the fabric over (11 - 12).

With the help of a safety pin, thread the elastic band into the waistband, through the gap you left without stitches (13).

Let the elastic band slide along the whole waistband until it comes out at the same place (14), then weld it with a machine stitch. The length of the elastic band must be slightly shorter than the waist circumference.

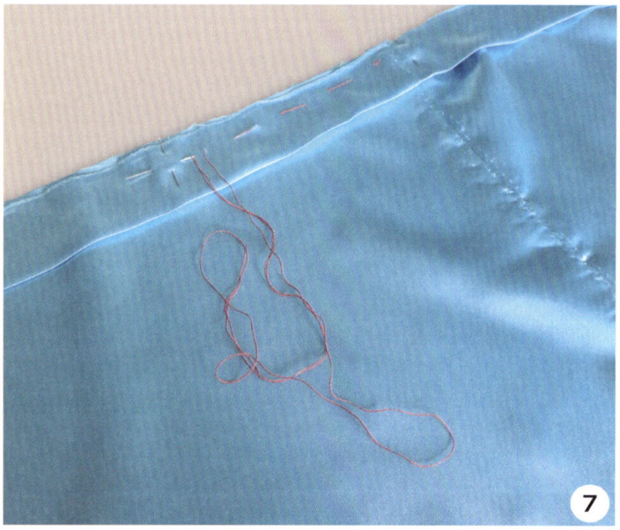
7

8

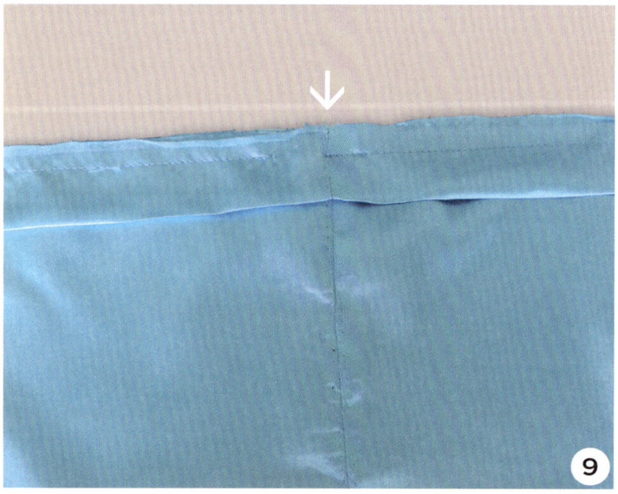
9

10

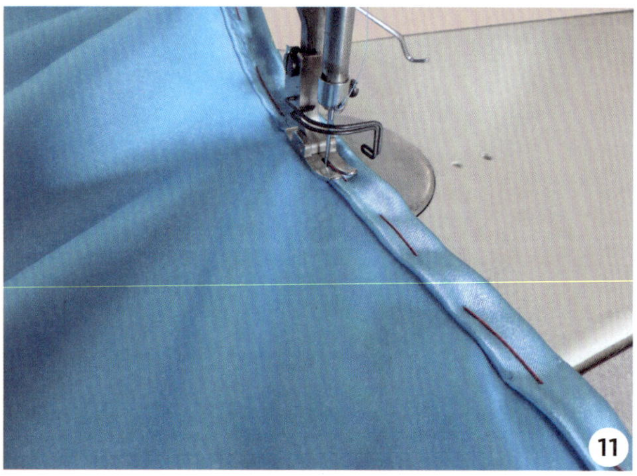
11

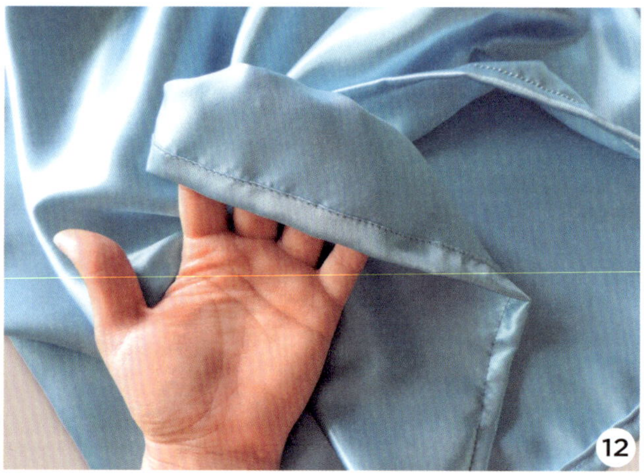
12

Sew up the gap (15) and then finish the edges off with a zig-zag stitch or with the cut-and-sew-machine. The skirt is ready to wear... in just half an hour!

CLASSIC OFFICE SKIRT

To make a classic office skirt, you need to make a pattern. Once you have taken the measurements, make a basic skirt pattern as explained on page 58. The classic office skirt can be made using the basic skirt pattern; you just have to add the slit to the middle of the back of the skirt, at the bottom, like in the diagram below:

- A1_A23 = from 12 to 14 cm / from 4.72" to 5.51".

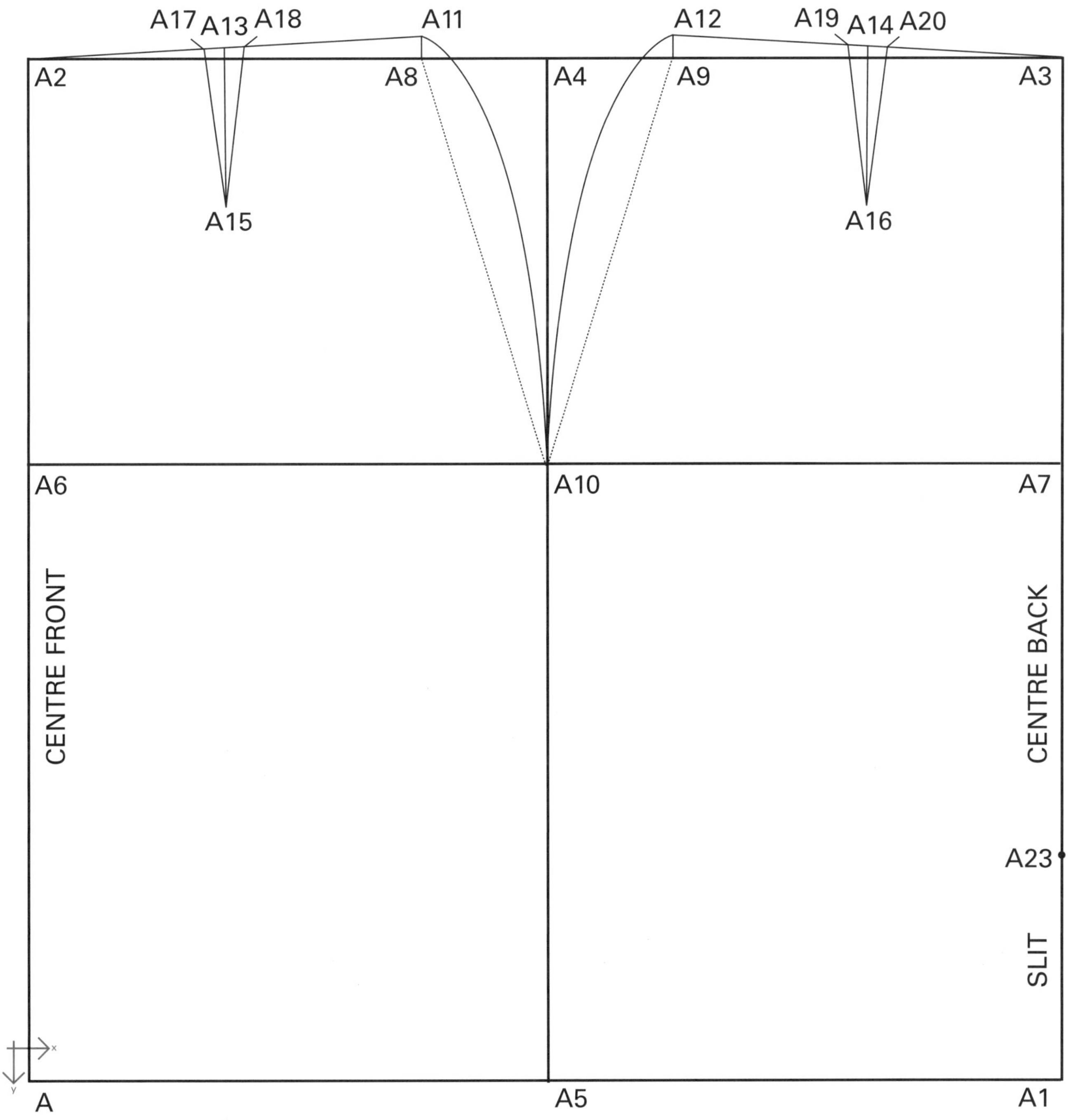

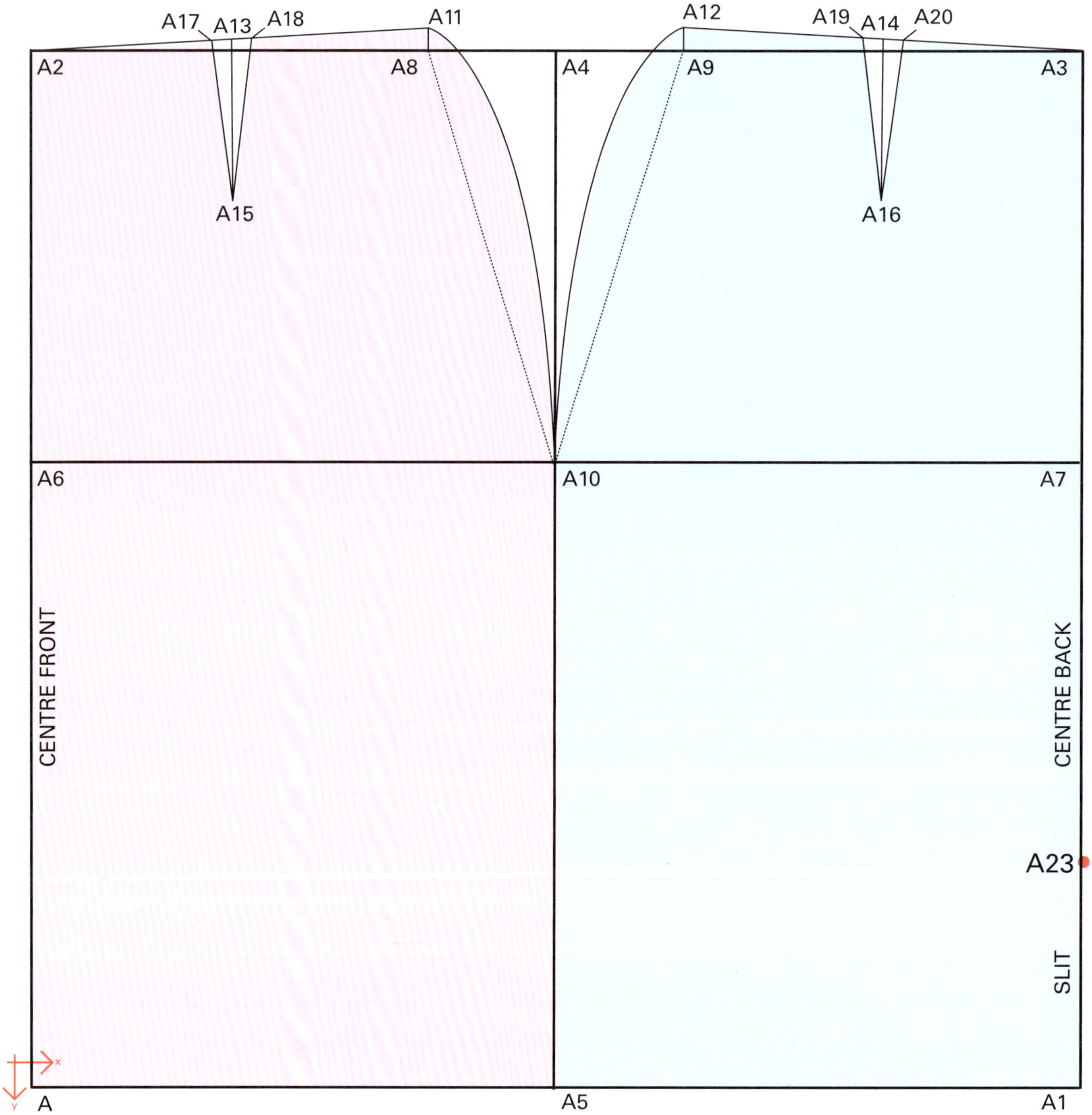

Once you have drawn the basic skirt and waistband, use different coloured pencils for the front and back of the skirt, then cut out the pattern as shown in the diagram above.

The pink part is the pattern for the front of the skirt, while the blue part is the pattern for the back. Cut out the patterns along all sides, separating them from each other. You will get two pieces: one for the front and one for the back of the skirt.

Choose a fabric you like and place it folded on a tabletop, with the fabric's right side facing inwards, and the two selvedges touching (1).

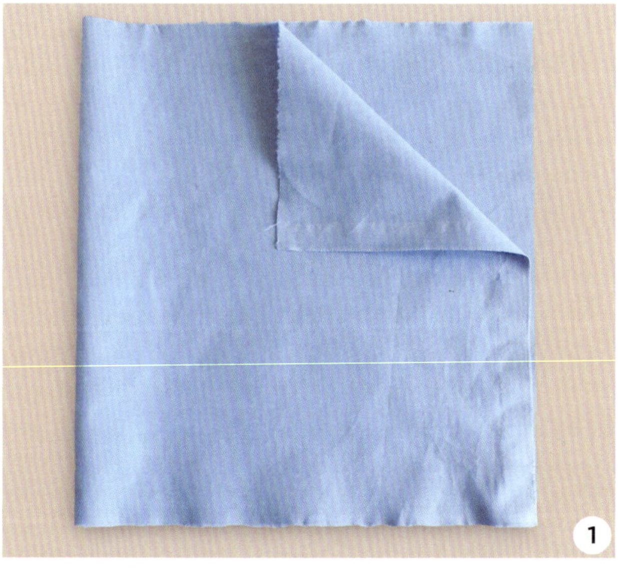

2

Position the two paper patterns so that the middle of the front part of the skirt lines up with the crease in the fabric. Then position the rear part in a perfect straight line so that there is enough room to make seam allowances along the perimeter (2). Pin the pattern onto the fabric, then with the chalk and tape measure to help you, add the seam allowances (3): usually 1 cm (0.39") along the waist line, 2 cm (0.78") along the hips and in the middle at the back, 5 cm (1.96") along the bottom if the hem is done by hand (or 2 cm / 0.78" along the bottom if the hem is done by machine, such as for a sports skirt).

3

4

5

Cut along the lines drawn in chalk (4). Sew guide stitches around the patterns for all the pieces that are still pinned to the fabric.

Once you have done this, detach the patterns from the fabric and open out the pieces of the skirt, cutting the stitches you made in the middle part, thereby marking out the seam allowances on each art of the skirt (5).

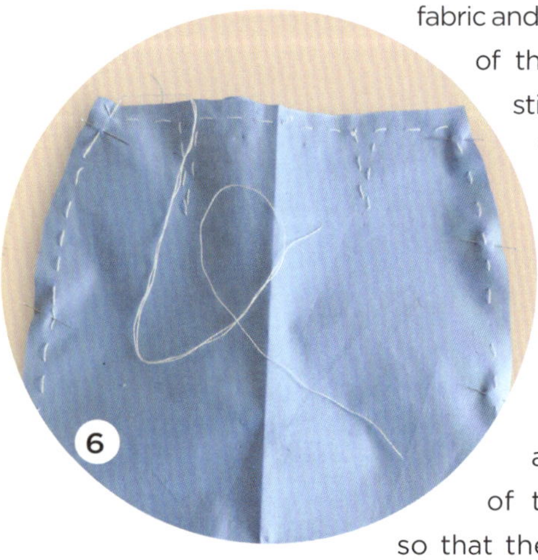

6

Put the front and two back parts of the skirt together, so that the right side of the fabric is facing inwards. In tailoring, this is called "Right Sides Together" (on the right side of the fabric, you now have cut guide stitches). Use pins to attach the parts together and then use tacking stitches to sew exactly on top of the marks you made previously (6).

Leave a gap at the bottom of the back of the skirt for a slit (at least 11 cm / 4.33") and another gap for a zip to be inserted at the waist (at least 20 cm / 7.87"). Sew exactly along the tacking stitches you made earlier and, if you find it easier, remove these loose stitches (7).

Tack and then sew the darts (8). Finish off the edges with a cut-and-sew-machine (9) or with zig-zag stitches and then iron them open. Insert the zip (10) and prepare the waistband as explained on page 42. For classic office skirts, I find an invisible zip looks better than a classic one. Finally, attach the waistband and add the finishing touches by hand on the wrong side of the skirt fabric (11). Finish the hem by hand or machine, as explained on page 50.

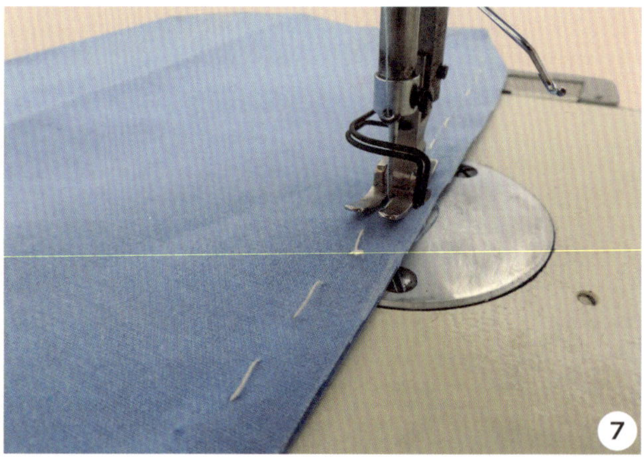

7

8

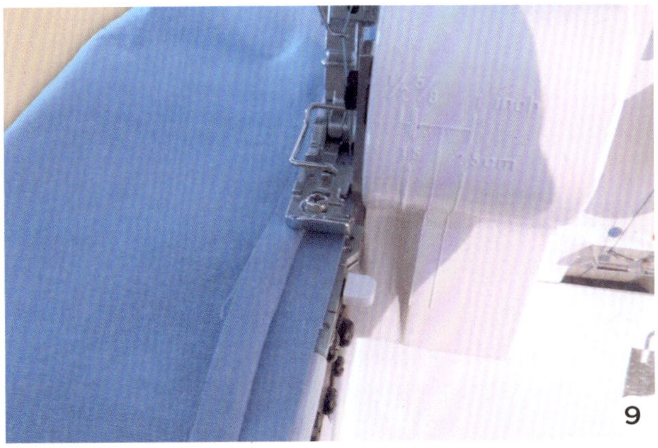

9

10

11

The mock-up skirt was made of a medium-weight cotton fabric, but you can use any fabric you like for the classic office skirt. I would recommend using Cool Wool for an elegant skirt.

MINI SKIRT

The mini skirt is made in exactly the same way, using the same skirt pattern; the only difference is that it will be shorter. So, once you have taken the measurements, draw out the skirt pattern with the length of the quadrature equal to the length of the mini skirt (for example, 40 cm / 15.74"). To draw the waistband, follow the explanation on page 42.

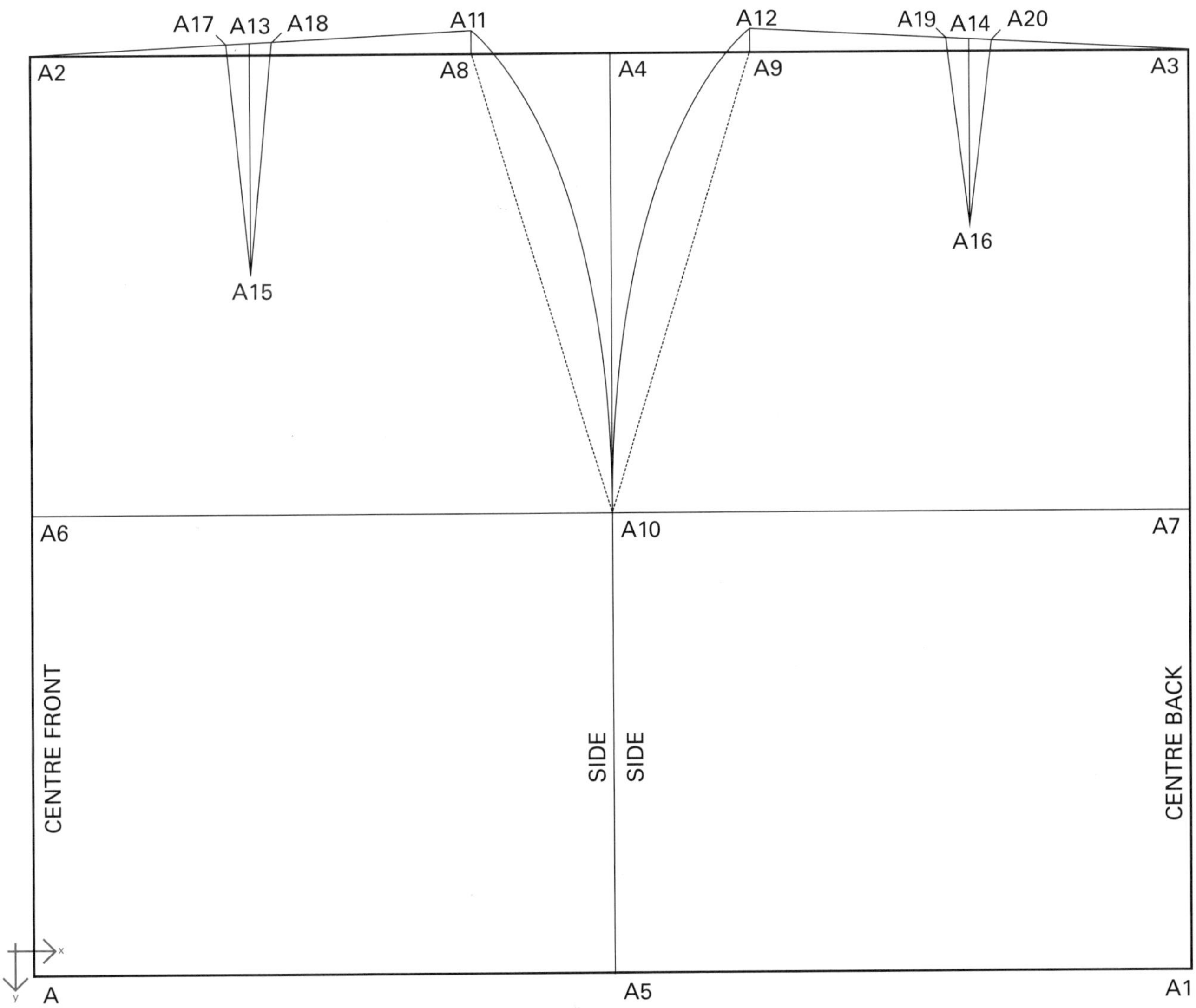

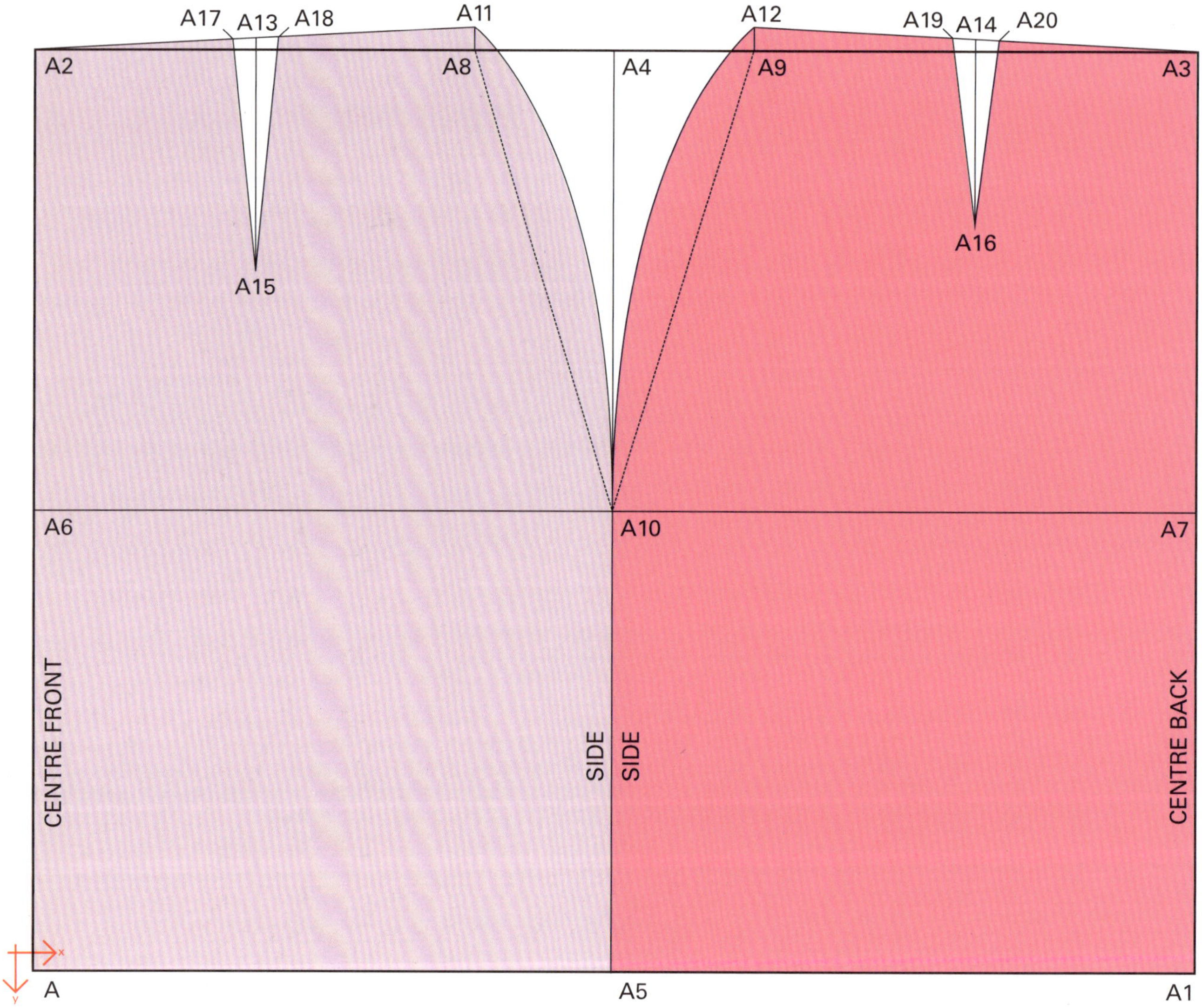

Use different coloured pencils for the front and back of the mini skirt, then cut out the two parts of the pattern. The purple part is the pattern for the front of the mini skirt, while the fuchsia part is for the back.

Choose a fabric you like and place it folded on a tabletop, with the fabric's right side facing in, and the two selvedges touching. Pin the pattern in place on the fabric, according to where you want to insert the zip on the mini skirt. If you want to insert the zip along the hip, position the middle part of the pattern so that it lines up with the fold on the fabric; or, if you want the zip to be in the middle at the back, line the pattern up with the middle part of the fabric so you have room for the seam allowances. Then, using chalk and a tape measure, add the seam allowances (1). Usually: 1 cm (0.39") on the waist, 2 cm (0.78") at the hip and the middle of the back, 3 cm (1.18") on the bottom if you are going to do the hem by machine, or 5 cm (1.96") if you want to do the hem by hand. Cut along the lines drawn in chalk, thereby obtaining the front and back of the skirt and the waistband (2). Sew tacking stitches around the patterns (3).

Detach the patterns from the fabric, open the parts obtained on the inside and cut the tacking stitches in the middle, thereby obtaining the marks for the seam allowances. Join the pieces together, keeping the marks as a reference and leave a gap so you can insert the zip in the middle of the back or on the hip, according to where you decided. Pin the pieces together (4): for greater accuracy, it is better to sew tacking stitches first and then sew a seam along those (5).

1

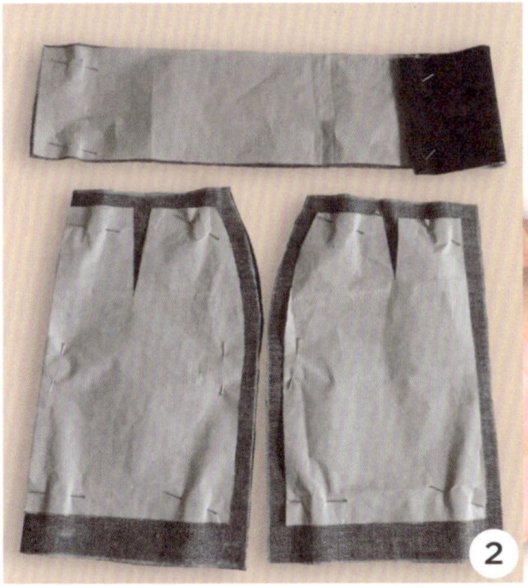

2

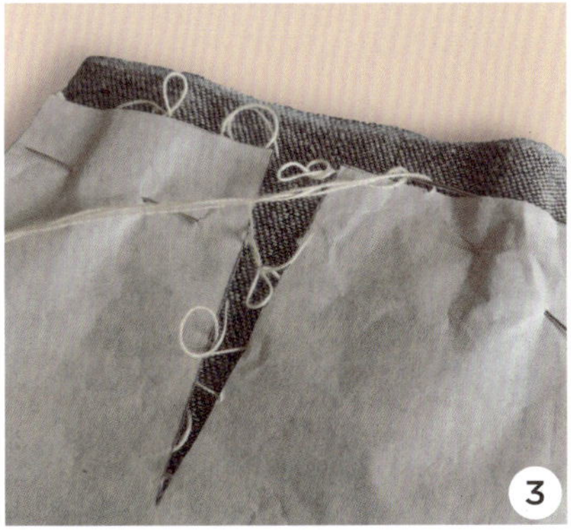

3

4

5

6

7

Finish off the seam allowances using the cut-and-sew-machine (6) or zig-zag stitches, then iron them open (7). Insert the zip (8 - 9 - 10) and prepare the waistband.

Attach the waistband (11 - 12) and do the finishing touches by hand or machine, following the explanations on pages 49 and 50. Once you've done the hem by hand or machine, as you prefer, the skirt will be ready to wear.

8

9

10

The mock-up was made in denim. The mini skirt can be made with any fabric that you like; each kind will give you a different style. Here are some suggestions:

- Faux leather
- Leather
- Denim
- Wool
- Cool Wool

PENCIL SKIRT

To make a pencil skirt, draw out the pattern once you have taken the measurements.

Look at the diagram and make the following changes to the pattern:

- A5_A21 = 1.5 cm (0.59") (this size will vary, depending on how narrow you want the bottom of the pencil skirt to be).
- A5_A22 same as A5_A21.
- Draw a line between A10_A21 and A10_A22.
- A1_A24 = 4 cm (1.57").
- A23_A25 same as A1_A24.
- Draw a line between A_24 and A25.
- A23_A26 = 3 cm (1.18").
- Draw a line between A26_A25.

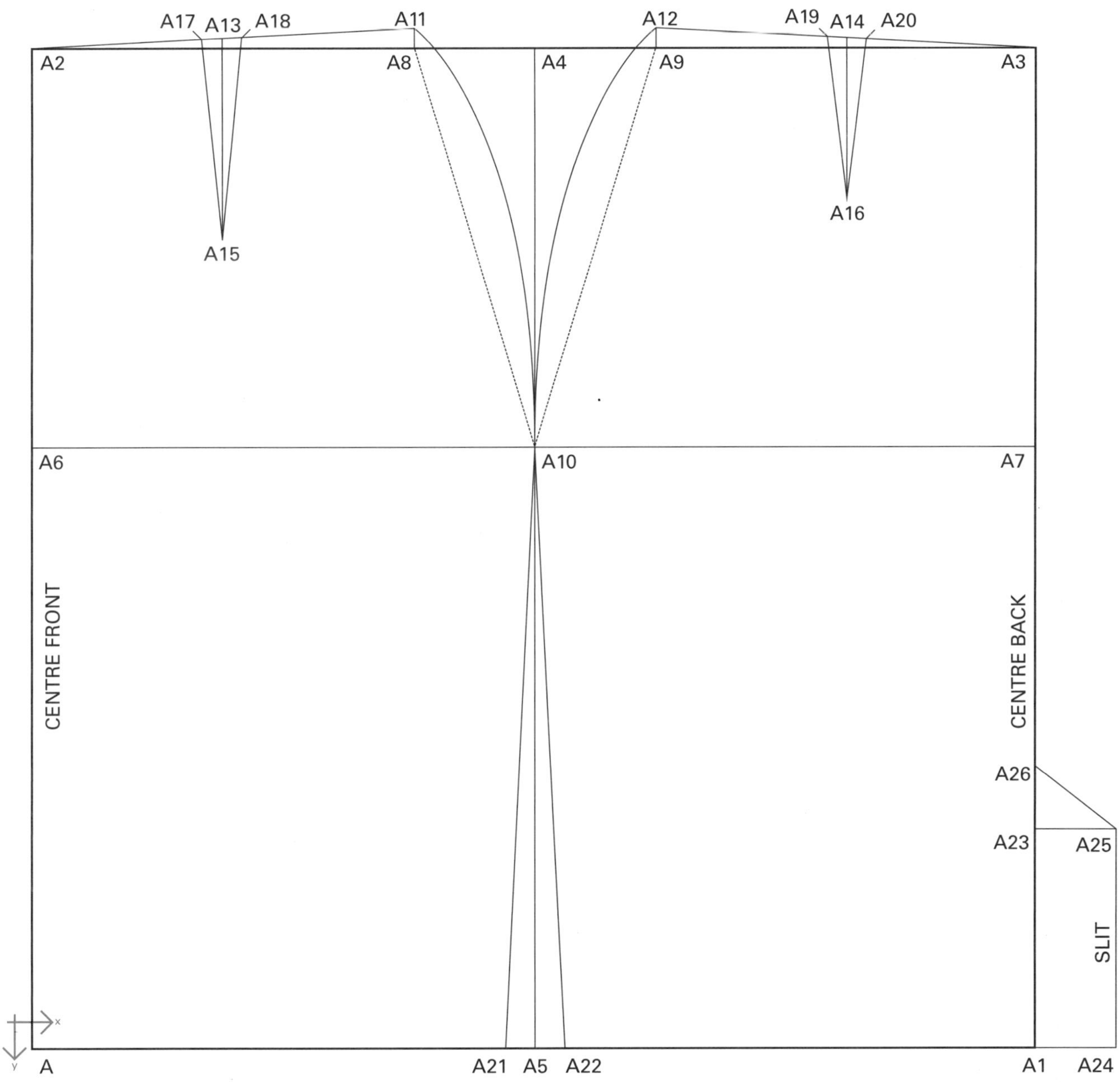

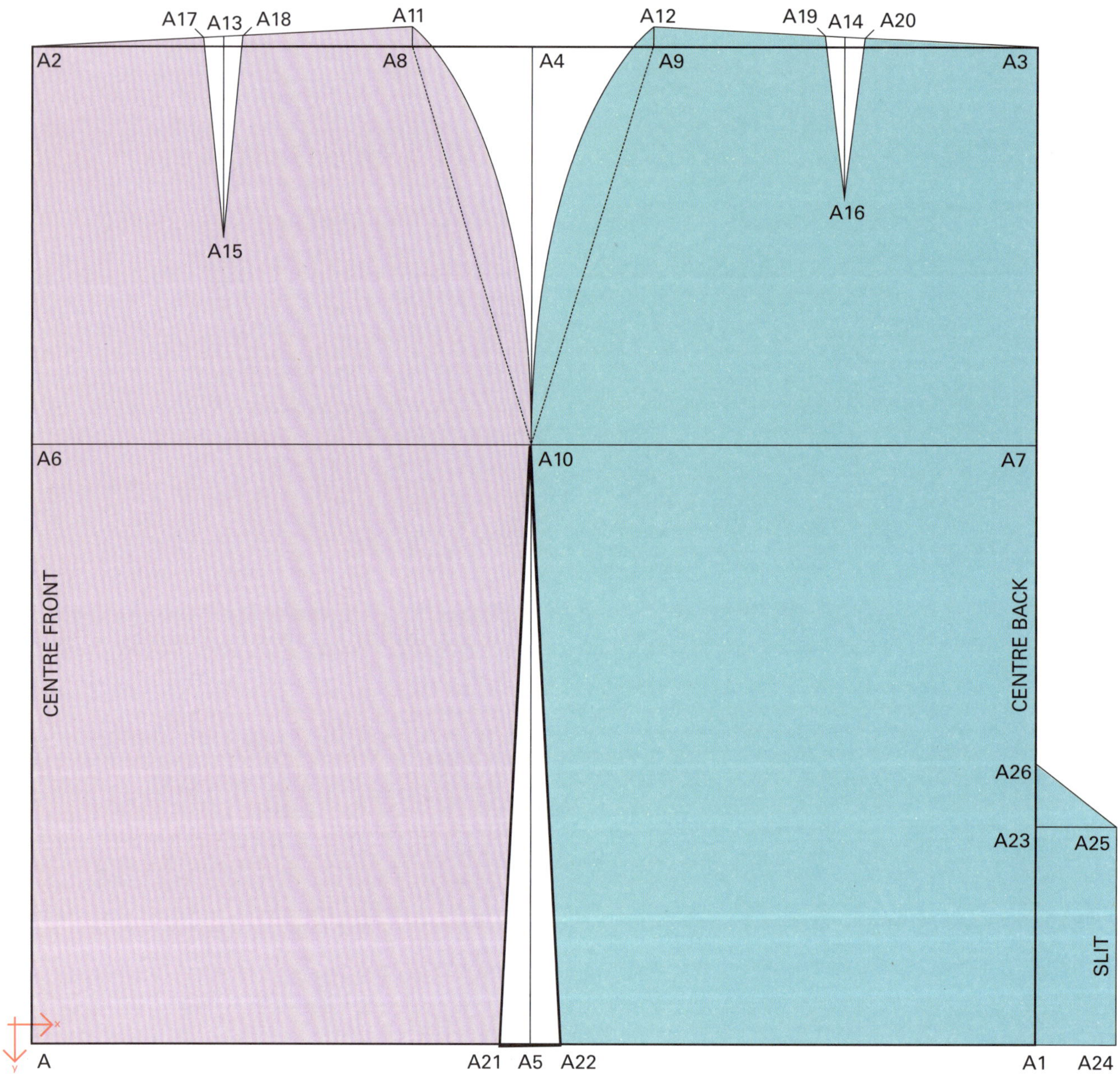

Use coloured pencils to differentiate between the patterns obtained and then cut out the front and back of the skirt. The purple coloured pattern is for the front of the skirt, while the green pattern is for the back. A gap is featured on the pattern.

Choose a fabric you like, join its selvedges together, with the right side of the fabric facing inwards and place it on a tabletop. Pin the pattern to the fabric, just like you did for the mini skirt and the classic office skirt. Using chalk and a tape measure, add the seam allowances: usually, 1 cm (0.39") on the waist, 2 cm (0.78") at the hip and the middle of the back, 5 cm (1.96") on the bottom for a hem made by hand (1).

Cut along the chalk marks and sew tacking stitches on each piece, around the patterns still pinned to the fabric (2). Detach the patterns from the fabric and open the parts inside them, cutting the stitches previously made in the middle, thereby obtaining all the markings that will be useful for sewing the seams. Assemble the pieces so that the right side of the fabric on the front matches the right side of the fabric on the back, and pin them together using the marks made by the tacking stitches as a guide (3).

Sew tacking stitches, leaving a gap for a slit and a gap for the zip (at least 20 cm / 7.87"), then sew a linear seam exactly along the tacking stitches (4).

1

2

3

4

Finish off the edges with a cut-and-sew-machine (5) or with zig-zag stitches and then iron them open (6). At the slit, make a small cut so that it can easily be folded onto one side only (7).

On the right side of the skirt, at the top of the slit, use a machine to sew a linear seam to keep it in place (8).

Insert the zip (9) and prepare the waistband, as explained on page 42. For the pencil skirt, I recommend using an invisible zip.

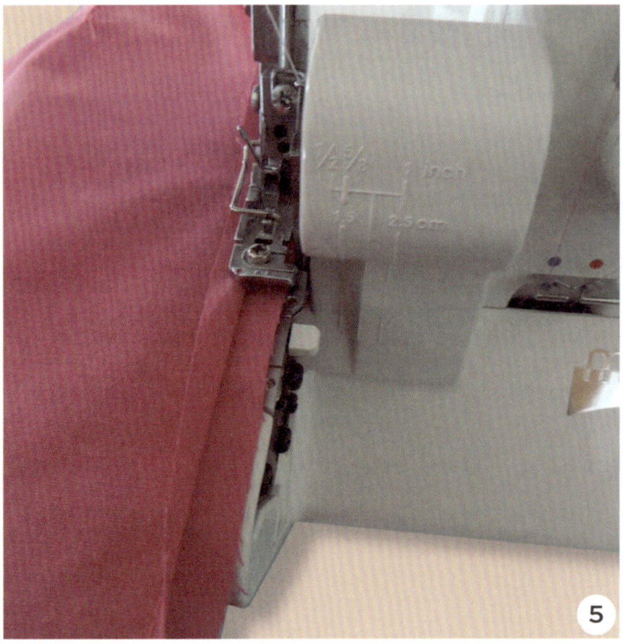

Attach the waistband and do the finishing touches by hand, with invisible stitches on the wrong side of the fabric (10). Also sew the hem with understitches by hand.

For the mock-up skirt, I used cotton; for an elegant pencil skirt, I would advise you to use Cool Wool. Other types of fabrics can also be fine, but remember that each type of fabric creates a different style of skirt.

A-LINE SKIRT

There are two versions of the A-line skirt: the simple one, that is, slightly flared, and the wider kind.

Draw the pattern of the A-line skirt starting from the basic design, using your own measurements.

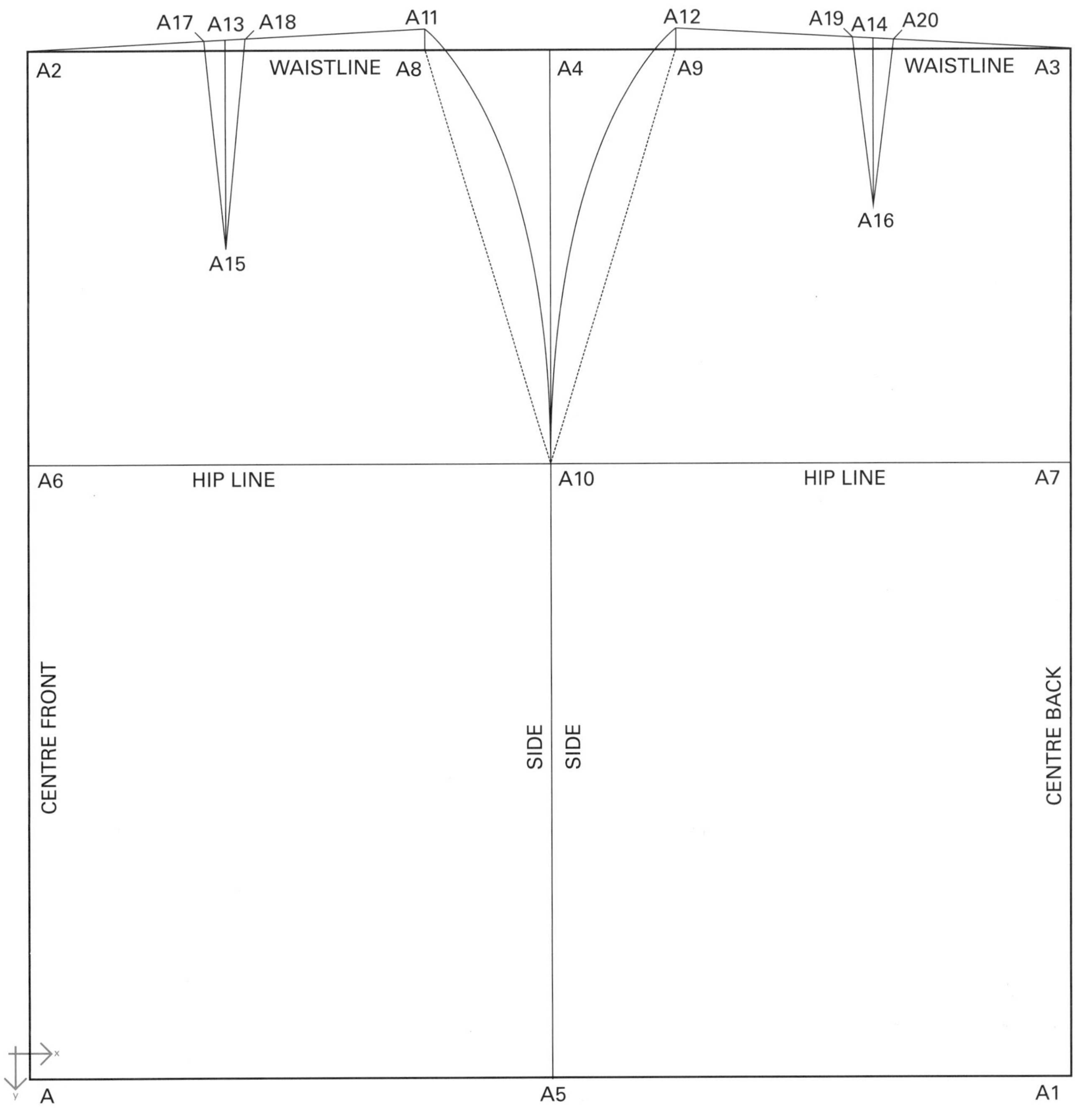

SIMPLE A-LINE SKIRT - FRONT

Using another sheet of paper, draw the front and back of the basic skirt pattern separately so you can modify it later, as described in the diagrams below.

- A3_A12 = 5 cm (1.96") (this size may vary, according to how flared you want it to be, however I advise you not to exceed 5 cm / 1.96").
- Draw a line between A5_A12 and colour this part of the pattern in crayon, to identify it as the front, and cut it out as shown in the following diagram.

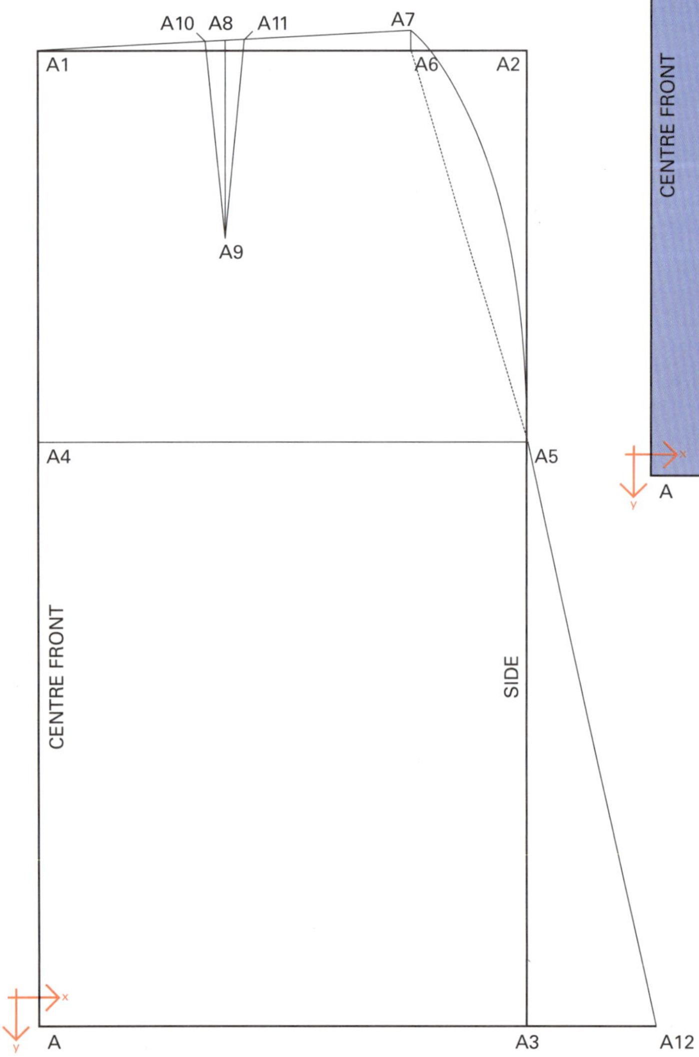

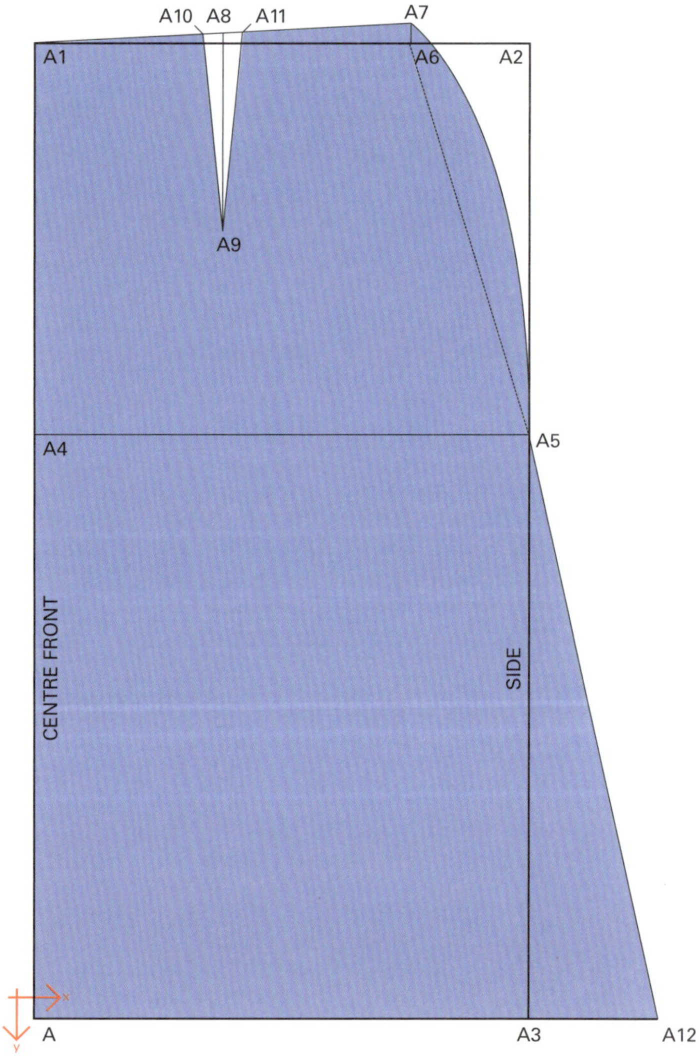

SIMPLE A-LINE SKIRT - BACK

Once you have copied the back of the pattern onto another sheet, you can make the following changes:

- A_A12 = 5 cm (1.96") (this size may vary according to how flared you want it to be, however I advise you not to exceed 5 cm / 1.96").
- Draw a line between A4_A12 and colour this part of the pattern in crayon, to identify it as the back, and cut it out as shown in the following diagram.

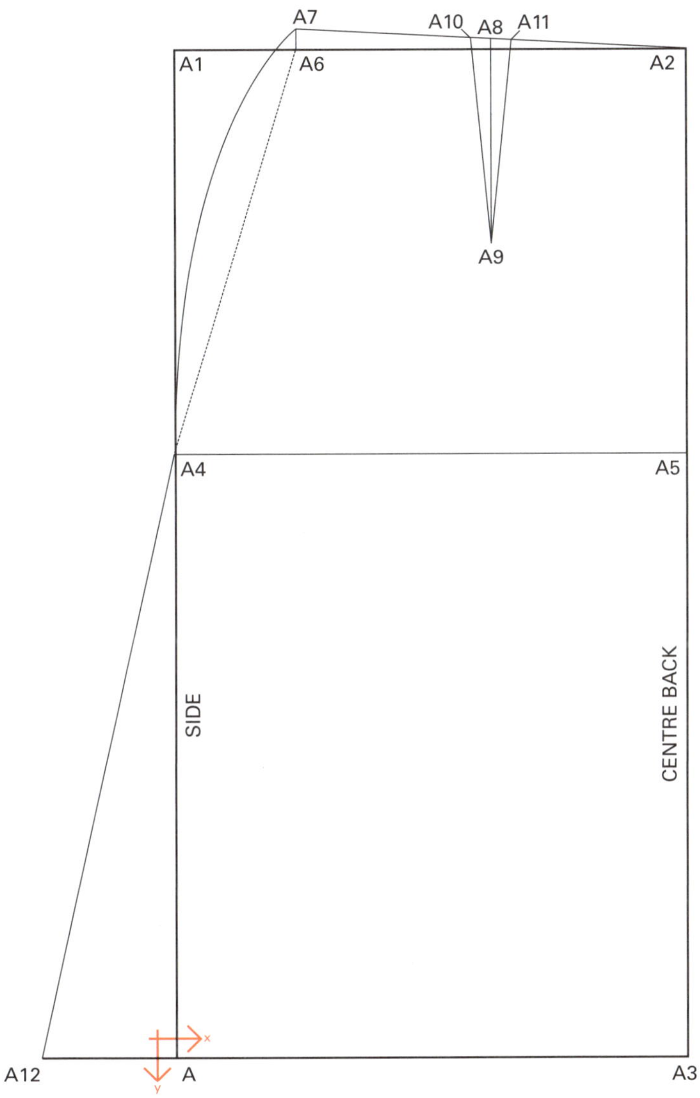

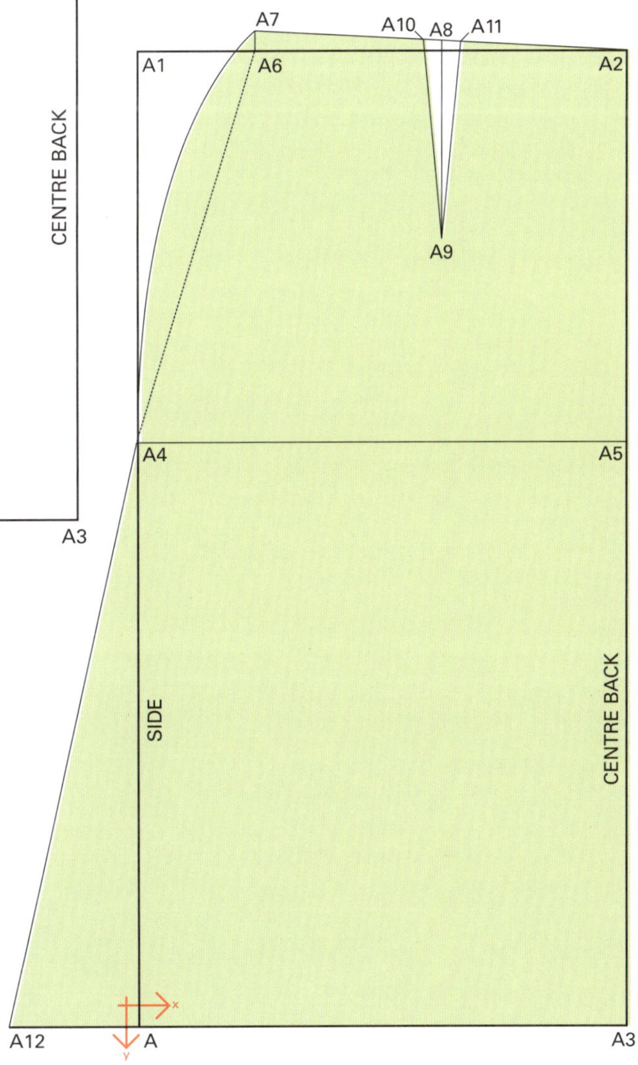

WIDE A-LINE SKIRT – FRONT

- A_A12 same as A1_A8.
- Draw a line between A9_A12 (this line defines how wide the skirt will be; it must be cut from the bottom up to the top of the dart). Then, while the dart closes on the paper, the cut section automatically opens up, giving shape to the skirt.

Using a pencil crayon, colour in the paper pattern to identify it as the front.

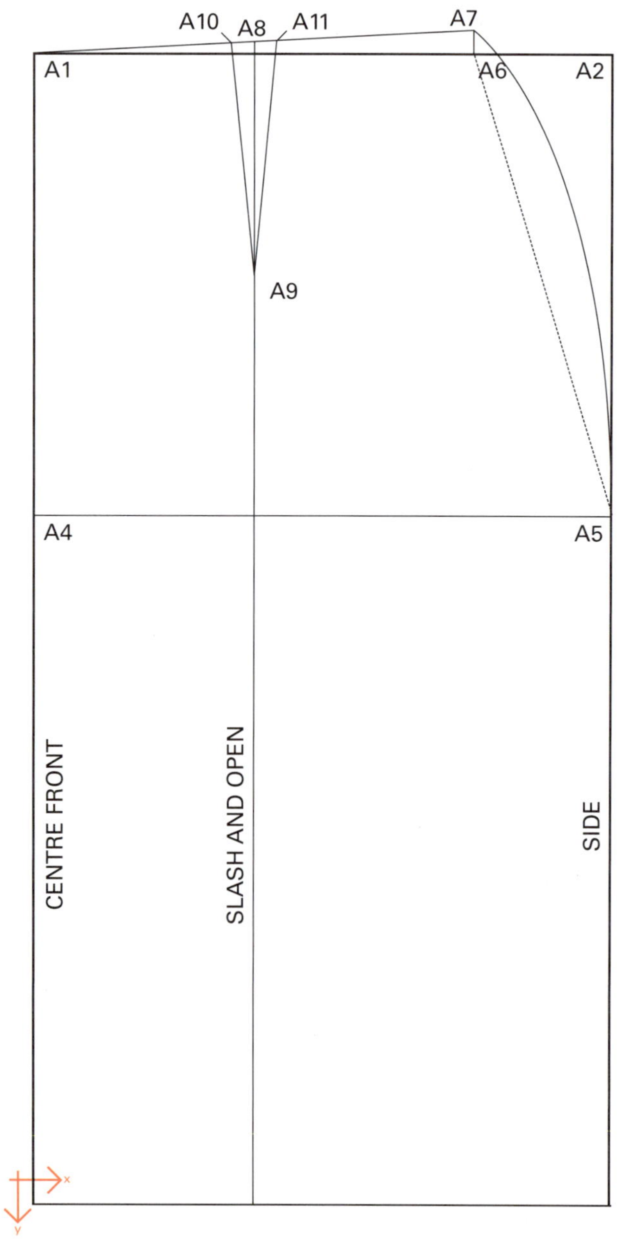

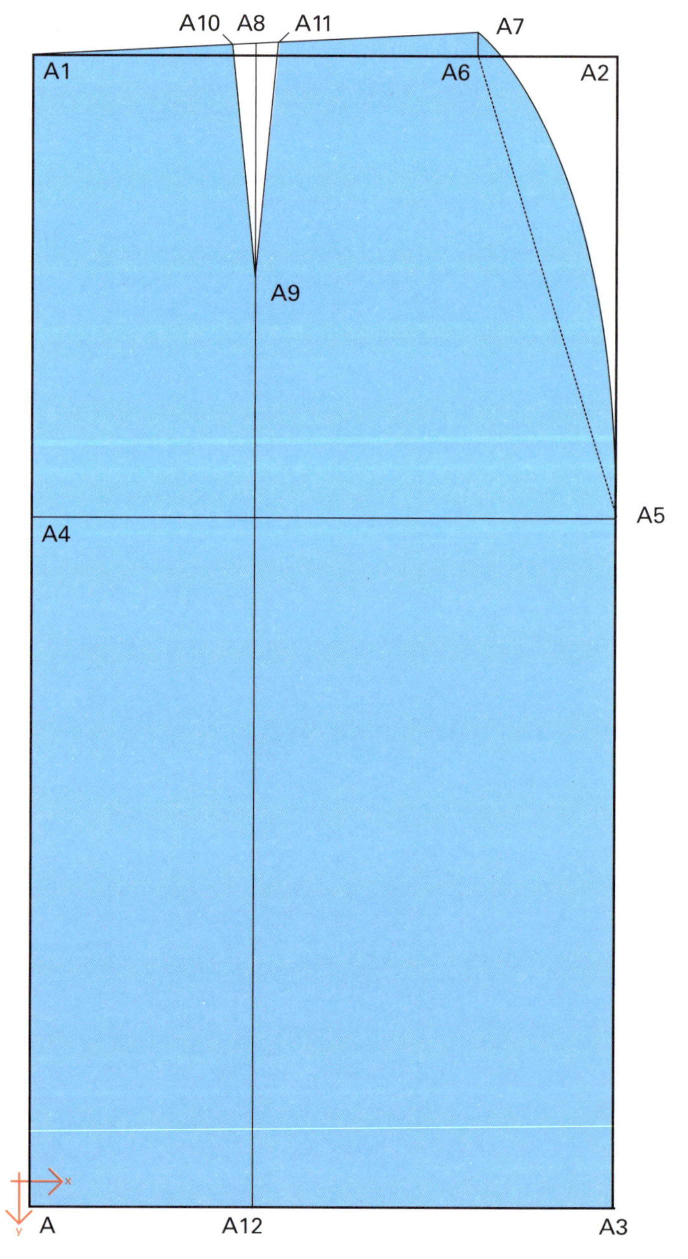

WIDE A-LINE SKIRT - BACK

- A3_A12 same as A2_A8.
- Draw a line between A9_A12 (this line defines how wide the skirt will be; it must be cut from the bottom up to the top of the dart). Then, while the dart closes on the paper, the cut section automatically opens up, giving shape to the skirt.

Using a pencil crayon, colour in the paper pattern to identify it as the back.

Since the simple A-line skirt is easier to make, I decided to demonstrate how to make the wide A-line skirt.

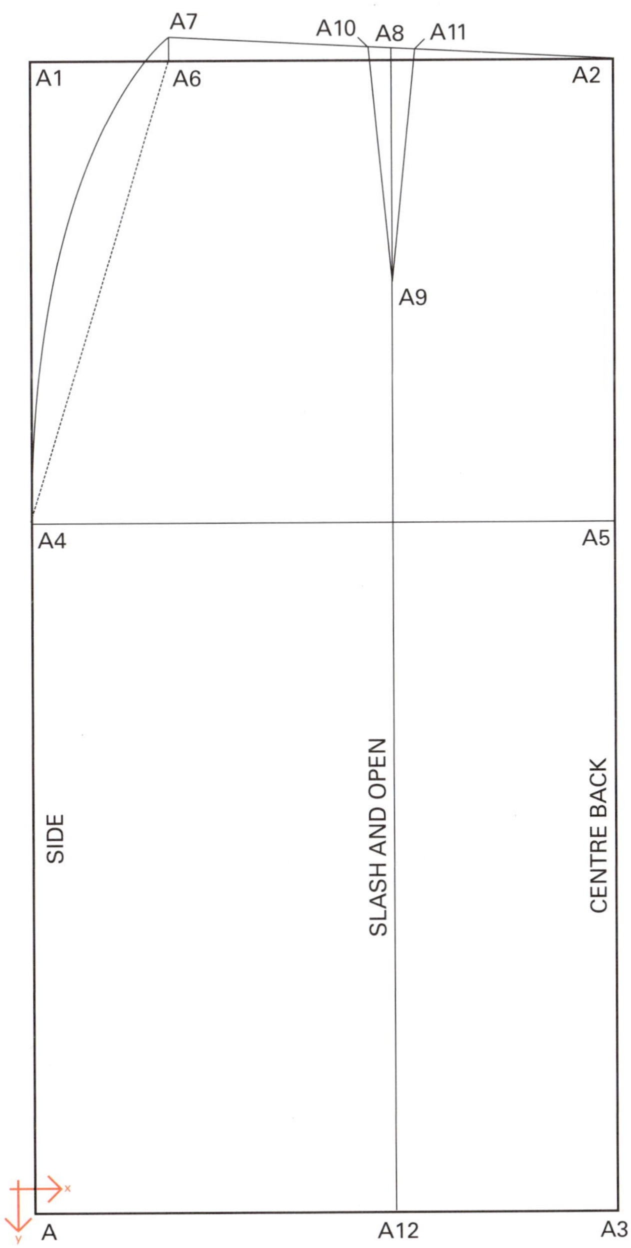

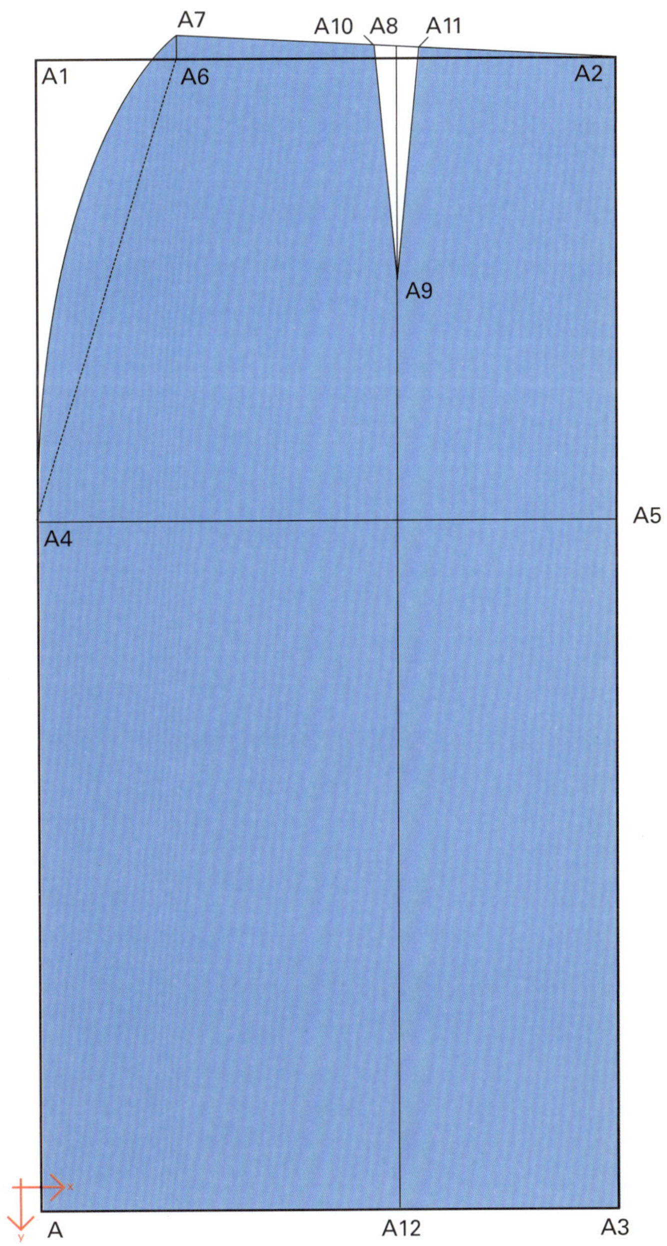

MAKING AN A-LINE SKIRT

Once you have cut out the pattern and cut along the traced line that defines the width, close the respective darts on the patterns for both the front and back: the parts of the skirt separated by the line will open automatically (1).

Use pins to position the pattern on the fabric that you have folded in two, with the selvages touching; the middle of the front and the middle of the back of the pattern must line up with where the fabric folds, since the zip is positioned on the side, for aesthetic reasons.

Using the chalk and measuring tape, insert the seam allowances: usually 2 cm (0.78") at the hip; 1 cm (0.39") on the waist; 3 cm (1.18") on the bottom, if you want to machine sew the hem, or 5 cm (1.96") if you want to do it by hand (2). Cut out all parts of the skirt exactly along the chalk marks.

Sew tacking stitches around each piece of the pattern (3), then detach the patterns and cut open the tacking stitches, thereby creating marks that are useful when sewing the seams. Join the parts together and sew tacking stitches, leaving a space on

1

3

2

the top left for the zip, then machine sew with linear stitches and finish off the edges with the cut-and-sew-machine or with zig-zag stitches. Iron the skirt on the wrong side, with the edges splayed open. Machine sew the hem, insert the zip and the waistband (4), as explained on page 42. Do the finishing touches of the inside of the waistband by hand or using a sewing machine, if you prefer (5).

Sew a press stud or normal button with buttonhole onto the overlapping part of the waistband. If you prefer, you can put the zip in the middle of the back of the skirt.

4

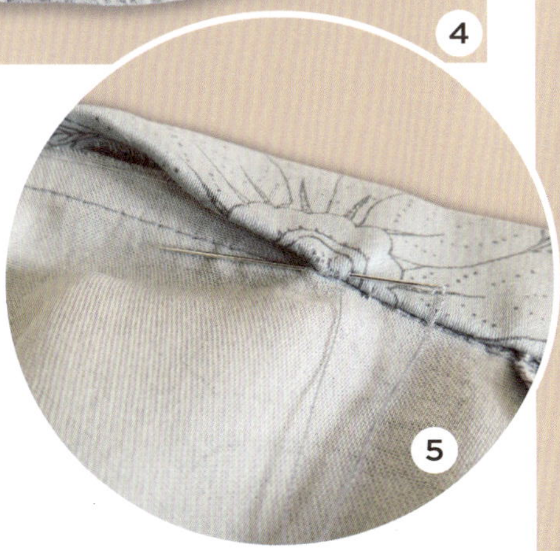

5

For the mock-up skirt, I chose to use medium-weight cotton, but for this type of skirt you can use whatever fabric you like. Each type of fabric gives the skirt a different look: if made with very light fabrics, the skirt will tend to "fall" and won't have the "fuller" effect that heavier fabrics have.

HALF-WHEEL SKIRT

To make a half-wheel skirt, you only need to take two measurements: the waist circumference and however long you want the skirt to be.

Looking at the diagram, draw the pattern out using the following calculations:

- A_A2 is at least double the length of the skirt.
- A_A1 is at least double the length of the skirt.
- A_A4 = 1/3 of waist circumference (for example 68 : 3 = 22.6 / 26.77" : 3 = 8.92").
- A_A3 same as A_A4.
- Draw a line between A3_A4.
- A7 = 1/2 of A3_A4.
- Draw a line between A_A8 passing through A7.
- A8 is at least twice the length of the skirt.
- A_A9 = 1/3 of waist circumference.

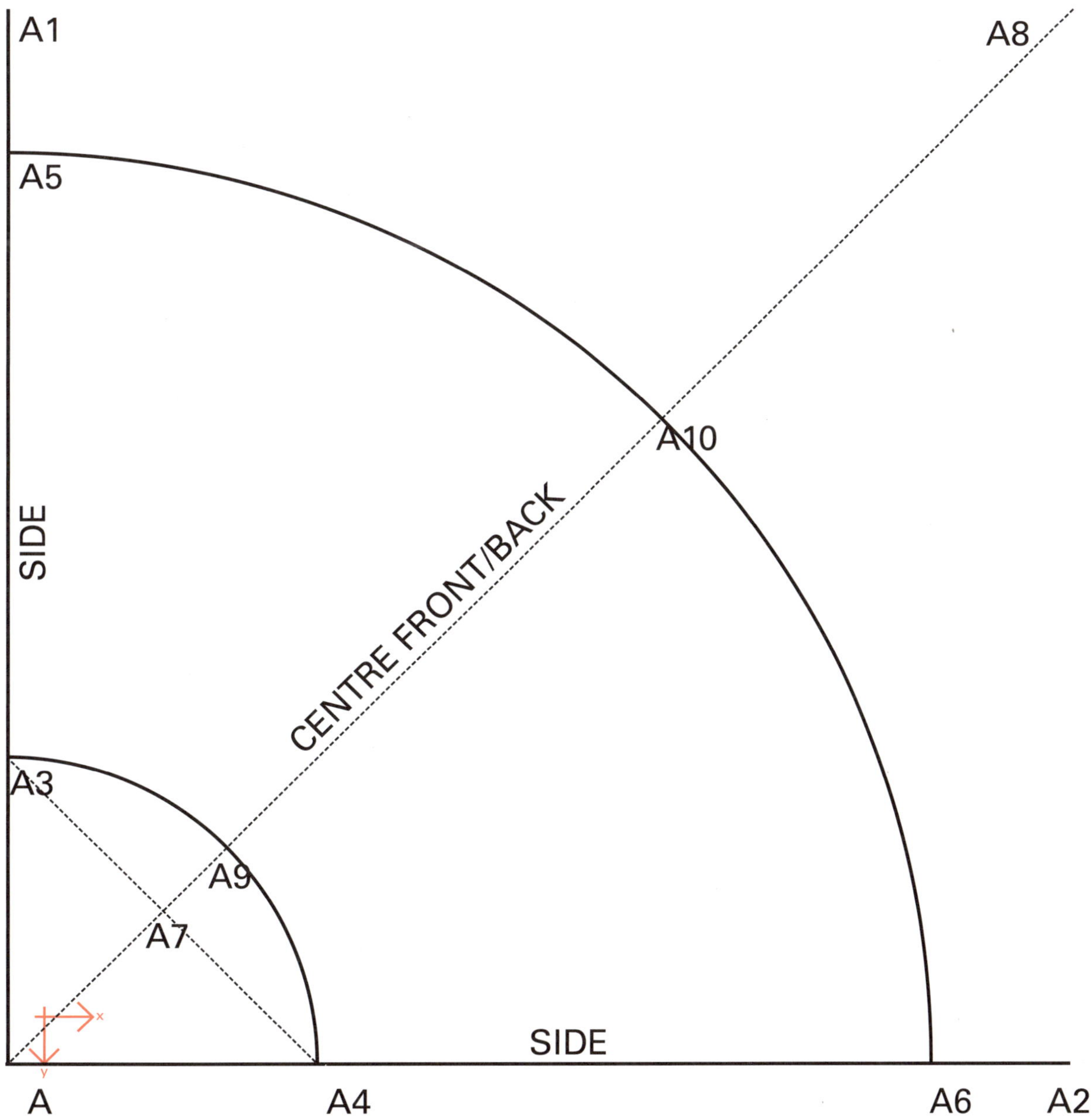

- Use a ruler and, considering point A as the vertex, join points A3_A9_A4 together with the same measurement as A_A3, A_A4 and A_A9, therefore 1/4 of the circumference.
- A4_A6 is the length of the skirt (for example, 50 cm / 19.68").
- A3_A5 same as A4_A6.
- A9_A10 same as A4_A6.
- Using a ruler and considering point A as the vertex, join points A5_A10_A6 together, with the same measurements as A3_A5, A9_A10, A4_A6, therefore 1/4 of the circumference.
- A9_A10 is the middle of the front or the middle of the back of the skirt.
- A3_A5 and A4_A6 are the sides of the skirt.

With a pencil crayon, colour in the paper pattern you've just drawn. Once you have cut out the pattern, place it on top of the fabric you have chosen, which was previously folded in two, with the selvedges touching and the right side of the fabric facing inwards. The line down the middle of the front or back is equidistant from each of the sides, so measure the distance from the selvedges to be sure

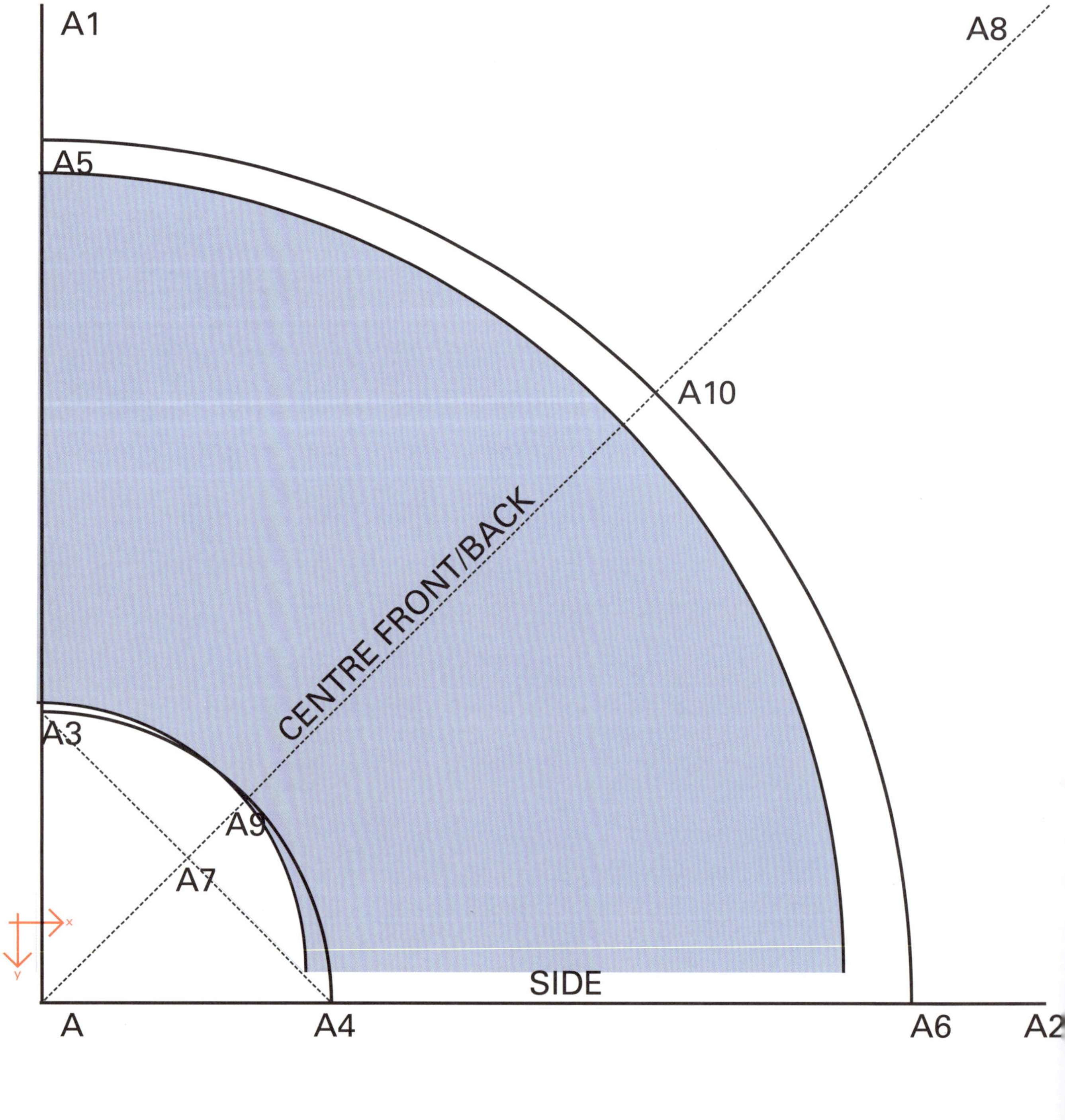

1

that you have positioned the pattern in perfect alignment with them (1).

Add the seam allowances using chalk: usually 2 cm (0.78") at the hip, 1 cm (0.39") on the waist and 2 cm (0.78") on the bottom, then cut along the marks you've made (2).

Sew guide stitches around the pattern while it is still positioned on the fabric (3), then detach the pattern,

2

cut open the guide stitches and put the front and back of the skirt together, so that the right side of the fabric is facing inwards and the marks left by the guide stitches line up perfectly. Then, pin the marks left by the guide stitches and use tacking thread to sew the materials together.

Sew along the marks left by the guide stitches (4), leaving a gap (at least 20 cm / 7.87") for a zip on the top left of the skirt.

Finish off the edges with a cut-and-sew-machine (5) or with zig-zag stitches and then iron them open (6). Insert the zip (7) and prepare the waistband, as explained on page 42.

3

4

5

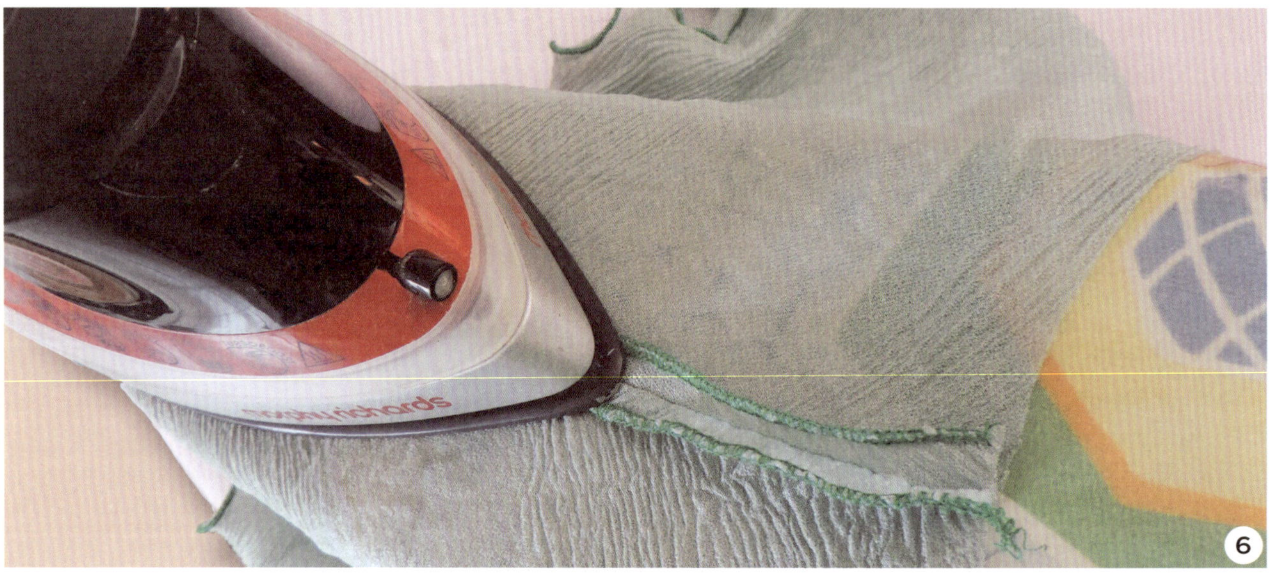
6

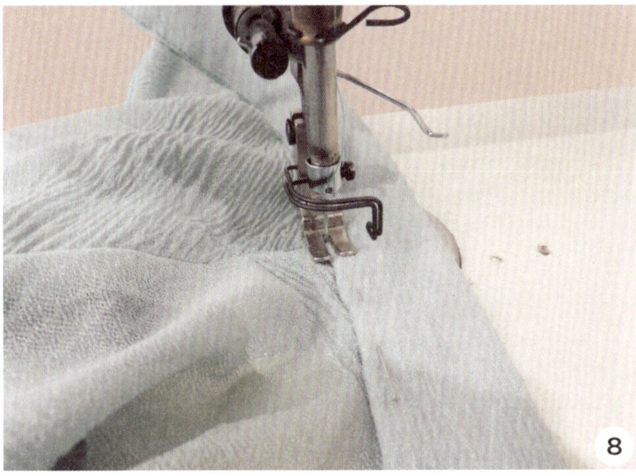

Attach the waistband and finish it off as you prefer (8). For this type of skirt, it is best to make the hem using the special hemming function on the cut-and-sew-machine, as it is cut on the bias.

To make the mock-up skirt, I chose a lightweight crêpe fabric made from mixed synthetic elastane. To get the same effect, I recommend using one of the following fabrics:

- Satin
- Viscose
- Khadi
- Georgette
- Crêpe
- Chiffon

However, you can make it with other fabrics if you want to try out different effects.

FULL-WHEEL SKIRT

Looking at the diagram, draw out the paper pattern for a full skirt. To make this type of skirt, you only need to take two measurements: the waist circumference and however long you want the skirt to be.

- Draw a horizontal line at least three times the desired length of the skirt (A7_A9).
- A2 = half of A7_A9.
- A2_A5 = 1/3 of waist circumference (for example, 68 cm : 3 = 22.6 / 26.77" : 3 = 8.92").
- A2_A4 same as A2_A5.
- A2_A6 same as A2_A5 and A2_A4.
- Use a ruler to join points A4_A6_A5 together and, considering A2 as the vertex, use the same measurements to get a semicircle: this represents the skirt's waist.
- A4_A7 same as the length of the skirt;
- A5_A9 same as A4_A7.
- A6_A8 same as A5_A9 and A4_A7.
- Use a ruler to join points A7_A8_A9 together and, considering A2 as the vertex, use the same measurements to get a semicircle: this represents the length of the skirt.
- A6_A8 represents the middle of the front or back of the skirt; A4_A7 and A5_A9 are the sides.
- With a pencil crayon, colour in the paper pattern you've just drawn.

Once you've cut the pattern out, position it on top of the fabric you've chosen, with the selvedges touching and the right side of the fabric facing inwards. Pin the paper pattern to the fabric, aligning the sides

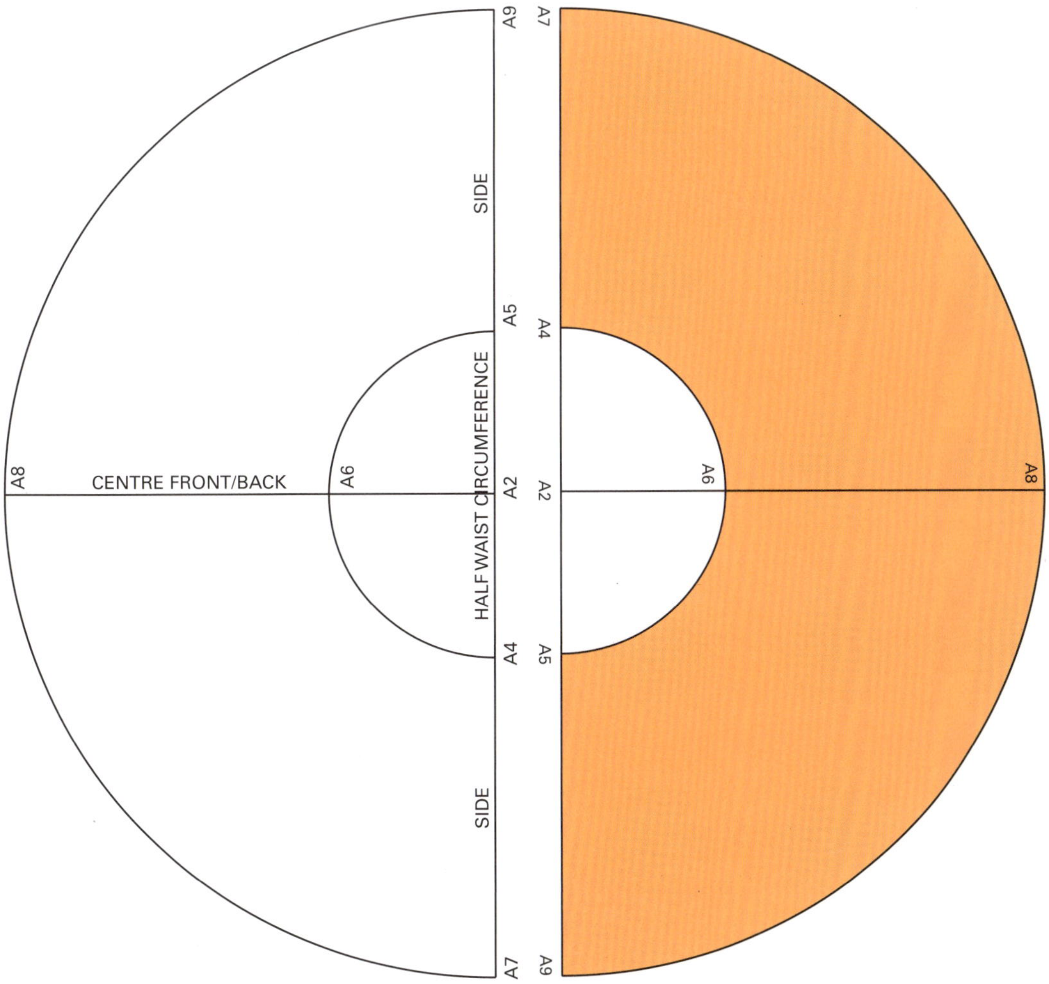

perfectly with the selvedges. Add seam allowances in chalk: usually 2 cm (0.78") along the sides, 1 cm (0.39") on the waist and 2 cm (0.78") on the bottom (1). Cut along the chalk marks, then sew guide stitches around the pattern (2).

Detach the pattern from the fabric, cut open the guide stitches and join the front of the skirt with the back, so that the right side of the fabric is facing inwards and the marks made by the guide stitches match up perfectly. Pin it all together, sew tacking stitches and then sew a seam exactly over them (3).

Along the top left of the skirt, leave a gap at the waist (at least 20 cm / 7.87") for a zip to be inserted.

Finish off the edges with a cut-and-sew-machine (4) or with zig-zag stitches and then iron them open (5). Sew the zip and prepare the waistband as explained on page 42, then attach the waistband and do the finishing touches as you prefer (6). For this type of skirt, too, it is best to make the hem using the special hemming function on the cut-and-sew-machine, as it is cut on the bias.

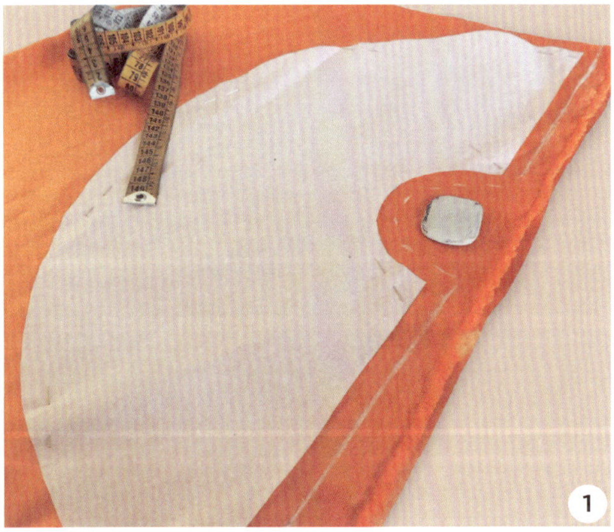

1

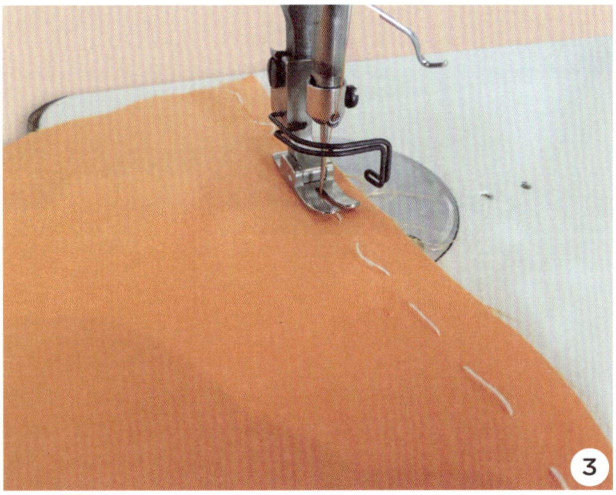

3

2

4

The mock-up skirt was made in satin. To achieve the same effect, I recommend using the following fabrics:

- Satin
- Khadi
- Viscose
- Crêpe
- Chiffon
- Georgette

Remember that the lighter the fabric, the more it tends to "fall"; thicker fabrics tend to have a fuller effect. You can choose to use other fabrics too, if you want to experiment with different effects.

BALLOON SKIRT

There are a few different ways to make a balloon skirt: draw the pattern of a full- or half-wheel skirt (pages 95 and 101), or even draw the pattern of a wide A-line skirt (page 90) and make several cuts to add width to the skirt. You'll get the same result, whichever one you choose.

Once you have chosen the type of pattern you want to use, draw it according to the rules already addressed in the previous chapters, then cut it out and position it on the fabric folded over twice, so that its selvedges are touching and the right side of the fabric is facing inwards (1). The middle of the front and the middle of the back of the patterns must line up with the fold of the fabric.

Once you have inserted the seam allowances - usually 2 cm (0.78") along the sides, 2 cm (0.78") on the bottom and 1 cm (0.39") on the waist - cut out the parts of the pattern you now have and sew guide stitches (2).

Detach the patterns and cut open the guide stitches. Join the front of the skirt to the back, so that the right side of the fabric is still facing inwards and the marks left by the guide stitches line up perfectly. Hold the fabric together with pins and tacking stitches, then sew a linear seam exactly along the tacking stitches (3), leaving enough space to insert a zip along the top left side of the skirt, at the waist.

1

2

3

Finish off the edges with a cut-and-sew-machine (4) or with zig-zag stitches and then iron them open (5). Sew the hem by machine, as explained on page 50, leaving a small gap to insert the elastic band (6) which creates the balloon skirt's characteristic inflated effect.

Using a safety pin to help you, insert the elastic band (7), sliding it inside the hem along its entire circumference, until it emerges from the same point it started at. The elastic must be at least 10 cm (3.93") shorter than the circumference of the waist.

4

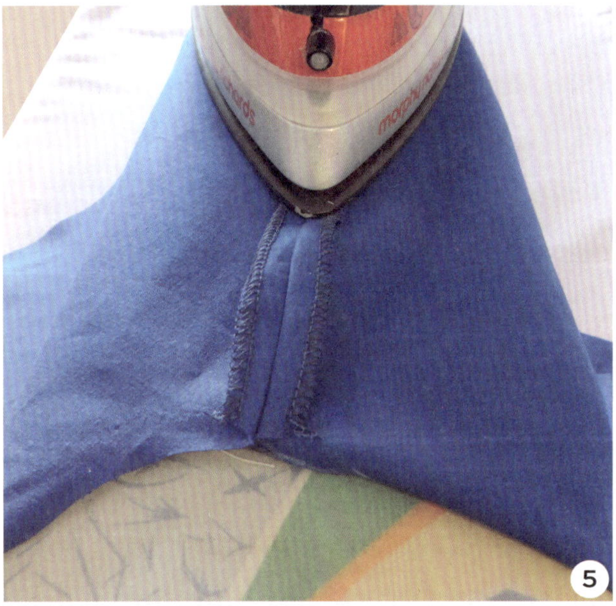

5

6

7

8

Pull the elastic to wrinkle up the fabric (8) and weld it in place with a machine stitch (9), then close the gap with a linear stitch.

Insert the zip and prepare the waistband as explained on page 42, then attach the waistband and finish it off as you like.

By the way: if you want to increase the balloon effect, you can wear the skirt upside down, ie. with the elasticated bottom around your waist and the top of the skirt around your legs.

The mock-up skirt was made of a medium-weight cotton fabric. To achieve a similar result, you can use the following fabrics:
- Satin
- Khadi
- Taffeta
- Mikado
- Duchesse

You can also try out new effects, using different fabrics.

FISHTAIL SKIRT

1

By combining the pencil skirt with the full-wheel skirt, you can get the much-loved fishtail skirt. Original, if not exactly comfortable, this skirt is perfect for showing off on special occasions.

To make it, you have to draw two paper patterns: one for the pencil skirt without the slit and one for the full-wheel skirt.

The pattern for the full-wheel skirt must be designed by measuring the circumference of the bottom of the pencil skirt - not the circumference of the waist - since it will be attached to the bottom of the pencil skirt. To do this, first draw out the pattern for the pencil skirt, usually with the bottom reaching below the knee and wide enough to be able to walk in it, unless you make it in a stretchy fabric. Then, once you've taken the measurements of the bottom of the pencil skirt with the tape measure directly on the pattern, go on to draw the pattern for the full-wheel skirt.

Now you have both patterns, position them on the fabric that you've folded in two with the selvedges touching and the right side of the fabric facing inwards. Add the seam allowances with chalk: for the pencil skirt, this is usually 2 cm (0.78") along the sides, 1 cm (0.39") on the waist, 1 cm (0.39") on the bottom and 2 cm (0.78") for the middle of the back; for the full-wheel skirt, 2 cm (0.78") on the bottom. Cut along the marks drawn in chalk until you have all the parts you need to make the skirt (1).

Sew guide stitches, then detach the paper patterns, cut open the guide stitches and join the front parts of the skirt with the corresponding back parts, so that the right side of the fabric is facing inwards. Use pins and sew tacking stitches exactly along the marks left by the guide stitches. Sew linear seams, thereby obtaining two skirts, one pencil skirt and one full-wheel skirt (2). Remember to finish off the edges with a zig-zag stitch or the cut-and-sew-machine and iron them open.

Join the full-wheel skirt to the bottom of the pencil skirt, matching up with the right side of the fabric of both skirts. Use pins and tacking stitches to join them together (3).

Sew exactly along the tacking stitches (4), then finish the edges off with the cut-and-sew-machine or a zig-zag stitch.

Prepare the waistband and insert the zip (5) as explained on page 47, then finish off the waistband as you wish.

2

3

The mock-up skirt was made in corduroy, but you can choose whichever fabric you like, knowing that each kind will give a different final effect.

CLASSIC FLOUNCED SKIRT

First draw the basic skirt pattern and apply the changes in accordance with the instructions explained below, carefully observing the diagram.

- Divide both the front and back of the skirt into four equal parts. If the width of the front is 25 cm (9.84"), do the calculation 25 cm : 4 = 6.25 cm / 9.84" : 4 = 2.46". For example: A1_A15, A15_A8, A8_A22 and A22_A7 are equal to 6.25 cm (2.46") respectively.
- A_A14, A14_A12, A12_A23 are also 6.25 cm (2.46") in width.
- Follow the same procedure for the back of the skirt. Then join the upper points with the lower points (for example: A15_A14, A8_A12, A22_A23, A5_A3, etc.).
- Once you have divided the front and back of the skirt into four equal parts vertically, divide them into three equal parts horizontally. For example, if the skirt is 50 cm (19.68") long, proceed by calculating 50 cm : 3 = 16.6 cm / 19.68" : 3 = 6.56".

In this case we have: A1_A4 = 16.6 cm (19.68"), A4_A13 = 16.6 cm (19.68"), A16_A18 = 16.6 cm (19.68"), A18_A19 = 16.6 cm (19.68").

- Join points A4_A18 and A13_A19 together.
- This will give you three flounces of equal size, as shown in the diagram (part 1, part 2 and part 3).
- Using pencil crayons, colour in the three parts of the front of the skirt in one colour and the three parts of the back in another, each of which are also divided vertically, as shown in the following diagrams; this will give you three patterns for the front and back of the skirt.

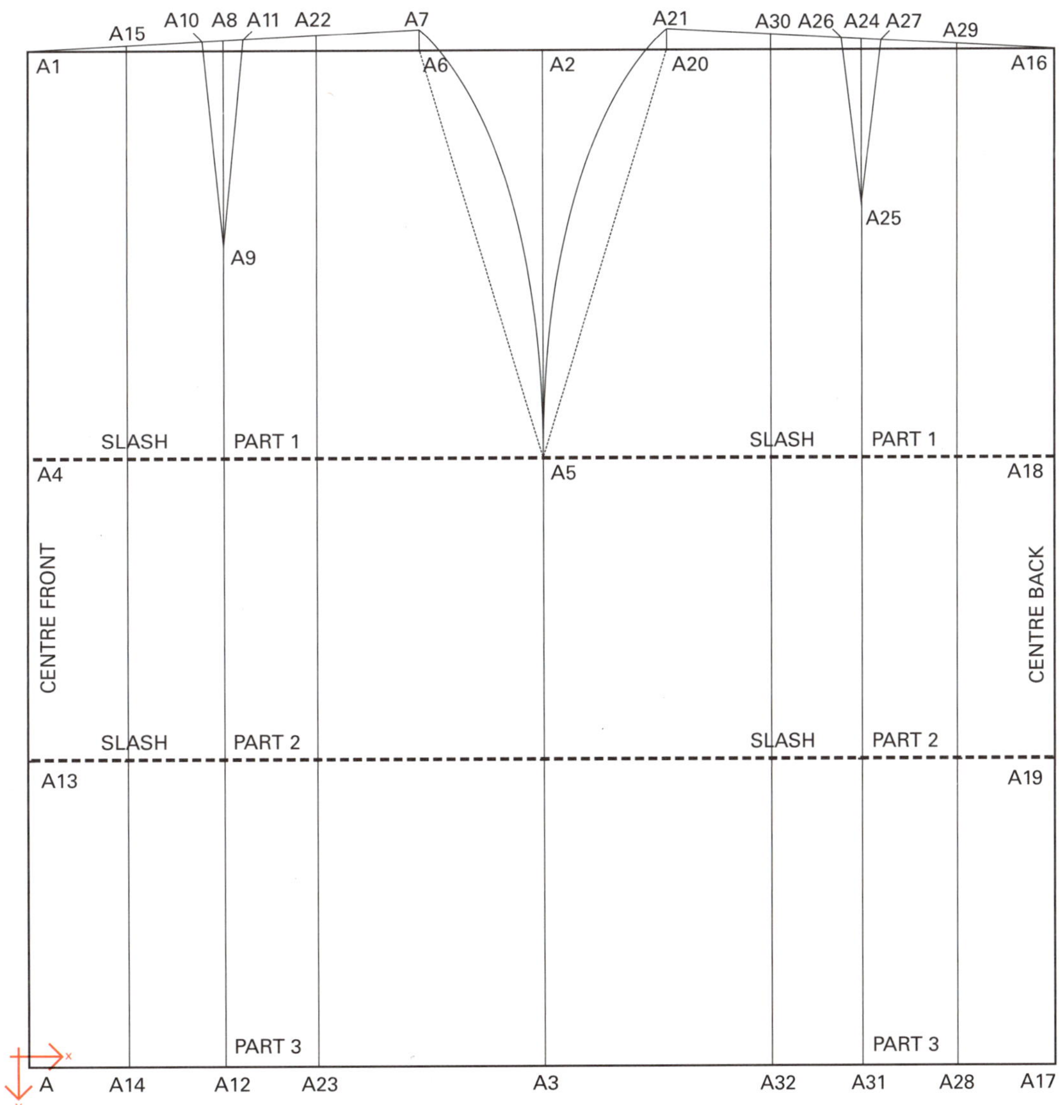

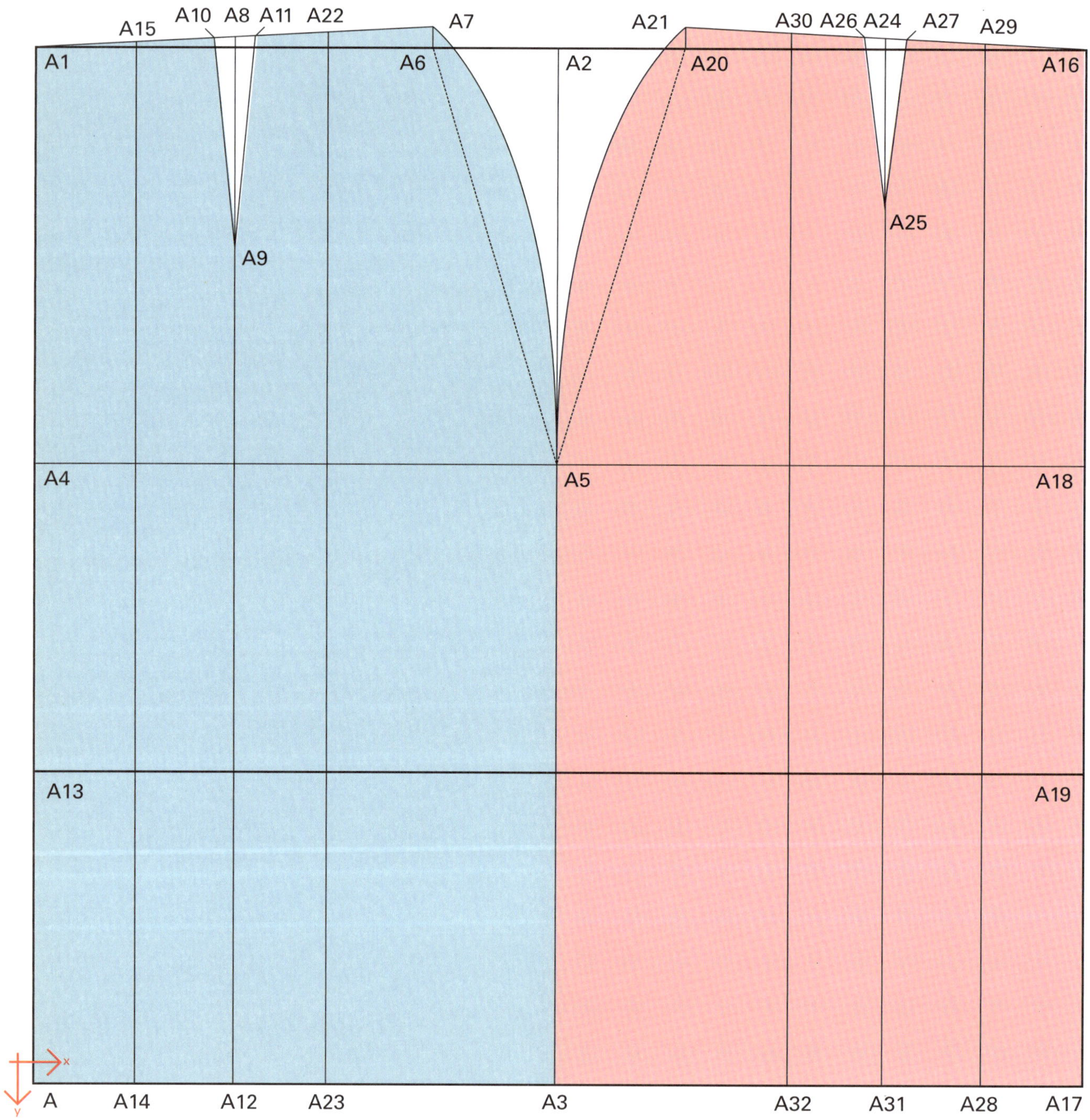

Cut out the respective pieces: you will have to make three skirts that overlap to create one (1).

Before you position the patterns on the fabric, cut along the vertical lines you've drawn, starting from the bottom of each piece. Along these lines, at the darts, put the paper together to give the skirt a flared effect. Position the patterns on the fabric that you have folded in two, with its selvedges touching and the right side of the fabric facing inwards.

The fabric can also be folded on the bias, as seen in the photo: this will give the skirt more of a wavy effect.

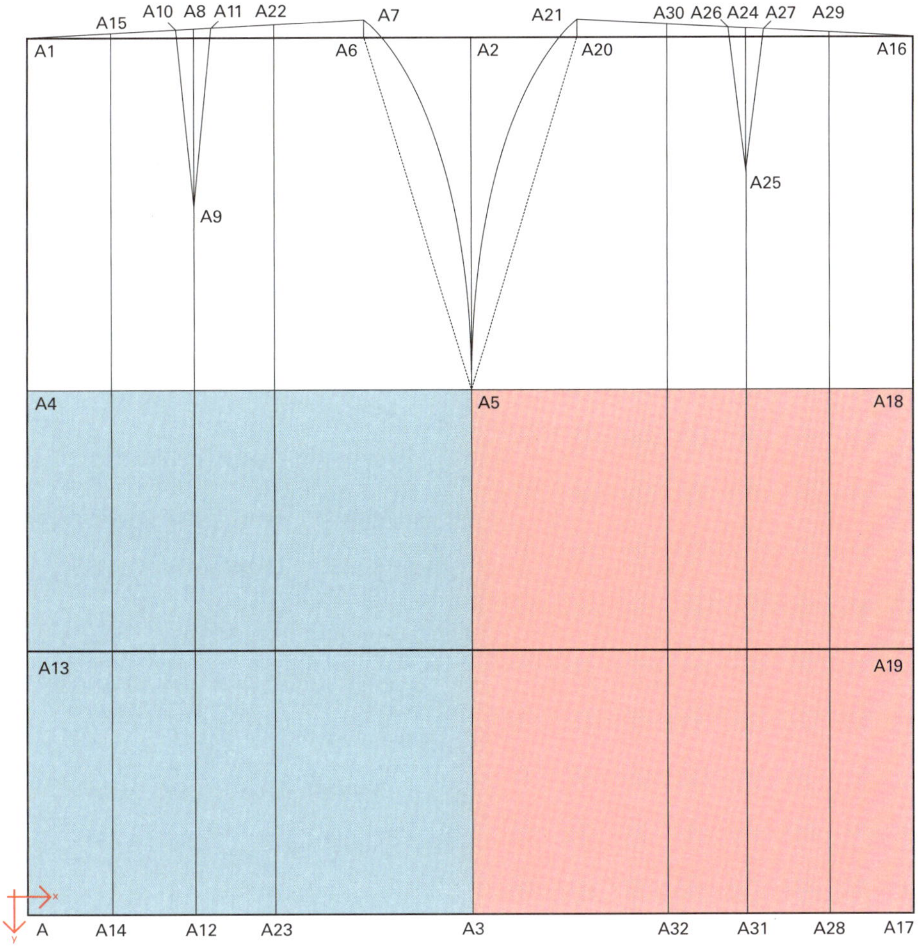
A15 A10 A8 A11 A22 A7 A21 A30 A26 A24 A27 A29
A1 A6 A2 A20 A16
A9
A25
A4 A5 A18
A13 A19
x
y
A A14 A12 A23 A3 A32 A31 A28 A17

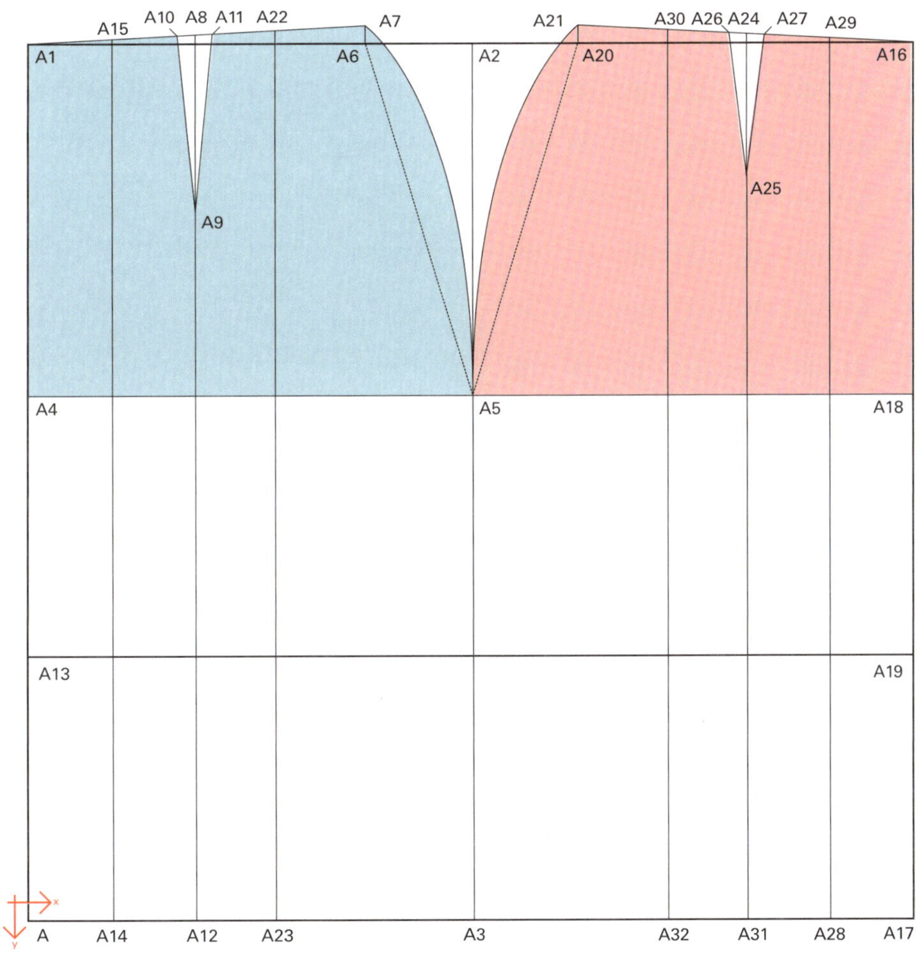
A15 A10 A8 A11 A22 A7 A21 A30 A26 A24 A27 A29
A1 A6 A2 A20 A16
A25
A9
A4 A5 A18
A13 A19
x
y
A A14 A12 A23 A3 A32 A31 A28 A17

Position each part of the pattern so that the middle of the front and the middle of the back line up with where you have folded the fabric (2).

Using chalk, insert the seam allowances: usually 2 cm (0.78") along the sides, 1 cm (0.39") on each upper part and 1 cm (0.39") on each bottom part, then cut along the marks you've made (3).

Sew guide stitches along the perimeter of each pattern (4). Detach the patterns, cut open the guide stitches and assemble each front with its respective back.

1

2

3

Sew tacking stitches and then sew each part of the skirt (5). At the top of the skirt, on the left side, leave a 20 cm (7.87") gap so you can insert a zip.

Make the hem of each part of the skirt with a cut-and-sew-machine (6) and iron the edges (7).

Assemble all of the pieces to obtain a flounced skirt; join the pieces along the waist circumference with tacking stitches and then sew a linear seam (8 - 9).

Insert the zip and waistband as explained on page 42, then finish off the latter as you like (10).

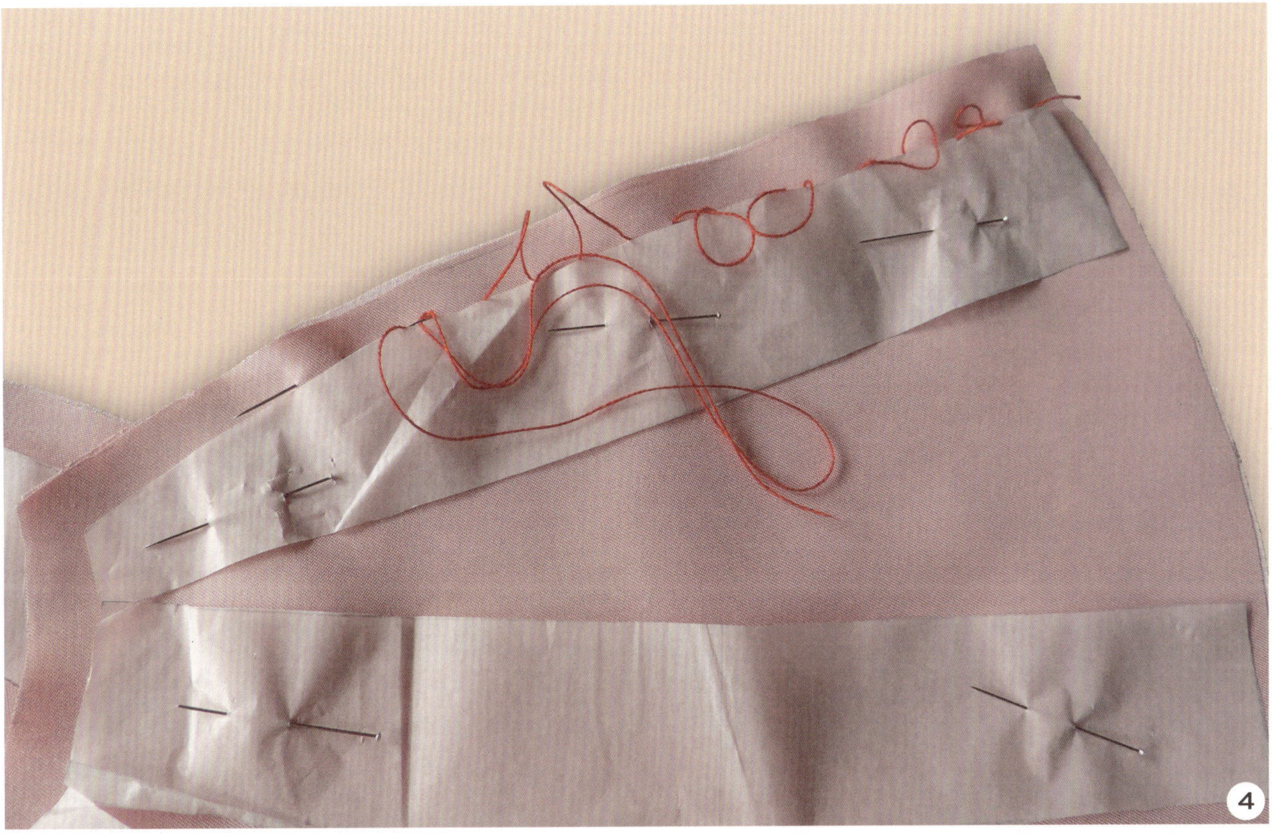
4

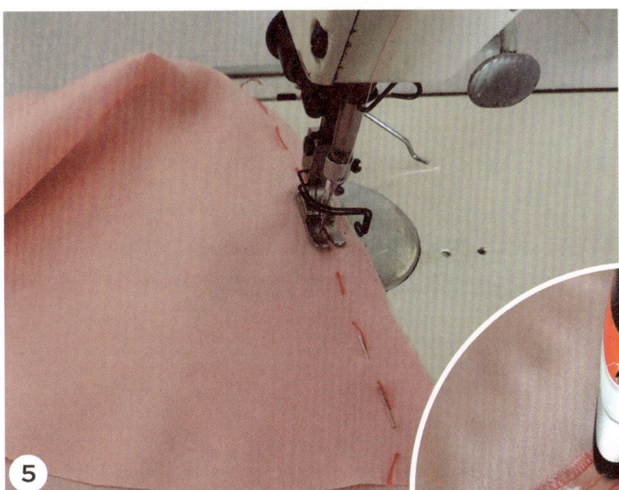
5

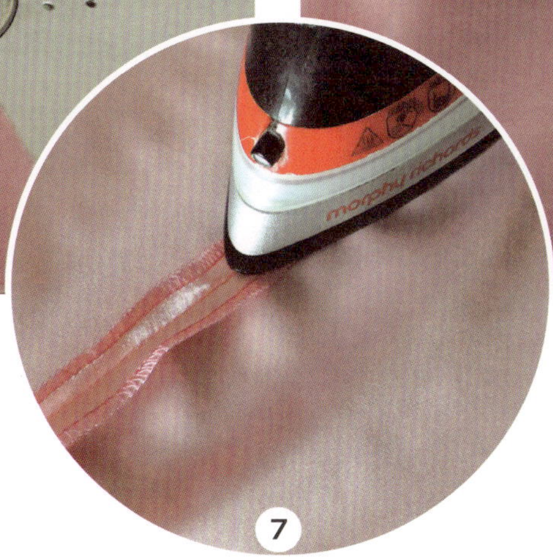
7

6

By the way: this type of skirt can also be made using the half-wheel or full-wheel skirt pattern. To do this, you must have three different lengths on the pattern, so as to create the effect of overlapping flounces.

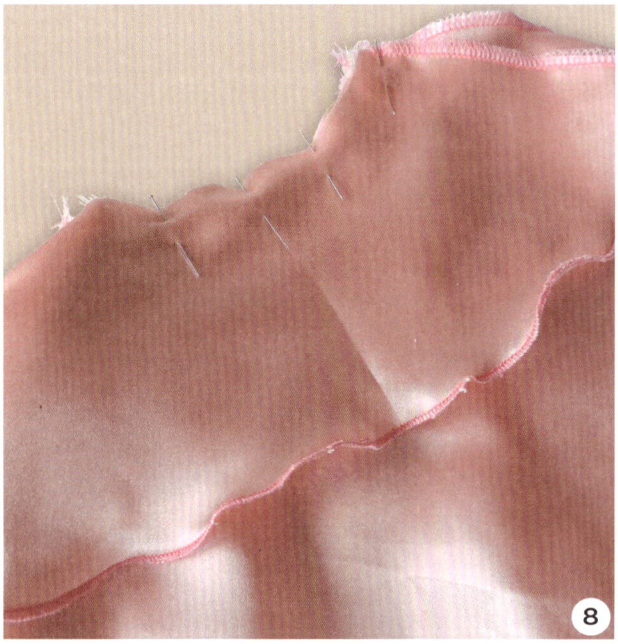

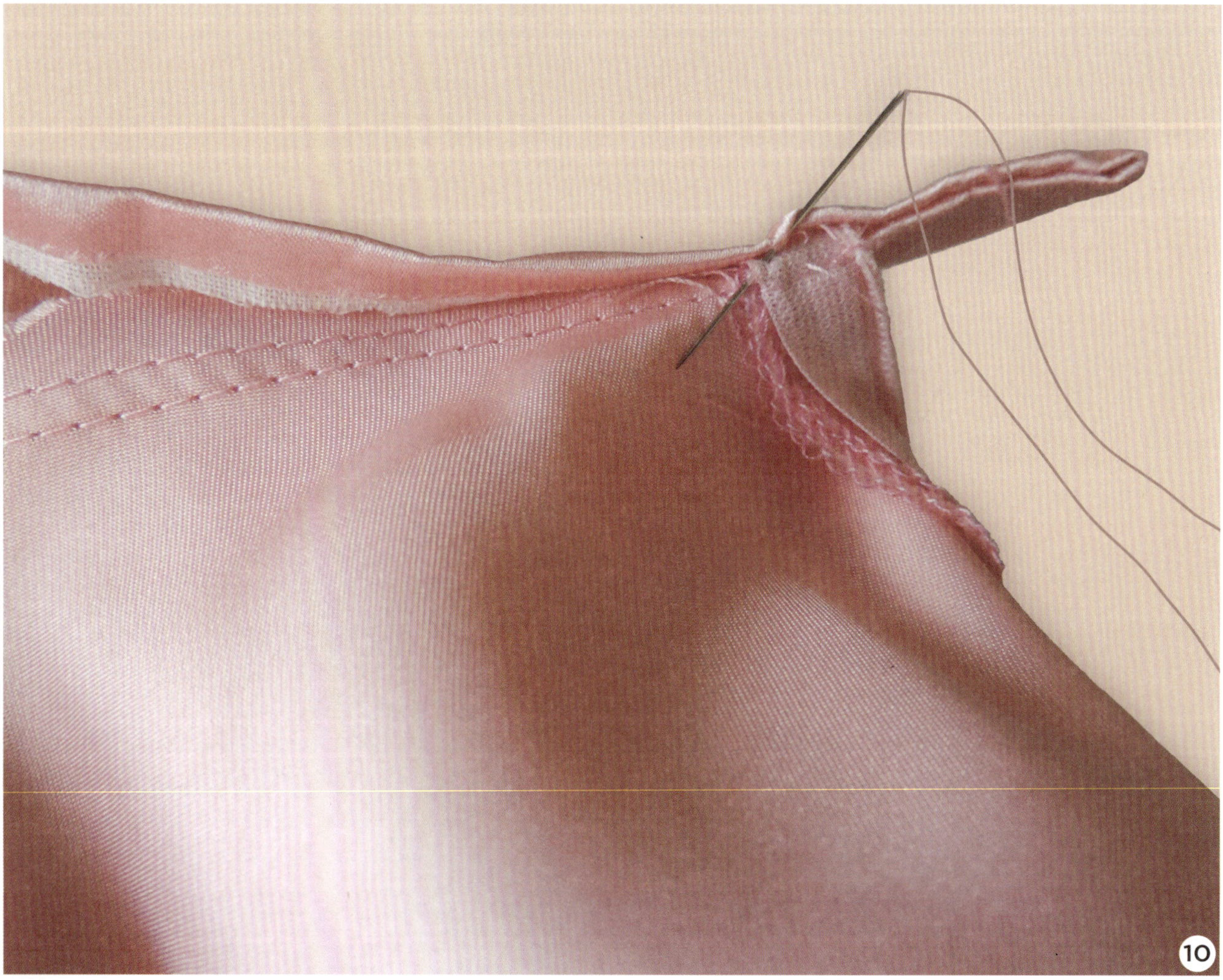

The mock-up skirt was made of medium-weight satin. To get the same effect, you can choose fabrics of similar consistency, such as:

- Viscose
- Khadi
- Duchesse

Have fun trying out different effects by choosing alternative fabrics.

FLOUNCE SKIRT WITH YOKE

To make the pattern of the flounced skirt with yoke, draw the basic pattern of the classic skirt.

Looking at the diagram, below, and carefully following the explanation given, make the following changes to make the relevant transformations:

- A_A21 is 1/2 of A_A6.
- A3_A22 is 1/2 of A3_A7.
- Draw a line between A21_A22.
- Divide the width of the front and back parts of the skirt vertically into eight equal parts.
- A6_A23 same as 1/8 of A6_A7.

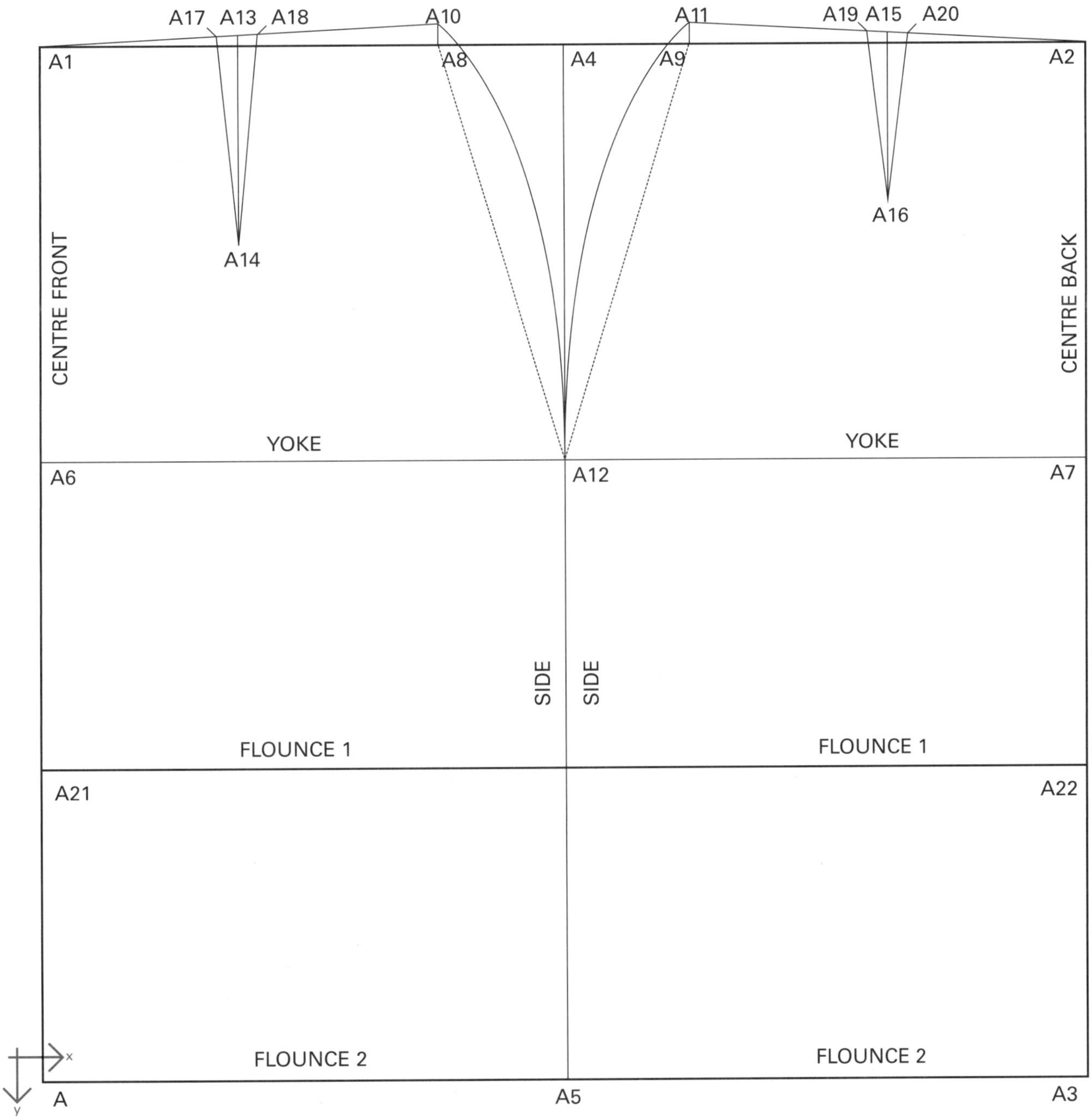

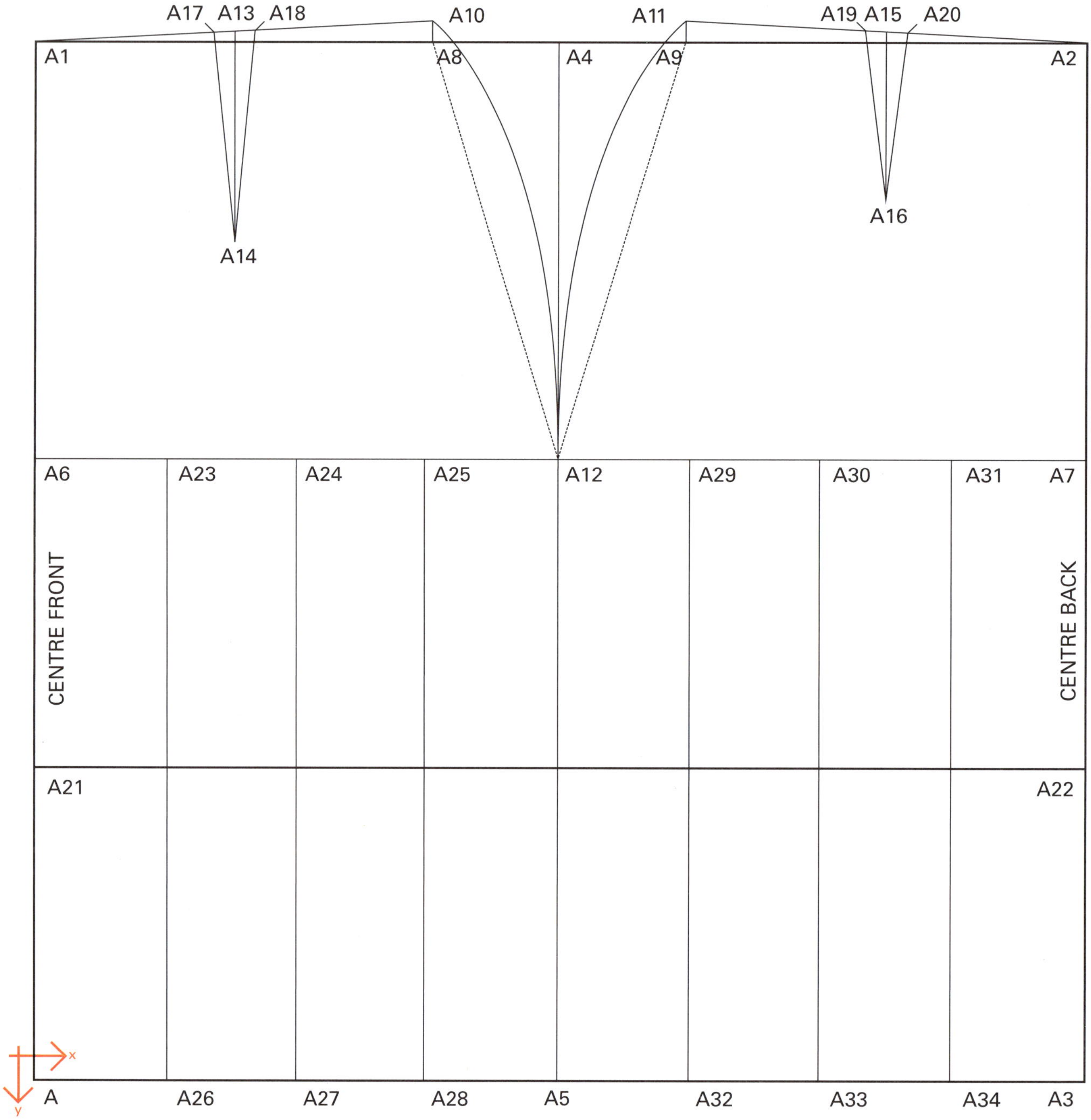

- A23_A24 same as 1/8 of A6_A7.
- A24_A25 same as 1/8 of A6_A7.
- A25_A12 same as 1/8 of A6_A7.
- A12_A29 same as 1/8 of A6_A7.
- A29_A30 same as 1/8 of A6_A7.
- A30_A31 same as 1/8 of A6_A7.
- A_A26 same as 1/8 of A_A3.
- A26_A27 same as 1/8 of A_A3.
- A27_A28 same as 1/8 of A_A3.
- A28_A5 same as 1/8 of A_A3.
- A32_A33 same as 1/8 of A_A3.
- A33_A34 same as 1/8 of A_A3.
- A34_A3 same as 1/8 of A_A3.
- Join the following points together: A_A6, A23_A26, A24_A27, A25_A28, A5_A12, A29_A32, A30_A33, A31_A34.

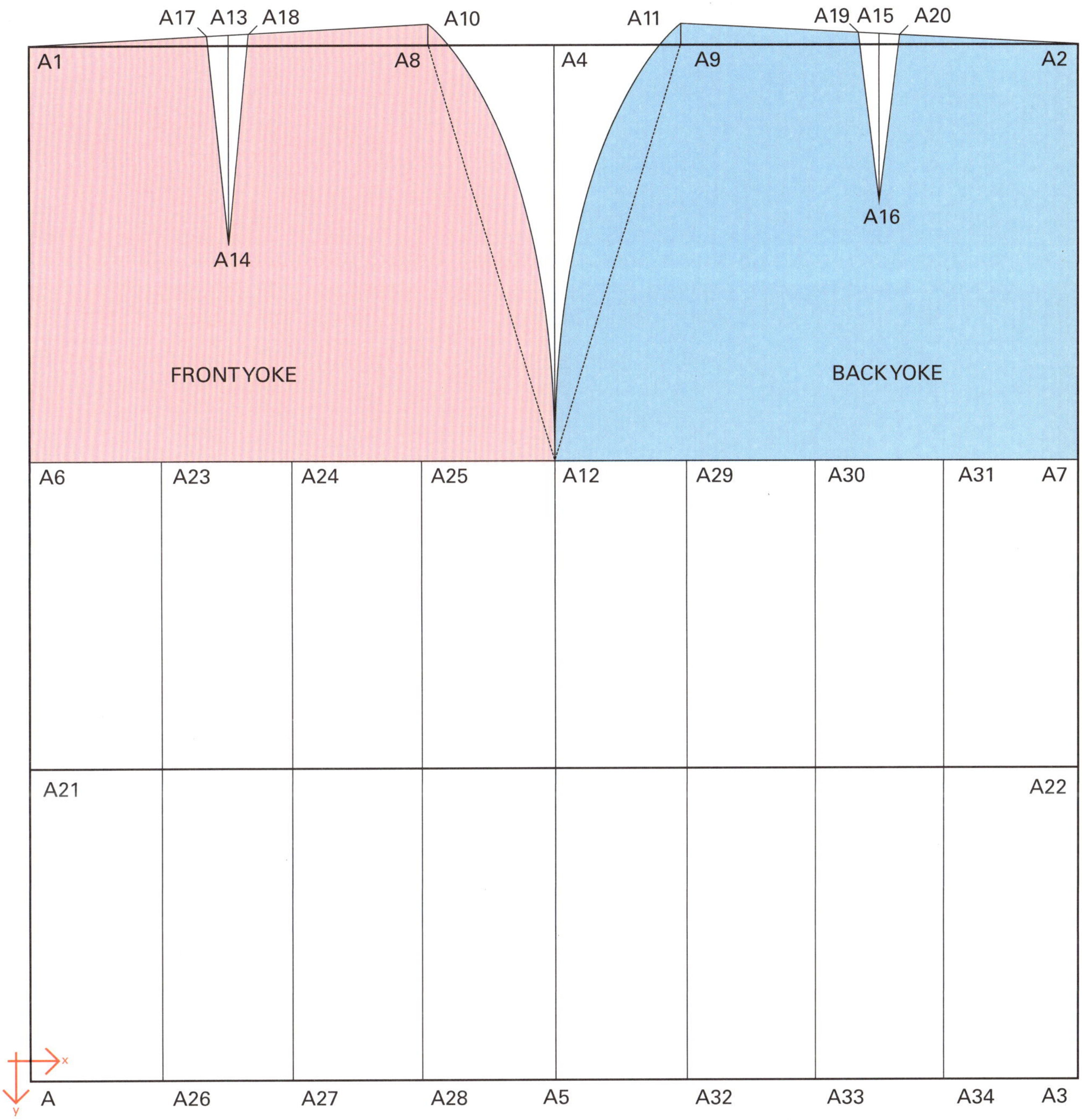

Using a pencil crayon, colour in all the parts relating to the skirt - for both the front and the back - the yoke and the two parts relating to the flounces, to get four patterns altogether: a front and back of the yoke, an upper flounce and a flounce that is overlapped.

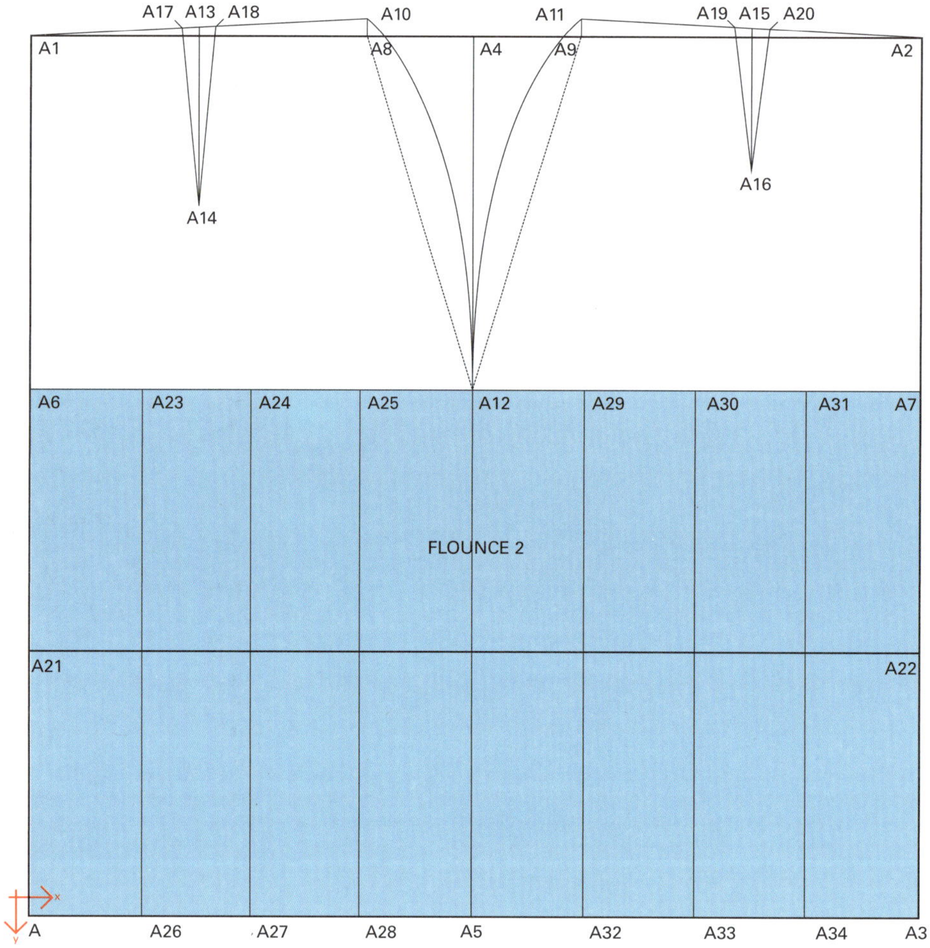
A17 A13 A18
A10
A11
A19 A15 A20
A1
A8
A4
A9
A2
A14
A16
A6 A23 A24 A25 A12 A29 A30 A31 A7
FLOUNCE 2
A21
A22
A A26 A27 A28 A5 A32 A33 A34 A3

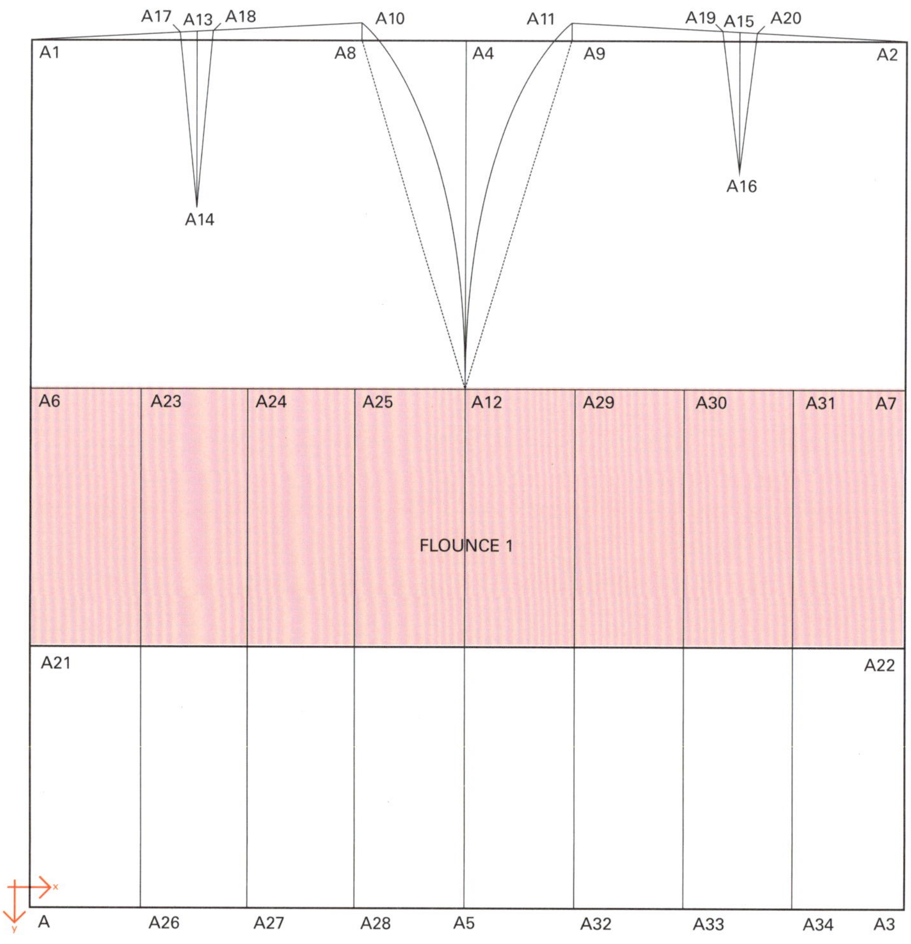
A17 A13 A18
A10
A11
A19 A15 A20
A1
A8
A4
A9
A2
A14
A16
A6 A23 A24 A25 A12 A29 A30 A31 A7
FLOUNCE 1
A21
A22
A A26 A27 A28 A5 A32 A33 A34 A3

Cut out the patterns and position the ones for the yokes on the fabric that you have folded in two, with the selvedges touching and the right side of the fabric facing inwards. Hold in place with pins and add the seam allowances, which for the yokes are: 2 cm (0.78") along the sides, 1 cm (0.39") on the waist, 1 cm (0.39") on the bottom and 2 cm (0.78") on the middle of the back (1).

Cut the flounces along the vertical lines, starting from the bottom and open them up to create width, then position the patterns on the fabric with the middle of the front positioned on the fold of the fabric, and insert the seam allowances: 1 cm (0.39") on the upper and lower parts and 2 cm (0.78") on the middle of the back (2 - 3).

Cut along the marks you have drawn in chalk to get two yokes, one for the front and one for the back, two flounces and the waistband (4). With the patterns still attached to the fabric, sew guide stitches along their perimeters, then detach the patterns and cut the guide stitches open and then tack the parts together.

Leave room for a zip in the middle of the back of the yoke. Sew a linear seam exactly along the tacking stitches (5). Finish the edges off with the cut-and-sew-machine (6) or with a zig-zag stitch, and then make a rolled hem on the bottom of each flounce (7).

4

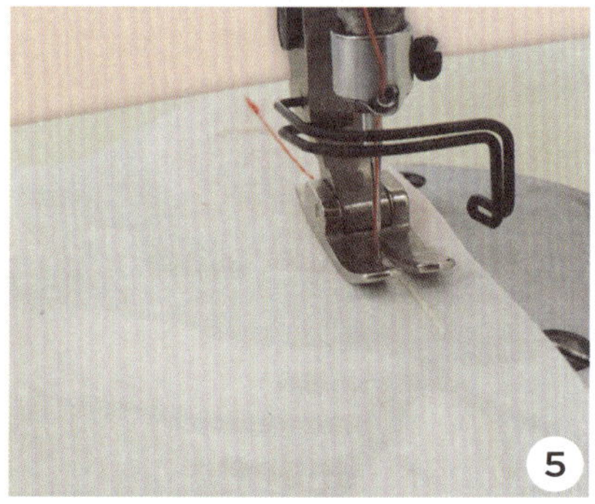
5

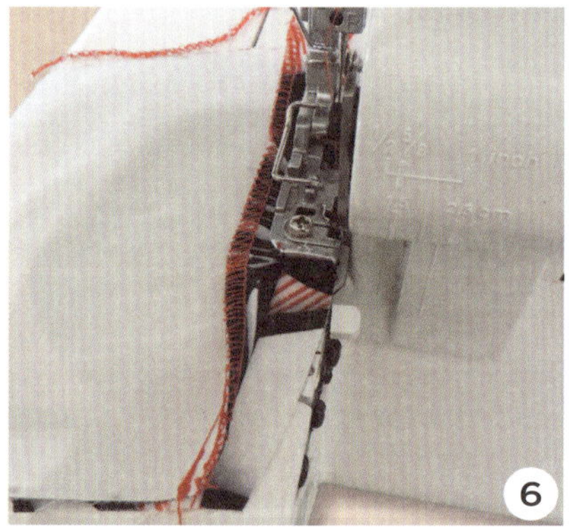
6

7

Iron the edges of the yoke open. Join the two flounces together. Join the flounces to the yoke, sewing on the wrong side of the flounces with a 1 cm (0.39") margin, then insert the zip (8) and attach the waistband as explained on page 42, then finish off the waistband how you prefer.

By the way: the flounces can also be made using the paper pattern for the full-wheel or half-wheel skirt in two different lengths.

The mock-up skirt was made of polyester and chiffon, but you can have fun trying out various other fabrics. If you want to achieve this effect, I recommend using lightweight fabrics for the flounces, such as chiffon, crêpe, georgette, voile or viscose.

SKIRT WITH EXTRA FLOUNCES

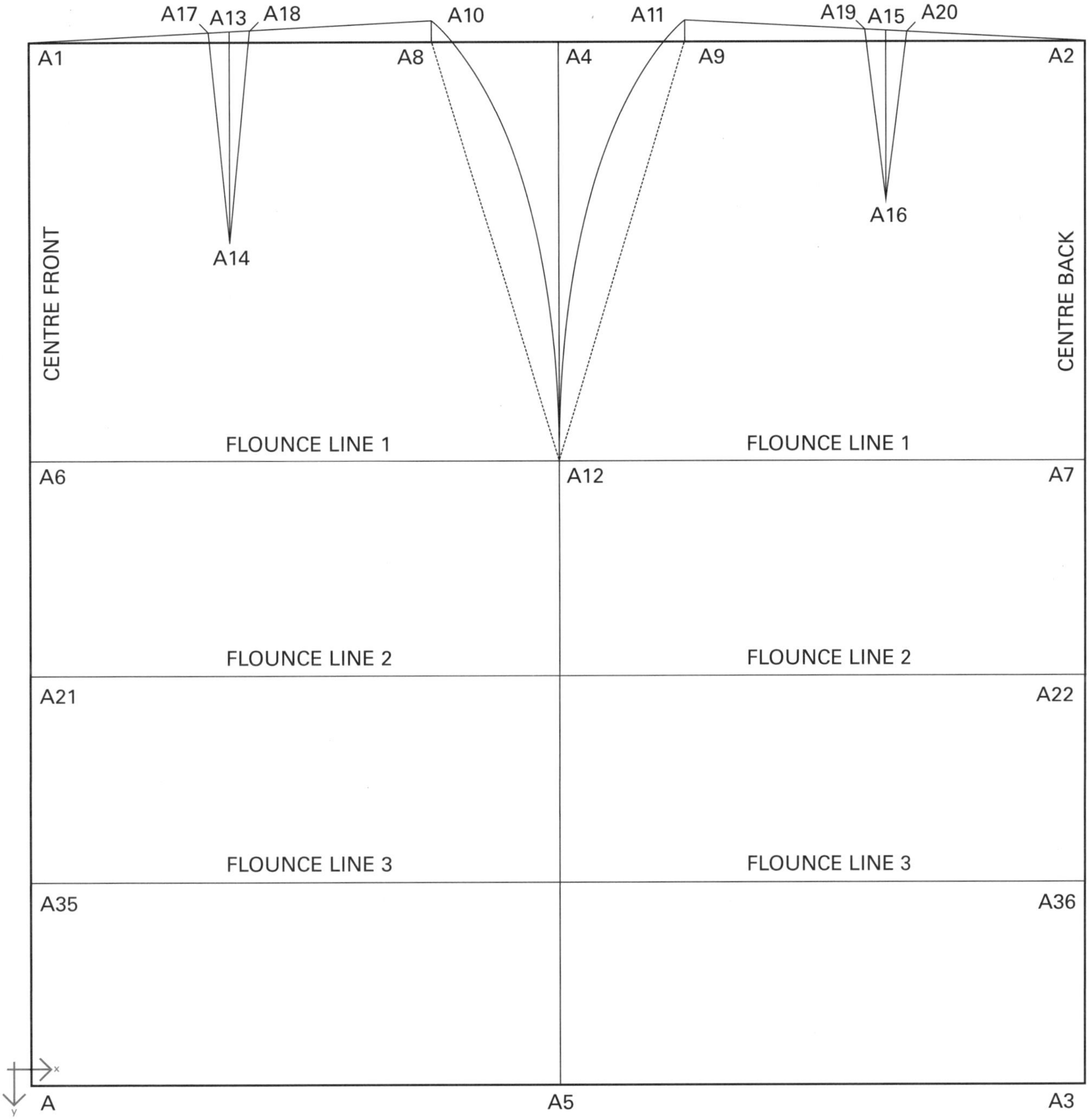

To create the pattern for the skirt with extra flounces, first draw the pattern for the basic skirt. Follow the explanation carefully and look at the diagram showing the necessary changes.

- Below the hip line, divide the length of the skirt into three equal parts. If, for example, the length from the hip line to the bottom, or A_A6 or A3_A7, is 30 cm (11.81"), divide 30 cm (11.81") into three equal parts of 10 cm (3.93").
- A6_A21 is 1/3 of A_A6.
- A21_A35 same as A6_A21.
- A_A35 same as A21_A35.
- A7_A22 is 1/3 of A3_A7.
- A22_A36 same as A7_A22.
- A3_A36 same as A22_A36.
- Join points A6_A7, A21_A22, A35_A36 together.
- Using a pencil crayon, colour in the paper pattern for the front and back of the skirt.

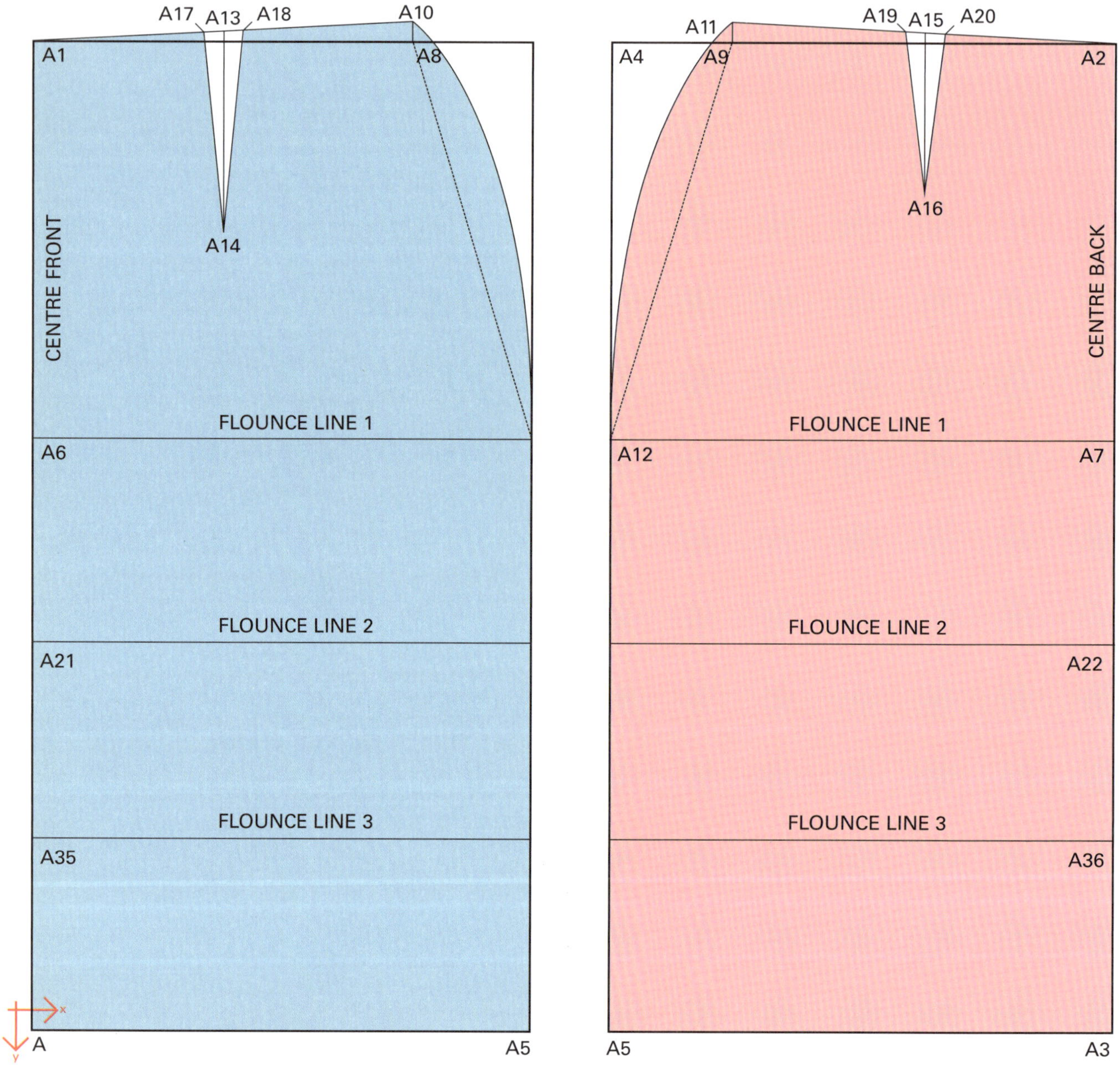
A17
A13
A18
A10
A1
A8
A14
CENTRE FRONT
FLOUNCE LINE 1
A6
FLOUNCE LINE 2
A21
FLOUNCE LINE 3
A35
x
y
A
A5
A11
A19
A15
A20
A4
A9
A2
A16
CENTRE BACK
FLOUNCE LINE 1
A12
A7
FLOUNCE LINE 2
A22
FLOUNCE LINE 3
A36
A5
A3

1

The skirt with extra flounces can also be flared. Once you have got the two patterns for the front and back of the skirt, cut the lines representing the flounces with scissors, being careful not to detach them from the rest of the pattern (1).

Position the patterns on the double folded fabric, so that the selvedges line up perfectly and the right side of the fabric is facing inwards. The middle of the front and middle of the back of the respective patterns must line up with where the fabric is folded. Pin it together and draw the seam allowances in chalk (2).

Cut along the lines drawn in chalk (3) and sew guide stitches around the paper patterns that are still attached to the fabric (4).

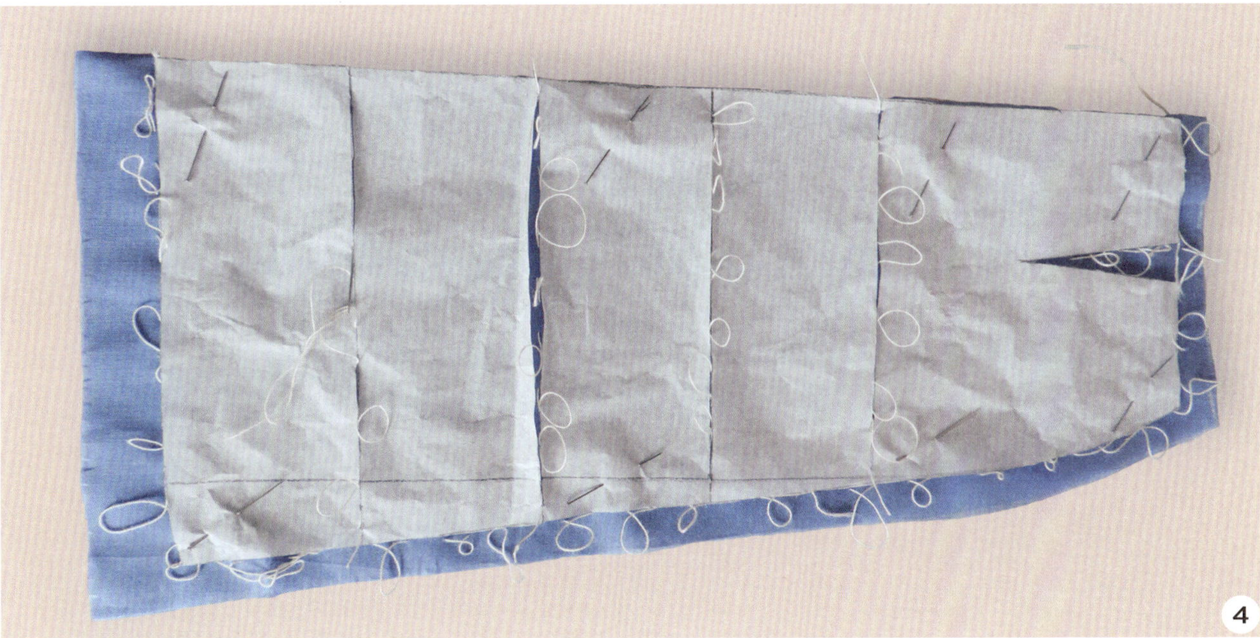

Guide stitches should also be sewn within the lines of the previously cut flounces. Detach the patterns and cut open the guide stitches (5).

Measure the width of the flounces and their length (6 - 7), then cut strips of fabric that are slightly wider than you want the flounces on the skirt to be and at least twice the length (8). The strips can be made of the same fabric as the skirt or of a different fabric.

Add the finishing touches to the strips using the cut-and-sew-machine. On the lower part of the strips, always roll the hem with the cut-and-sew-machine if it is an especially light fabric, as is the case for organza (9). Alternatively, use the sewing machine to

5

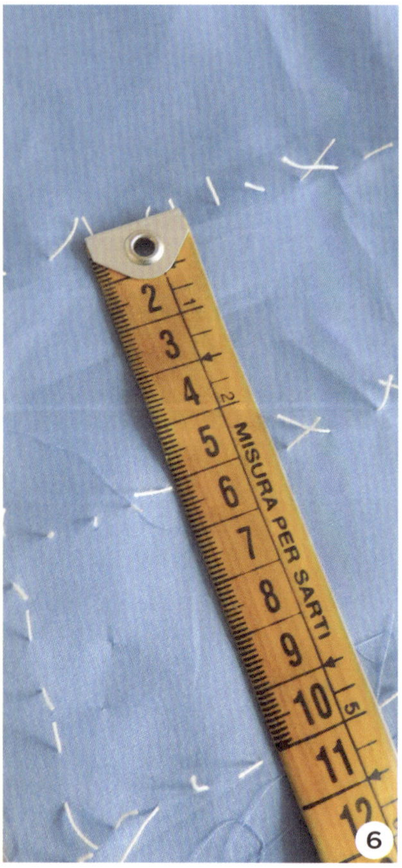

6

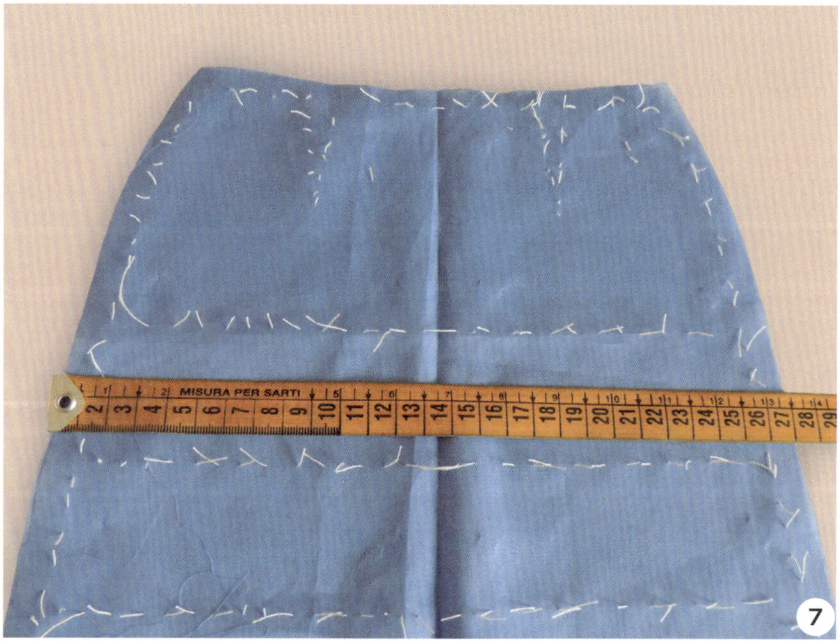

7

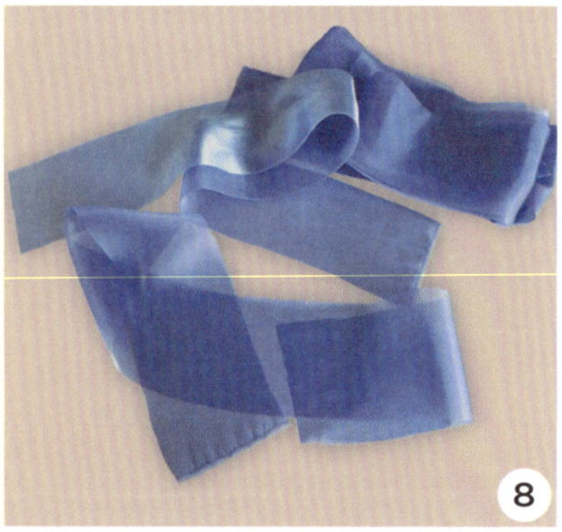

8

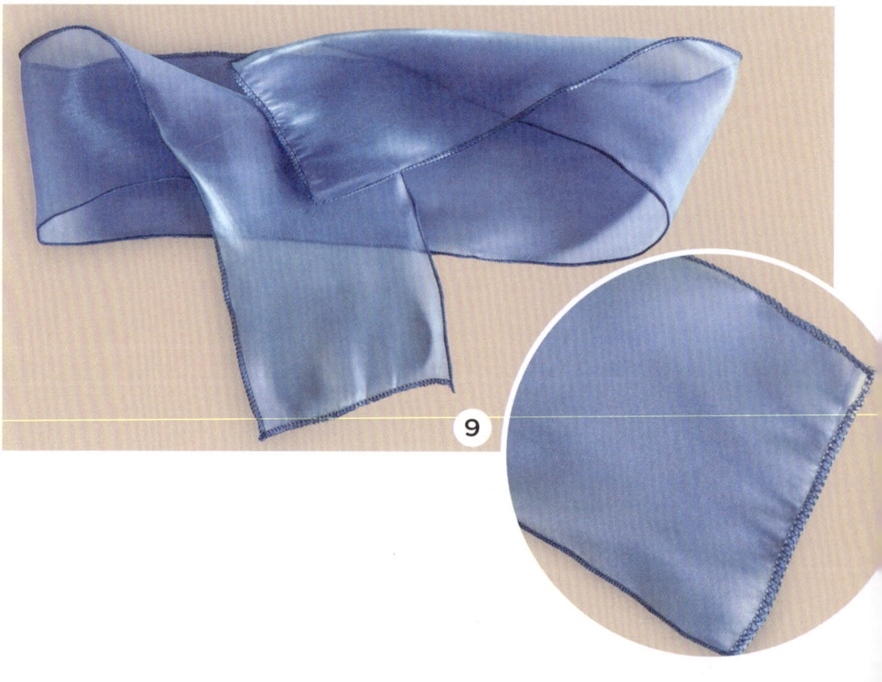

9

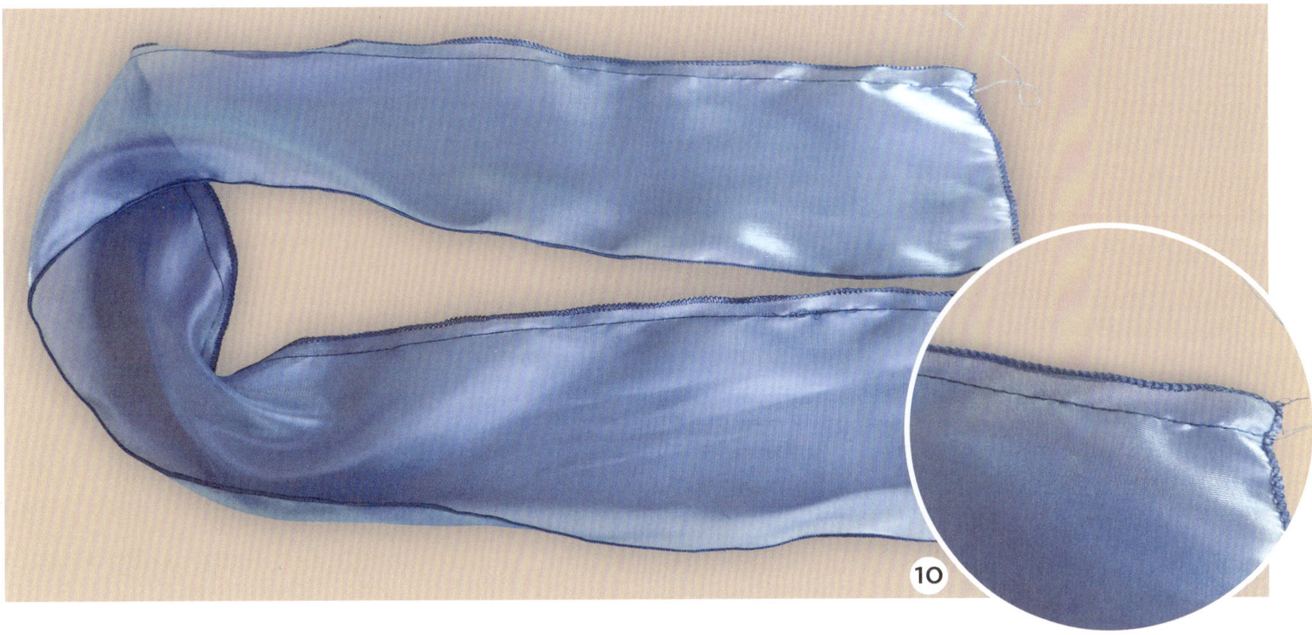

attach bias binding to finish off the bottom, and finish the rest of the strip with a zig-zag stitch.

On the upper part of each strip, sew a linear seam with a very long stitch 1 cm (0.39") from the upper edge, leaving "tails" of thread at the beginning and at the end of the seam: you can pull on these threads to wrinkle up the strip (10).

Once you have pulled the "tails" of thread, attach each strip along the lines drawn with guide stitches on the front and back of the skirt, adjusting the wrinkled up fabric to their width. Pin the strips to the lines on the skirt so as to match the seam of the strip with the guide stitches on the skirt line (11).

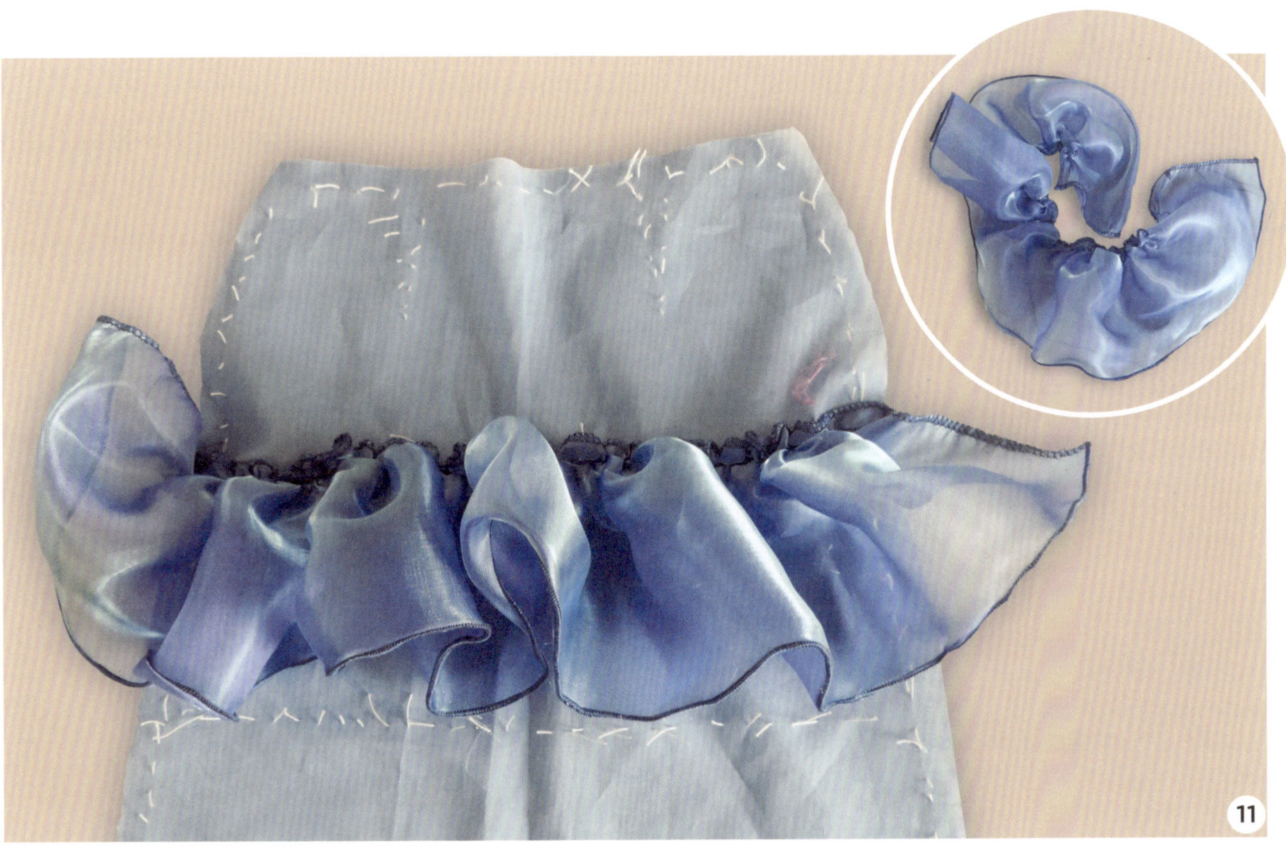

Using pins and tacking stitches, attach each strip to the line on the front and back of the skirt and then sew them on. Once all the strips have been sewn on, pin the sides of the skirt together on the wrong side of the fabric, so that the flounces on the right side of the fabric are on the inside. First sew tacking stitches and then sew a seam (12 - 13), leaving a gap for a zip on the upper left side (at least 20 cm / 7.87").

Finish off the edges with a cut-and-sew-machine (14), then attach the zip and the waistband to the skirt, as explained on page 42.

12

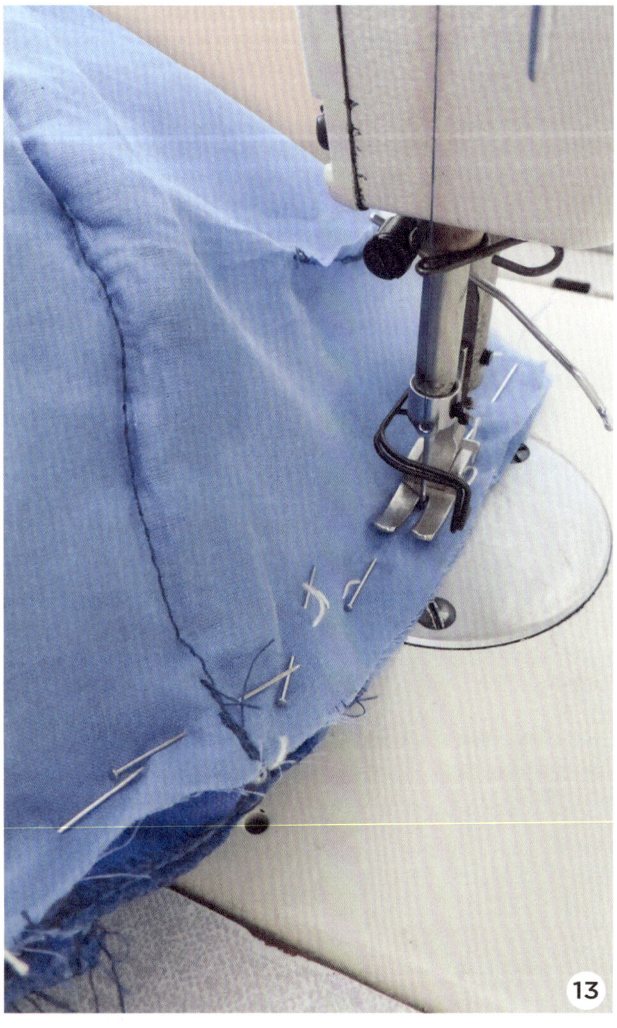

13

14

The mock-up skirt was made of cotton and organza. To achieve the same effect, I recommend using any fabric for the main part of the skirt, but using organza for the flounces. You can also use different fabrics for the flounces, if you want to try out some other effects.

SKIRT WITH WIDE PLEATS

For the skirt with wide pleats, first draw the basic skirt pattern and then add the alterations that are explained in the diagram, below. Once you have decided how many pleats you want the skirt to have, divide the skirt's width by the number of pleats. To get a better understanding, I recommend following the example given in this chapter, ie. for a skirt with ten wide pleats in total, five on the front and five on the back.

In the specific case shown here, the skirt has a hip circumference equal to 100 cm (39.37") and 10 folds have been made, using the following calculation: 100 cm : 10 = 10 cm / 39.37": 10 = 3.93", which corresponds to the width of each pleat.

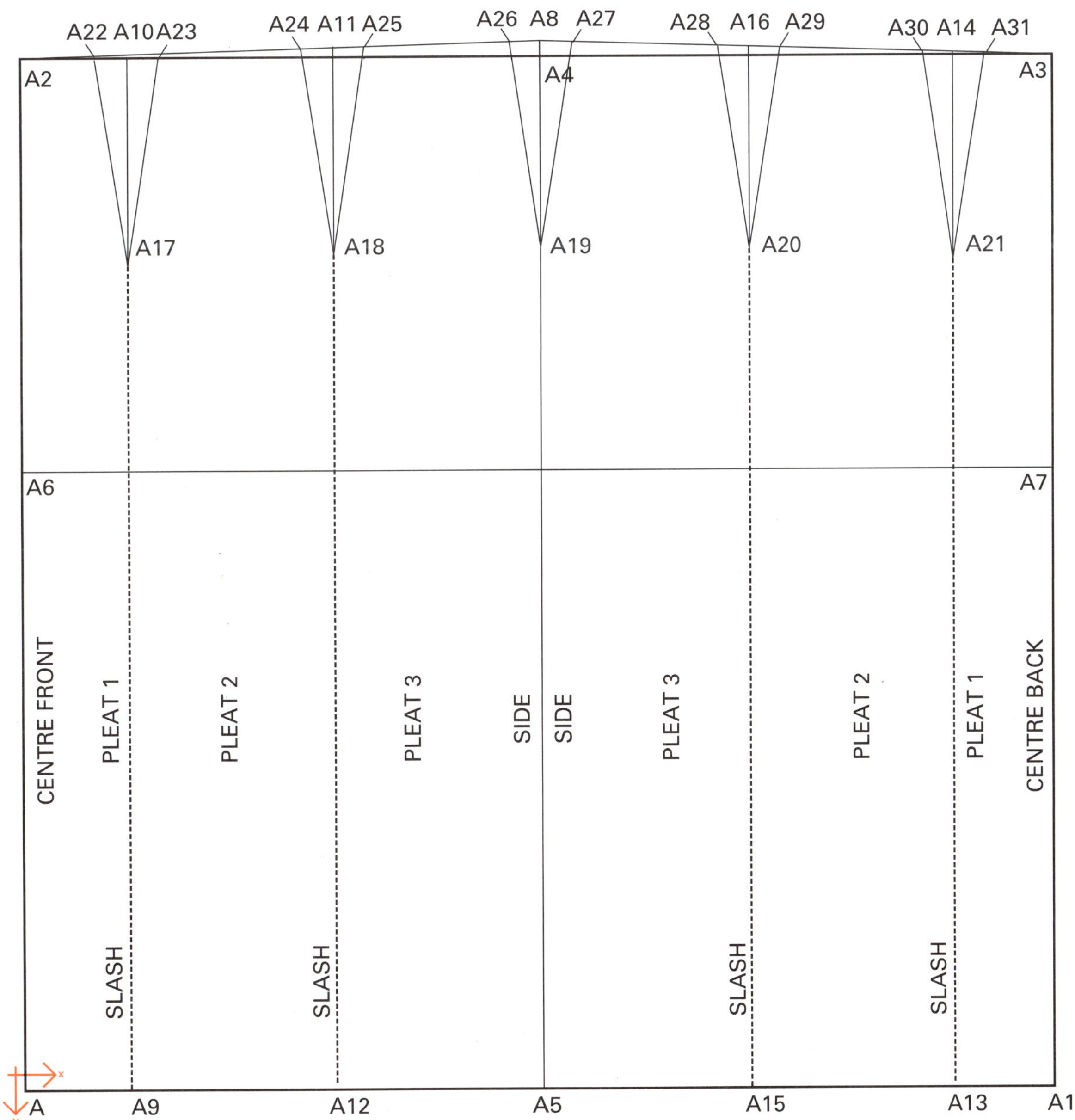

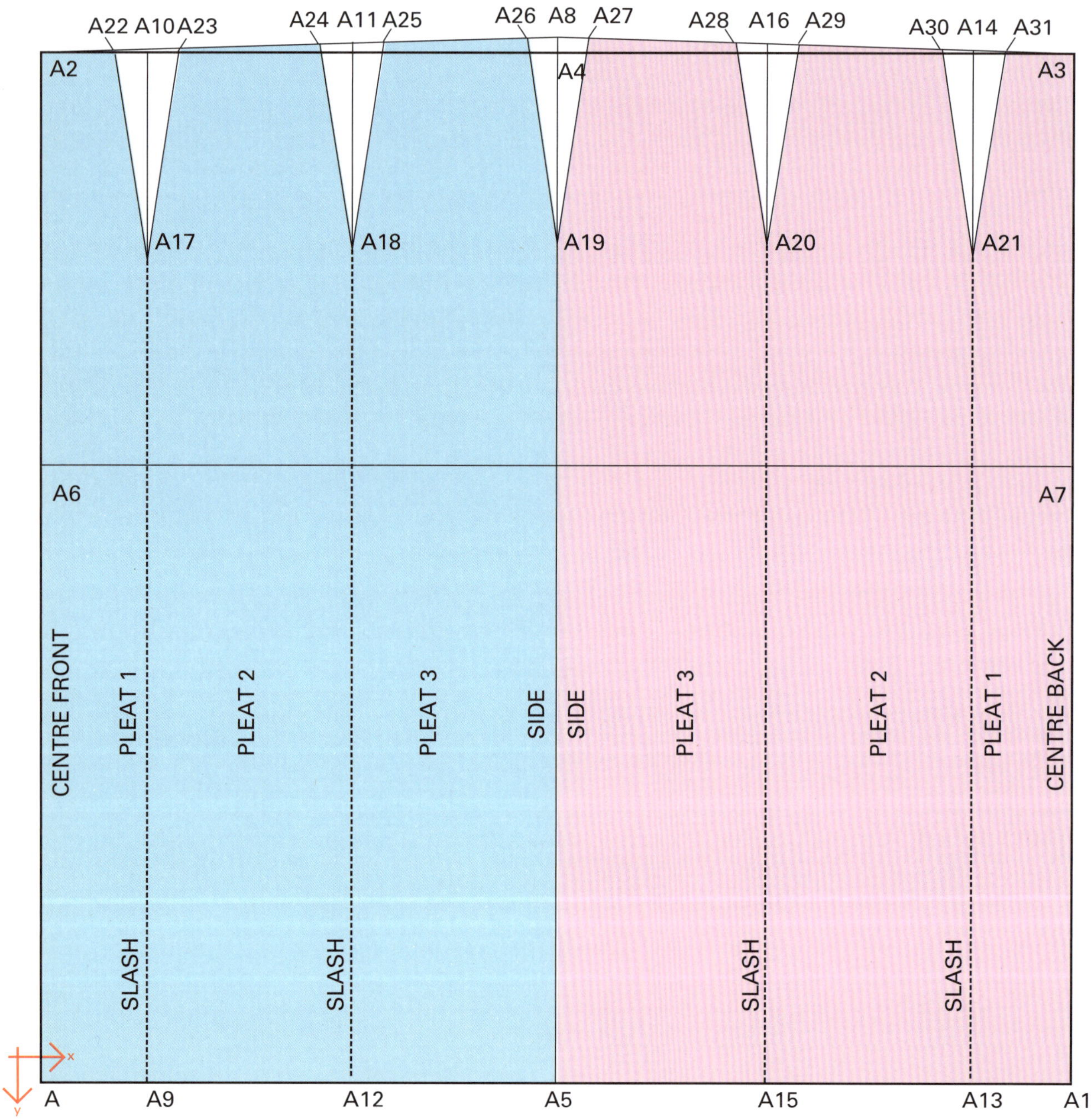

Once you have drawn the basic skirt pattern, join the waist lines at the top of the hips. This is because the pleated skirt does not need to be shaped on the hips, rather, the difference between the waist and hip circumference is distributed between several darts that are inserted between the pleats of the skirt.

For a better understanding, follow these steps:

- A_A2 is the desired length.
- A1_A3 same as A_A2.
- A_A1 = 1/2 of hip circumference.
- A2_A3 same as A_A1.
- Join the points together and draw the quadrature.
- A2_A4 = 1/2 of A2_A3.
- A4_A8 = 1.5 cm (0.59").
- Join points A2_A8 and A3_A8 together.
- A_A5 same as A2_A4.
- Draw a line between A4_A5 (hip line).

Assuming, therefore, that you want to insert 10 pleats in total, ie. 5 pleats on the front of the skirt and 5 on the back, and that the hip circumference of the skirt is 100 cm (39.37"), proceed as follows:

- 100 cm / 39.37" (hip circumference) : 10 (pleats) = 10 cm / 3.93" (width of each pleat).
- A2_A10 = 5 cm / 1.96" (half fold on the middle of the front, which will be cut in two where the fabric is folded).
- A10_A11 = 10 cm (3.93").
- A11_A8 = 10 cm (3.93").

- A8_A16 = 10 cm (3.93").
- A16_A14 = 10 cm (3.93").
- A14_A3 = 5 cm (1.96") (half fold on the middle of the back, which will be cut in two where the fabric is folded).
- A_A9 same as A2_A10.
- A9_A12 same as A10_A11.
- A12_A5 same as A11_A8.
- A5_A15 same as A8_A16.
- A15_A13 same as A16_A14.
- A13_A1 same as A14_A3.

To calculate the width of each dart, you must subtract the waist circumference from the hip circumference. Example: hip circumference 100 cm (39.37") - waist circumference 70 cm (27.55") = 30 cm (11.81"); divide this by 2, since we are working on the pattern for half the skirt (30 cm : 2 = 15 cm / 11.81" : 2 = 5.90"); divide this by the number of pleats there are on the pattern, in this case 5, (15 cm : 5 = 3 cm / 5.90" : 5 = 1.18").

Each pleat will therefore be 3 cm (1.18") wide and 10 cm (3.93") long. Insert the darts as follows:
- A10_A17 = 10 cm (3.93").
- A10_A22 = 1.5 cm (0.59").
- A10_A23 = 1.5 cm (0.59").
- A11_A18 = 10 cm (3.93").
- A11_A24 = 1.5 cm (0.59").
- A11_A25 = 1.5 cm (0.59").
- A8_A19 = 10 cm (3.93").
- A8_A26 = 1.5 cm (0.59").
- A8_A27 = 1.5 cm (0.59").
- A16_A20 = 10 cm (3.93").
- A16_A28 = 1.5 cm (0.59").
- A16_A29 = 1.5 cm (0.59").
- A14_A21 = 10 cm (3.93").
- A14_A30 = 1.5 cm (0.59").
- A14_A31 = 1.5 cm (0.59").
- Using pencil crayons, colour in the paper patterns to identify which one is for the front and which one is for the back of the skirt.

Cut out the patterns for the front and back of the skirt and the individual pleats, which I recommend you give numbers to. Fold the fabric in half, with the selvedges touching and the right side of the fabric facing inwards. Position the pattern for the middle of the front and the middle of the back so that it lines up exactly with where the fabric is folded. Then, between one pleat and the next, leave a distance equal to twice the width of the pleat (for example: if each pleat is 10 cm (3.93") wide, leave 20 cm (7.87") between one pleat and the next). Using chalk, add the seam allowances: usually 1 cm (0.39") along the waist, 2 cm (0.78") along the bottom for a machine hem or 5 cm (1.96") for a hand-stitched hem, and 2 cm (0.78") along the sides; then cut exactly along the lines you've drawn (1).

1

Sew guide stitches around each pleat (2), then detach the patterns and create the pleats by ironing exactly along the marks left by the guide stitches (3).

For convenience, sew a seam along the upper edge of the front and back of the skirt, to hold the pleats in place (4).

Join the sides of the front and back of the skirt together, so that the right side of the fabric is on the inside and held in place with pins and tacking stitches. Then sew it together, leaving a gap of at least 20 cm (7.87") on the left hip for a zip (5). Finish off the edges with a cut-and-sew-machine or zig-zag stitch (6) and then iron them open.

Add a zip (7) and prepare the waistband (8) as explained on page 42, then attach it and finish it off as you like (9). Sew the hem by hand or by machine, as you prefer.

2

3

4

5

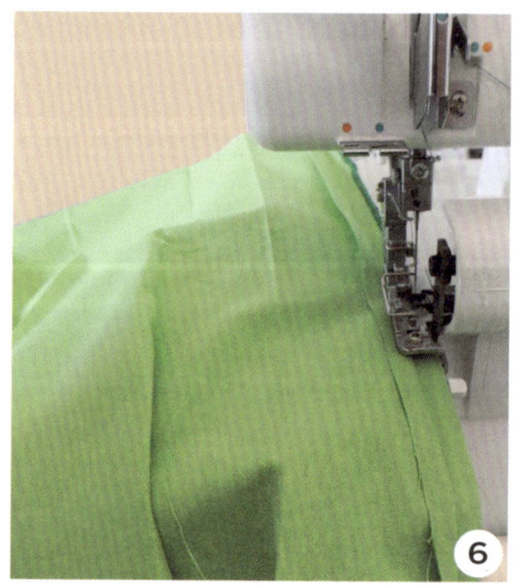

6

7

8

The mock-up skirt was made from medium to light cotton fabric. You can make this type of skirt from any fabric you like, but of course, the yield and overall effect will be different for each sort of fabric.

SKIRT WITH NARROW PLEATS

Making a skirt with narrow pleats is pretty similar to what you have already seen for the skirt with wide pleats. Start off by drawing the basic skirt pattern, then carry out all the alterations by following the explanations, below, and looking at the diagram.

Once you have decided how many pleats you want the skirt to have, divide the skirt's width by the number of pleats. To get a better understanding, I recommend that you follow the example shown in this book, which is a skirt with thirty-four narrow pleats in total: seventeen on the front and seventeen on the back.

Let's assume that in this example, the skirt has a hip circumference of 100 cm (39.37"). In order to make 34 pleats, you must use the following calculation: 100 cm (39.37") : 34 = 2.9 cm (1.14"), so each pleat will be 2.9 cm (1.14") wide.

Once you have drawn the basic skirt pattern, join the waist lines at the top of the hips. This is because the pleated skirt does not need to be shaped on the hips, rather, the difference between the waist and hip circumference is distributed between several darts that are inserted between the pleats of the skirt.

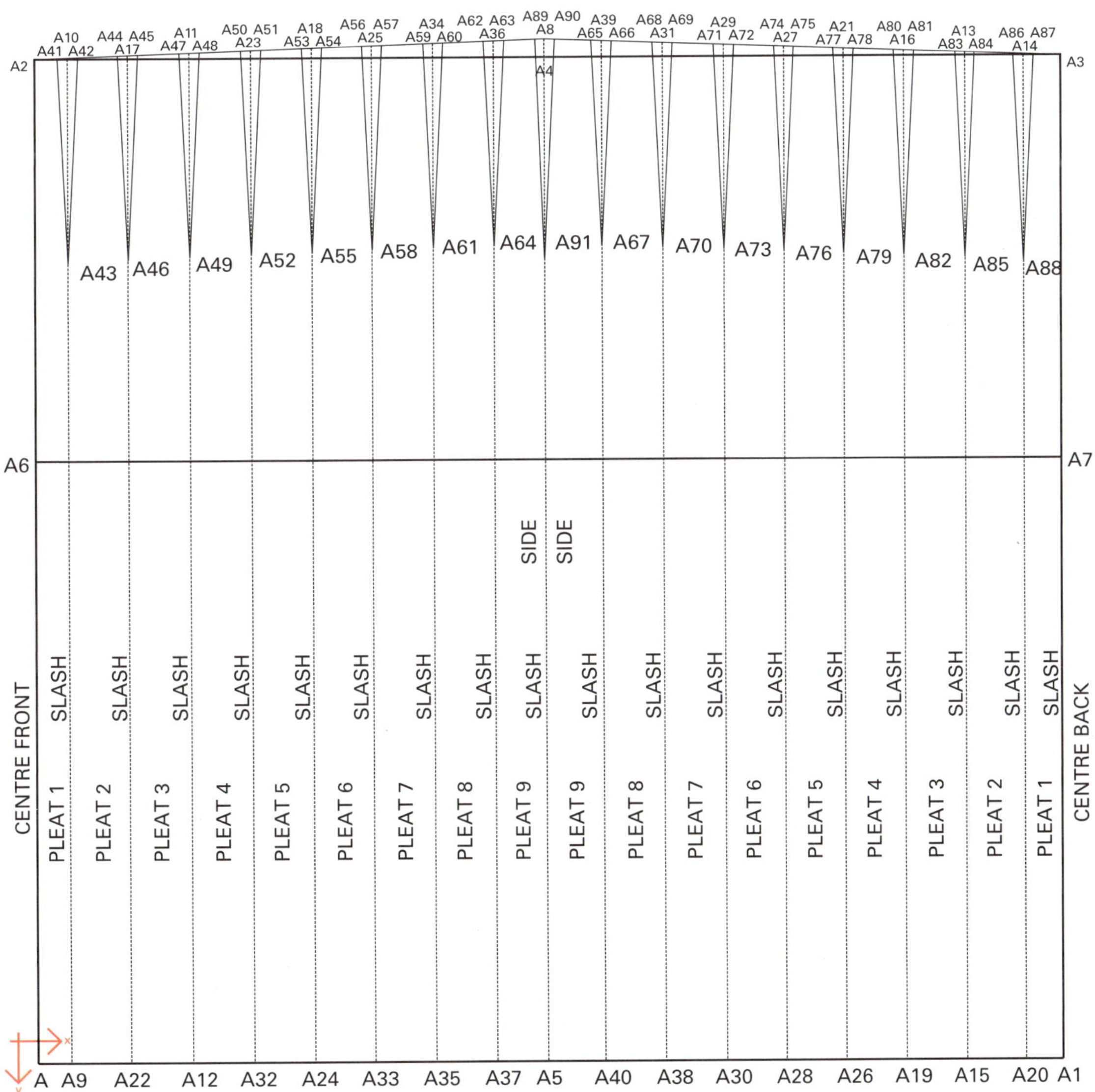

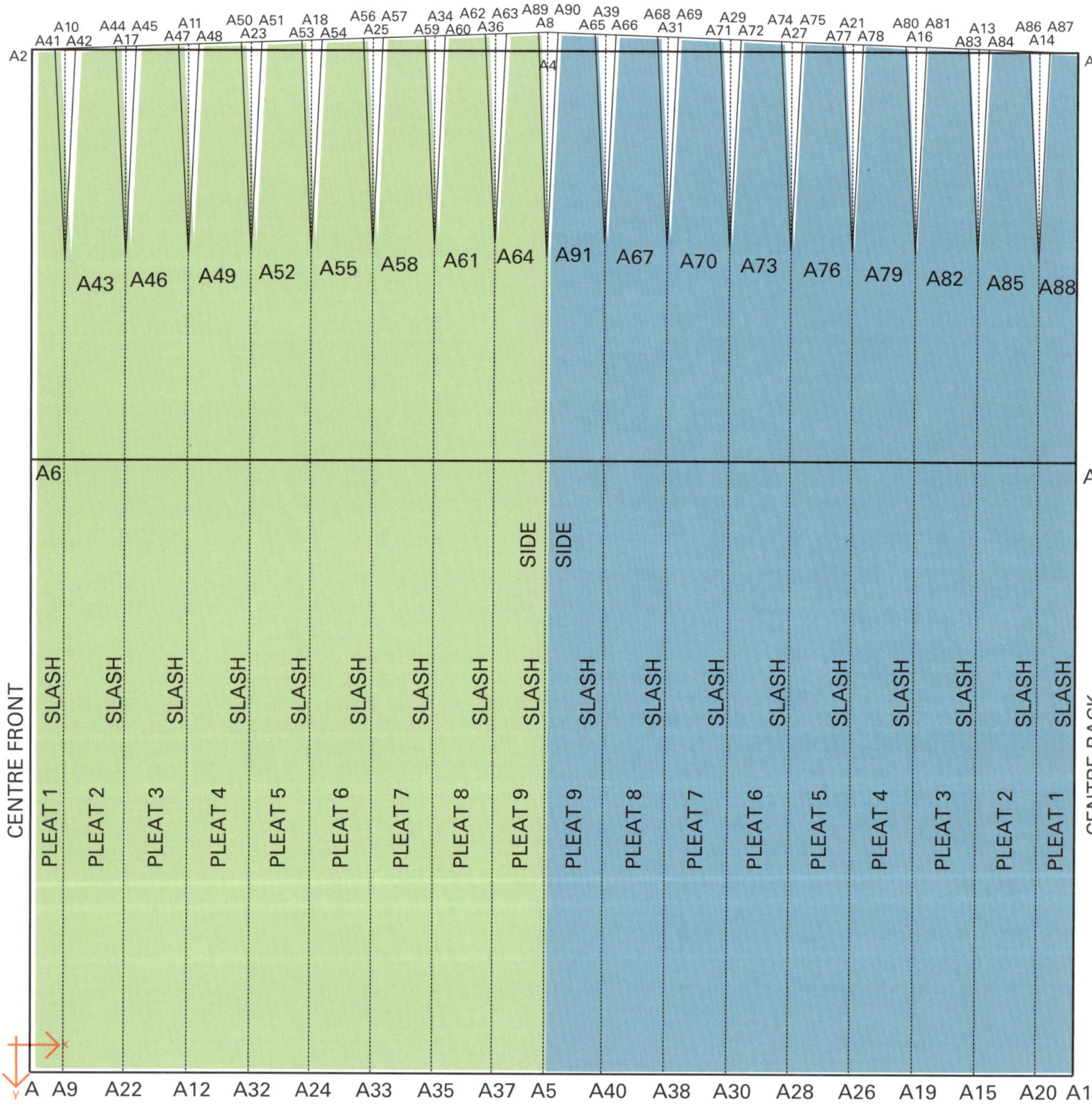

For a better understanding, follow these steps:

- A_A2 as the desired skirt length.
- A1_A3 same as A_A2.
- A_A1 = 1/2 of hip circumference.
- A2_A3 same as A_A1.
- Join the points together and draw the quadrature.
- A2_A4 = 1/2 of A2_A3.
- A4_A8 = 1.5 cm (0.59").
- Join points A2_A8 and A3_A8 together.
- A_A5 same as A2_A4.
- Draw a line between A4_A5 (hip line).

Assuming, therefore, that you want to insert 34 pleats in total, ie. 17 pleats on the front of the skirt and 17 on the back, and that the hip circumference of the skirt is 100 cm (39.37"), proceed as follows:

- 100 cm (39.37") (hip circumference) : 34 (pleats) = 2.9 cm (1.14") (width of each pleat).
- A2_A10 = 1.45 cm (0.57") (half fold on the middle of the front, which will be cut in two where the fabric is folded).
- A_A9 same as A2_A10.
- A10_A17 = 2.9 cm (1.14").
- A9_A22 same as A10_A17.
- A17_A11 = 2.9 cm (1.14").
- A22_A12 same as A17_A11.
- A11_A23 = 2.9 cm (1.14").
- A12_A32 same as A11_A23.

- A23_A18 = 2.9 cm (1.14").
- A32_A24 same as A23_A18.
- A18_A25 = 2.9 cm (1.14").
- A24_A33 same as A18_A25.
- A25_A34 = 2.9 cm (1.14").
- A33_A35 same as A25_A34.
- A34_A36 = 2.9 cm (1.14").
- A35_A37 same as A34_A36.
- A36_A8 = 2.9 cm (1.14").
- A37_A5 same as A36_A8.
- A8_A39 = 2.9 cm (1.14").
- A5_A40 same as A8_A39.
- A39_A31 = 2.9 cm (1.14").
- A40_A38 same as A39_A31.
- A31_A29 = 2.9 cm (1.14").
- A38_A30 same as A31_A29.
- A29_A27 = 2.9 cm (1.14").
- A30_A28 same as A29_A27.
- A27_A21 = 2.9 cm (1.14").
- A28_A26 same as A27_A21.
- A21_A16 = 2.9 cm (1.14").
- A26_A19 same as A21_A16.
- A16_A13 = 2.9 cm (1.14").
- A19_A15 same as A16_A13.
- A13_A14 = 2.9 cm (1.14").
- A15_A20 same as A13_A14.
- A14_A3 = 1.45 cm (0.57") (half fold on the middle of the back, which will be cut in two where the fabric is folded).
- A20_A1 same as A14_A3.
- Join the following points: A10_A9; A17_A22; A11_A12; A23_A32; A18_A24; A25_A33; A34_A35; A36_A37; A39_A40; A31_A38; A29_A30; A27_A28; A21_A26; A16_A19; A13_A15; A14_A20.

To calculate the width of each dart, you must subtract the waist circumference from the hip circumference. For example: hip circumference 100 cm (39.37") - waist circumference 70 cm (27.55") = 30 cm (11.81"). Divide this by 2, since we are working on the pattern for half the skirt (30 cm : 2 = 15 cm / 11.81" : 2 = 5.9"); then divide this by the number of pleats there are on the pattern, in this case 17, (15 cm : 17 = 0.8 cm / 5.9" : 17 = 0.34"); each pleat will be 0.8 cm (0.31") wide and 10 cm (3.93") long.

Add a dart to each pleat, as shown in the diagram; each dart will be 10 cm (3.93") long and 0.8 cm (0.31") wide, as in the example below:
- A10_A43 = 10 cm (3.93").
- A10_A41 = 0.4 cm (0.15") (half of 0.8 cm / 0.31", total width of one dart).
- A10_A42 = 0.4 cm (0.15") (half of 0.8 cm / 0.31", total width of one dart).
- Join points A41_A43_A42 together.
- Add a dart to each pleat, exactly as shown in the example on the opposite page.
- Using pencil crayons, colour in the paper patterns to identify which one is for the front and which one is for the back of the skirt. Then cut everything out, including the pleats. To make things easier, I recommend that you number each pleat.

Position each pleat on the double folded fabric with the selvedges touching and the right side of the fabric facing inwards (1). For the front and back of the skirt, the middle of the front and the middle of the back of the first fold must line up exactly with the fold of the fabric. Each pleat must be twice as far from the other as its width (for example: if each pleat is 3 cm / 1.18" wide, the distance between one pleat and the next will be 6 cm / 2.36"). Draw in the seam allowances with chalk: usually 1 cm (0.39") along the waist, 2 cm (0.78") on the hips and 2 cm (0.78") along the bottom for a machined hem or 5 cm (1.96") for a hand-stitched hem. Then cut exactly along the lines you've drawn.

Sew guide stitches around each pleat pattern (2), then detach them and cut the guide stitches open. Fold the pleats along the guide stitches (3) and then iron the pleats to keep their shape (4).

In order to keep the pleats in place, sew a seam along the top of the skirt, about 1 cm (0.39") from the edge.

2

3

If you want to get a different effect from that of the large pleated skirt, you can close the pleats on the wrong side of the fabric, with seams on the top of the skirt: this will allow you to shape the skirt a little more at the waist. The seams must be no more than 5-8 cm (1.96-3.14") long (5).

Using tacking stitches and then sewing actual seams, join the front and back of the skirt together at the sides, keeping the right side of the fabric facing inwards (6). Leave a gap on the top left (at least 20 cm / 7.87") for a zip.

4

5

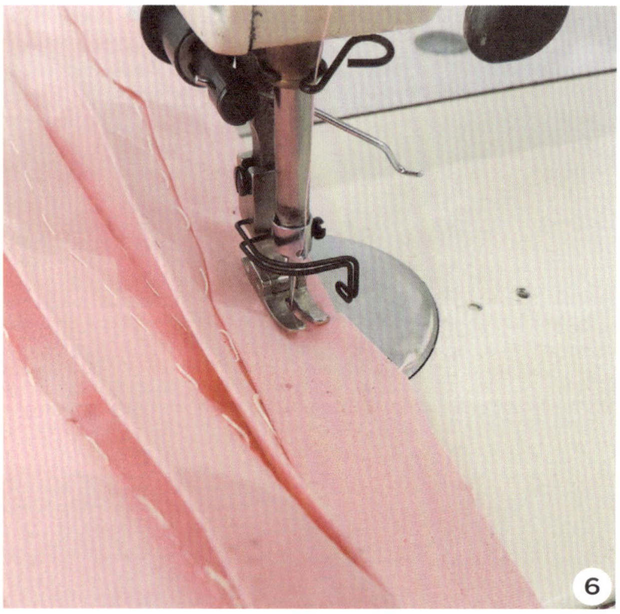

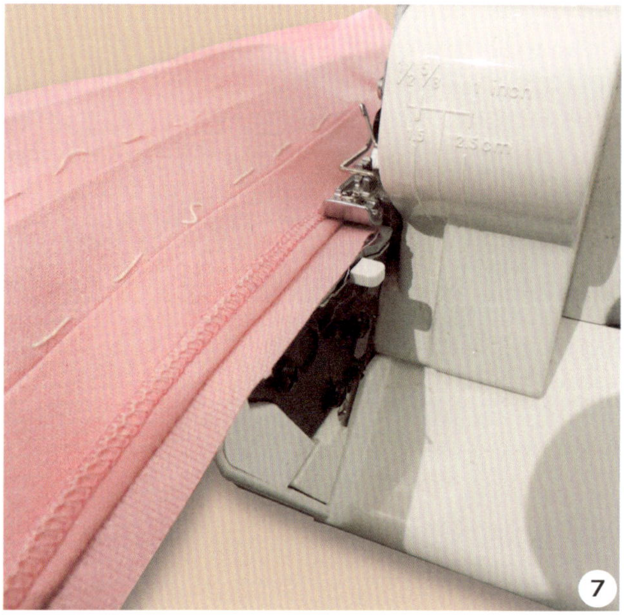

Finish off the edges with a cut-and-sew-machine (7) or zig-zag stitch and then iron them open. Add the zip and waistband (8) once you have prepared them, as explained on page 42. Add the finishing touches to the waistband (9) and then sew the hem, either by hand or using the sewing machine, as you prefer.

The mock-up skirt was made of medium-light cotton fabric. You can make this type of skirt from any fabric you like, but of course, the yield and overall effect will be different for each sort of fabric.

WRAPAROUND SKIRT

The procedure for designing the pattern for the wraparound skirt is somewhat different to the patterns for all the other skirts we've looked at so far, because it looks asymmetrical at the front. First, start by drawing the basic design for the classic skirt. Then, using another sheet of paper, just copy the front part of the skirt on the right-hand side of the sheet.

Next, fold the sheet exactly along the centre line of the front of the skirt and copy it onto the left-hand side of the sheet. Turn the sheet over and trace out the part of the skirt you drew on the reverse. This will give you the entire front of the skirt.

The front of the wraparound skirt is made of two parts that cross over: usually, the covered part comes in from the left, while the other part overlaps from the right.

Use pencil crayons in various colours to distinguish the two front parts of the skirt from the rest.

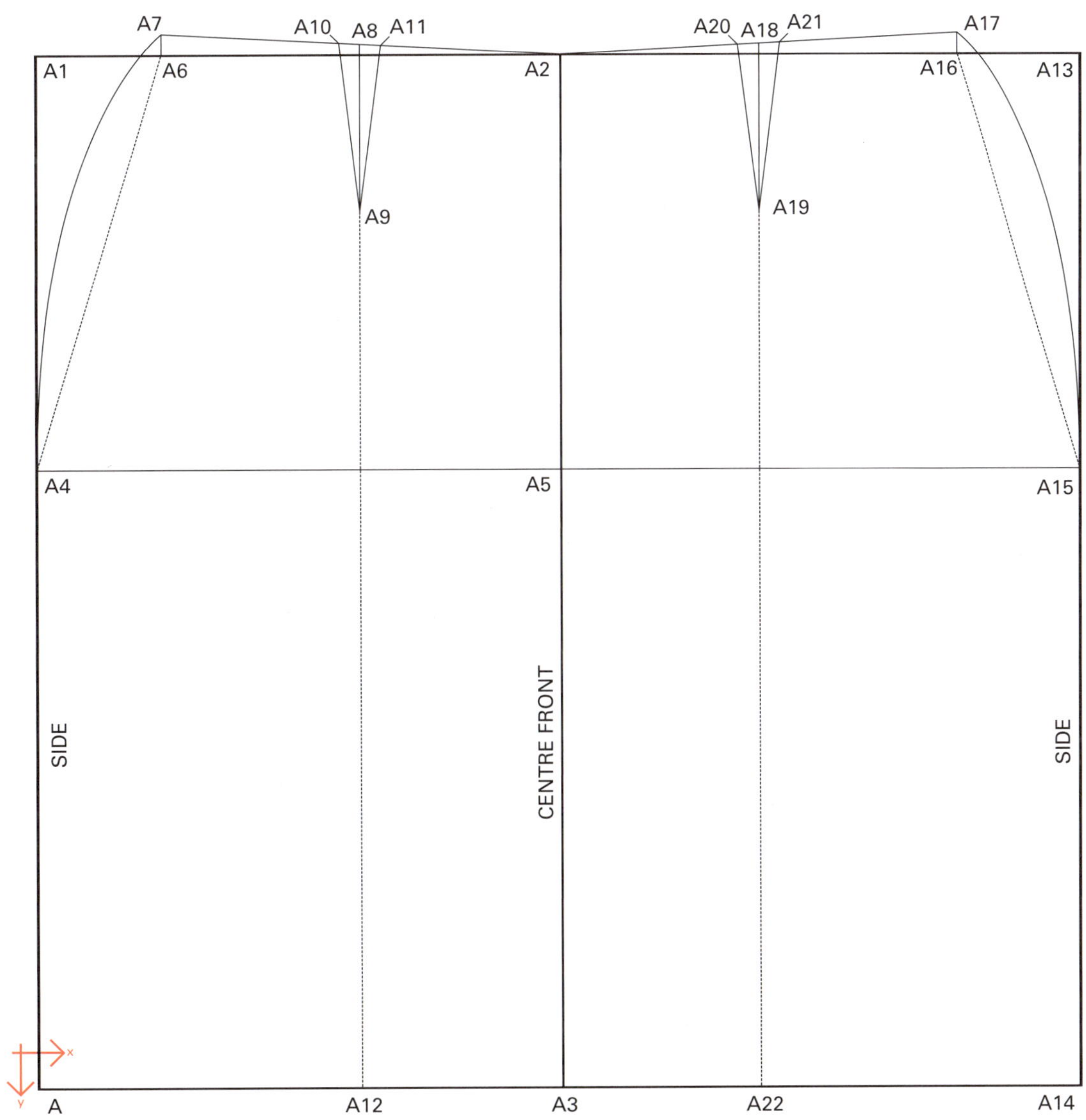

COVERED PART

- Join points A8_A2; A2_A17; A17_A15; A15_A14; A14_A12; A12_A8 together.

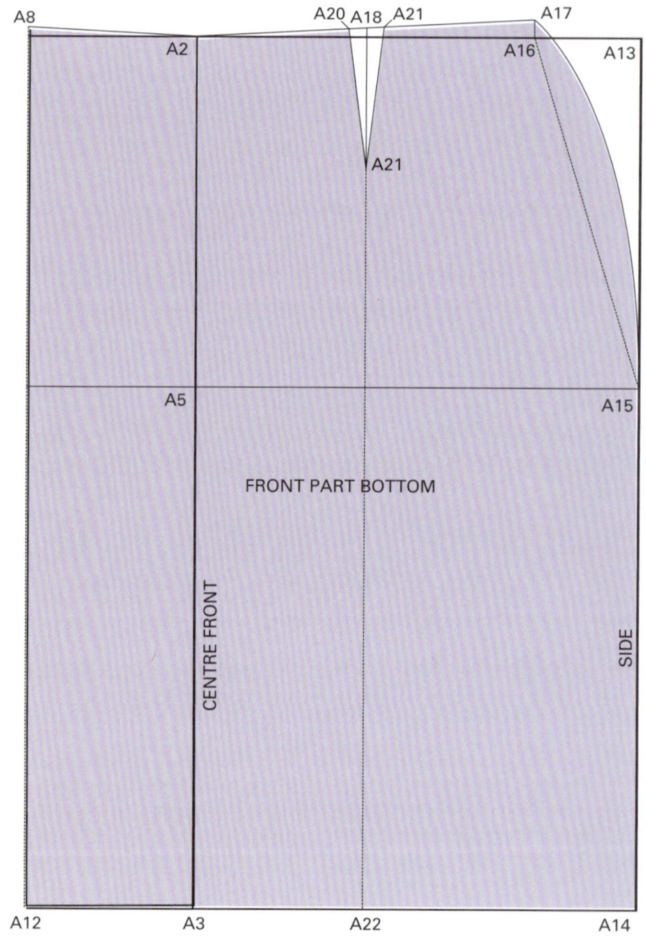

OVERLAPPING PART

- Join points A7_A2; A2_A18; A18_A22; A22_A; A_A4; A4_A7 together.

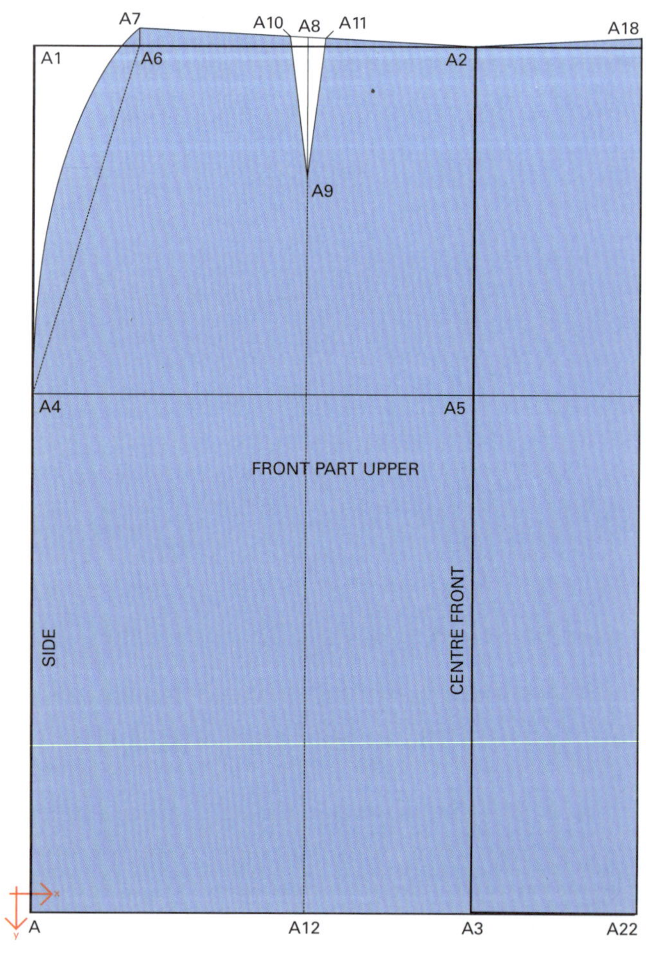

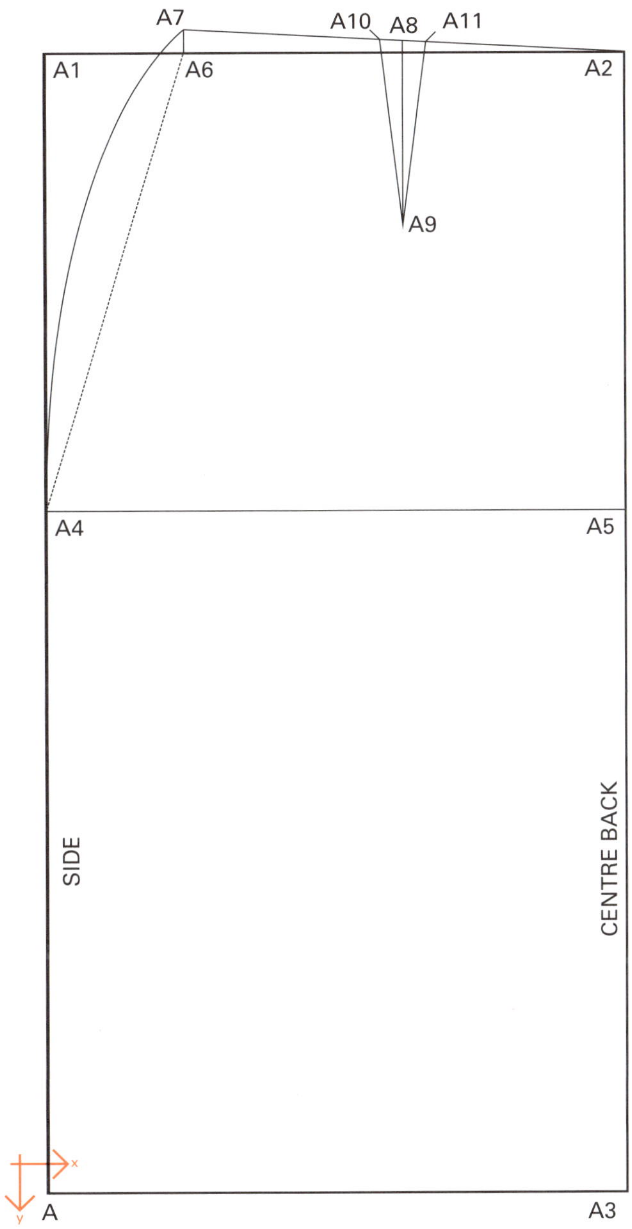

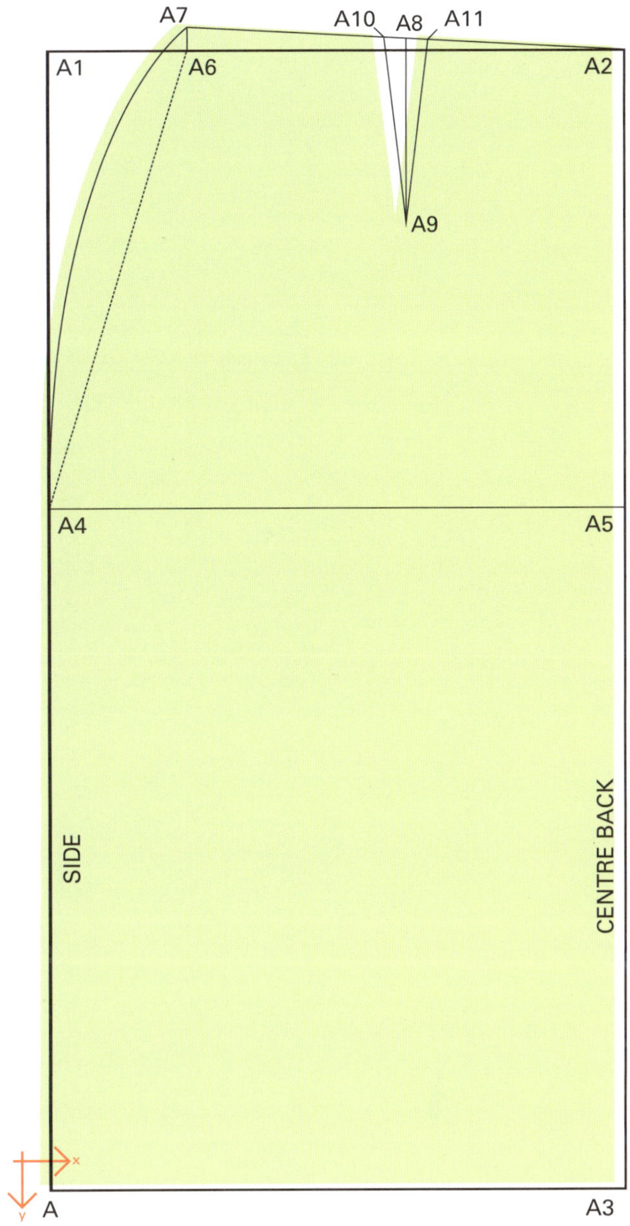

On the pattern, use a pencil crayon to identify which part is the back of the skirt. This will be identical to the back of the pattern for the classic office skirt.

Cut out all parts of the pattern. Spread the fabric you have chosen out on a tabletop without folding it and position the patterns for the front of the skirt so that they perfectly align with the selvedge of the fabric. Pin them in place and draw the seam allowances in chalk: usually 2 cm (0.78") on each side, 1 cm (0.39") along the waist, 5 cm (1.96") along the bottom and on the outer edge, adjacent to the middle of the front (1).

Cut out the front parts of the skirt, then fold the fabric in two and position the pattern for the back section according to where you want to put the zip. If you would prefer to have the zip on the side, line

up the middle of the back of the pattern with the fold in the fabric. If, on the other hand, you want to have the zip in the middle of the back, position the pattern so that there is also a seam allowance on the middle of the back. Assuming you want to put the zip in the middle of the back of the skirt, add the following seam allowances in chalk: 2 cm (0.78") along the sides and middle of the back, 1 cm (0.39") along the waist and 5 cm (1.96") along the bottom.

By cutting along the marks you've drawn in chalk, you will get two front parts, one part for the back and one waistband (2).

Since the front parts of the skirt have been cut separately and not with the fabric that you folded in two, instead of sewing guide stitches around the patterns, you can sew tacking stitches to make the marks to guide your subsequent seams (2).

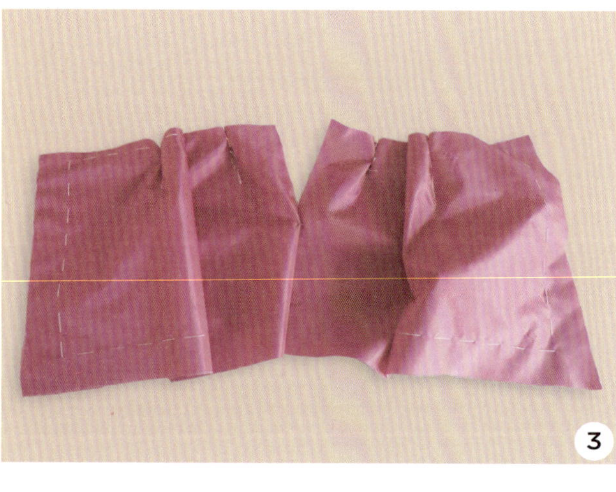

5

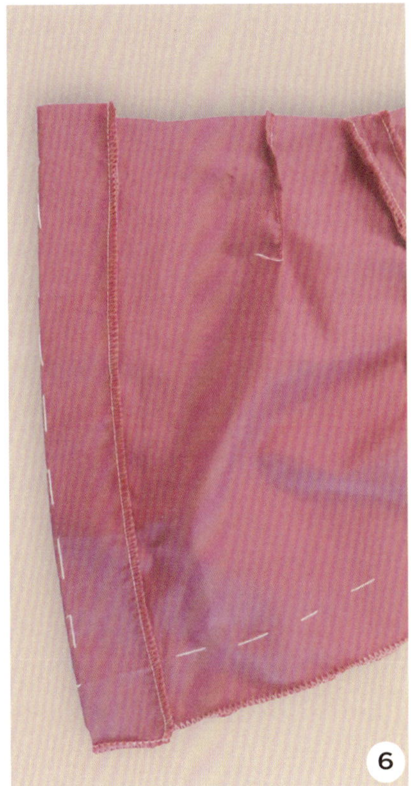

6

On the back, however, sew guide stitches. Detach the patterns and cut open the guide stitches on the back of the skirt, pin together all the parts (the front with the back), then sew tacking stitches before sewing the final seam (3 - 4). In the middle of the back section, leave a gap on the waistband for a zip. Finish off all the edges and the bottom of the skirt with a cut-and-sew-machine or a zig-zag stitch, then iron them open. Add the zip, as explained on page 47 (5).

Before you sew the hem by hand, use the iron to make a "corner" where the seam allowances of the front parts and the bottom meet. Creating a corner like this is a high-level tailoring skill.

To do it, iron the front edge on the wrong side of the fabric, exactly along the marks left by the tacking stitches (6).

Then, iron the hem along the marks left by the tacking stitches which, meeting with the front edge, create a "square" that is overlapped by both edges (7). Cut open the edges of the "square" (8), then fold it so that the crease created by ironing both sides lines up with the fold line on the bottom part of the fabric and the fold line on the front of the fabric (9).

7

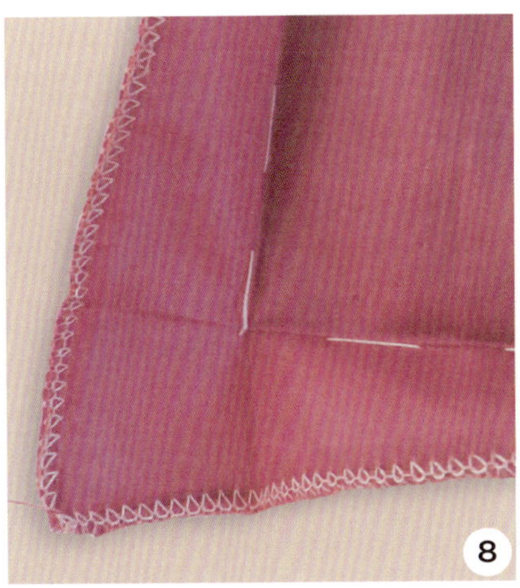

8

9

Close the corner by exactly lining up the folds created by ironing (10 - 11).

Hold the corner in place with an invisible stitch - by hand or using the sewing machine - on the wrong side of the fabric (12). Hand sew stitches to keep all the edges of the skirt in place on the wrong side of the fabric (13).

Prepare and attach the waistband as explained on page 42, then do the finishing touches as you prefer (14). If you like, you can make this design without the classic back zip, adding a button on the overlapping part on the front instead. In this case, the waistband will be different to the ones seen on the skirts we have looked at so far, not so much in how you make it but in how you design the pattern. To draw it, measure the waist circumference of the skirt you've made rather than your waist circumference, because the overlaps will make it longer than your waist circumference.

Then draw a rectangle as long as the measurement of the waist circumference of the skirt, plus at least 2 cm (0.78") for seam allowances, and twice the width of the final measurement of the waistband (for example: if the final waistband is going to be 4 cm / 1.57" wide, draw it as 8 cm / 3.14" wide), plus at least 2 cm (0.78") for the seam allowance. The process for making and attaching the waistband is exactly the same as for the other skirts we have seen thus far.

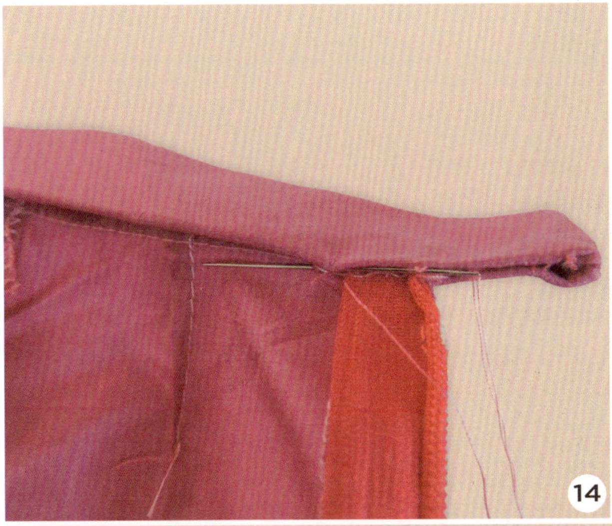

The mock-up skirt was made of silk shantung fabric. You can make this type of skirt from any kind of fabric you like. There are many variations of the wraparound skirt, in both fabric and design. So, using the basic skirt design as a starting point, you can try out lots of different versions.

ASYMMETRIC SKIRT

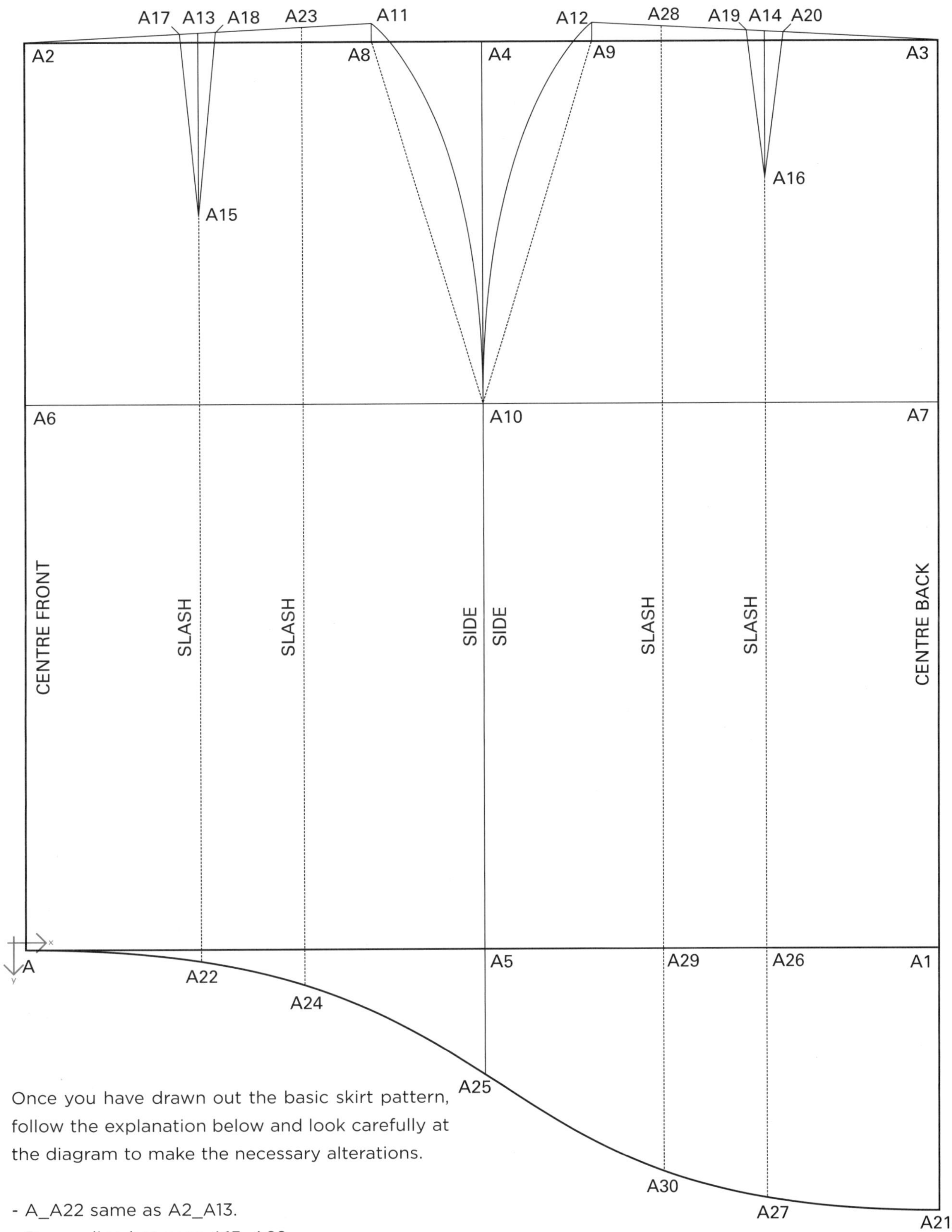

Once you have drawn out the basic skirt pattern, follow the explanation below and look carefully at the diagram to make the necessary alterations.

- A_A22 same as A2_A13.
- Draw a line between A15_A22.
- A13_A23 same as A2_A13.
- A22_A24 same as A13_A23.
- Draw a line between A23_A24.

- A1_A21 = the length of the back of the skirt can be as long as you like (for example, 20 cm / 7.87" longer than the central front part).
- A1_A26 same as A3_A14.
- Draw a line between A16_A27.
- A14_A28 same as A3_A14.
- A26_A29 same as A14_A28.
- Draw a line between A28_A30.
- Join points A_A22; A22_A24; A24_A25; A25_A30; A30_A27; A27_A21 together.
- Draw a smooth line to join the points together, creating the curve that connects the front to the back.
- Using pencil crayons, colour in the paper patterns to identify the various sections.

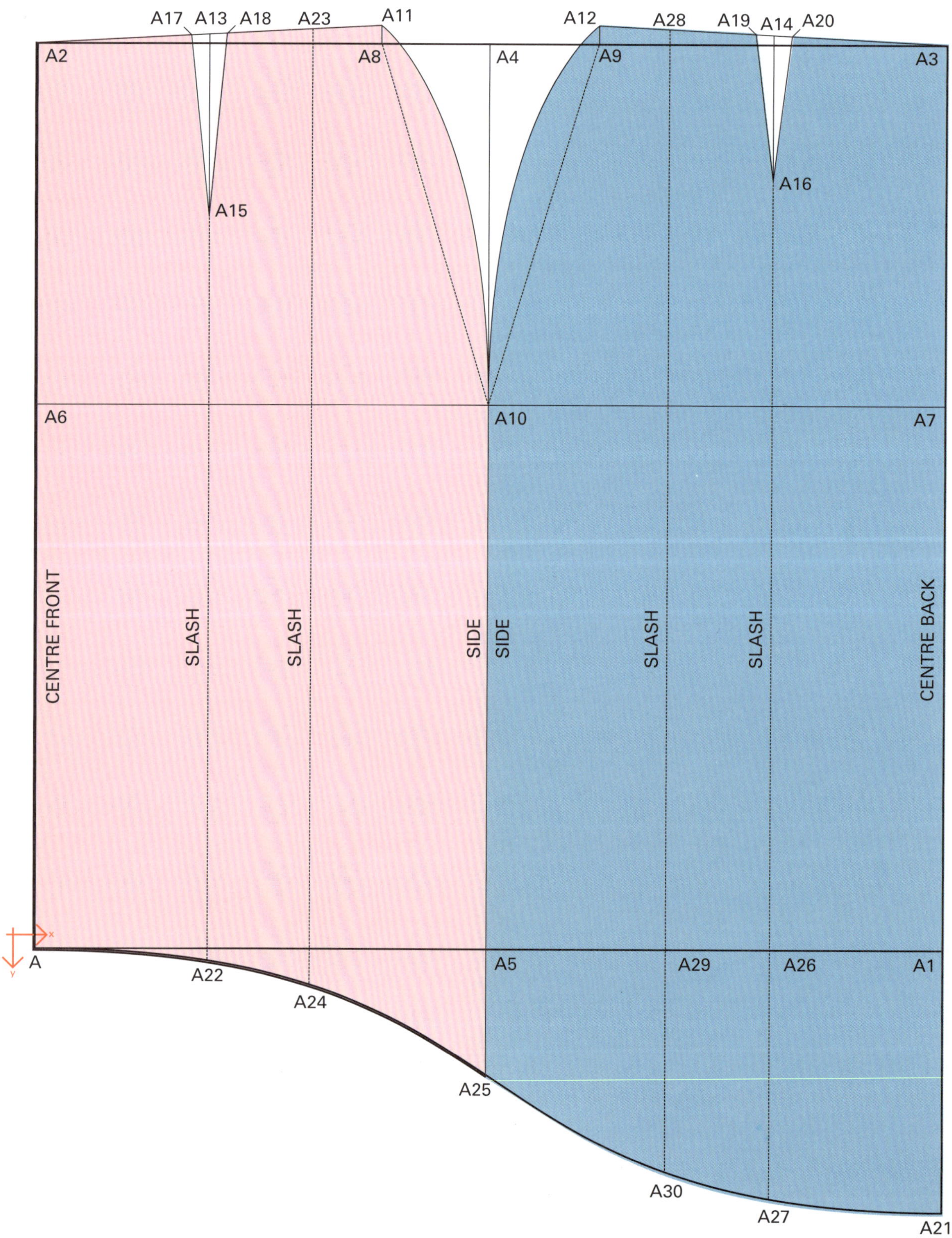

Starting from the bottom, cut out the patterns along the lines you have drawn on the fabric, which will later give the skirt its width (1).

Position the patterns on the folded fabric, with the selvedges touching and the right side of the fabric facing inwards. The middle of the front and the middle of the back must line up with the fold on the fabric. Open the cut out sections on the patterns to give the skirt extra width.

Alternatively, to give it more movement, rather than folding the fabric along the straight grain, you can fold it along the bias, as shown in this book (2).

Once you have chalked out the seam allowances, (usually 2 cm / 0.78" long on the hips, 1 cm / 0.39" along the waist and 1 cm / 0.39" along the bottom), cut along the markings, then sew guide stitches around the patterns (3).

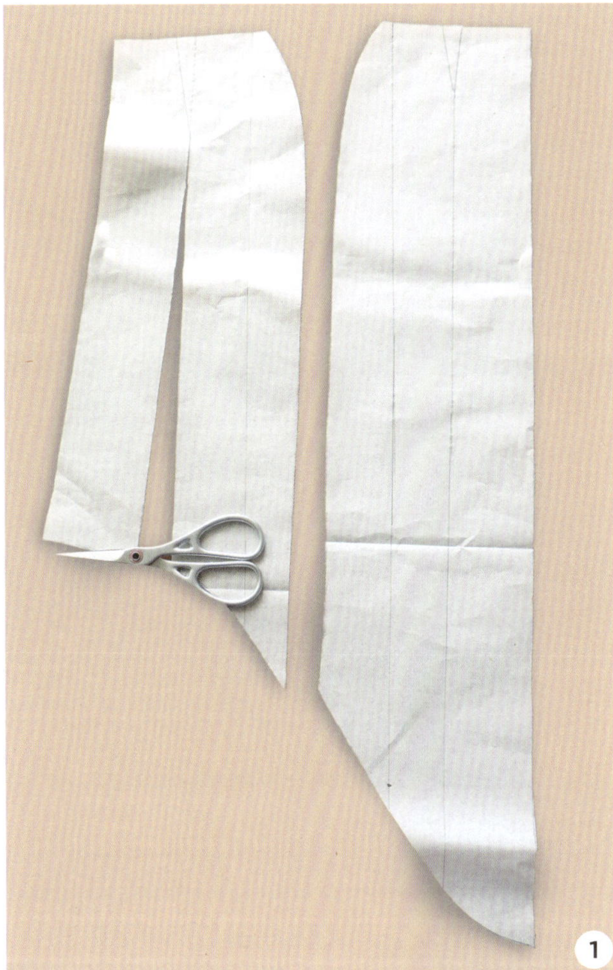

1

2

Detach the patterns, cut open the guide stitches and put the front and back of the skirt together so that the right side of the fabric is facing inwards and the guide stitches line up. Pin them together and sew tacking stitches, leaving a gap at the top on the left (at least 20 cm / 7.87") for a zip. Sew a linear seam exactly over your tacking stitches (4).

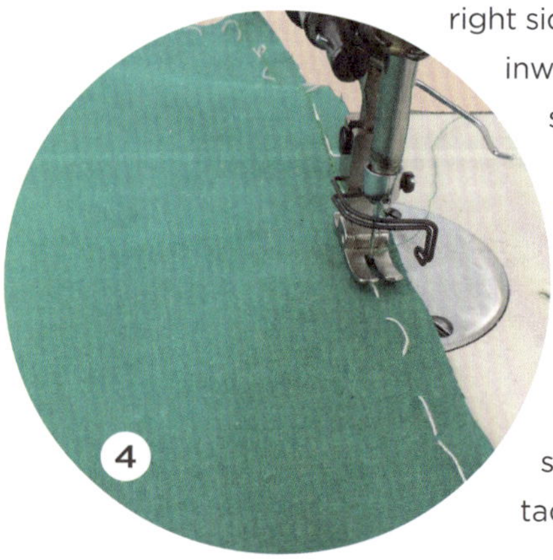

Finish off the edges with the cut-and-sew-machine (5) and then iron them open (6).

Attach the zip (7) and the waistband as explained on page 42, then finish off the waistband as you prefer. For light fabrics, it is best to sew the hem with the cut-and-sew-machine, using the special "rolled edge" function. Alternatively, if you do not have a cut-and-sew-machine, you can attach bias binding to finish off the bottom.

7

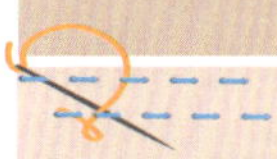

The mock-up skirt was made in a medium-weight cotton fabric. This type of skirt is ideal for special occasions and formal events, so it is important to choose an appropriate fabric. For the best results, I recommend the following fabrics:

- Satin
- Taffeta
- Khadi
- Mikado
- Duchesse
- Brocade
- Damask

TRAIN SKIRT

The train skirt is best suited to special occasions and elegant settings. From a design point of view, it is very similar to the asymmetrical skirt, because the back is longer than the front, although it has a few more details. Start by drawing out the basic skirt pattern, then follow the explanation, below, looking carefully at the diagram to make the necessary alterations.

- A_A22 same as A2_A13.
- Draw a line between A15_A22.
- A13_A23 same as A2_A13.
- A22_A24 same as A13_A23.
- Draw a line between A23_A24.
- A1_A21 is the desired length of the train (for example, 30 cm / 11.81" longer than the middle of the front of the skirt).

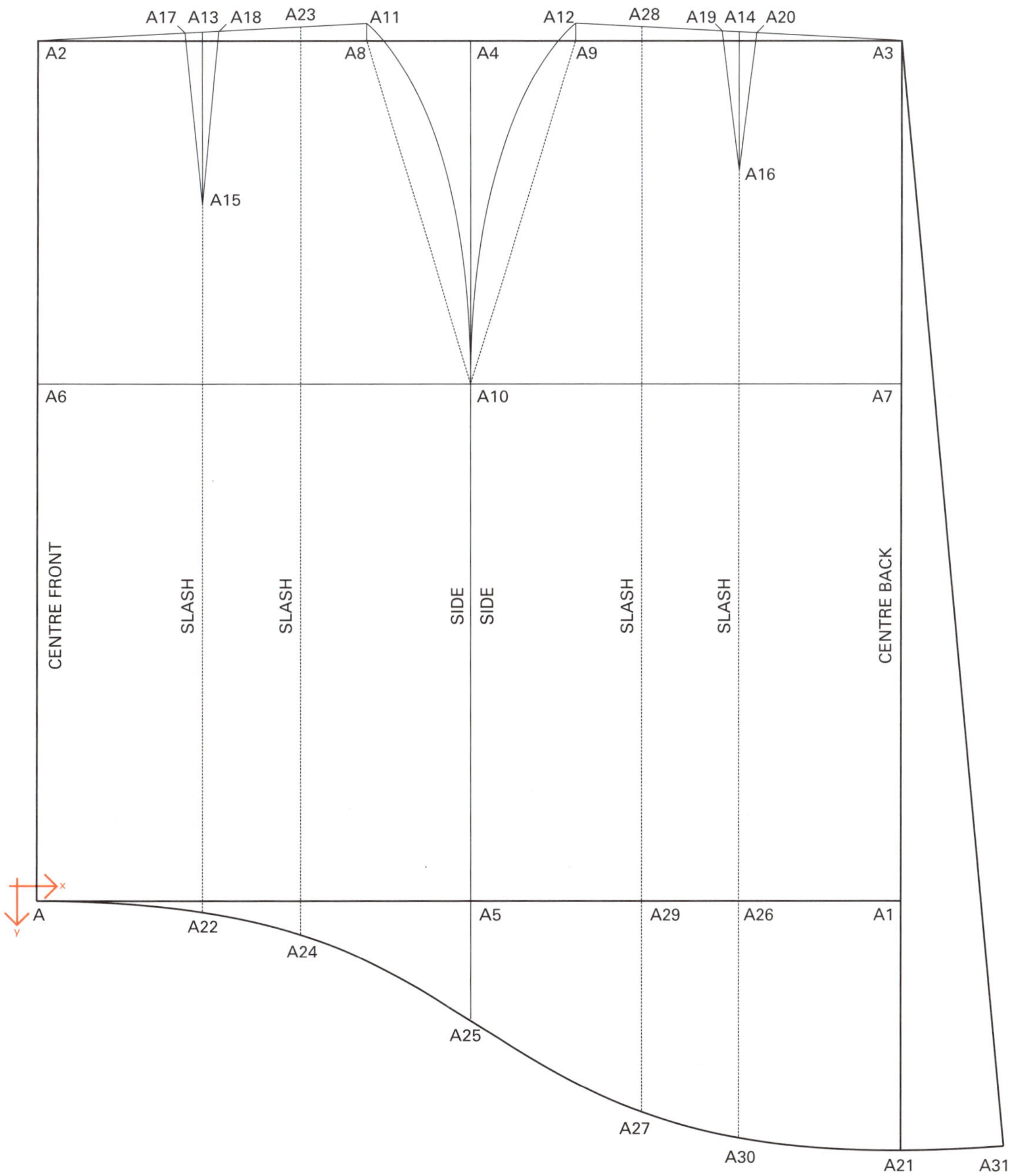

- A21_A31 is how flared you want it to be. It contributes to the length of the train (at least 10 cm / 3.93").
- Draw a line between A3_A31.
- A1_A26 same as A3_A14.
- Draw a line between A16_A30.
- A14_A28 same as A3_A14.
- A26_A29 same as A14_A28.
- Draw a line between A28_A27.
- Draw lines between the following points: A_A22; A22_A24; A24_A25; A25_A27; A27_A30; A30_A21; A21_A31. Line up the points precisely, to make sure that the front and back of the skirt are symmetrical.
- Using pencil crayons, colour in the paper patterns to identify the various sections.

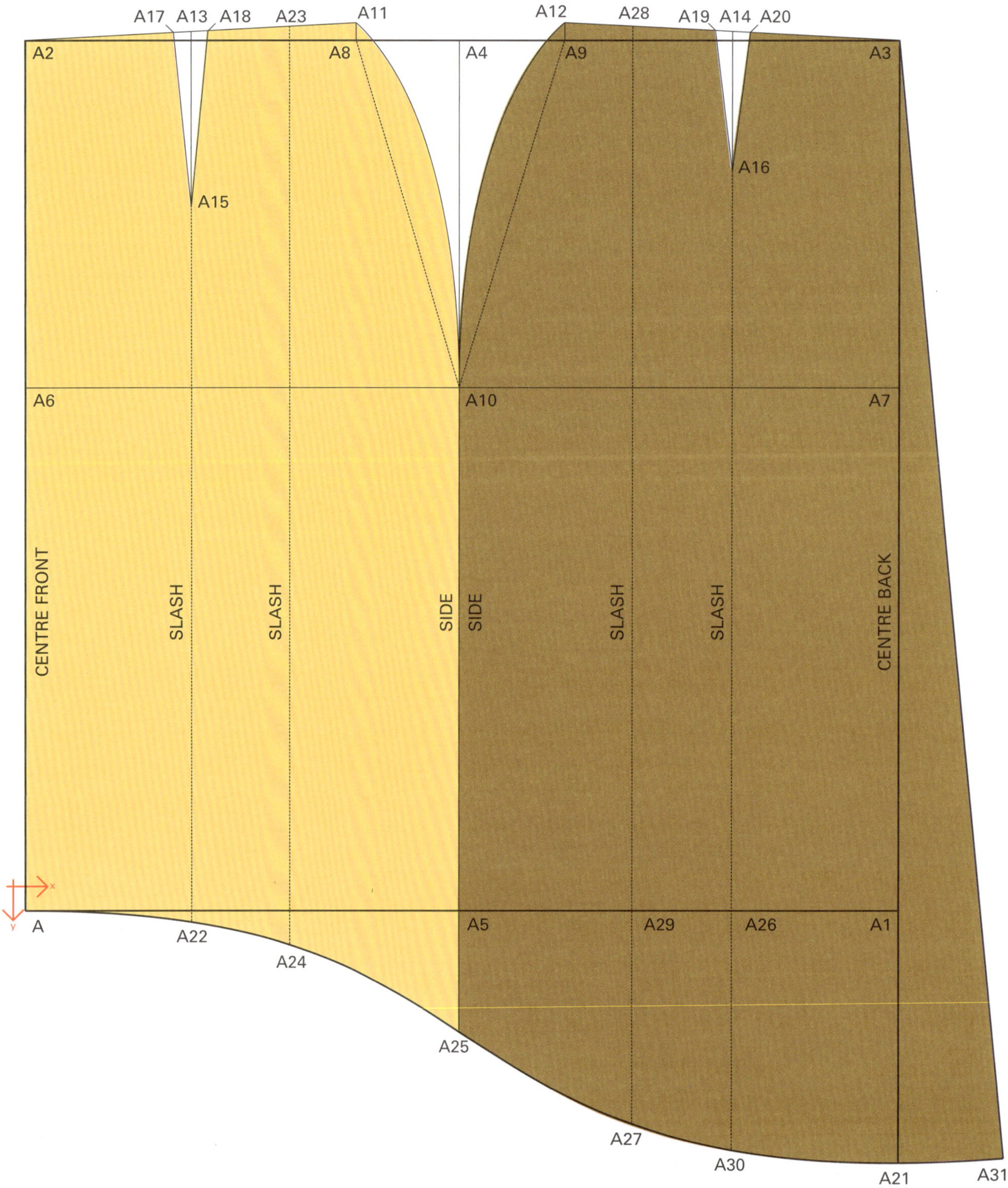

1

Starting from the bottom, cut out the patterns along the lines you have drawn: this will allow you to get the desired width of the skirt. Fold the fabric in two, with the selvedges touching and the right side of the fabric facing inwards; alternatively, the fabric can be folded on the bias to give the skirt more movement. Position the patterns on the fabric, making sure the middle of the front and middle of the back line up with the fold on the fabric (1).

Using chalk, draw in the seam allowances: usually 2 cm (0.78") on the sides, 1 cm (0.39") along the waist and 2 cm (0.78") along the bottom for a machined hem or 5 cm (1.96") for a hand-stitched hem.

Cut exactly along the marks made in chalk (2). Sew guide stitches around the patterns (3), then detach the patterns, cut open the guide stitches and put the front and back of the skirt together with the right

2

3

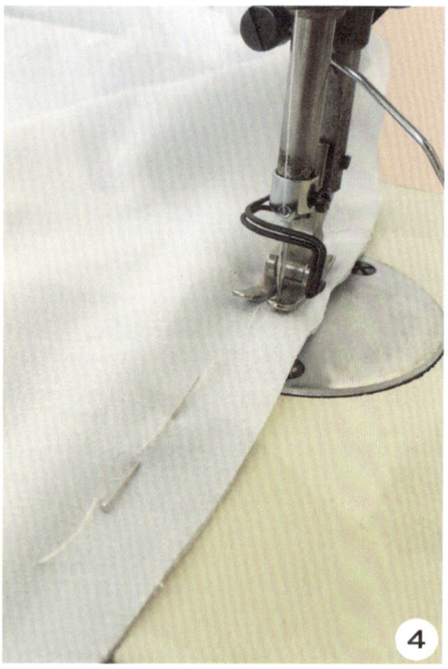

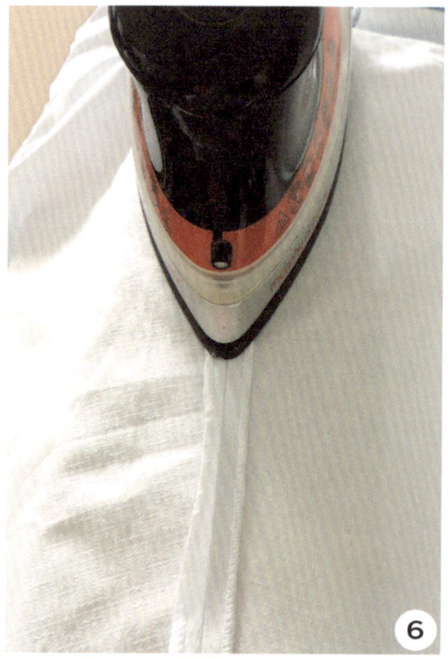

side of the fabric facing inwards. Finally, pin them together and sew tacking stitches. Then sew a linear seam exactly along the tacking stitches, leaving a gap on the upper left side for a zip (4).

Finish off the edges with a cut-and-sew-machine (5) or with zig-zag stitches, and iron them open (6). Attach the zip (7) and the waistband as explained on page 42, then finish off the waistband as you prefer.

The mock-up skirt was made in a medium- weight cotton fabric. This type of skirt is worn on special or important occasions, which is why I recommend using the following fabrics:

- Satin
- Khadi
- Taffeta
- Brocade
- Damask
- Duchesse
- Silk
- Tulle

LOWERING THE WAISTBAND

All of the skirts we have looked at so far in this book have high waists. Generally speaking, a high waist makes skirts and trousers look more elegant and sophisticated. However, other kinds of skirts exist that have a low waist, such as miniskirts, sports skirts and other styles, such as asymmetrical or patterned skirts. When designing a low-rise skirt, always start with the basic skirt pattern, and then make the adjustments to lower the waistband, as explained below and shown in the diagram.

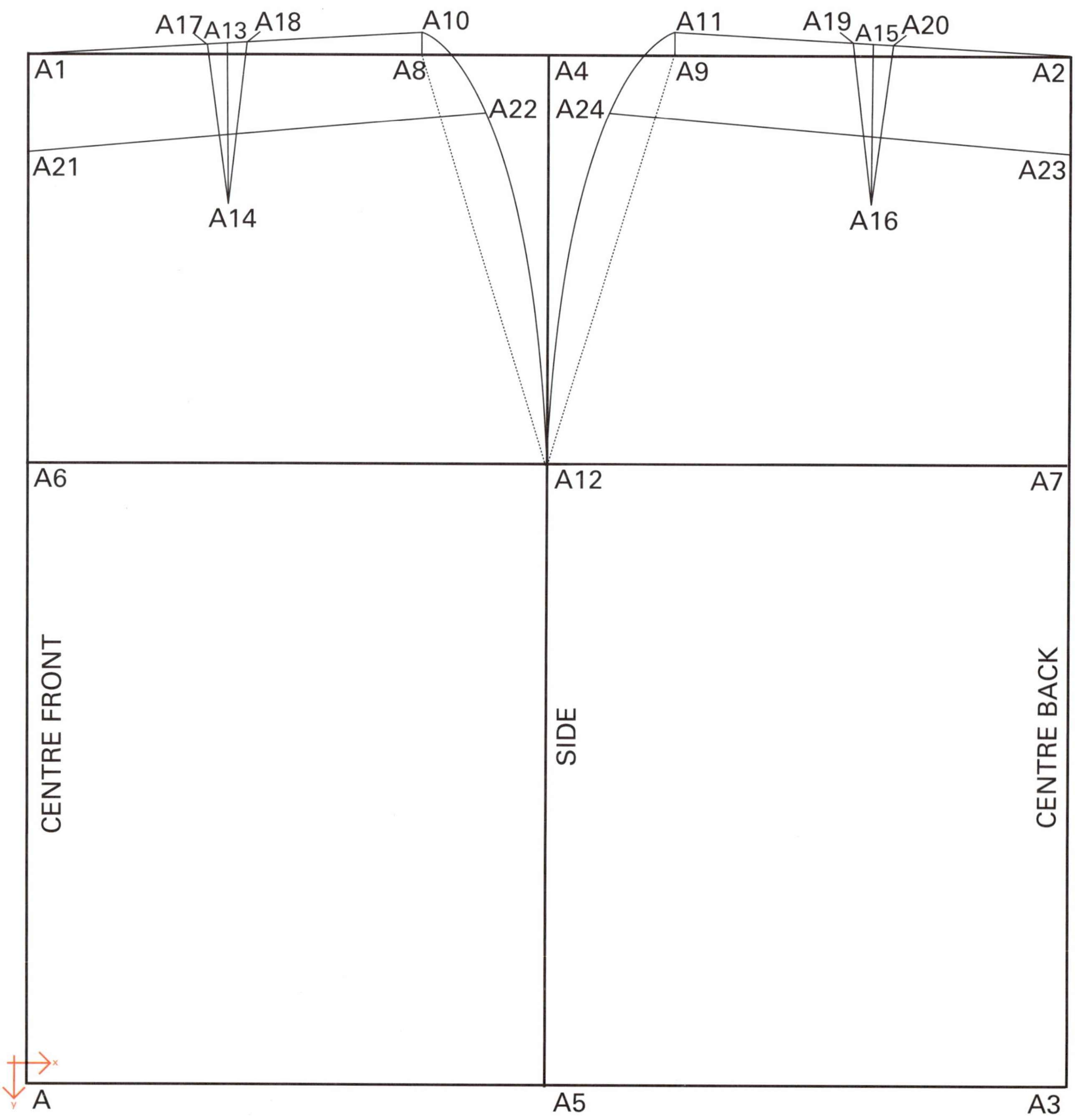

- A1_A21 is the measurement to lower the waistband by (for example, 5 cm / 1.96").
- A10_A22 same as A1_A21.
- Draw a line between A21_A22.
- A2_A23 is the measurement to lower the waistband by (for example, 5 cm / 1.96").
- A11_A24 same as A2_A23.
- Draw a line between A24_A23.

The skirt's new waistline now starts from points: A21_A22 and A23_A24; use pencil crayons to show where the skirt pattern now starts.

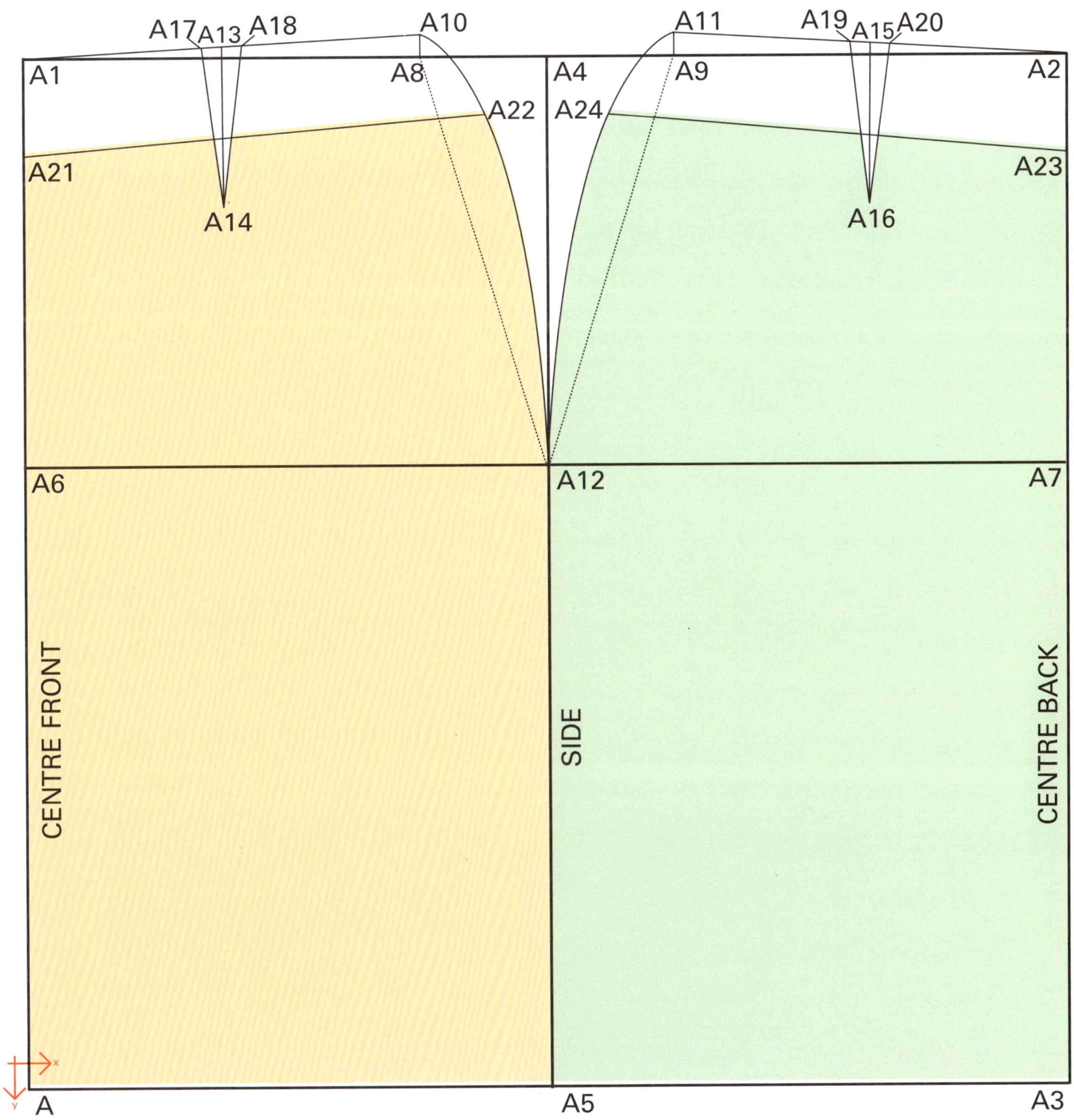

DESIGNING AND TAILORING A PAIR OF TROUSERS

TROUSERS: HISTORY AND DESIGNS

BRIEF HISTORY

The first trousers date back to about two thousand years ago, when a Eurasian nomadic population felt the need to invent a hard-wearing garment that covers the legs individually, so that they could move more easily on horseback. As such, for a long time trousers were an exclusively male item of clothing. It was only in the early nineteenth century that many women started wearing trousers as a sign of disapproval of the social system, giving rise to a gradual battle towards the conquest of equal rights. But it wasn't until the end of the 1970s that the world finally started to get used to the idea that women can also wear trousers, without it being considered "immoral". Indisputably, denim jeans are the symbol of a new era of emancipation. Today, trousers are worn daily by all genders, and are synonymous with comfort, practicality and elegance. There are all sorts of designs, each made in the most varied fabrics, with their own style and character: sporty or more elegant jeans, classic trousers, sweatpants, flared or palazzo pants, and so on.

BASIC DESIGNS

In this book, you can learn how to create patterns for all kinds of trousers so you can make them yourself. You will also find explanations on how to make pockets for trousers, such as seam pockets, patch pockets, welt pockets, etc.

To make things easier, the instructional examples displayed in this book are made to 1:2 scale, but the same rules apply when making trousers to full scale, using your own measurements. With the exception of a few styles, all trousers are made using the same basic design: a paper pattern that uses geometric methods, but based on your own measurements.

Once you have taken your measurements, as instructed in the previous chapter, equip yourself with tissue paper, a ruler, set square, pencil, rubber and sharpener, so you can draw the basic trouser pattern. Once you have studied the diagram and carefully followed the explanation, draw your basic design.

Front

- A_A1 = 1/4 of hip circumference.
- A1_A2 = 1/4 of hip circumference.
- A2_A3 same as A_A1.
- A3_A same as A1_A2.
- Combine A_A1, A1_A2, A2_A3, A3_A to get the quadrature.
- A3_A4 = 1/2 hip circumference : 12 (for example, hip circumference 100 cm : 2 = 50 cm / 39.37": 2 = 19.68"; 50 cm : 12 = 4.16 cm / 19.68" : 12 = 1.64"; the final result is the measurement for the crotch section at the front of the trousers).
- A3_A5 same as A3_A4.
- Draw a curved line between A4_A5 (for the crotch).
- A_A10 = 2 cm (0.78").
- A9_A10 = 1 cm (0.39").
- Draw a line between A5_A10.
- A1_A6 = 1/4 hip circumference + crotch size : 2 (for example, hip circumference 100 cm : 4 = 25 cm / 39.37": 4 = 9.84"; 25 cm + 4 cm = 29 cm / 9.84" + 1.57" = 11.41"; 29 cm : 2 = 14.5 cm / 11.41": 2 = 5.70"; the resulting measurement represents the crease line of the trousers and its straight grain).
- A6_A7 is the total length of the trousers, measured from the waist.
- A10_A11 = 1/4 waist circumference + 2 cm (0.78") (for example, waist circumference 70 cm : 4 = 17.5 cm / 27.55" : 4 = 6.88"; 17.5 cm + 2 cm = 19.5 cm / 6.88" + 0.78" = 7.66").
- Draw a curved line between A11_A2 (this represents the hip shape).
- A6_A19 = 1 cm (0.39").
- A6_A20 same as A6_A19.
- A6_A8 = 8 cm (3.14").
- Draw a line between A19_A8_A20.
- A6_A13 = knee height, measured from the waist.
- A13_A14 = 10 cm (3.93") (size depends on how wide you want the trousers to be).
- A13_A15 same as A13_A14.
- Draw a smooth line between A4_A15 and A2_A14.
- A7_A17 = 9 cm (3.54") (size depends on how wide you want the trousers to be).
- A7_A16 same as A7_A17.
- Draw a line between A15_A17 and A14_A16.
- Using a pencil crayon, colour in the paper pattern to identify it as the front.

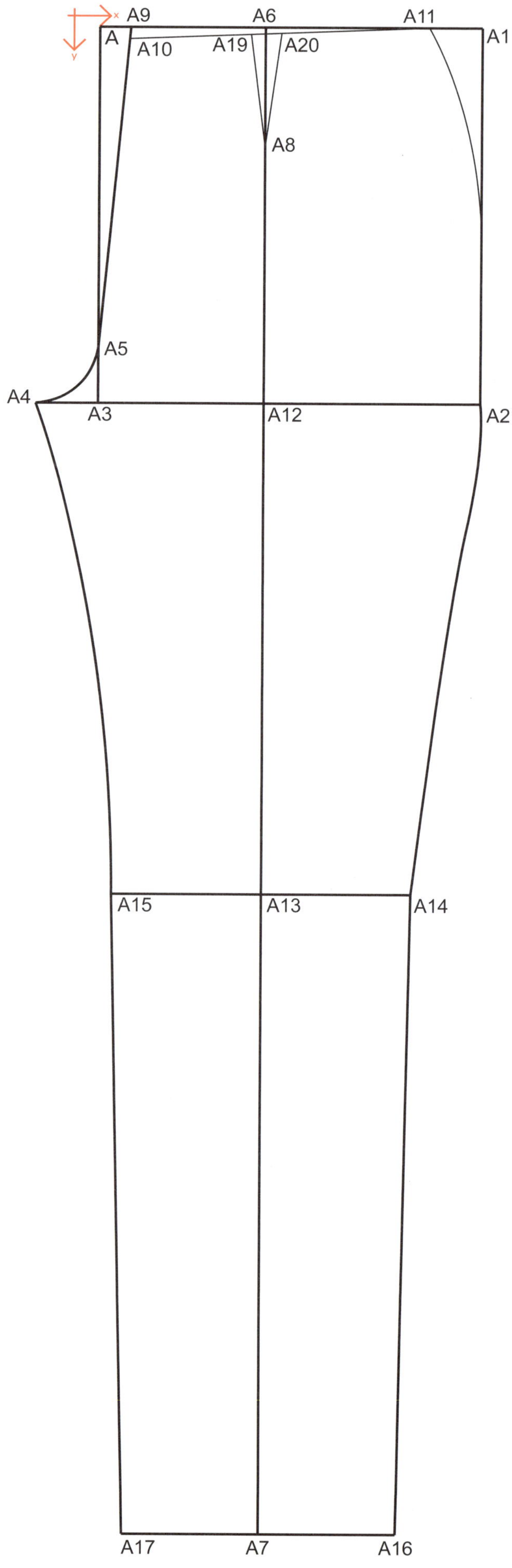

Back

- A_A1 = 1/4 of hip circumference.
- A1_A2 = 1/4 of hip circumference.
- A2_A3 same as A_A1.
- A3_A same as A1_A2.
- Combine A_A1, A1_A2, A2_A3, A3_A to get the quadrature.
- A2_A4 = 1/2 of hip circumference: 12 x 2 (for example, hip circumference 100 cm : 2 = 50 cm / 39.37" : 2 = 19.68"; 50 cm : 12 = 4.1 cm / 19.68" : 12 = 1.64"; 4.1 cm x 2 = 8.2 cm / 1.61" x 2 = 3.22", the final result is the measurement for the crotch section at the back of the trousers).
- A4_A5 = 1 cm (0.39").
- A2_A6 is half of A2_A4.
- Draw a curved line between A6_A5 (for the crotch).
- A1_A7 = 5 cm (1.96").
- A7_A8 = 3 cm (1.18").
- Draw a line between A8_A6.
- A_A10 = 1/4 hip circumference + crotch size : 2 (for example, hip circumference 100 cm : 4 = 25 cm / 39.37" : 4 = 9.84"; 25 cm + 4 cm = 29 cm : 2 = 14.5 cm / 9.84" + 1.57" = 11.41" : 2 = 5.74"; the resulting measurement represents the crease line of the trousers and its straight grain).
- A10_A11 is the total length of the trousers, measured from the waist.
- A8_A9 = 1/4 waist circumference + 2 cm (0.78") (for example, waist circumference 70 cm : 4 = 17.5 cm / 27.55" : 4 = 6.88"; 17.5 cm + 2 cm = 19.5 cm / 6.88" + 0.78" = 7.66").
- Draw a slightly curved line between A9_A3 (represents the hip shape).
- A9_A12 half of A9_A8.
- A12_A14 = 1 cm (0.39").
- A12_A15 same as A12_A14.
- A12_A13 = 12 cm (4.72") (draw the line on the waistline using a set square).
- Draw a line between A14_A13_A15.
- A10_A17 = knee height measured from the waist.
- A17_A18 = 12 cm (4.72") (size depends on how wide you want the trousers to be).
- A17_A19 same as A17_A18.
- Draw a smooth line between A5_A18 and A3_A19.
- A11_A20 = 10 cm (3.93") (size depends on how wide you want the trousers to be).
- A11_A21 same as A11_A20.
- Draw a line between A19_A21 and A18_A20.

The basic trouser pattern is ready and can be used to make all the different designs covered in this book.

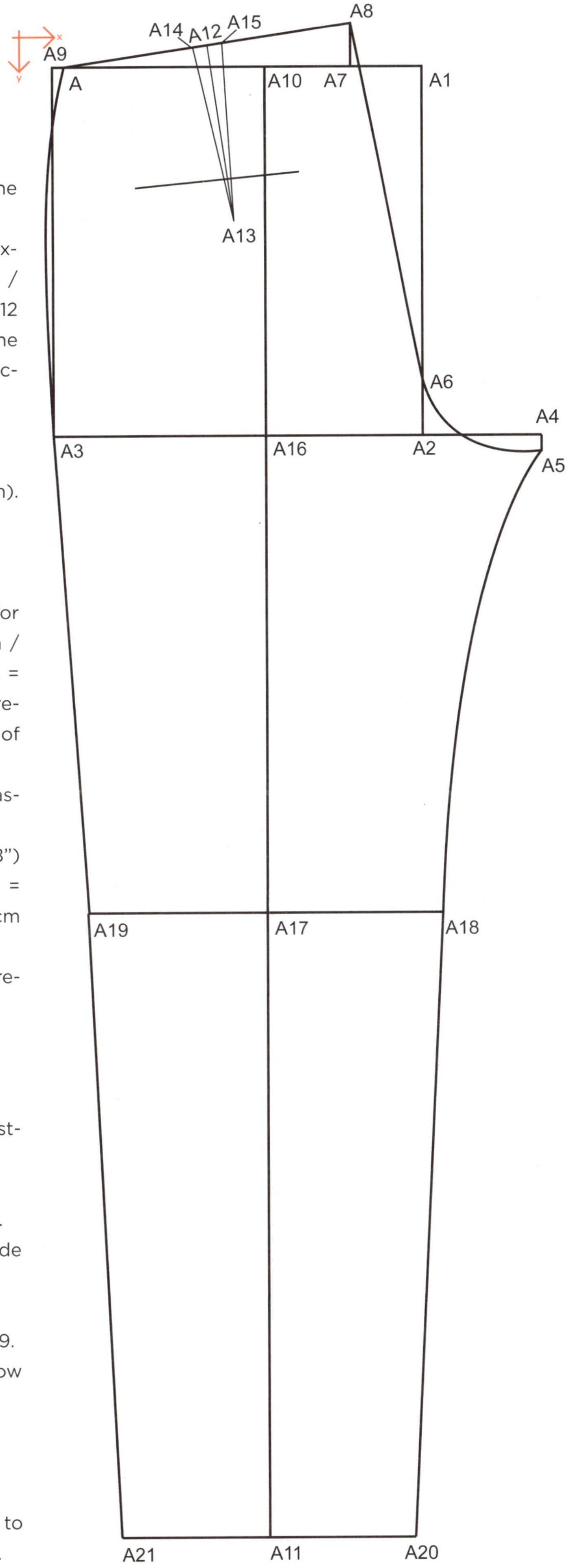

CLASSIC OFFICE TROUSERS

You are sure to find a pair of classic office trousers in most women's wardrobes. Ideal for special occasions or for work, they give an outfit an elegant look without compromising on comfort. There are all sorts of designs: with or without pockets; with a zip at the front, back or even at the side.

In this book, I explain how to use a pattern to make classic office trousers with various options: without pockets; with an invisible zip on the left side; with front and back welt pockets.

In this section, therefore, not only will I explain how to make classic office trousers, I will also show you how to make front pockets as well as single- and double-welt pockets.

CLASSIC TROUSERS WITHOUT POCKETS

In order to make a pattern for classic office trousers without pockets, just draw out the basic trouser pattern, as already seen in the previous chapter, without making further changes. Then, using pencil crayons, colour in the pattern to identify which part is for the front and which is for the back of the trousers.

Front

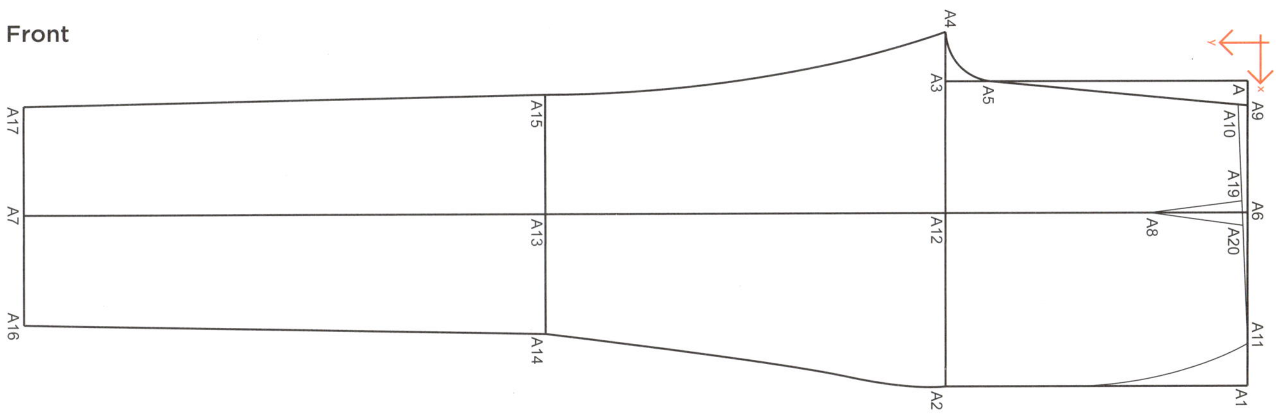

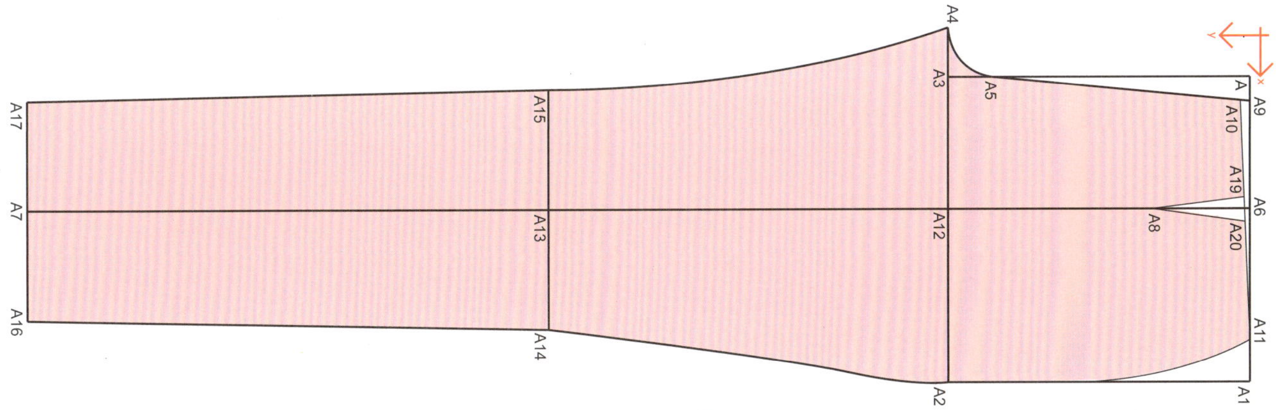

Back

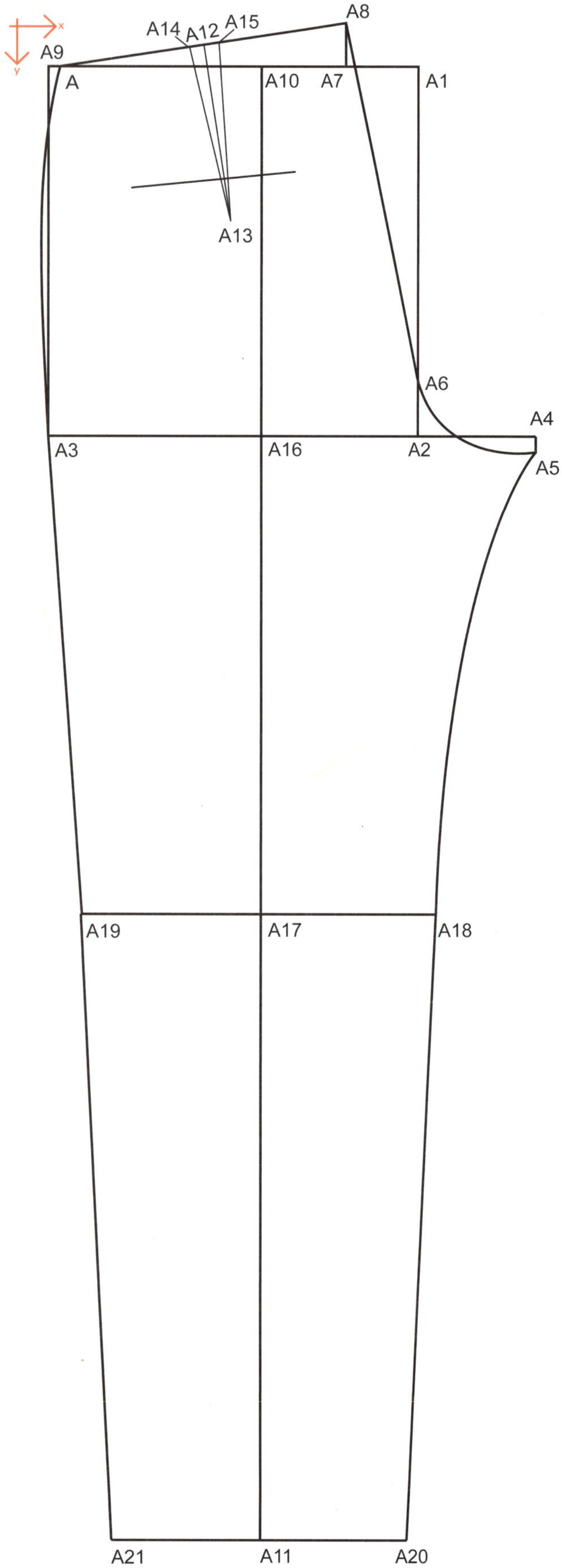
x
y
A9
A14
A12
A15
A8
A
A10
A7
A1
A13
A6
A4
A3
A16
A2
A5
A19
A17
A18
A21
A11
A20

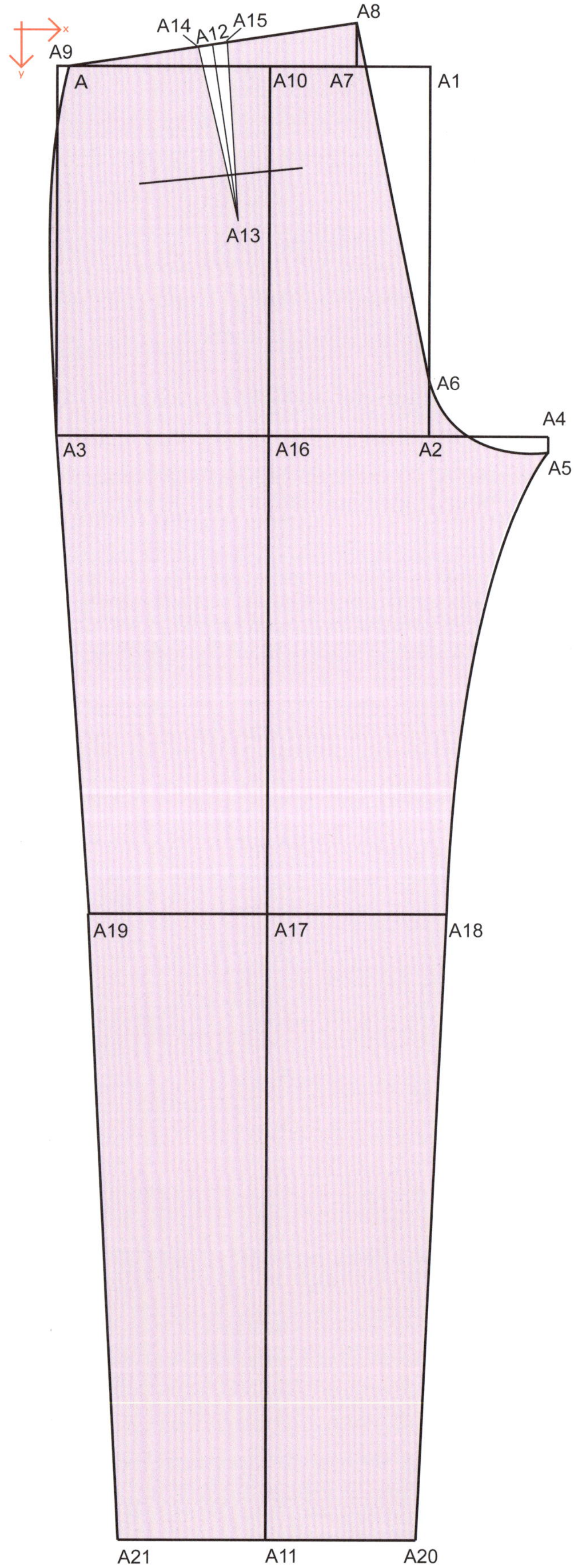
x
y
A9
A14
A12
A15
A8
A
A10
A7
A1
A13
A6
A4
A3
A16
A2
A5
A19
A17
A18
A21
A11
A20

Fold your chosen fabric in two so that the selvedges are touching and the right side of the fabric is facing inwards. Once you have cut out the respective patterns, position them on the fabric. When positioning the patterns on the fabric, make sure that the crease line is exactly parallel to the selvedges of the fabric. Pin the paper patterns to the fabric, then mark the seam allowances in chalk using the tape measure: usually 1 cm (0.39") on the waist, 2 cm (0.78") along the sides and on the middle of the front and the middle of the back of the patterns, 5 cm (1.96") along the bottom (1).

Cut along the lines you've just drawn, then sew guide stitches around each of the paper patterns while they are still attached to the fabric (2).

Detach the patterns from the fabric, cut open the guide stitches, then put the front and back of the trousers together, so that the right side of the fabric is facing inwards (3). Hold these parts together with pins and tacking stitches (4).

Sew a linear seam exactly along the tacking stitches you've just sewn, leaving a gap on the left side for a zip (5). Finish off the edges with a cut-and-sew-machine (6) or zig-zag stitches, and iron them open. Remember to remove the tacking stitches once you have finished machine sewing. Tack and then sew the darts (7). Now sew the middle of both of the newly assembled parts together (the crotch) with a linear seam, making sure that the seams of the inside leg line up perfectly (8).

Finish off the edges with the cut-and-sew-machine (9) or with zig-zag stitches, then iron them open (10).

3

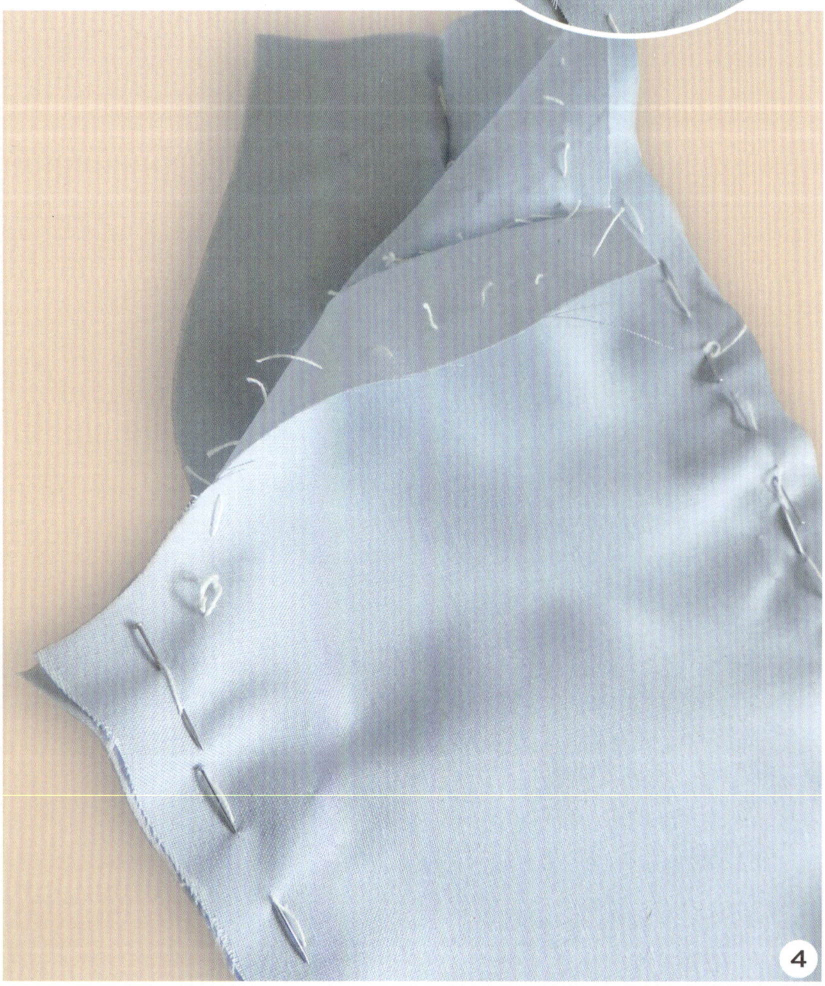
4

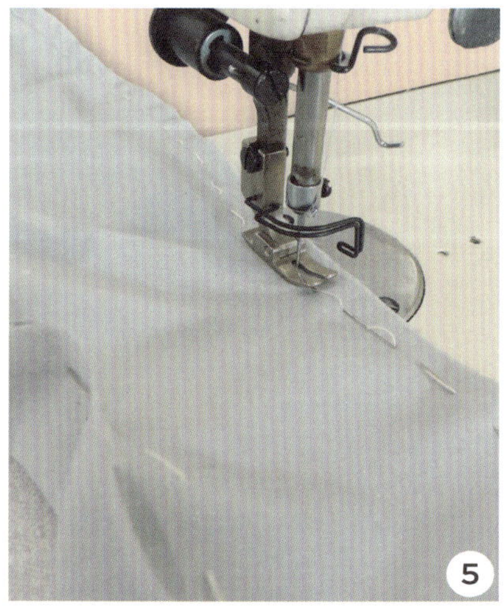
5

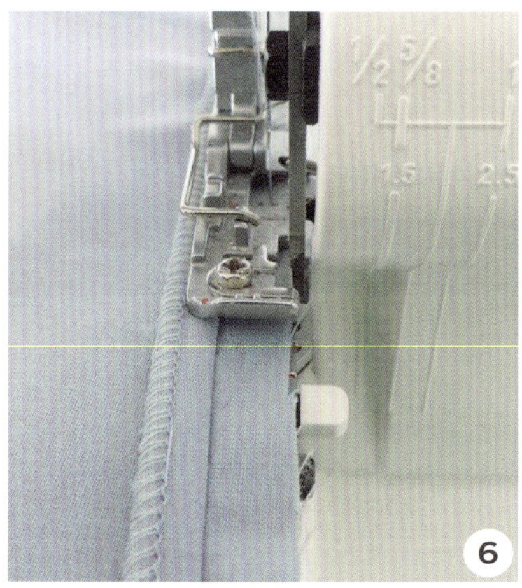
6

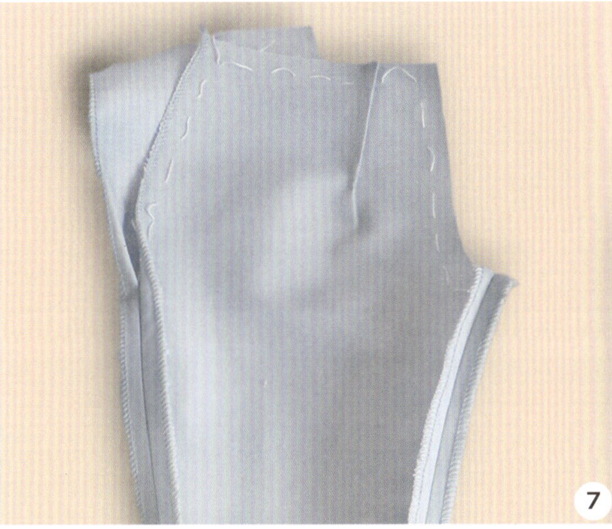
7

8

9

10

11

12

Attach the zip (11) and prepare the waistband as explained on page 42, then attach the waistband and finish it off by hand on the wrong side of the trousers (12). Sew the hem by hand with an understitch (13).

Hand sew a press stud onto the overlap of the waistband (14). Pull the trousers inside out again so they are the right way round, then fold them so that the seams on the sides and inside leg line up. Now iron the legs to get that classic crease that you always see down the front of elegant trousers (15).

13

14

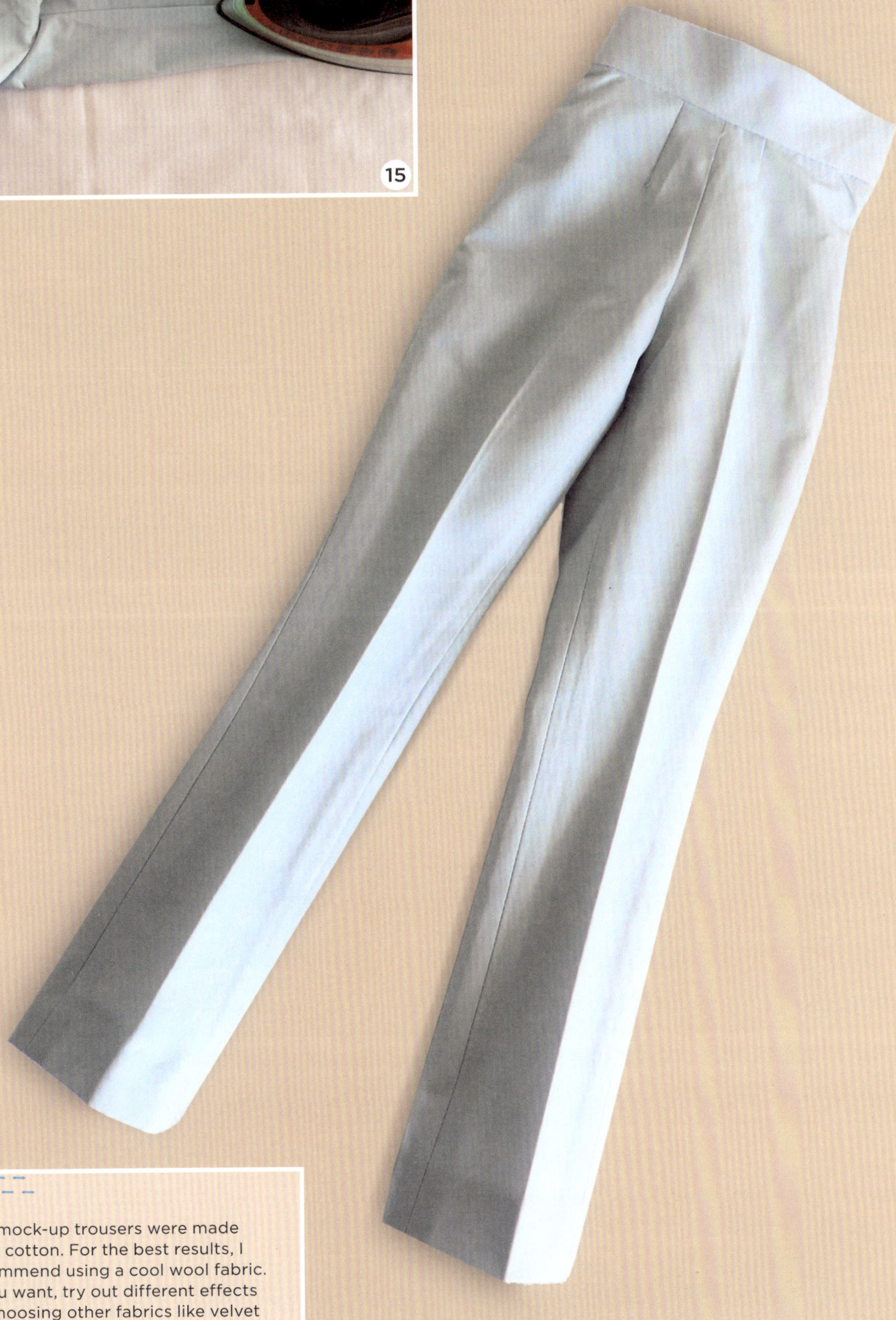

The mock-up trousers were made from cotton. For the best results, I recommend using a cool wool fabric. If you want, try out different effects by choosing other fabrics like velvet or Glen plaid.

CLASSIC OFFICE TROUSERS WITH POCKETS

In order to make a pattern for classic office trousers with pockets, just draw out the basic trouser pattern, and add whichever pockets you want. Classic trousers with pockets can have a zip in the middle of the front or back. In this book, the mock-up was made with a zip in the middle of the back. Once you have studied the diagram and carefully followed the explanation, you can make the necessary alterations.

- A8_A21 = 8 cm (3.14") (this measurement can vary according to the style and size of the trousers).
- A1_A27 = 18 cm (7.08") (this measurement can also vary according to the style and size of the trousers).
- Draw a line between A21_A27 (front pocket).
- A21_A23 = at least 4 cm (1.57").
- A27_A22 = at least 5 cm (1.96").
- Draw a line between A23_A22, as shown in the diagram, to draw the pocket.
- Using pencil crayons, colour in the trousers to show which parts represent the pocket openings and the pocket pouch, as shown in the following diagrams.

Front

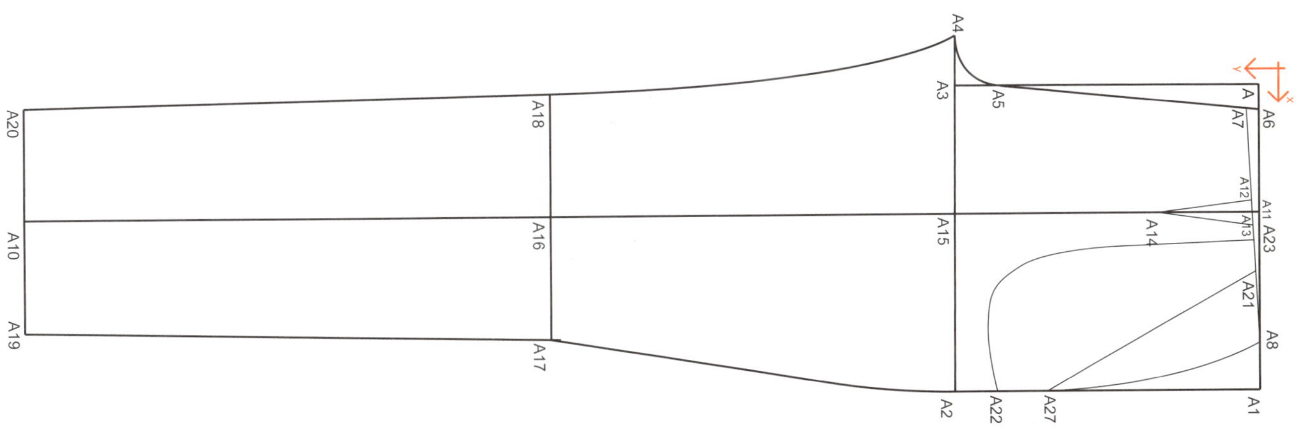

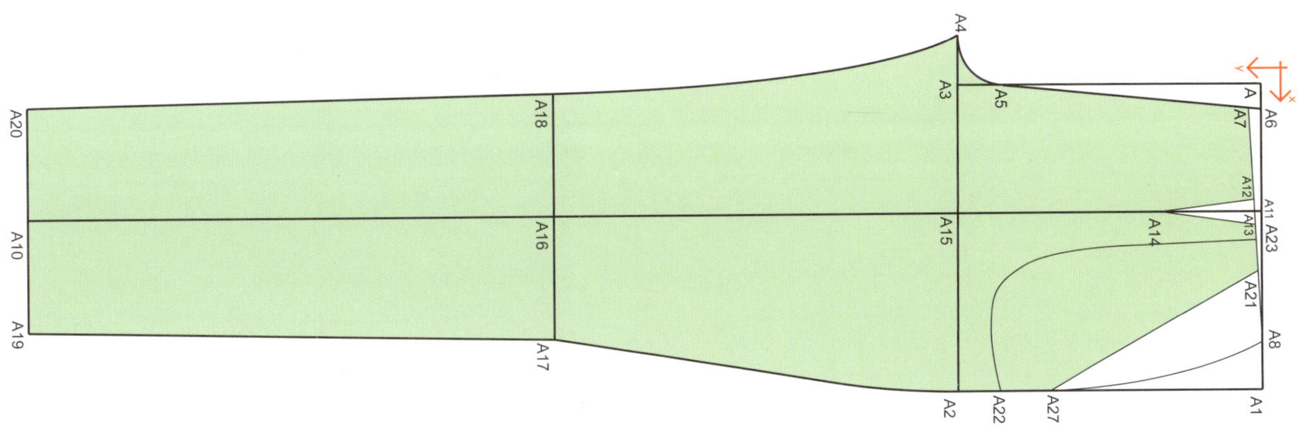

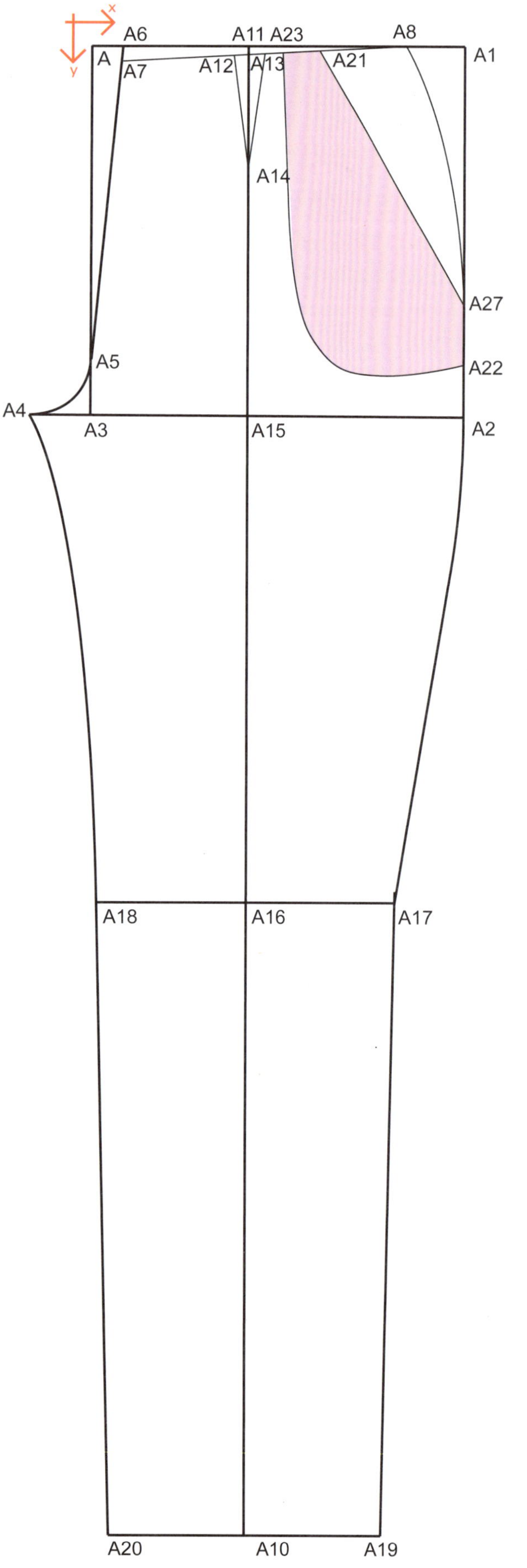

Sewing pattern for the pocket opening.

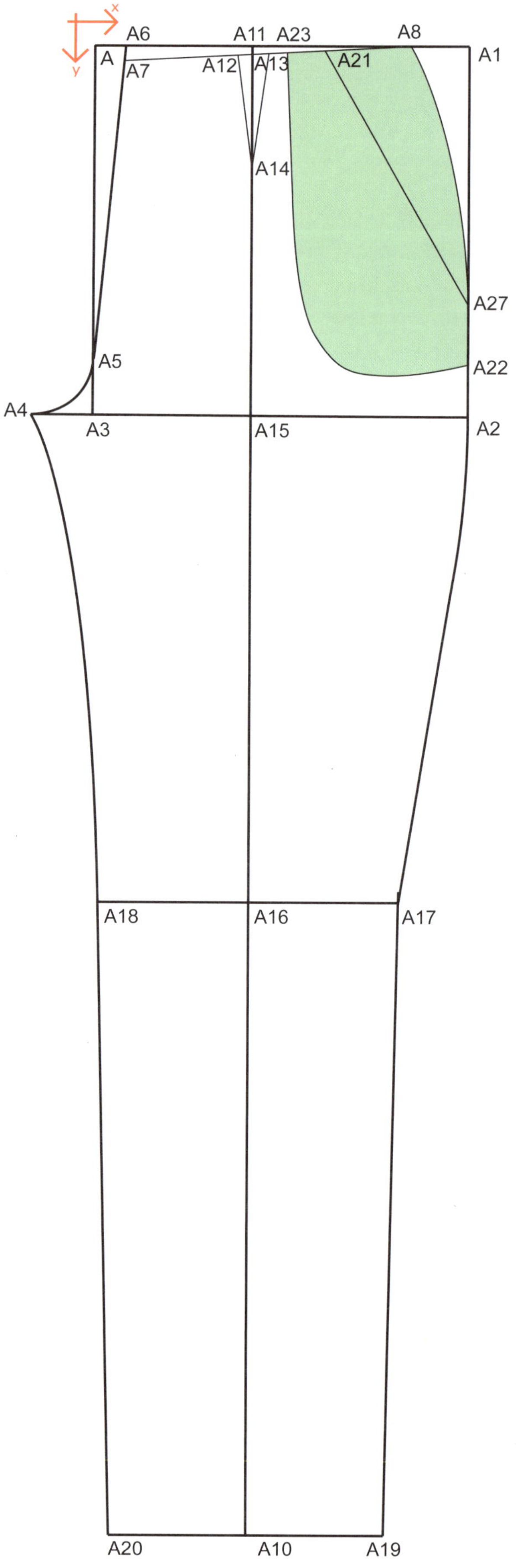

Sewing pattern for the pocket pouch.

Back

The back is identical to that of the classic office trousers with no pockets. If you want to add a welt pocket, a common feature on elegant trousers, just draw a simple horizontal line across the dart. It should be as long as you want the pocket size to be (for example, 14 cm / 5.51"). Using a pencil crayon, colour in the paper pattern to identify it as the back.

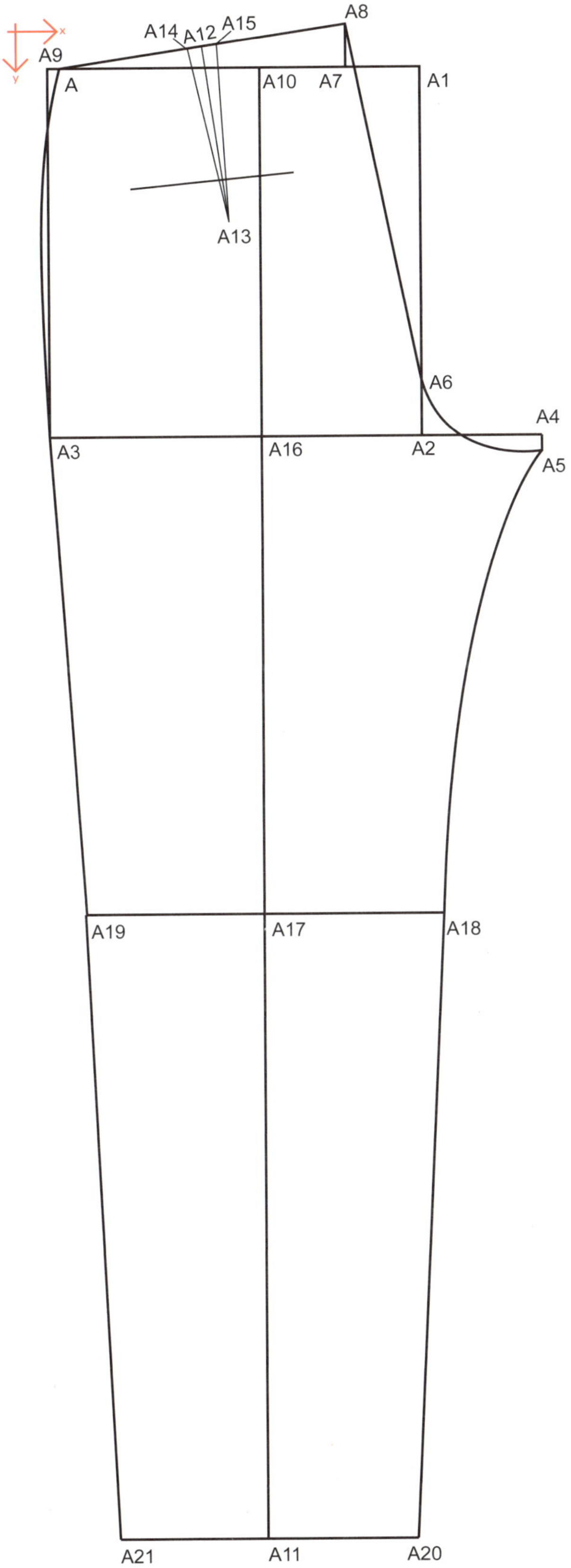

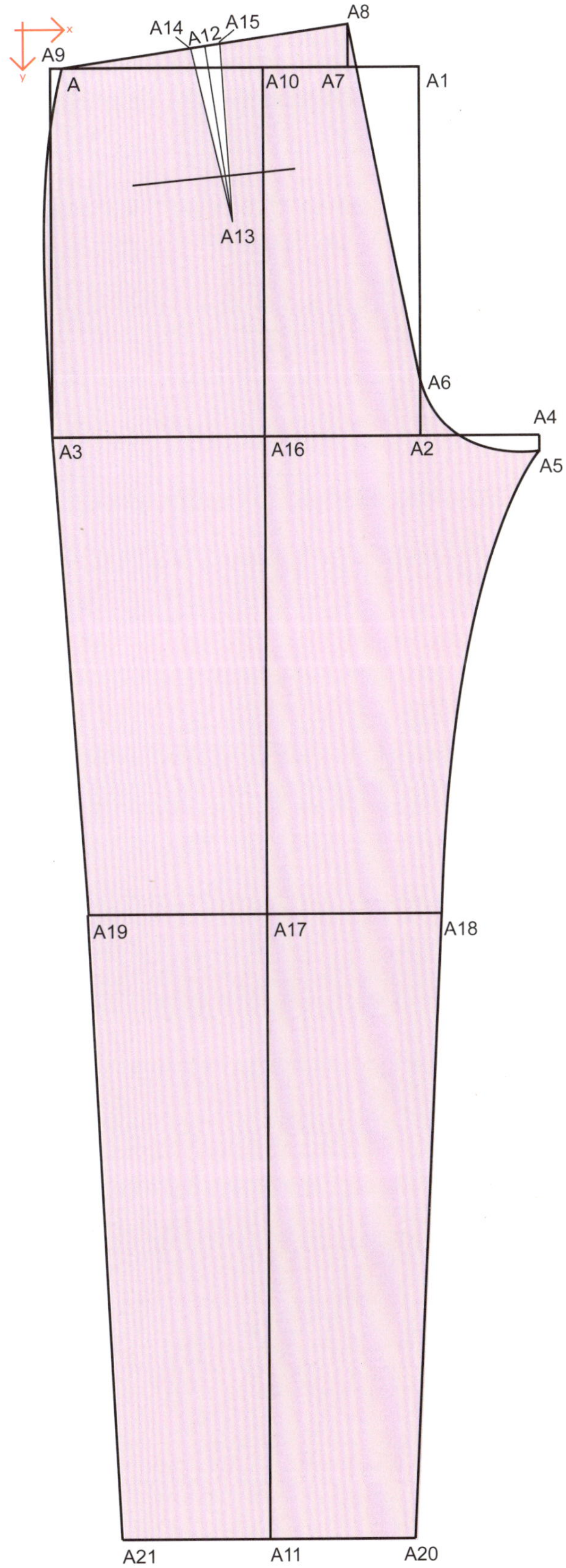

Cut out the respective patterns (1). With paper scissors, cut a line on the back to add the pocket (2).

Position the patterns on the fabric, which you have folded in two so that the selvedges are touching and the right side of the fabric is facing inwards. Make sure that the crease line is exactly parallel to the selvedges.

Draw the seam allowances in chalk: usually 1 cm (0.39") on the waist, 2 cm (0.78") along the sides and the middle of the front and back of the patterns, 5 cm (1.96") on the bottom (3).

Cut along the lines you have drawn (4) and sew guide stitches around the patterns (5). Sew guide

1

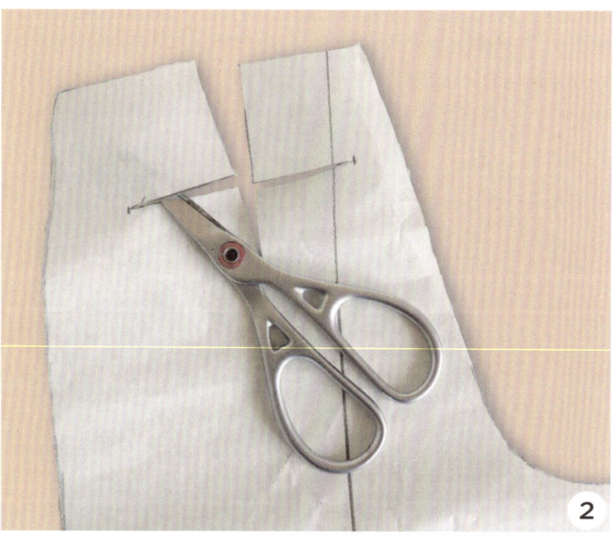

2

3

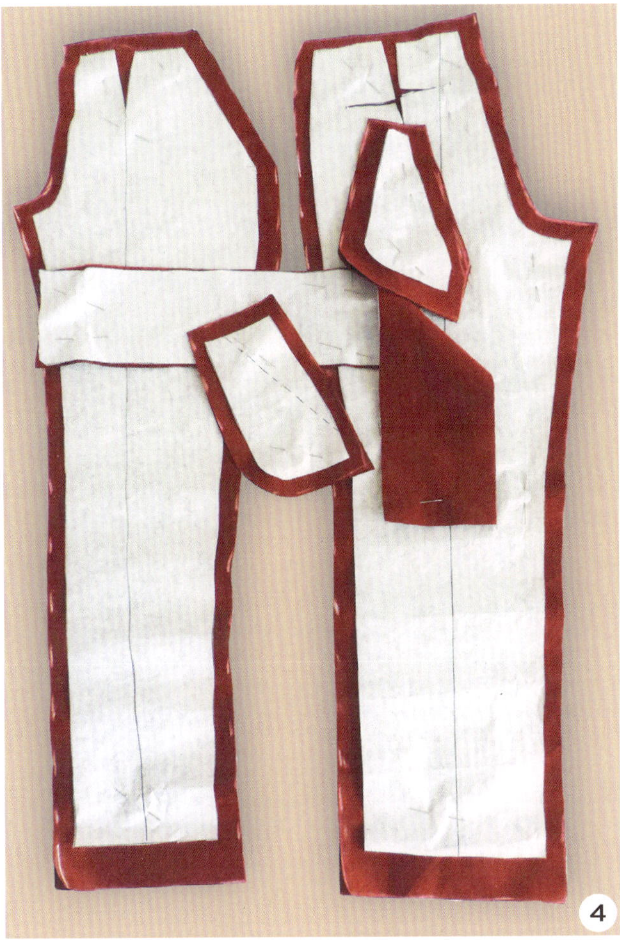
4

stitches inside the pocket lines (6) as well as around the pocket patterns (7).

Once the guide stitches are done, detach the sewing patterns from the fabric, cut open the guide stitches

5

6

7

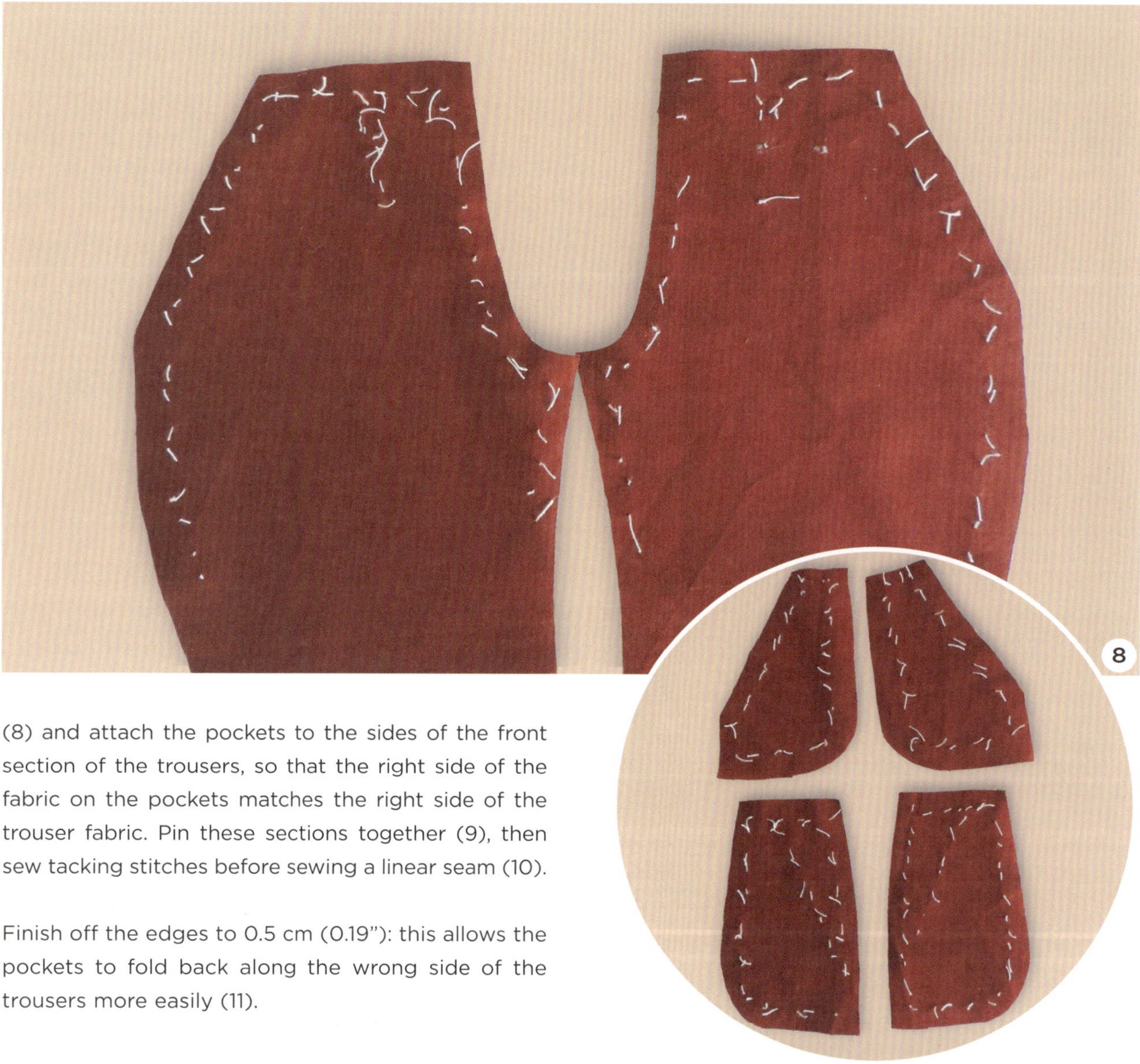

8

(8) and attach the pockets to the sides of the front section of the trousers, so that the right side of the fabric on the pockets matches the right side of the trouser fabric. Pin these sections together (9), then sew tacking stitches before sewing a linear seam (10).

Finish off the edges to 0.5 cm (0.19"): this allows the pockets to fold back along the wrong side of the trousers more easily (11).

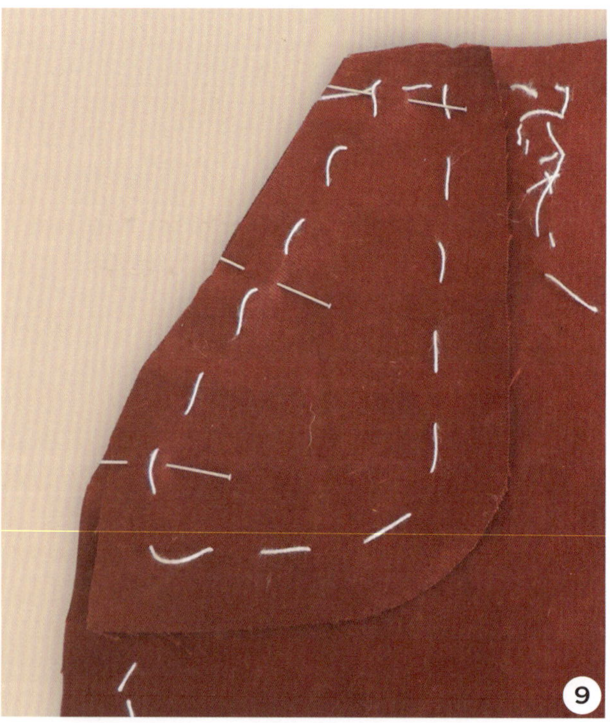

9

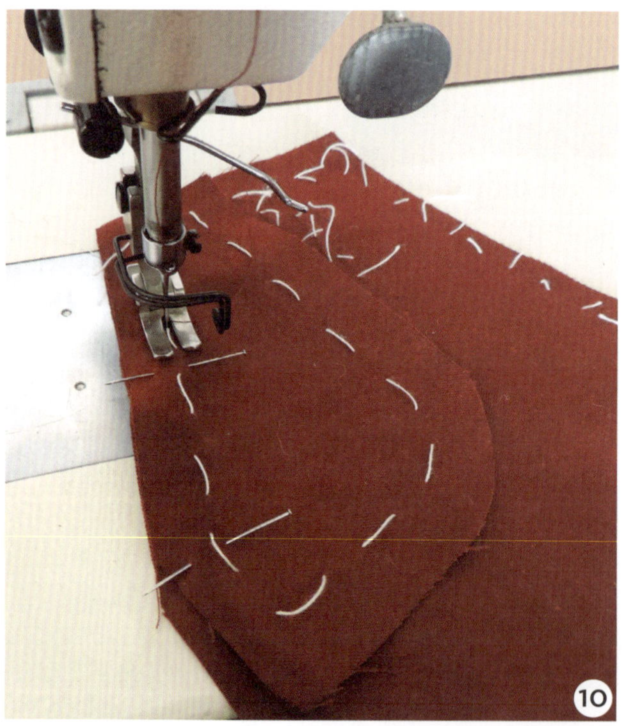

10

Place the pockets with the wrong side of the fabric on the front of the trousers (12). Attach the pocket pouch along the sides so as to complete the missing parts of the sides of the front section of the trousers (13 - 14).

Match up the pocket pouch to the pocket openings on the wrong side of the front of the trousers (15).

Hold these sections together with pins and sew tacking stitches before sewing the actual seam (16). Finish the joined edges off, using the cut-and-sew-machine or with zig-zag stitches (17).

If you have chosen to put the pockets on the back, attach them first before putting the front and back of the trousers together. For this procedure, see p. 196 or 200.

Once you have attached the pockets to the back of the trousers, you can put all the parts together. Then, pin the front and back of the trousers together so that the right side of the fabric is facing inwards. Sew tacking stitches and then sew the actual seams.

Finish off the edges with the cut-and-sew-machine or zig-zag stitches, and iron them open. Sew up the darts, too (18).

Now pin the middle parts of the trousers together and sew tacking stitches. Then sew the seams, leaving a gap for a zip (at least 18 cm / 7.08") in the middle of the back. Finish off the edges with a cut-and-sew-machine or zig-zag stitches, and iron them open (19). Attach the zip to the middle of the back (20), then prepare and attach the waistband (21) as explained on page 42. Finish the waistband as you wish, preferably by hand (22), and sew the hem by hand with an understitch.

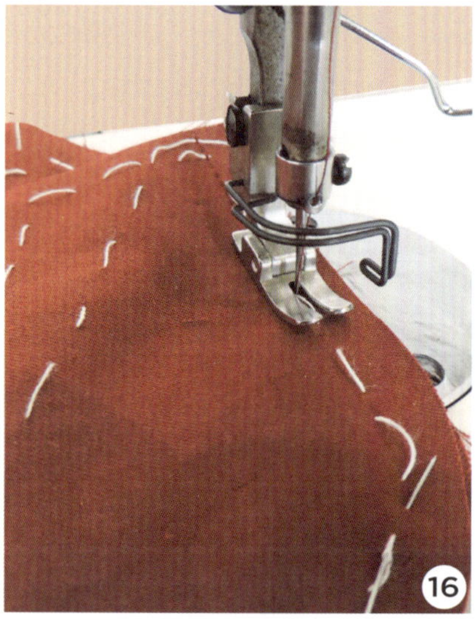

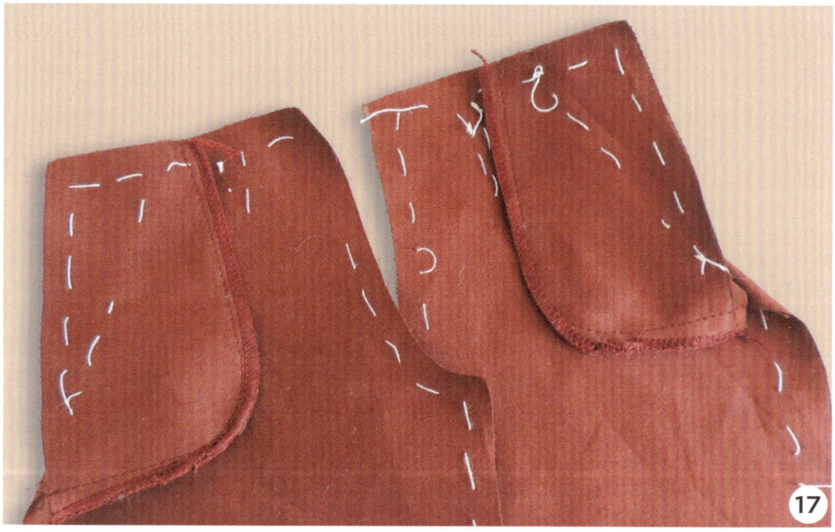

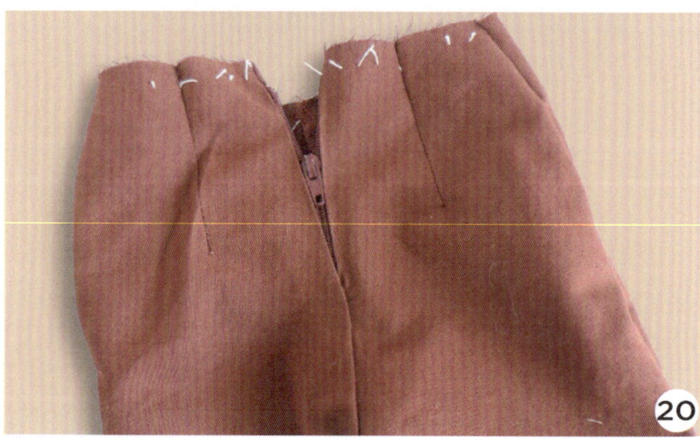

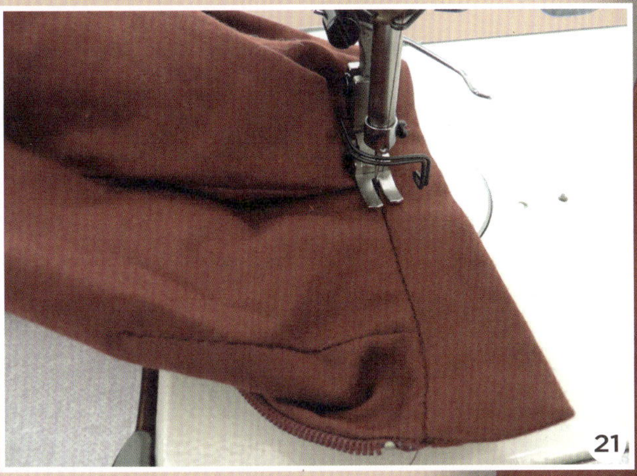

21

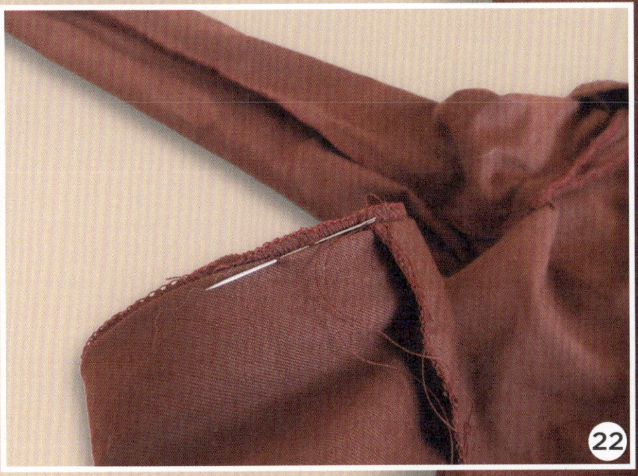

22

The mock-up trousers were made in a medium-weight cotton fabric. To get the best results, I recommend you use a cool-wool fabric. You can use different fabrics to try out other effects, like velvet or Glen plaid.

SINGLE-WELT POCKET

Below, you will find explanations on how to make the single- and double-welt pockets that feature on classic and elegant trousers. Please pay particular attention to the procedure, as it requires a lot of precision. To make things easier, the instructional example is made to 1:2 scale and is composed of pieces of fabric in different colours.

Measure the line drawn on the trousers where the pockets will be, then draw and cut out a strip of fabric (I recommend using the same fabric) that is the same length as the line, plus 2 cm (0.78") for the seam allowances and twice as wide as the final width, plus a 2 cm (0.78") seam allowance. For example: if the final width of the welt pocket is going to be 1 cm (0.39"), you will have to draw the width equal to 2 cm (0.78"), plus a 2-cm (0.78"), seam allowance, therefore the total width of the fabric strip will be 4 cm (1.57") (1).

Prepare four pocket pouches that are the same size as the final size of the pockets you are making, plus a 2 cm (0.78") seam allowance, making sure they are at least 10 cm (3.93") wide (2). Reinforce the strips of fabric with a piece of adhesive canvas of the same size. Iron the adhesive canvas onto the back of the fabric strips (3).

Fold the strips so that the right side of the fabric is facing inwards (4) and sew a seam 1 cm (0.39") from their outer edges (5), then turn the strips over onto

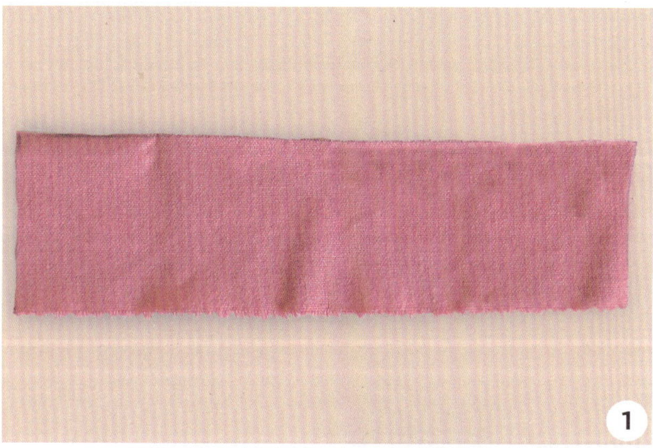
1

2

3

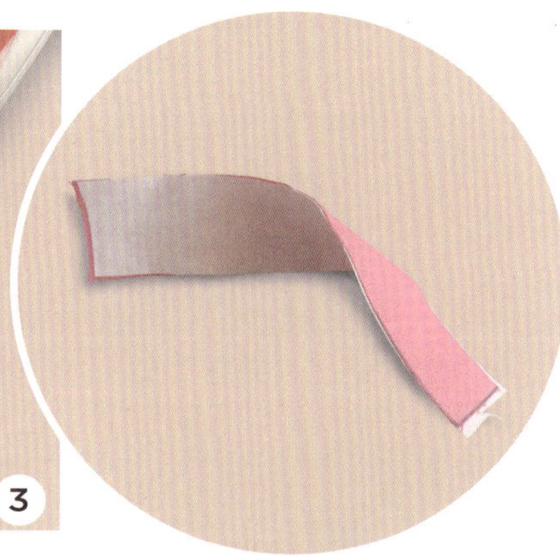

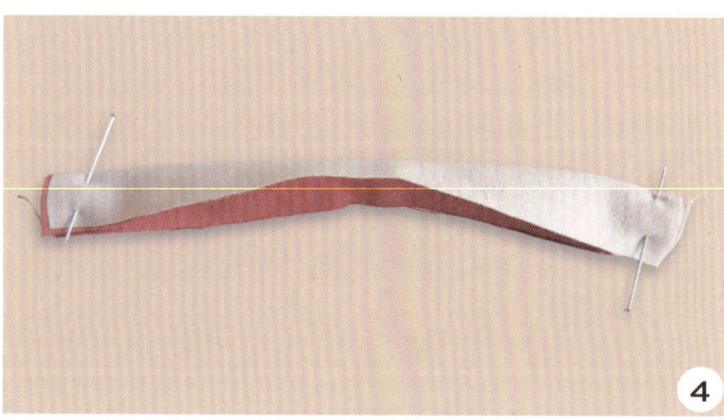
4

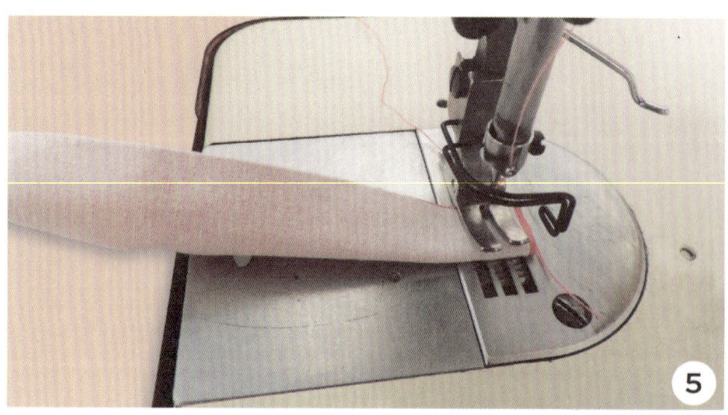
5

6

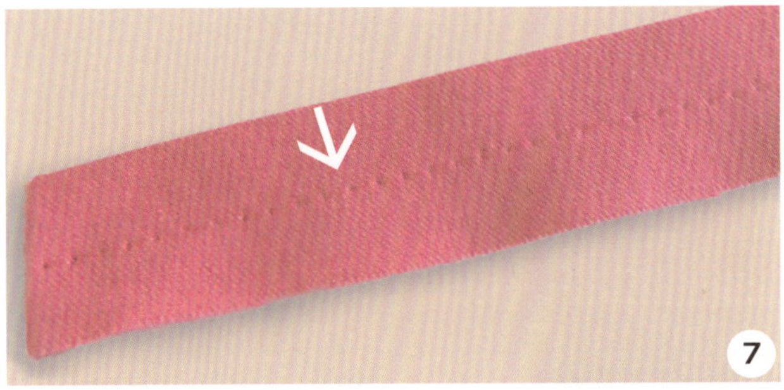
7

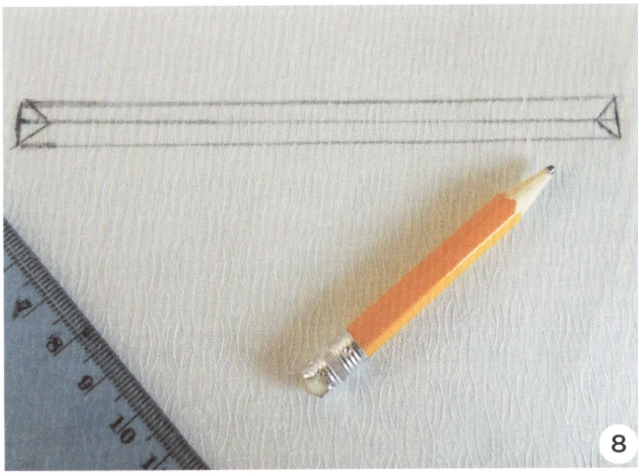
8

9

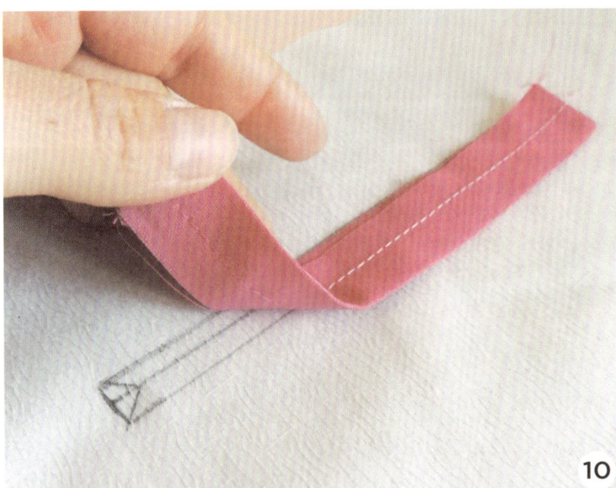
10

11

the right side of the fabric (6). Sew a 1 cm-long (0.39") linear seam horizontally: this will make it easier to make the pocket (7). Using chalk or a pencil, draw a rectangle on the right side of the fabric on the back of the trousers where you want the pocket to be. It needs to be as long as the pocket will be, and 1 cm (0.39") wide. Divide the rectangle horizontally into two identical parts and draw a little triangle on each end (8). Iron a piece of adhesive canvas onto the wrong side of the fabric rectangle you've just drawn out. This will make the pocket more hard-wearing (9).

On the right side of the fabric – lined up with the rectangle you've just drawn – position the strip of fabric so that the folded part is facing downwards and the seam is lined up with the base line of the rectangle (10).

Attach the pocket pouch to the strip of fabric, with the wrong side of its fabric facing the strip, so that its upper edge lines up with the upper edge of the strip (11).

12

13

Pin the pocket onto the strip and then sew tacking stitches 1 cm (0.39") from the edge, exactly along the seam you just made on the strip of fabric (12). Sew a seam along the tacking stitches (13).

Along the upper line of the rectangle you've just drawn, attach the second pocket pouch so that the right side of its fabric matches that of the trouser fabric. Its upper edge must line up with the upper line of the rectangle (14). Pin the pouch onto the strip and sew tacking stitches (15) before sewing a seam 1 cm (0.39") away, exactly along the upper line of the rectangle (16).

Using scissors, cut open the line in the middle of the rectangle, along with the triangles on either side (17).

14

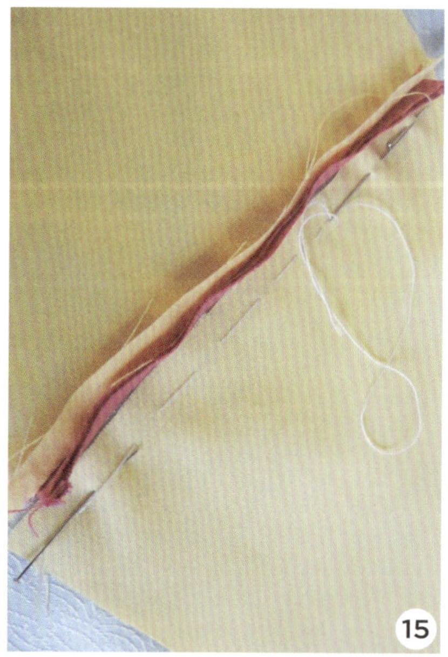
15

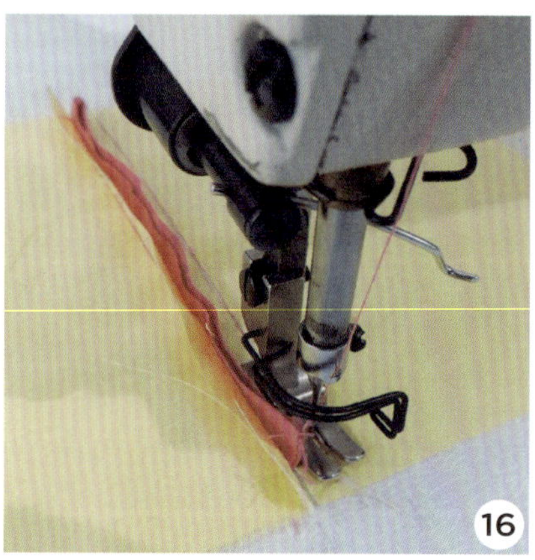
16

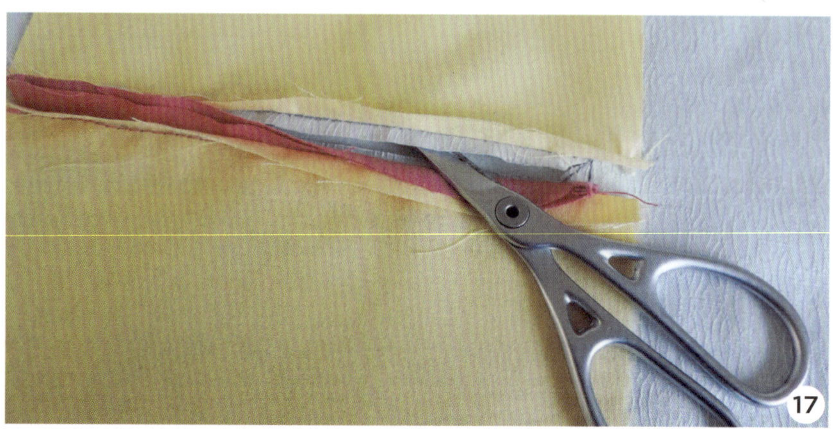
17

Turn the fabric strip and its pocket pouches over from the cut you just made, onto the wrong side of the trouser fabric (18-19).

Then, still on the wrong side of the fabric, pin the pocket pouches together and sew 1 cm (0.39") from the edge (20). To get the best result, iron the pocket on the right side of the fabric.

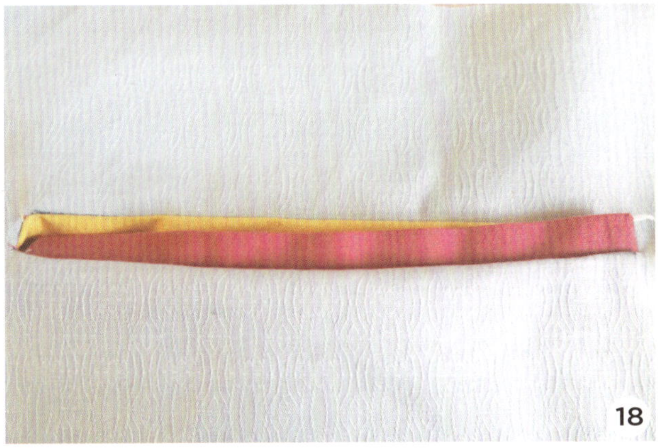

18

19

20

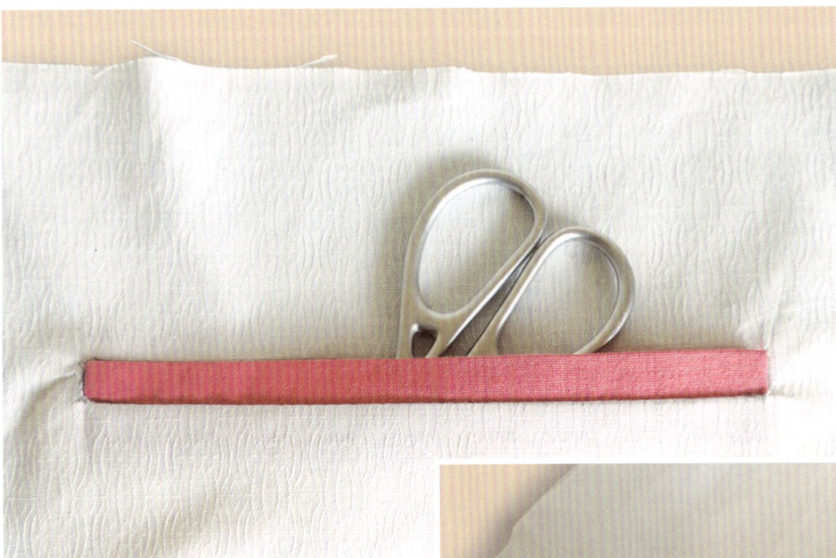

DOUBLE-WELT POCKET

Prepare two strips of fabric in the same way as you did for the single-welt pocket. Then, on the right side of the fabric, use chalk or a pencil to draw a rectangle on the right side of the fabric on the back of the trousers where you want the pocket to be. It should be as long as you want the pocket to be and 2 cm (0.78") wide. Divide the rectangle horizontally into two identical parts and draw a little triangle on each end (1).

Position the two strips of fabric so as to have the folded part oriented towards the outside of the rectangle, with the seams respectively positioned along the lines at the top and bottom of the rectangle (2). Lie the pocket pouches over the strips so that their upper edges line up with the edge of each strip. The wrong side of their fabric needs to face both the strips and the right side of the trouser fabric (3).

Pin together and sew tacking stitches (4), then sew 1 cm (0.39") from the edges, exactly along the seam you just made on the strips (5 - 6).

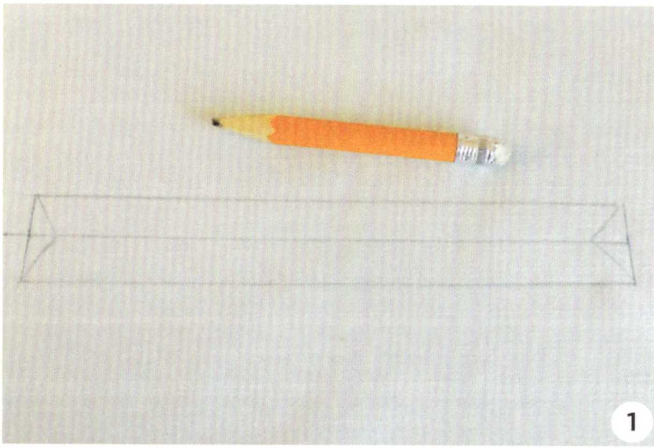

1

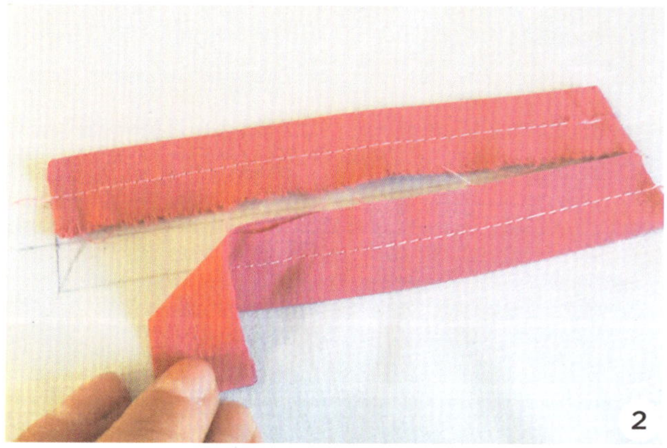

2

3

4

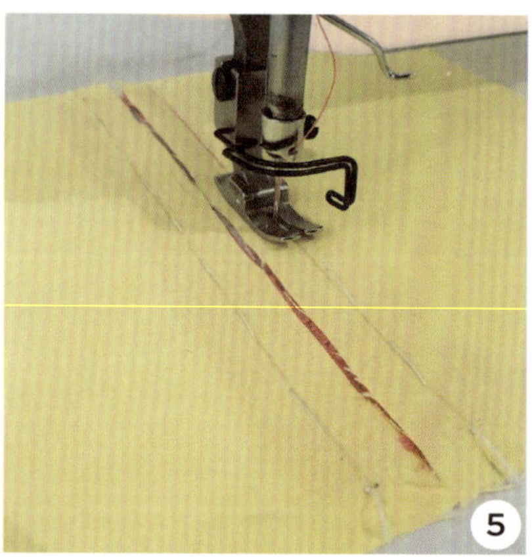

5

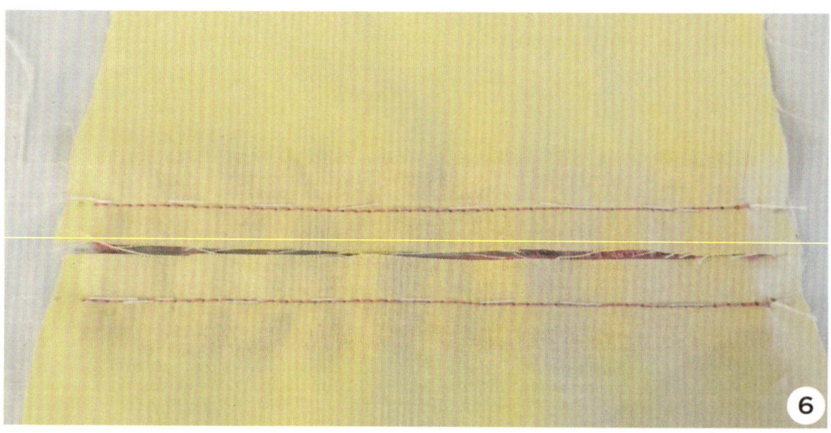

6

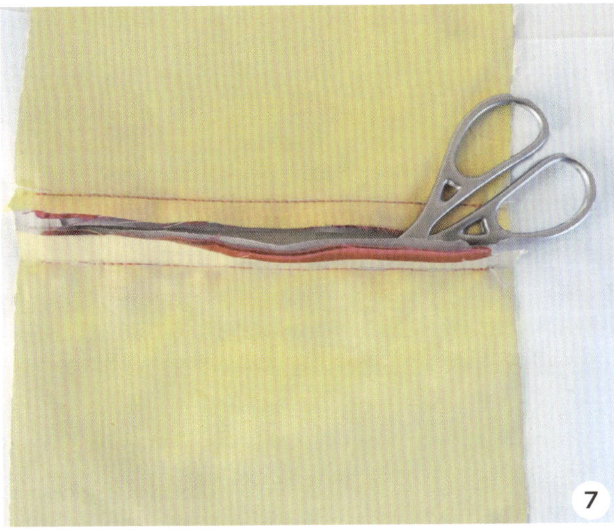

Cut open the line in the middle of the rectangle, along with the triangles on either side (7).

Turn the pocket pouches and strips over onto the wrong side of the fabric (8), then pin them in place and sew the pocket pouches together, 1 cm (0.39") from the edge (9).

To get the best result, iron the pocket on the right side of the trouser fabric.

SKINNY-FIT TROUSERS, STRAIGHT-LEG TROUSERS, FLARES AND PALAZZO PANTS

Since the procedure for making these trousers is the same as for classic office trousers, I will only explain the respective alterations.

SKINNY-FIT TROUSERS

Skinny-fit trousers are usually very elegant, but they can sometimes be casual, such as skinny jeans, for example. These trousers appear to be a little wider on the thigh, becoming tighter on the legs and tapered at the ankles.

Draw the basic trouser pattern according to your measurements. Then, using the following diagram and explanation as a guide, make the relevant design alterations for the kind of trousers you want to make.

Front

- A7_A16 same as A13_A14 - 2 cm (0.78") (this measurement depends on how tapered you want the bottom of the trousers to be).
- A7_A17 same as A7_A16.
- Draw a line between A14_A16 and A15_A17.
- Using a pencil crayon, colour in the paper pattern to identify it as the front.

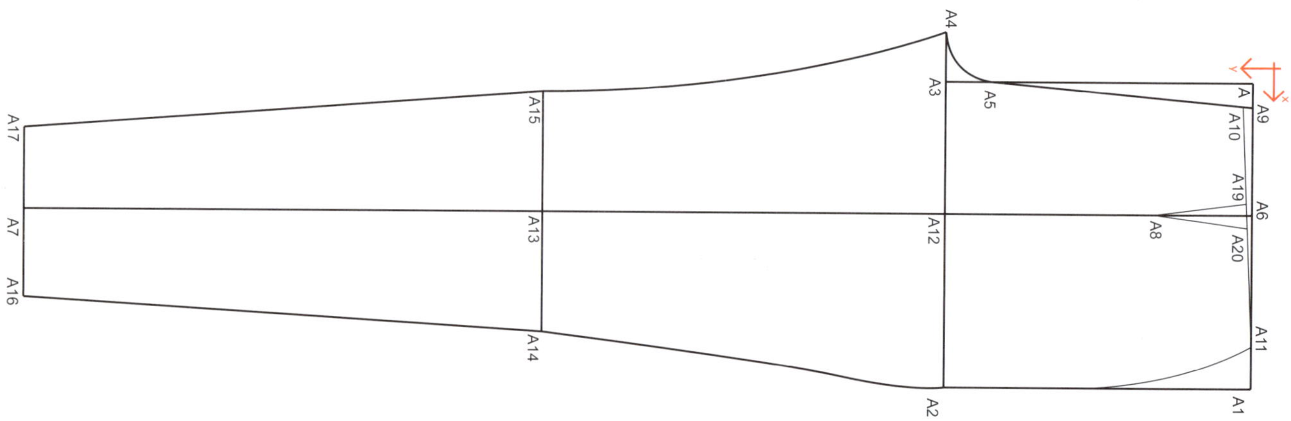

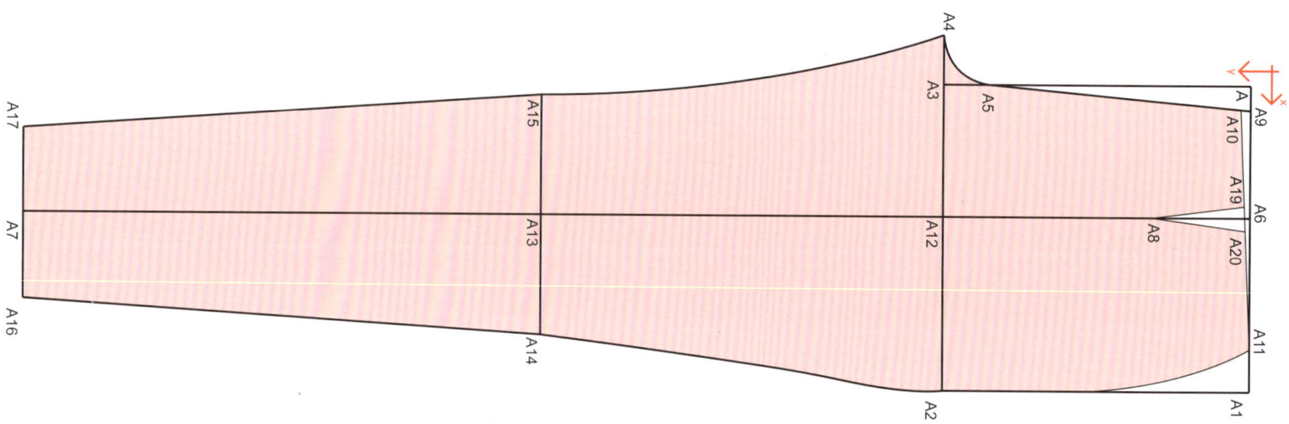

Back

- A11_A20 same as A7_A16 on the front + 2 cm (0.78") (this size may vary depending on how tapered you want the bottom of the trousers to be).
- A11_A21 same as A11_A20.

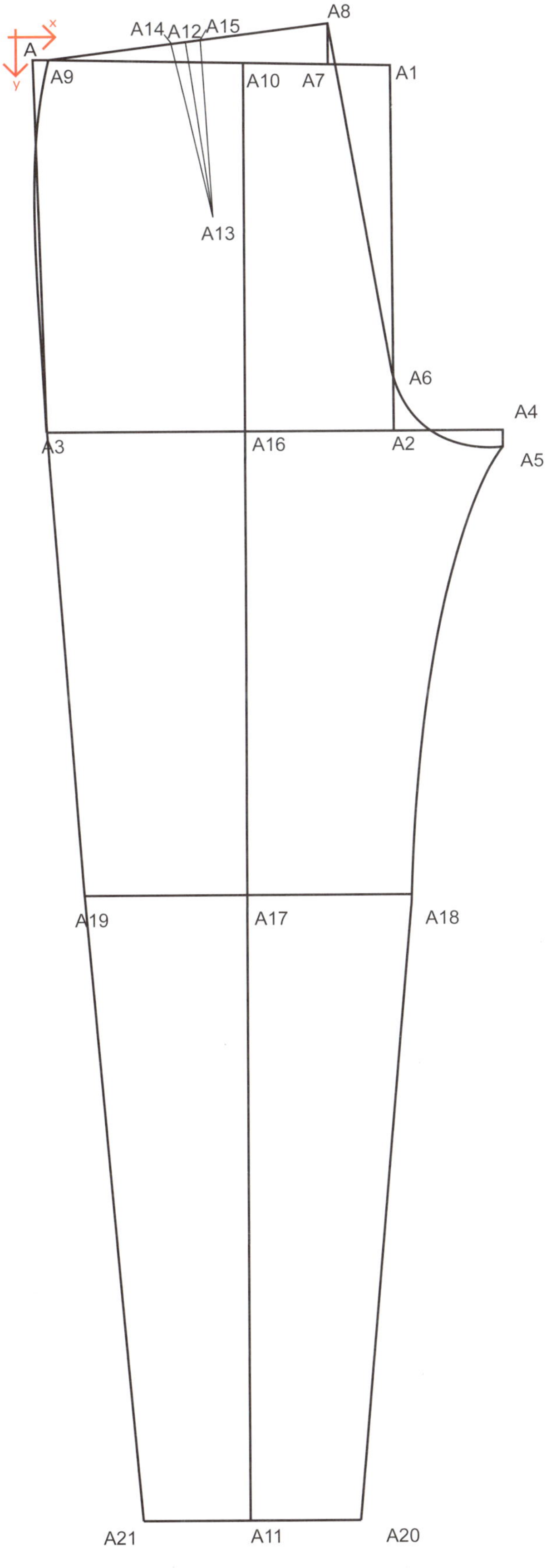

- Draw a line between A18_A20 and A19_A21.
- Using a pencil crayon, colour in the paper pattern to identify the various sections.

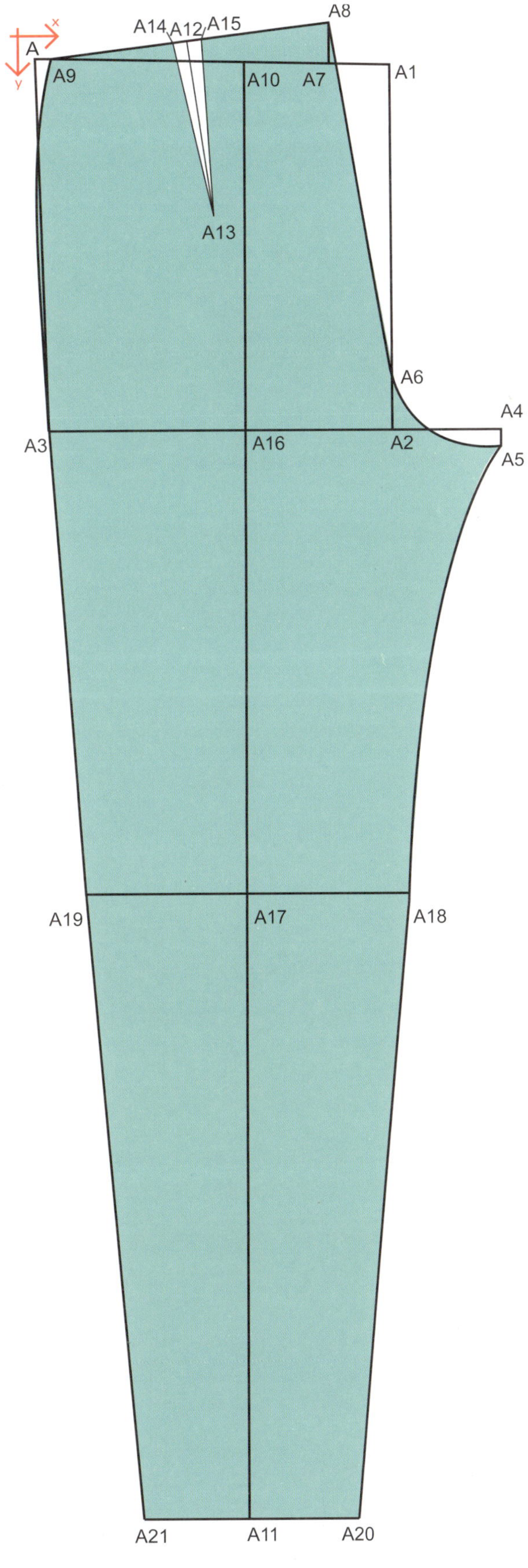

STRAIGHT-LEG TROUSERS

Straight-leg trousers are sometimes called "cigarette" trousers, because of their shape. The width at the bottom is the same as it is at the knee. They are usually very elegant trousers. Draw the basic trouser pattern according to your own measurements. Then, using the following diagram and explanation as a guide, make the relevant design alterations for the kind of trousers you want to make.

Front

- A7_A16 same as A13_A14.
- A7_A17 same as A13_A15.
- Draw a line between A14_A16 and A15_A17.
- Using a pencil crayon, colour in the paper pattern to identify it as the front.

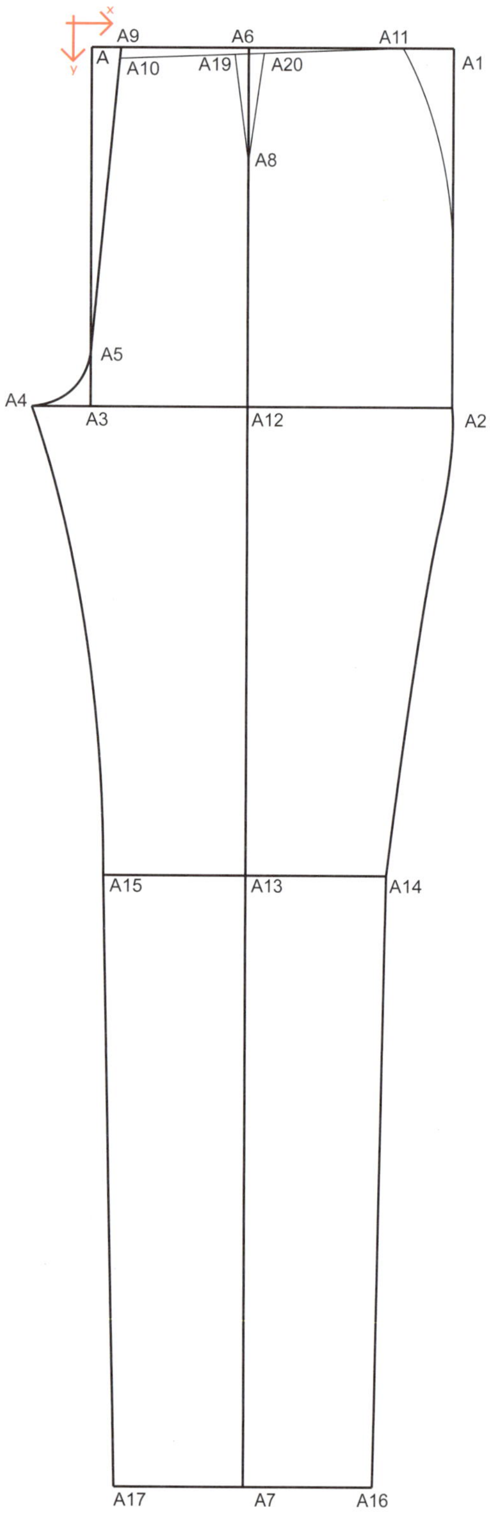

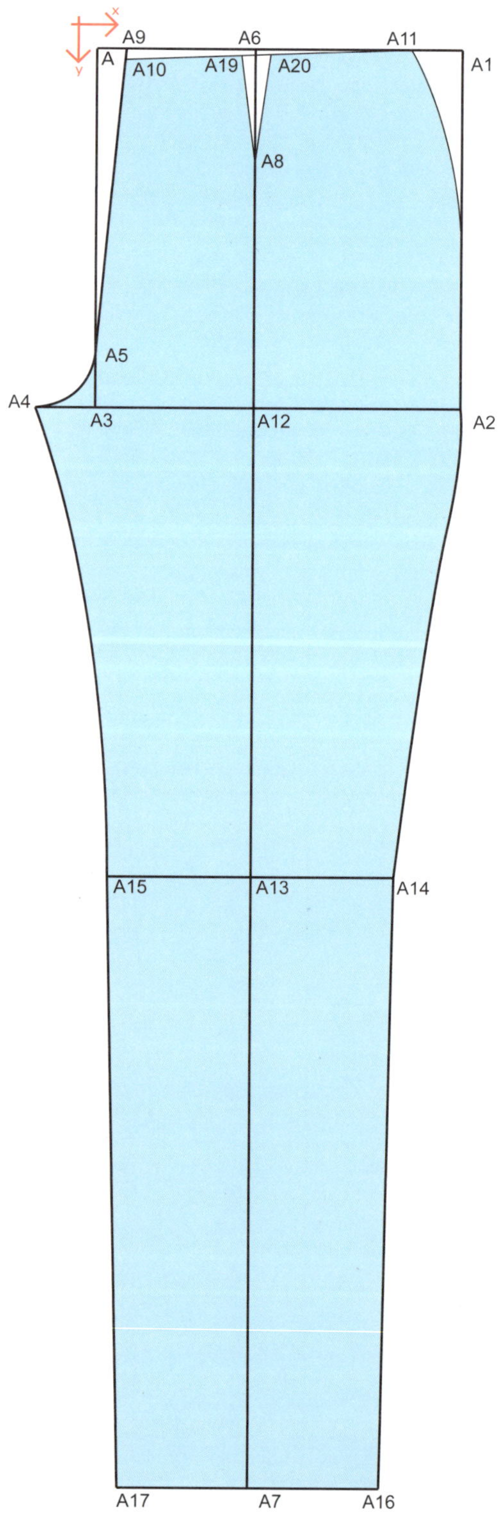

Back

- A11_A20 same as A17_18.
- A11_A21 same as A17_A19.

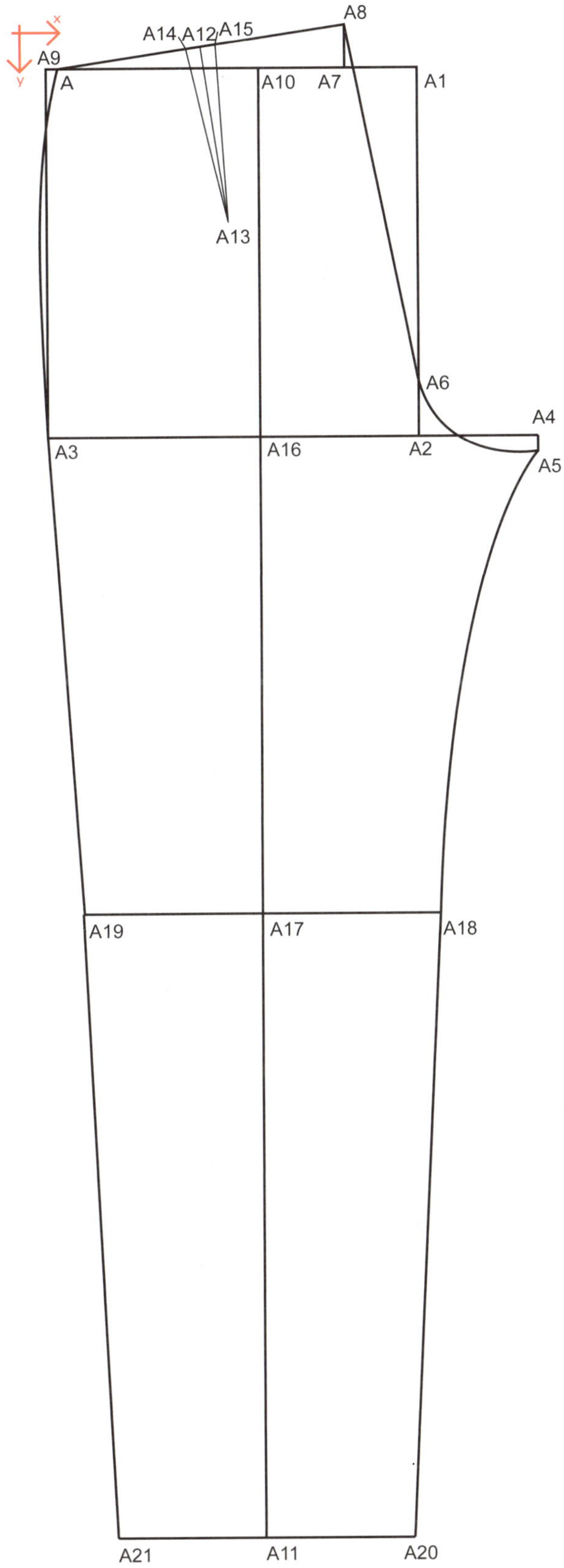

- Draw a line between A18_A20 and A19_A21.
- Using a pencil crayon, colour in the paper pattern to identify it as the back.

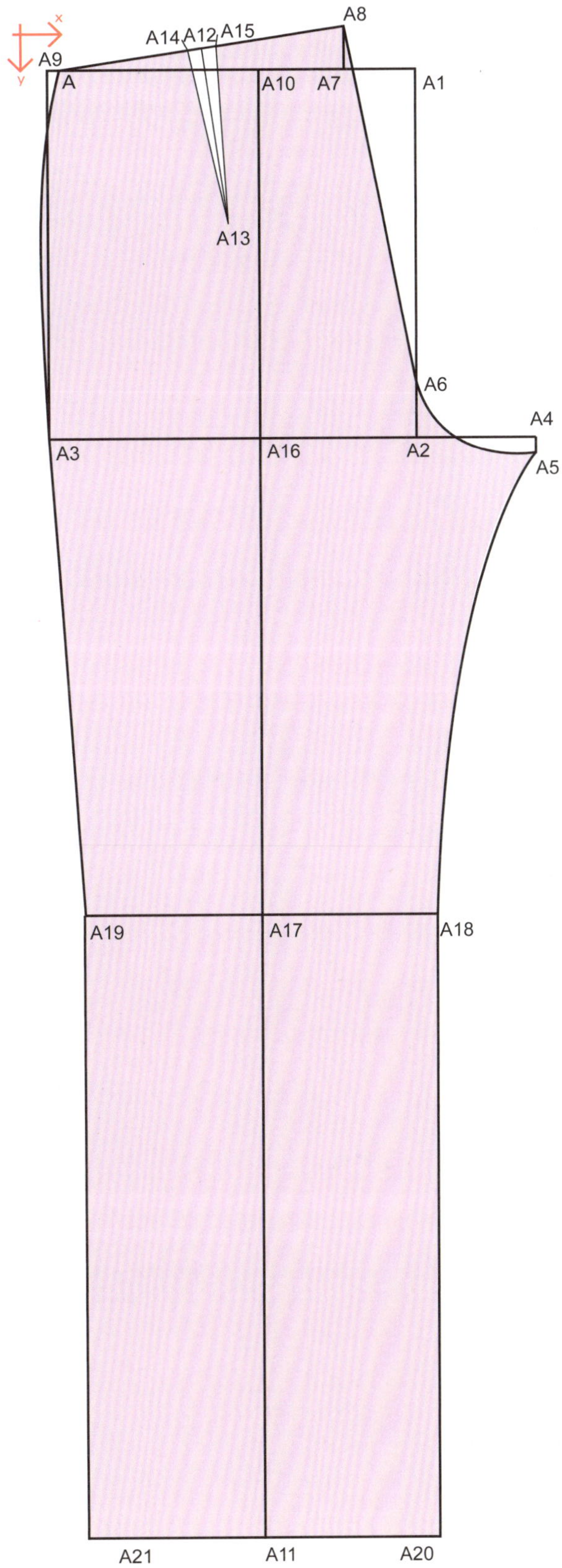

FLARES

These iconic trousers always come back into fashion, appearing cyclically on catwalks around the world before disappearing and reappearing again after a few years. Both the elegant and casual versions have a slimming effect on the figure, thanks to their distinctive shape: fitted on the thigh and gradually getting wider from the knee down to the bottom.

Front

- A7_A16 same as A13_A14 + 3 cm (1.18") (this measurement depends on how wide you want the bottom of the trousers to be).
- A7_A17 same as A7_A16.
- Draw a line between A14_A16 and A15_A17.
- Using a pencil crayon, colour in the paper pattern to identify it as the front.

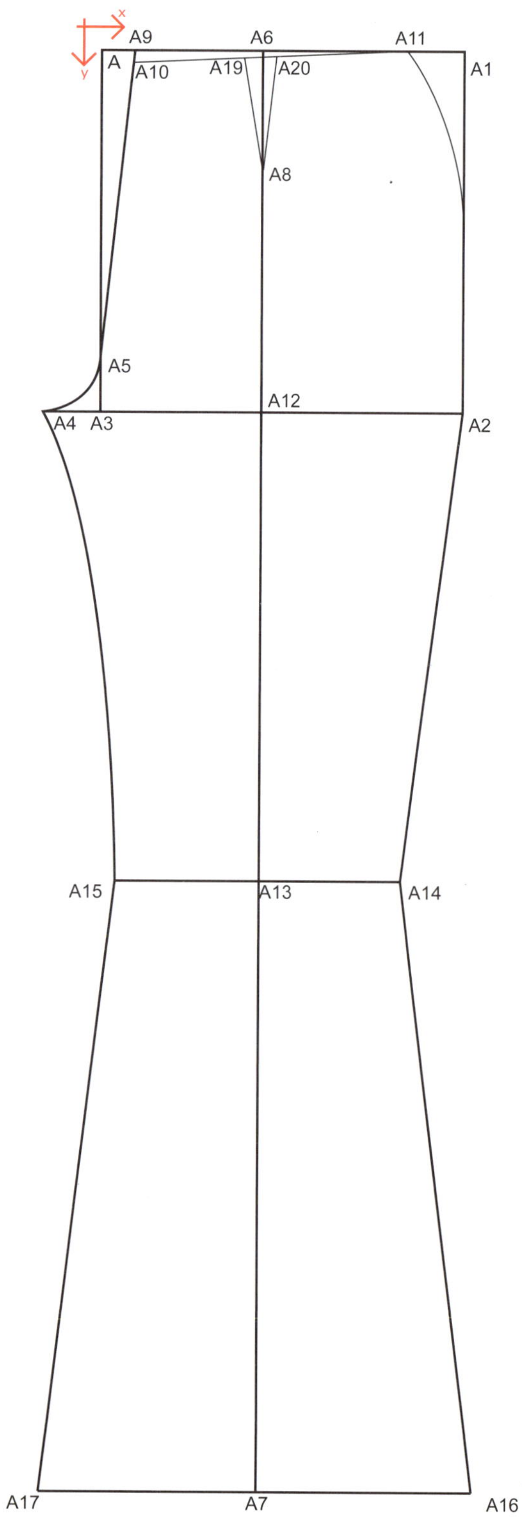

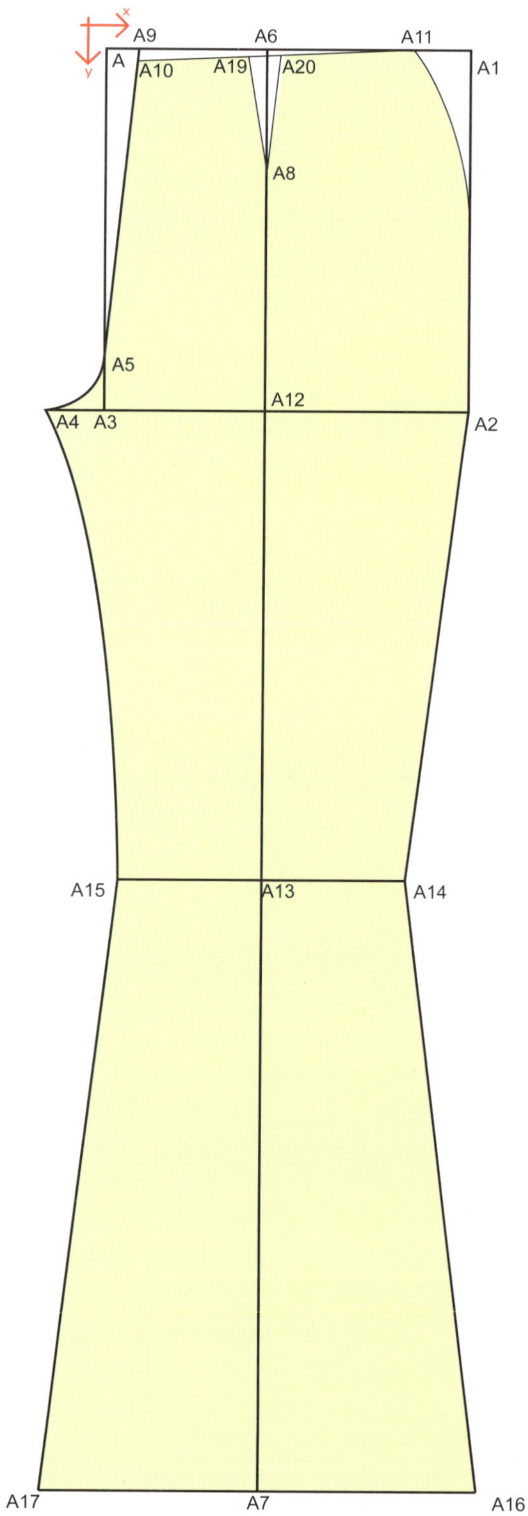

Back

- A11_A20 same as A17_A18 + 4 cm (1.57") (this measurement depends on how wide you want the bottom of the trousers to be).
- A11_A21 same as A11_A20.
- Draw a line between A18_A20 and A19_A21.
- Using a pencil crayon, colour in the paper pattern to identify it as the back.

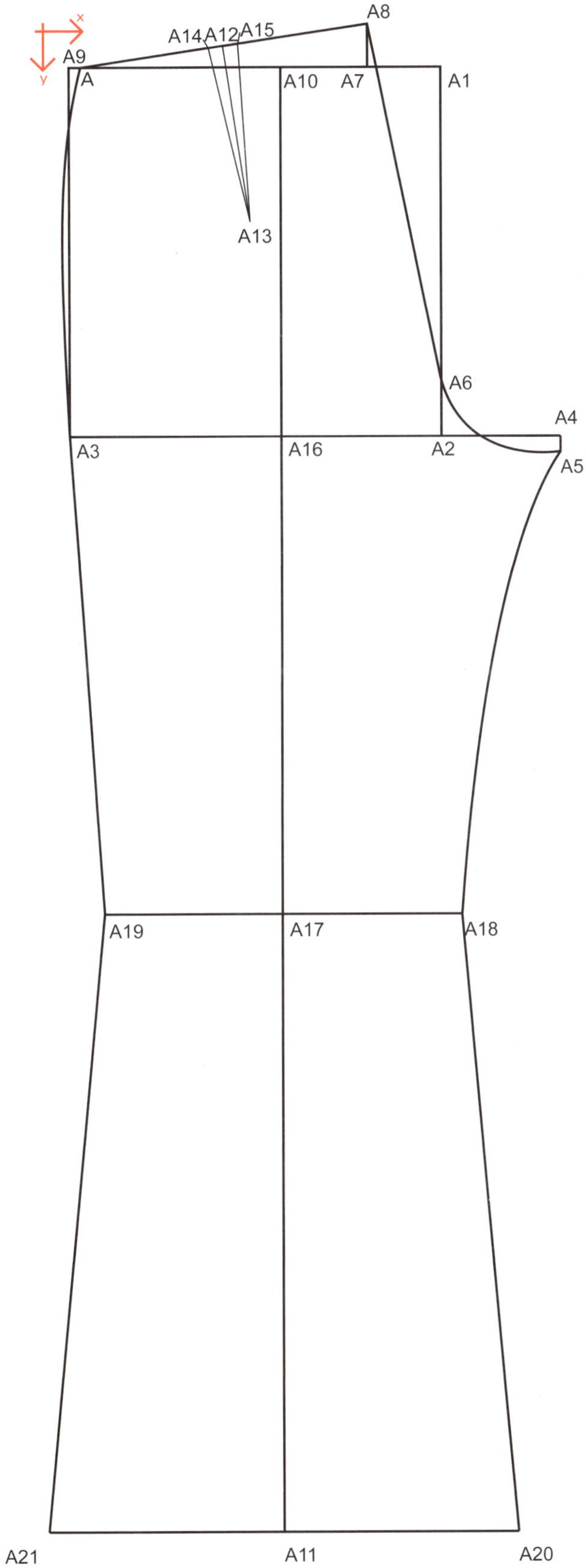

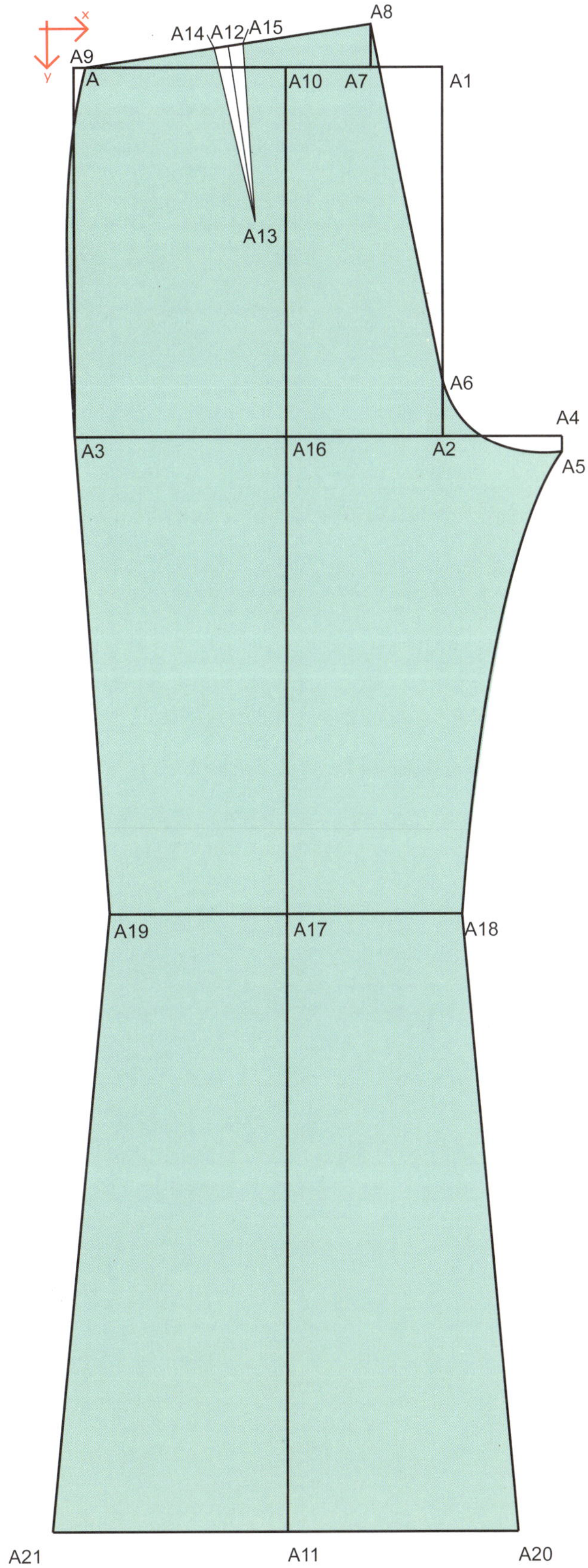

PALAZZO PANTS

Palazzo pants are usually very elegant and sophisticated, looking particularly good when worn with high heels.

They are very wide from top to bottom and feature a fitted waist. A real must have for every elegantly-dressed woman.

Front

- A13_A14 same as A12_A2 + 3 cm (1.18").
- A13_A15 same as A13_A14.
- A7_A16 same as A13_A14 + 3 cm (1.18") (this measurement depends on how wide you want the trousers to be).
- A7_A17 same as A7_A16.
- Draw a line between points A2_A14, A14_A16, A4_A15 and A15_A17.
- Using a pencil crayon, colour in the paper pattern to identify it as the front.

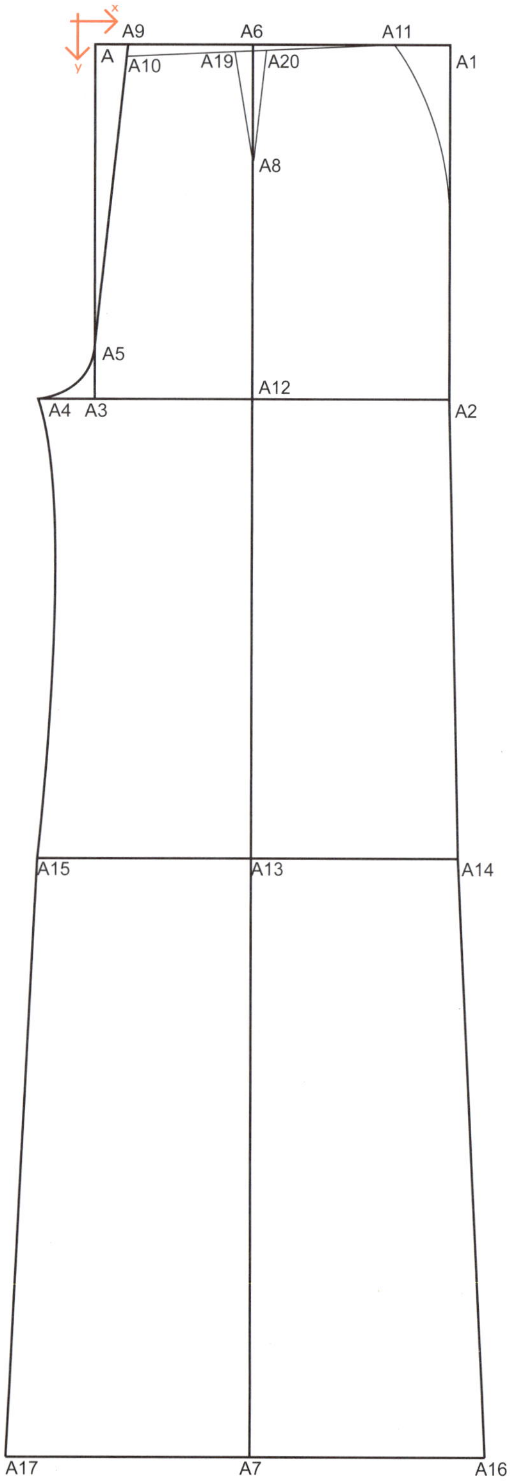

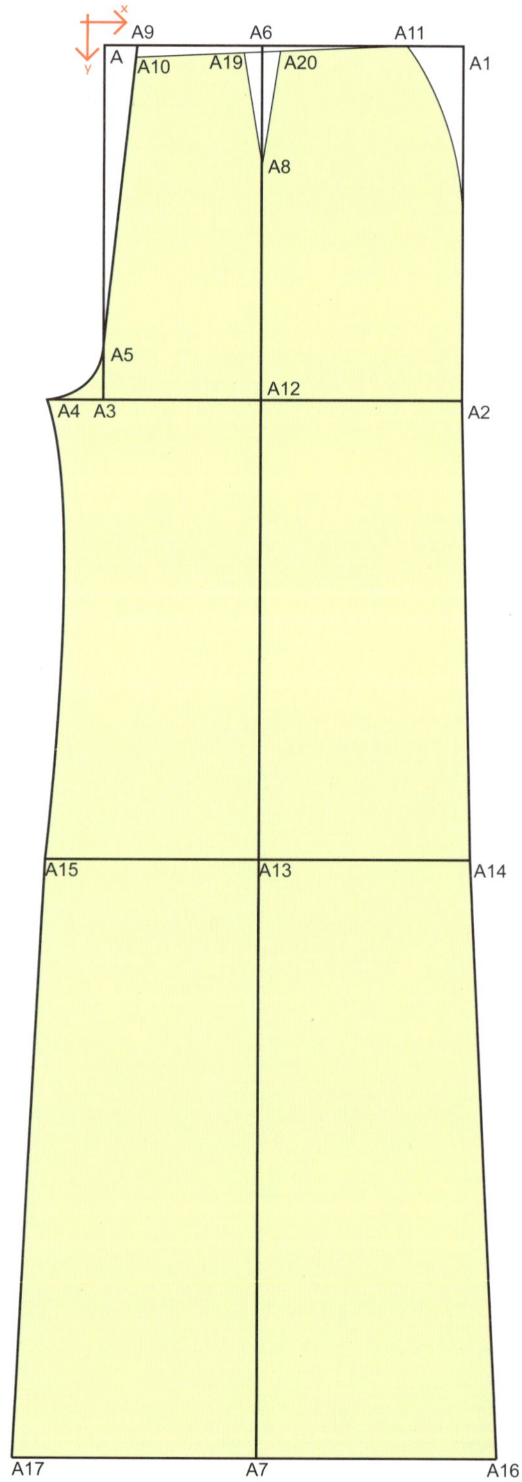

Back

- A17_A19 same as A16_A3 + 5 cm (1.96").
- A17_A18 same as A17_A19.
- A11_A20 same as A17_A18 + 4 cm (1.57") (this measurement depends on how wide you want the trousers to be).
- A11_A21 same as A11_A20.
- Draw a line between points A5_A18, A18_A20, A3_A19 and A19_ A21.
- Using a pencil crayon, colour in the paper pattern to identify it as the back.

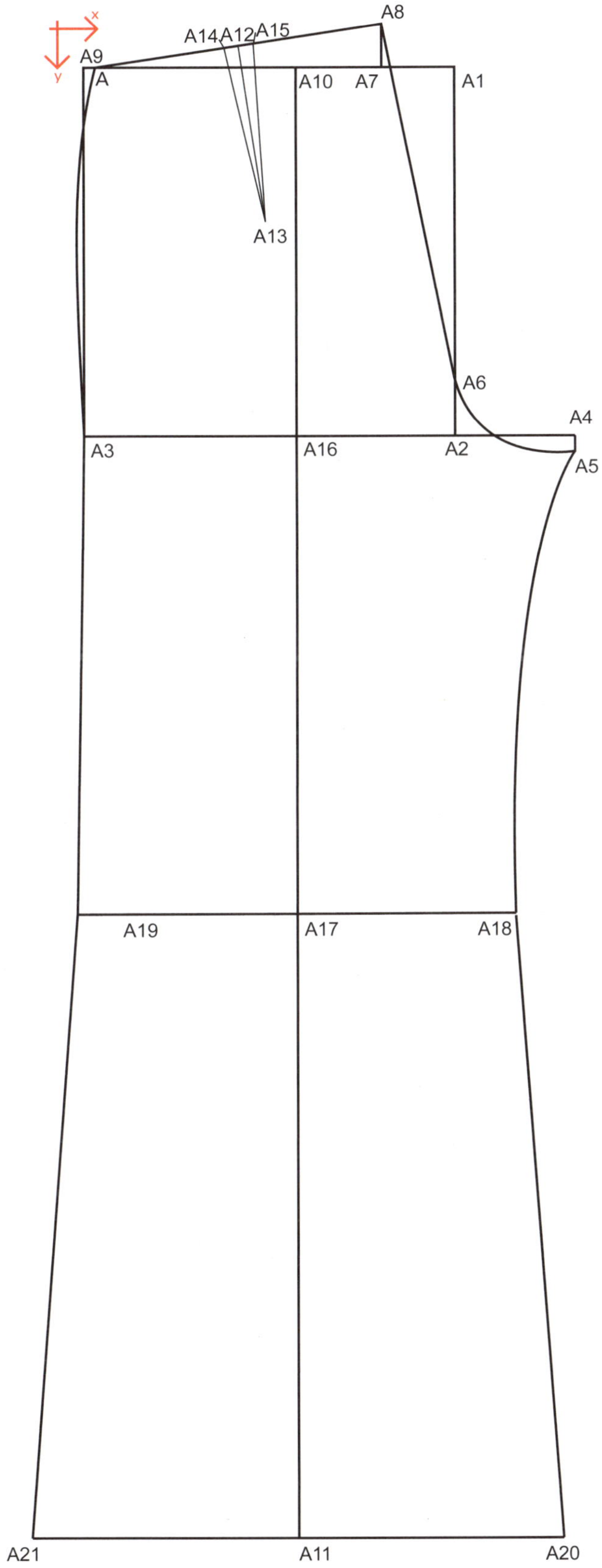

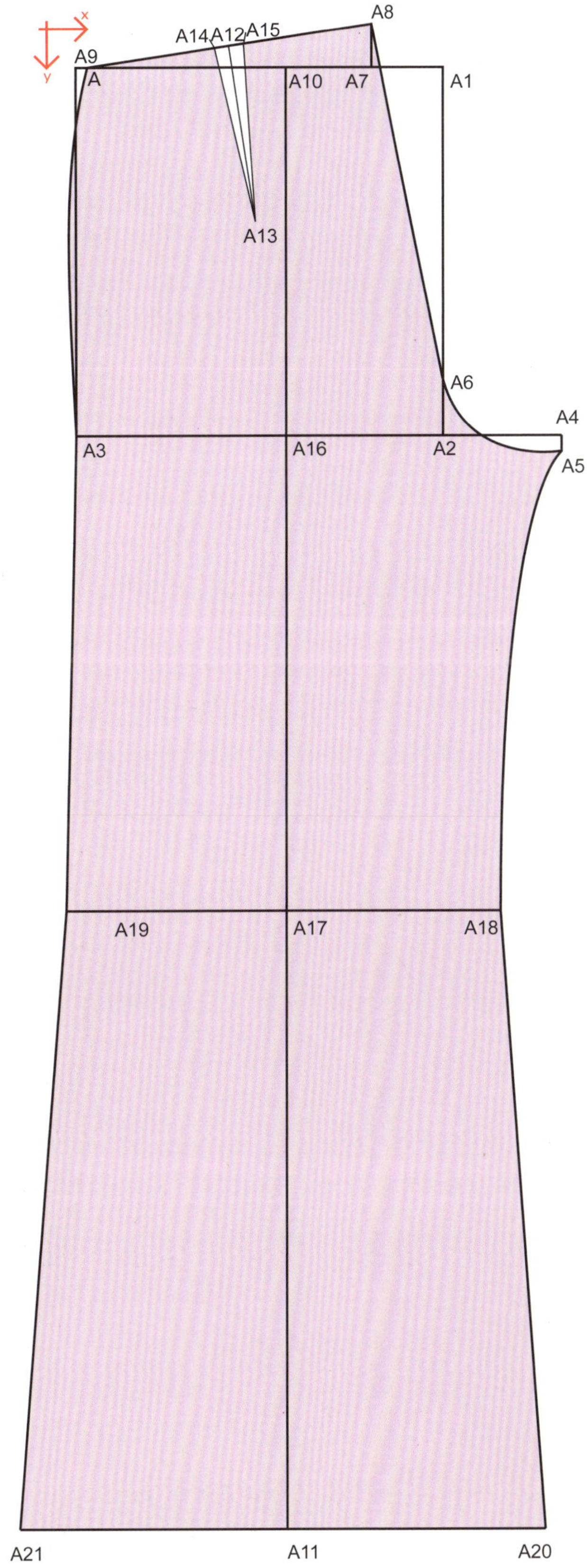

JOGGING BOTTOMS

These sporty trousers are an essential piece of clothing for leisure-time activities. Since they are extremely comfortable, they are ideal for informal occasions or taking part in sports. Jogging bottoms are not made in the same way as the other trousers we've looked at so far: in fact, now would be a good time to use the special four-thread and two-needle functions on the cut-and-sew-machine. If you don't have a cut-and-sew machine, you can just use a normal sewing machine to sew a linear seam, and then add the finishing touches to the margins with a zig-zag stitch, as we did for the classic office trousers. By doing it this way, however, you can sometimes tear the fabric as you sew, because stitches made by the normal sewing machine are less flexible than those made with a cut-and-sew-machine.

In this chapter, I will show you how to use the cut-and-sew-machine. As well as explaining how to make jogging bottoms, I would also like to share with you how to make seam pockets and zip-up pockets, which often feature on these types of trousers.

To make jogging bottoms, start by drawing the basic trouser pattern according to your own measurements. Then, using the following diagram and explanation as a guide, make the relevant design alterations for the kind of trousers you want to make.

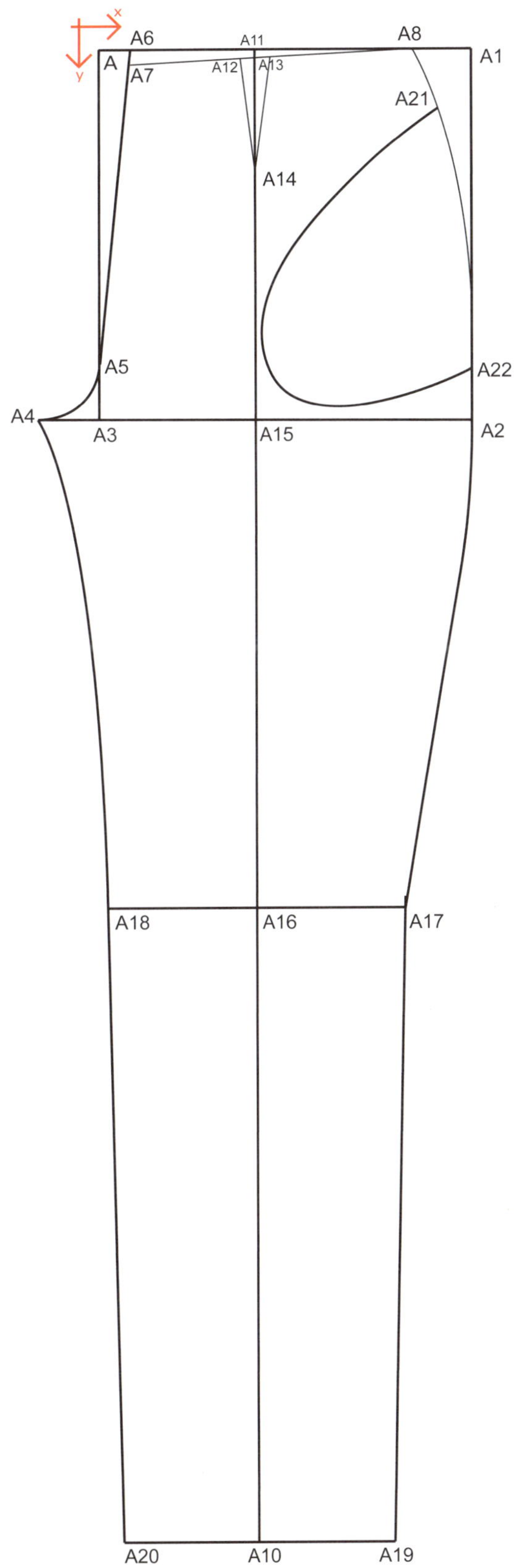

Front

- A8_A21 = 5 cm (1.96").
- A2_A22 = 3 cm (1.18").
- Draw a curved line between A21_A22 to represent the pocket pouch, as shown in the diagram.
- Using pencil crayons, colour in the paper patterns to identify the various sections.

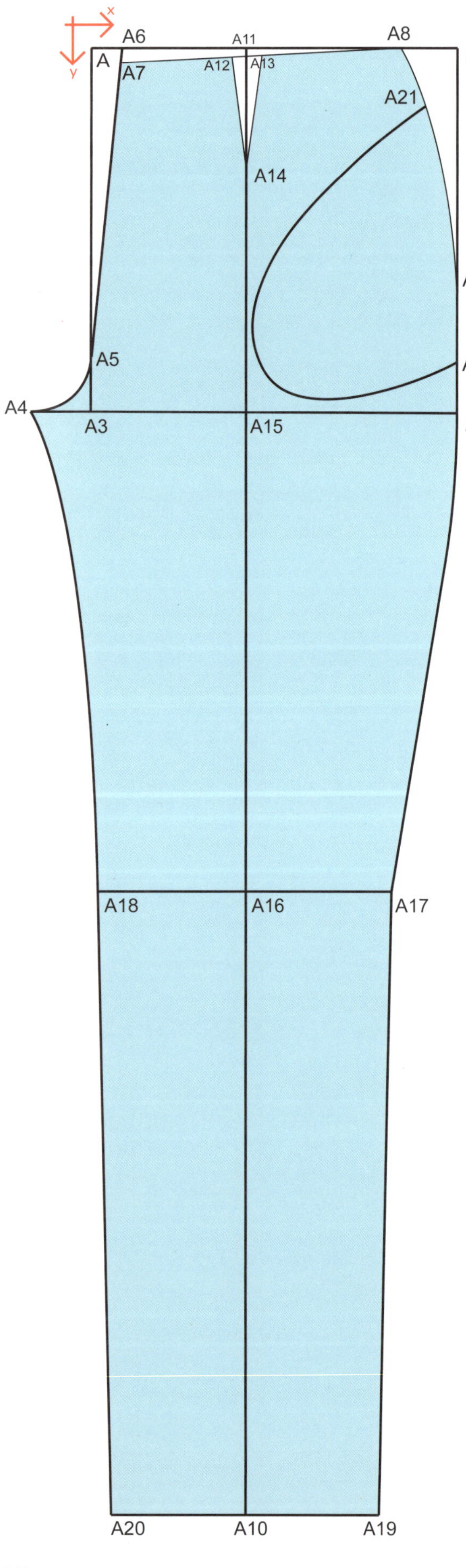
x
y
A6
A
A7
A11
A12
A13
A8
A1
A21
A14
A27
A5
A22
A4
A3
A15
A2
A18
A16
A17
A20
A10
A19

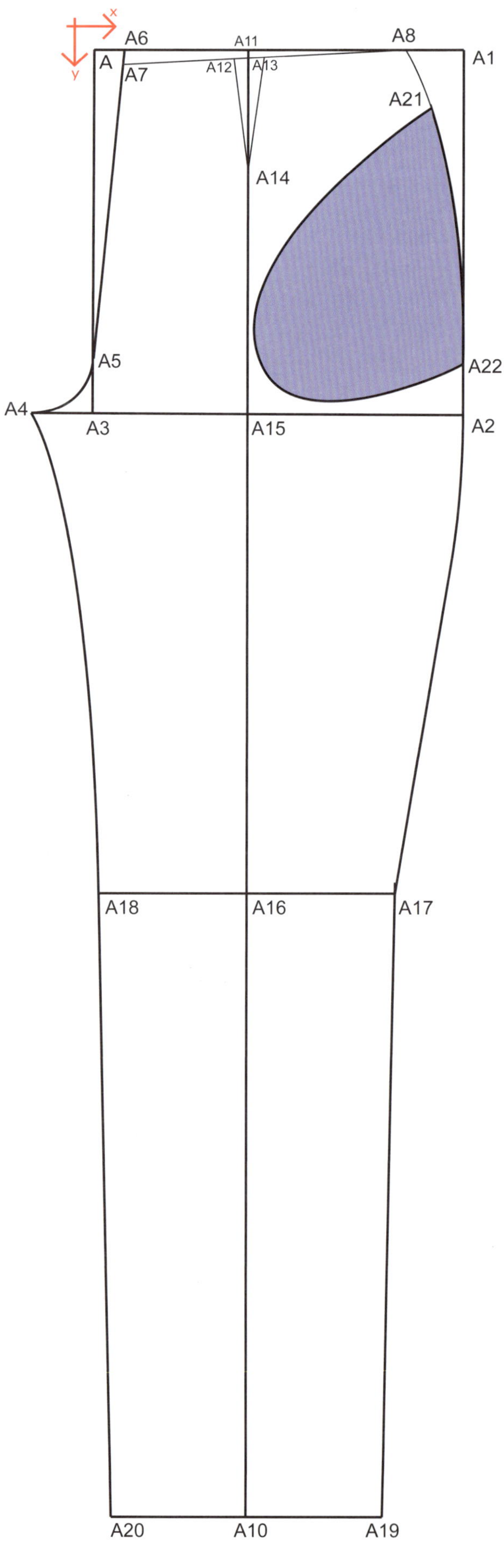
x
y
A6
A
A7
A11
A12
A13
A8
A1
A21
A14
A5
A22
A4
A3
A15
A2
A18
A16
A17
A20
A10
A19

Back

The back is identical to that of the classic office trousers.

- Using pencil crayons, colour in the paper patterns to identify the various sections.

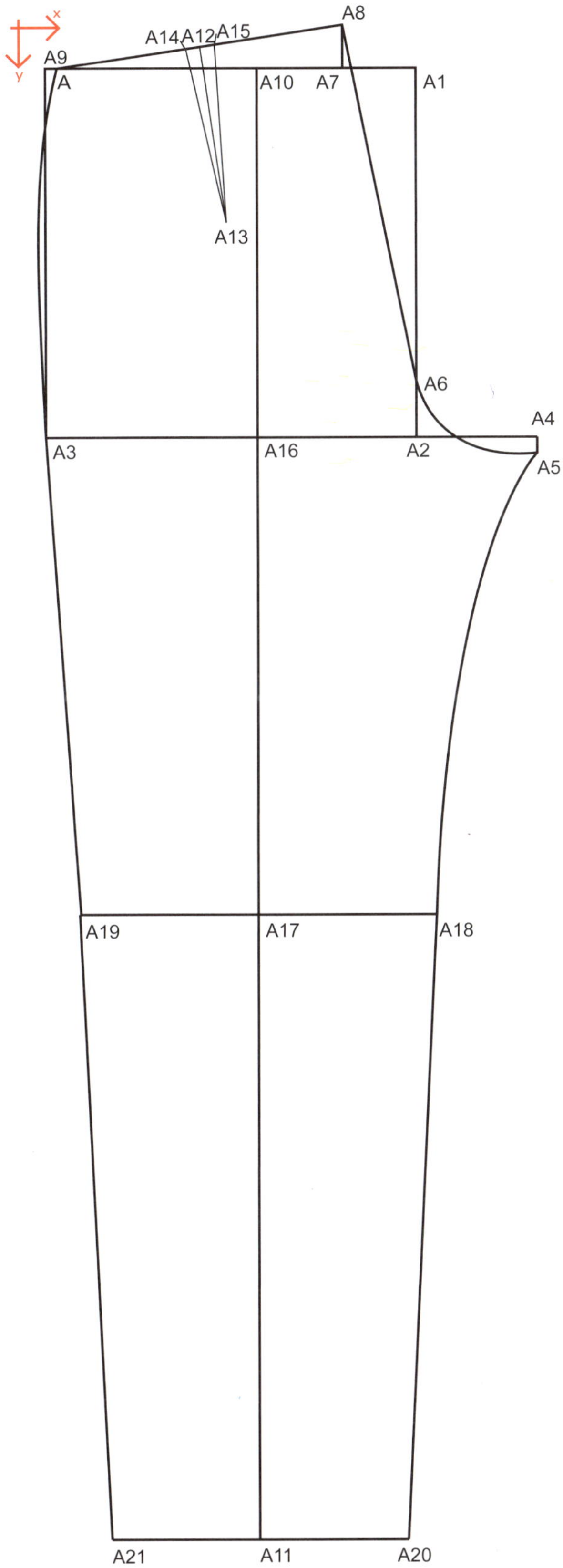

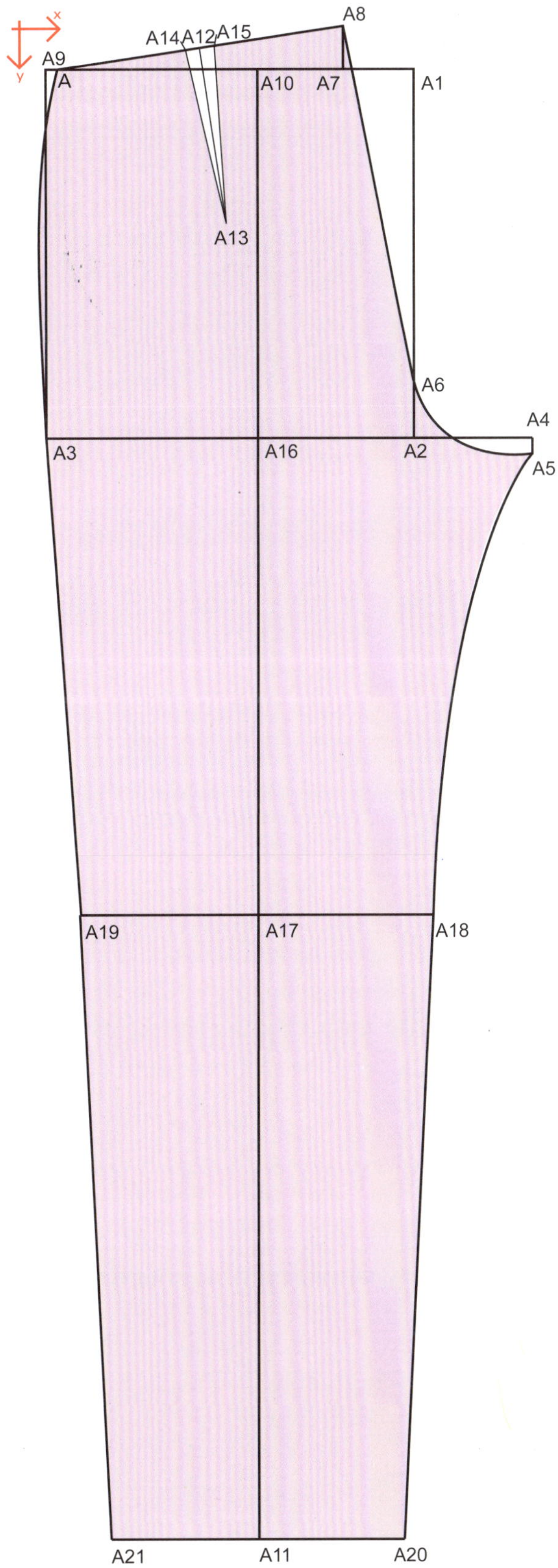

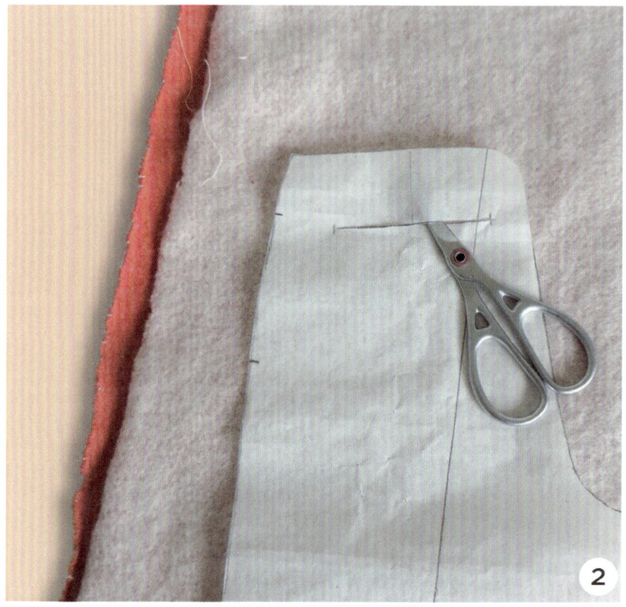

Cut out the respective patterns, without cutting the darts out: jogging bottoms are not shaped at the waist, so they do not need any darts. However, the extra width of the untailored waist can be pulled in by means of an elastic band inserted inside the waistband (1). If you decide to sew a pocket onto the back, cut the line that designates the correct position on the pattern, and then sew guide stitches inside as a reference (2).

Position the patterns on your chosen fabric, which you have folded in two, with its selvedges touching and the right side of the fabric facing inwards. As you position the paper patterns, make sure that the fold lines are exactly parallel to the selvedges of the fabric (3).

Pin the patterns to the fabric and add the seam allowances: usually 1 cm (0.39") for the entire perimeter of each pattern, and cut them out (4). You will have to cut out four pocket pouches: two for the front of the trousers and two for the back.

If you use a cut-and-sew-machine to make the trousers, you won't need to sew any guide stitches, except along the lines designating the back pockets, if there are any (5).

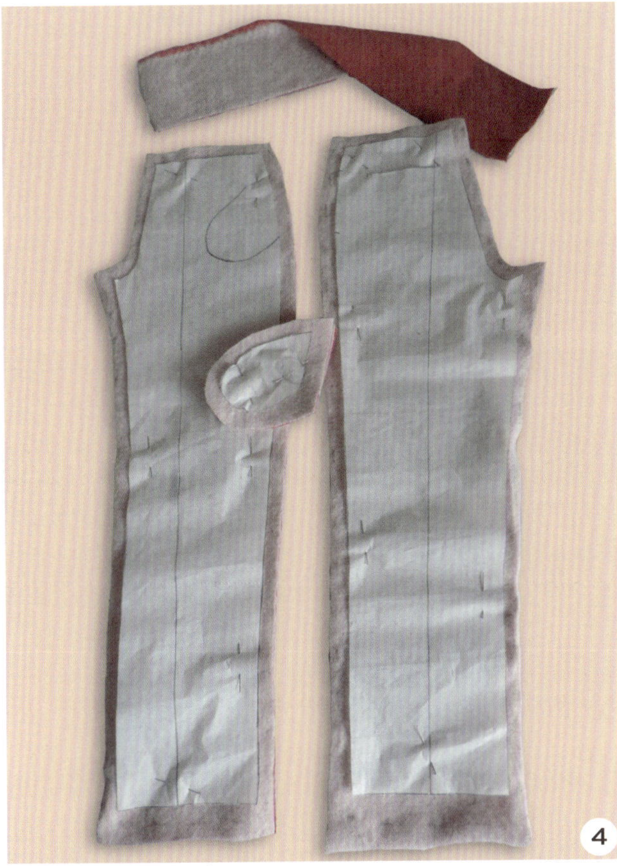
4

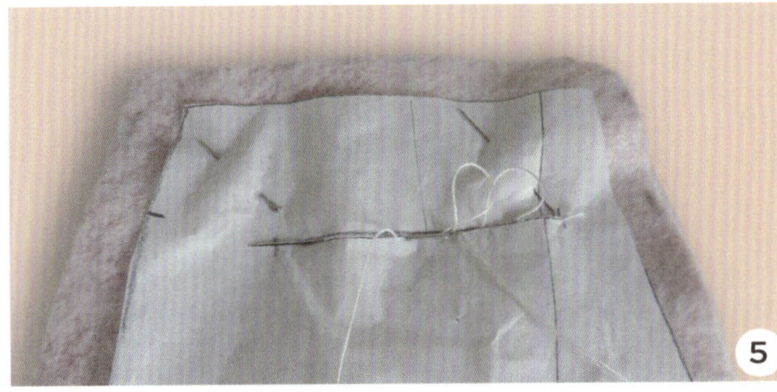
5

6

7

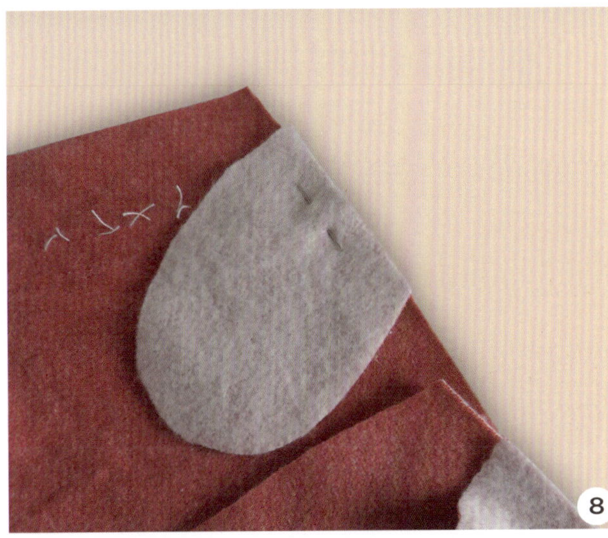
8

Use scissors to make a little cut where you want to attach the pocket pouches, both on the front and back of the trousers (6).

On each part of the trousers, attach a pocket pouch on the sides, as indicated by the cuts. The pocket pouch must be attached facing downwards and with the right side of its fabric lined up with that of the trousers (7).

Pin the pocket along the edges (8) and sew it on with the cut-and-sew-machine (9). If you have decided to attach pockets to the back of the trousers, do so before you put the front and back together.

When you make the pocket, measure the size of the zip with the tape measure (10).

On the back of the trousers, where you can see the marks left by the guide stitches, use chalk or a pencil to draw a line on the right side of the fabric that is the same length as the zip, with lateral triangles that are as wide as the teeth on the zip (11). On the wrong side of the fabric, where you have drawn the line, it is a good idea to reinforce the fabric with adhesive canvas, as seen for the welt pockets on page 196.

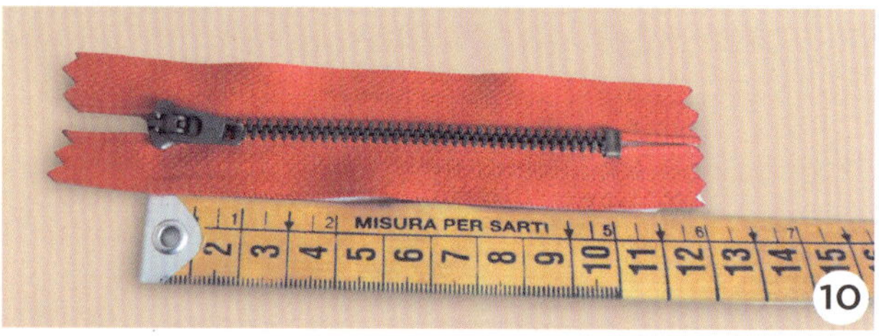

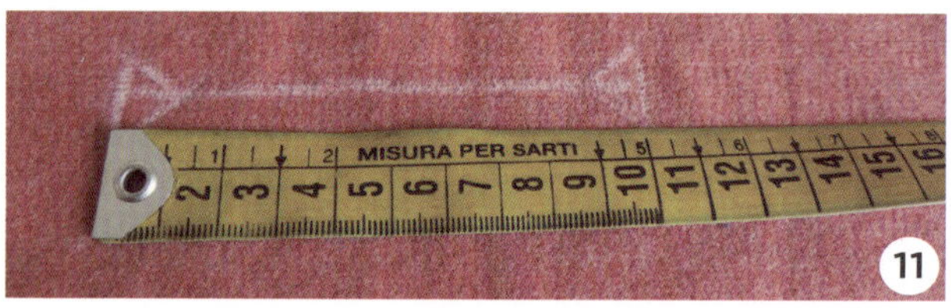

Cut along the line and the triangles you have drawn (12). Then draw and cut out pocket pouches that are the same width as the pocket width, plus a 2-cm (0.78") seam allowance, making sure they are at least 10 cm (3.93") wide (13).

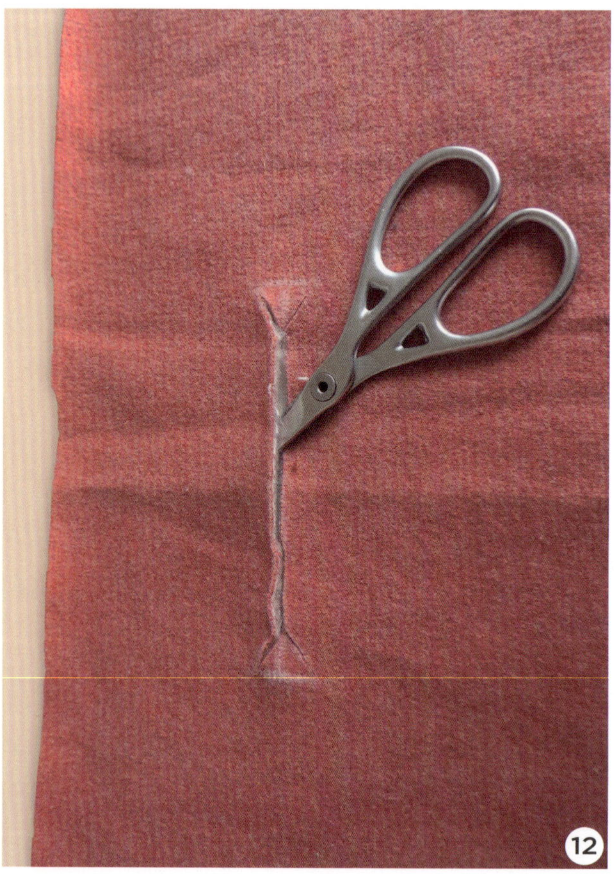

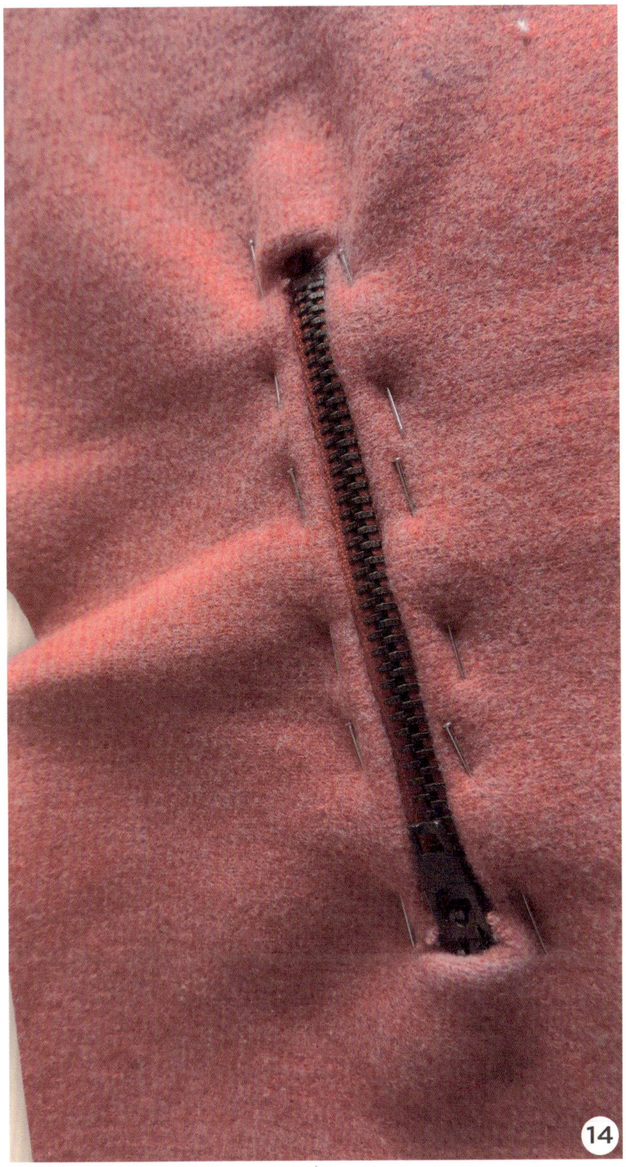

Insert the zip into the hole you have cut out, so that the tape is touching the wrong side of the fabric and is covered over, leaving only the teeth visible. Pin it in place (14).

On the wrong side of the fabric, position the two pocket pouches so that they cover up the tape of the zip. This makes sure that the seams are not visible when open and the right side of the fabric matches (15 - 16).

Sew the zip and the pocket pouches together with tacking stitches in such a way that you can sew along the edges (17).

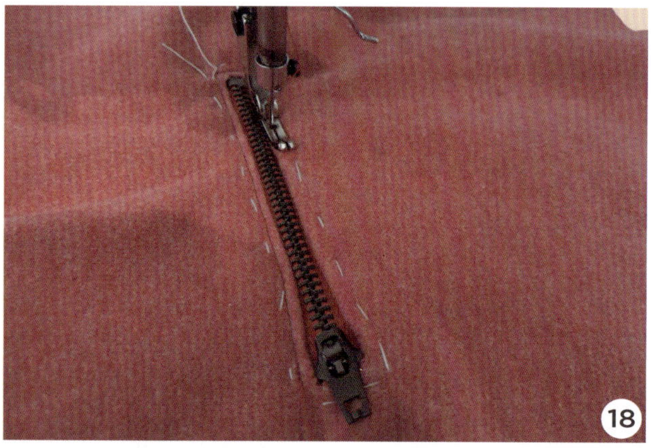

18

19

Use the special foot to sew around the zip (18). On the wrong side, join the edges of the pocket pouches together and sew them using the cut-and-sew-machine (19). Now continue to put the trousers together, joining the front parts with the back parts. Pin it together and use tacking stitches for better accuracy and then sew a seam using the cut-and-sew-machine. As you proceed to sew along the sides of the trousers, carry on along the edges of the pockets you have made, so that there is a single seam that holds all of the pieces together (20). Now put the two central pieces of the trousers together (21-22).

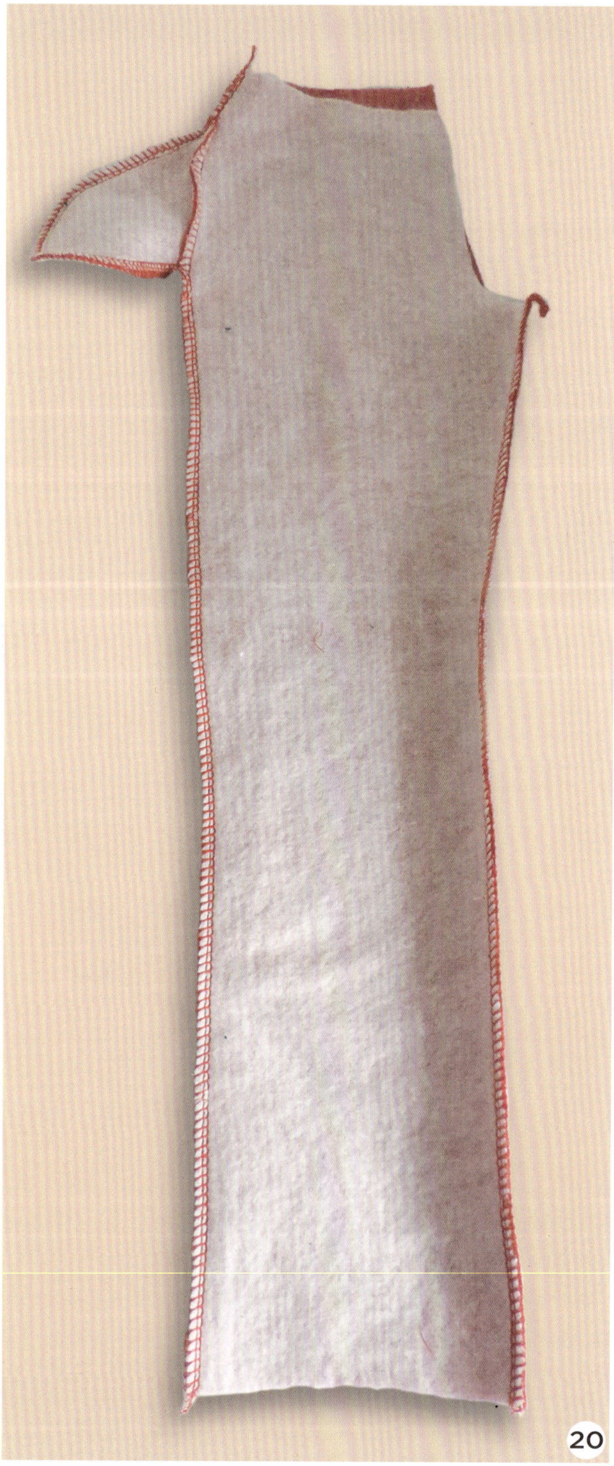

20

21

22

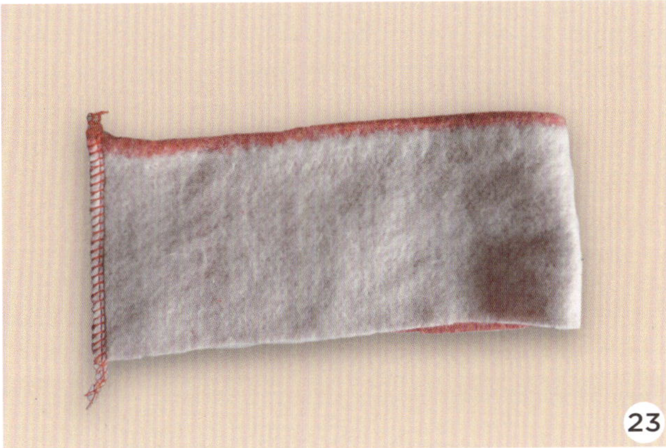

23

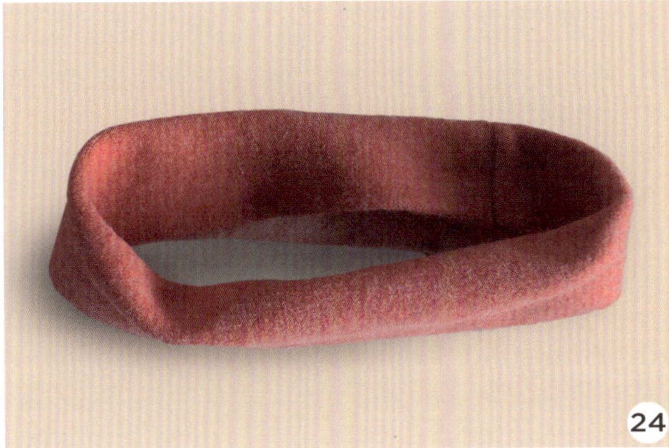

24

Make the waistband: this is just a rectangle of fabric that needs to be as long as the waist circumference of the trousers you have just made, plus 2 cm (0.78") for seam allowances, and twice as wide as the final waistband. For example: if the final waistband should be 4 cm (1.57") wide, draw it as 8 cm (3.14") wide, plus 2 cm (0.78") for seam allowances. Unlike the waistbands we have looked at so far, and since there will be an elastic band inside, this waistband should not be reinforced with adhesive canvas. Once cut, fold it with the right side of the fabric facing inwards so that it matches the edges. Sew it on with the cut-and-sew-machine (23).

Fold the waistband in two, with the outer layer of the fabric facing inwards (24) and attach it to the waist of the trousers so that its edges match up perfectly with those of the trousers. Hold it in place with pins (25) and tacking stitches for greater accuracy. Finally, sew it on using the cut-and-sew-machine, leaving a small gap for the elastic band to pass through. The seams on the waistband must match the central seam on the back of the trousers.

25

With the help of a safety pin, insert the elastic band through the small gap and slide it along the entire length until it re-emerges from the same place (26). The length of the elastic band should be a dozen centimetres shorter than your waist circumference.

Weld the edges of the elastic band with a linear machine stitch, then close up the gap using the cut-and-sew-machine. You can add a hem, like on a pair of jeans, or attach cuffs that are made from the same fabric or from jersey. To make the cuffs, draw and cut out rectangles of fabric that are as long as the circumference of the bottom of the trouser legs, plus a 2-cm (0.78") seam allowance. If the cuffs are made from stretchy jersey fabric, they must be shorter than the circumference of the bottom of the trouser legs, and twice their final width, plus a 2-cm (0.78") seam allowance (27). Proceed as you did before for the waistband (28). The seams on the cuffs must match the seams on the inside leg.

26

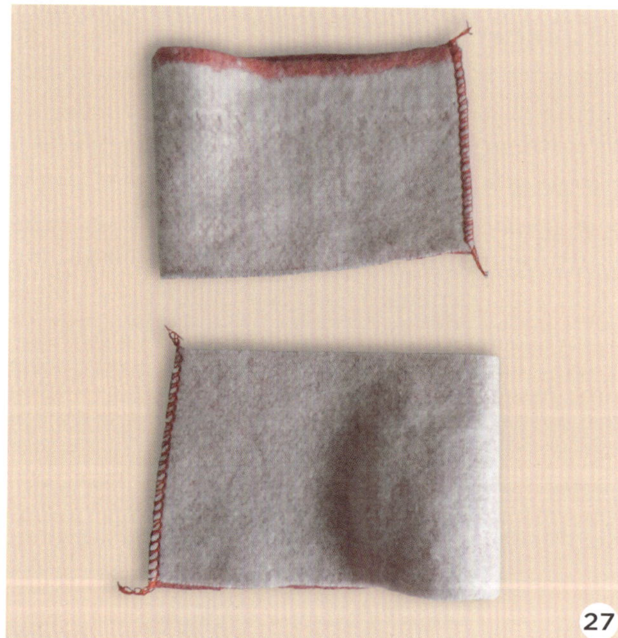

27

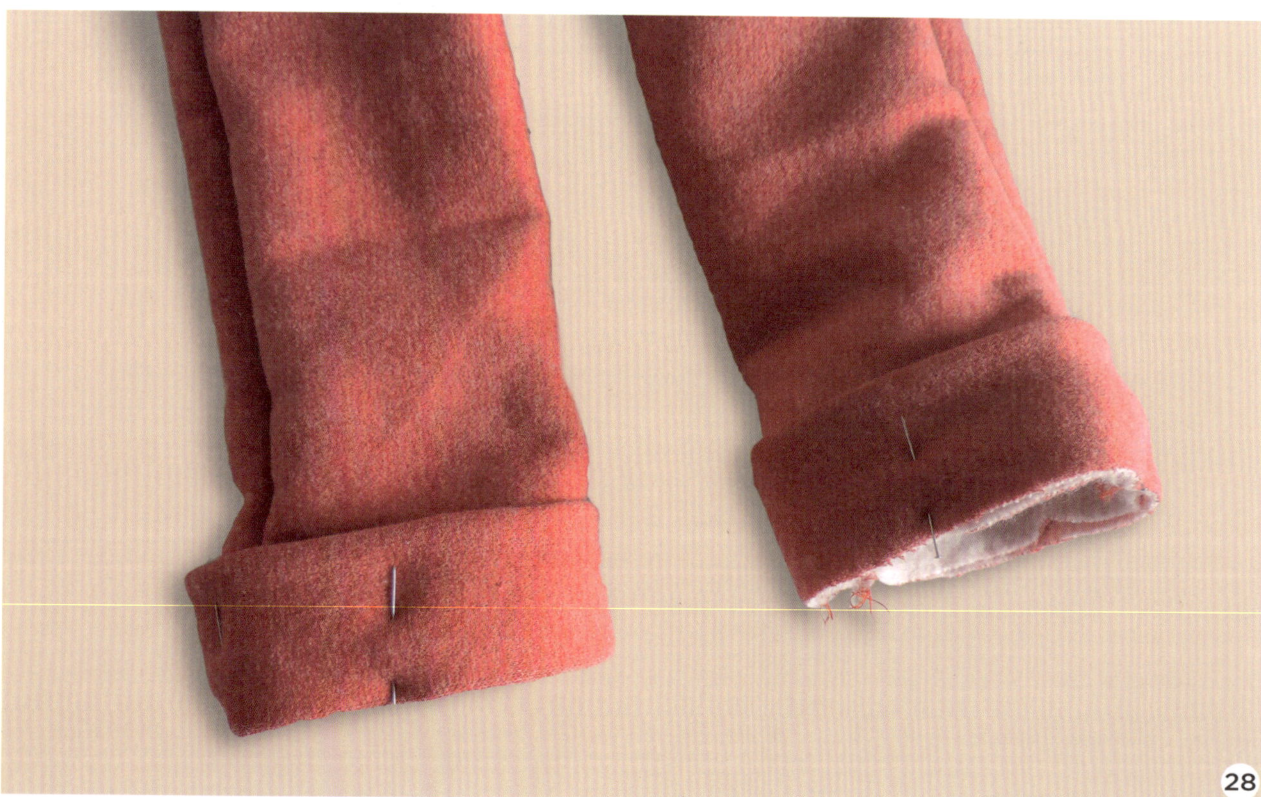

28

The mock-up trousers were made from fleece fabric. You can make the same design using jersey or technical textiles for sports clothing.

JEANS WITH PATCH POCKETS

Jeans are undoubtedly the best loved and most worn style of trousers - not just by women but also by men - because they are so practical, hard wearing and never go out of fashion. To make a pair of jeans, start by drawing the basic trouser pattern, then carefully follow the explanation and diagrams to make the necessary alterations for the kind of jeans you want to make. In this chapter, I will explain how to make a pair of jeans as well as the pockets to go with them, paying particular attention to patch pockets.

Front

- A7_A21 is the final width of the waistband (for example, 5 cm / 1.96").
- A8_A22 same as A7_A21.
- Draw a line between A21_A22 (waistband).
- A21_A23 = 4 cm (1.57").
- A24_A25 same as A21_A23.
- Draw a line between A23_A25 (the fly).
- A22_A26 = at least 8 cm (3.14") (this measurement will vary according to the style or cut of the jeans).
- A2_A27 = 10 cm (3.93") (this measurement can vary according to the type of pocket or cut of the jeans).
- Draw a line between A26_A27 (pocket).
- A26_A28 = at least 4 cm (1.57").
- Draw a line between A28_A27 to form the pocket pouch, as shown in the diagram.
- Using pencil crayons, colour in the patterns to distinguish the various sections: the legs, waistband and pockets.

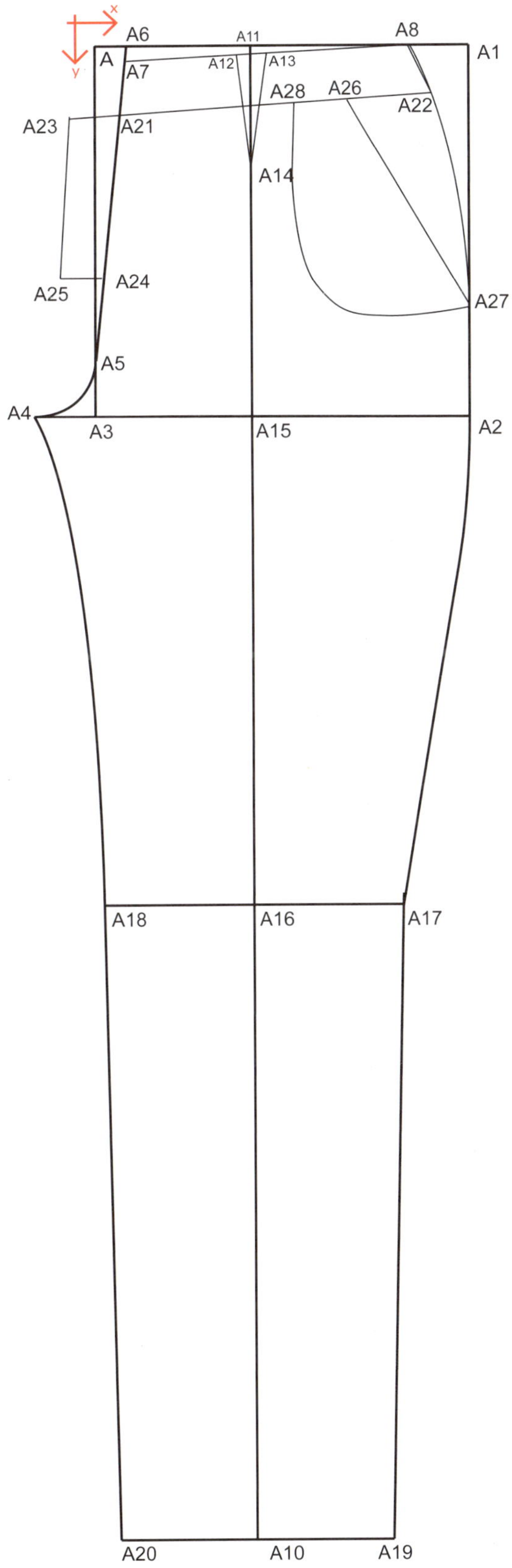

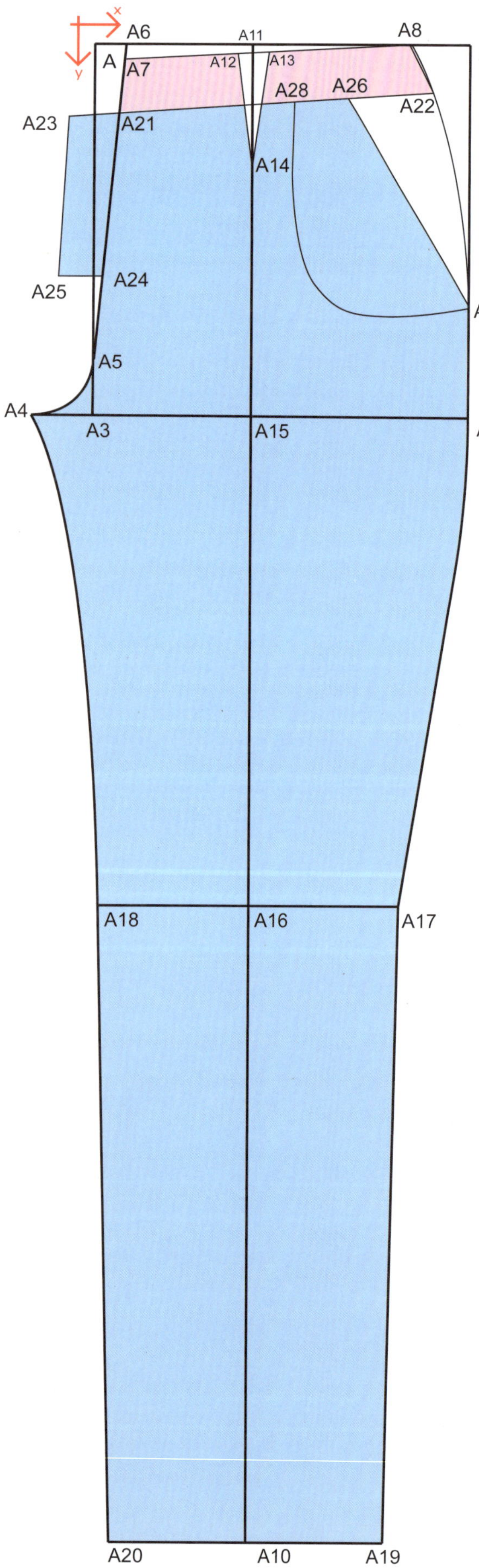

Pattern for jeans and waistband

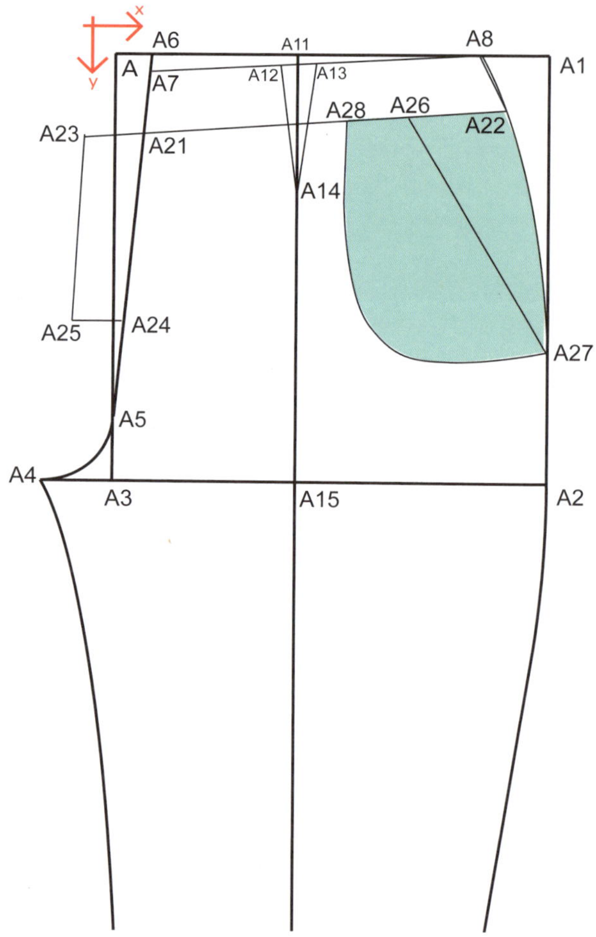

Pattern for the pocket pouch

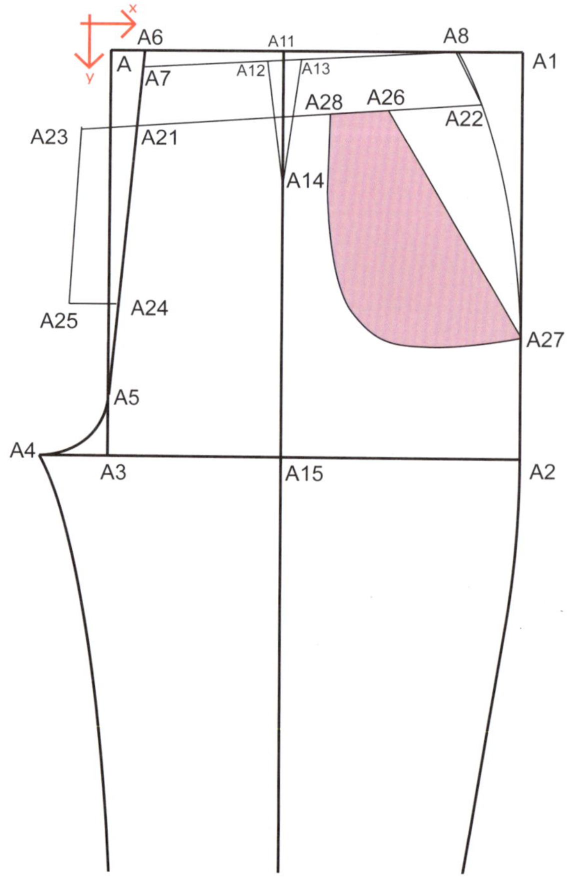

Pattern for the pocket

Back

- A_A22 is the final width of the waistband (for example, 5 cm / 1.96").
- A8_A23 same as A_A22.
- Draw a line between A22_A23 (waistband).
- A22_A24 = at least 3 cm (1.18") (this measurement can vary according to the style and design of the jeans you want to make).
- A23_A25 = at least 6 cm (2.36") (this measurement can vary according to the style and design of the jeans you want to make).
- Draw a line between A24_A25.

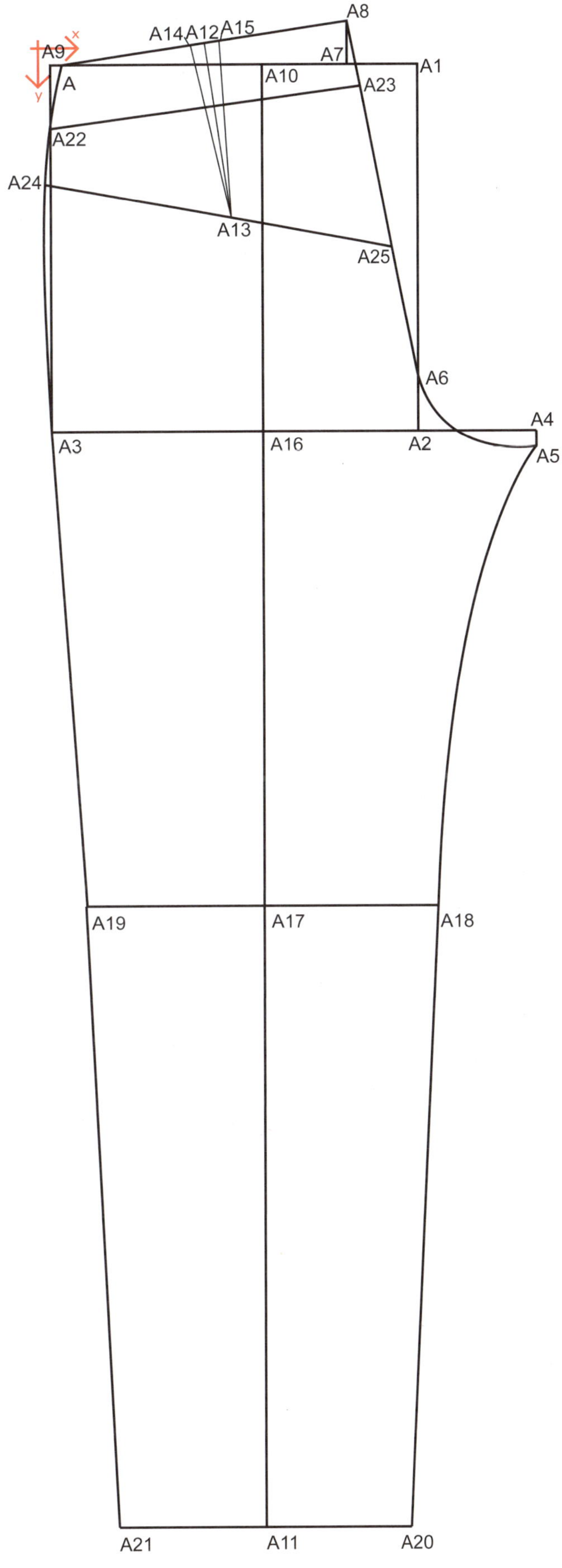

There are also patch pockets on the back.

To make these, all you need to do is draw a line on the pattern for the back of the jeans, to show where you want to put the pockets (as we did for the classic office trousers). Then, on a separate sheet, draw the patch pocket as shown in the following diagram.

- A1_A2 is the pocket width (at least 10 cm / 3.93").
- A_A3 same as A1_A2.
- A1_A8 is the width of the flap inside the pocket (at least 2 cm / 0.78").
- A2_A9 same as A1_A8.
- A8_A is the final height of the pocket (for example, 14 cm / 5.51").
- A9_A3 same as A8_A.
- A1_A4 = half of A1_A2.
- A_A5 same as A1_A4.
- Draw a line between A4_A5.
- A_A6 = 2 cm (0.78").
- A3_A7 same as A_A6.
- Join these points together and draw the pocket as shown in the diagram.
- Use a pencil crayon to identify it on the paper pattern.
- Also use pencil crayons to colour in the pattern for the back of the jeans, highlighting the various parts it is composed of.

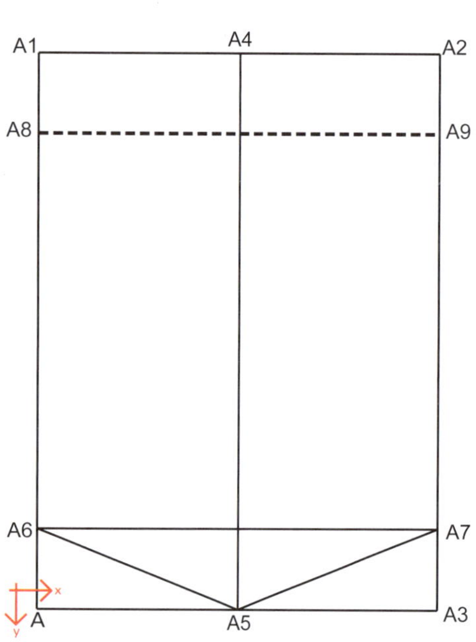

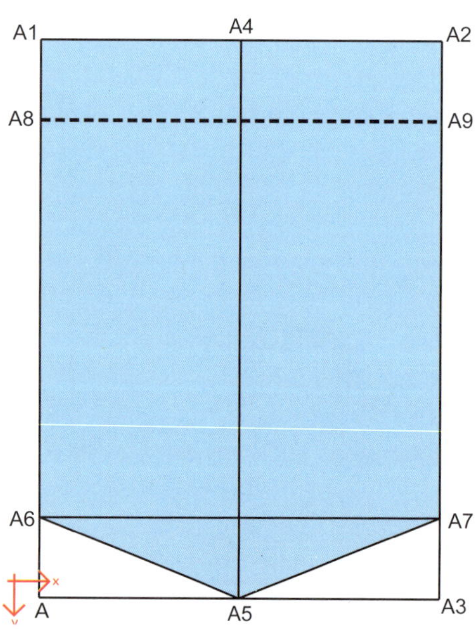

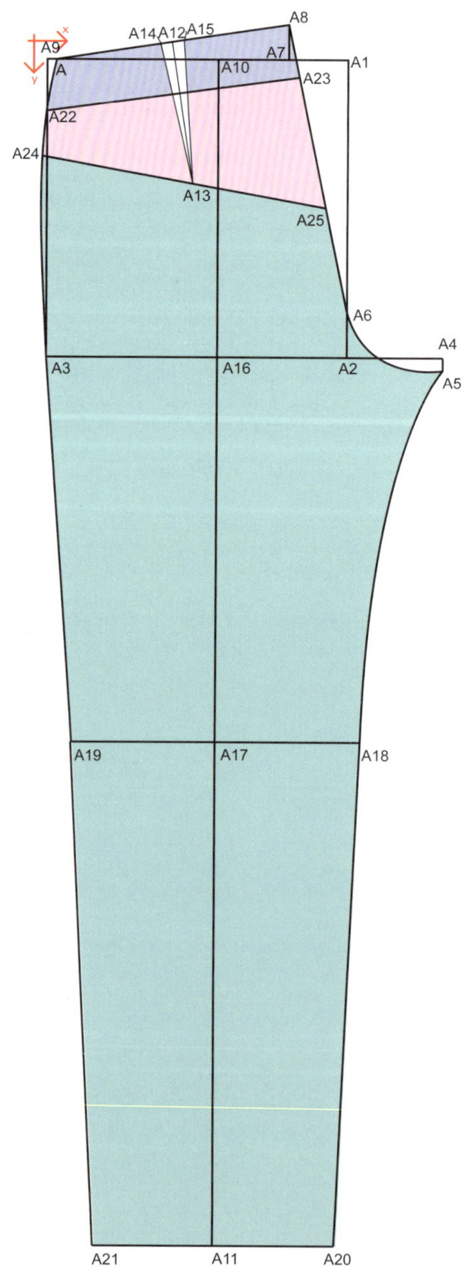

1

2

Cut out all the parts of the pattern (1), then position them on the fabric that you have folded in two, with the selvedges touching and the right side of the fabric facing inwards. Position the pattern for the front and back of the jeans so that the crease line is exactly parallel to the selvedges of the fabric. Pin the pieces together and then use chalk to mark out the seam allowances: usually 1 cm (0.39") along the waist and the pockets and central pieces on the back, 2 cm (0.78") along the sides and the middle of the front and back of the patterns, 3 cm (1.18") on the bottom. On the pattern for the waistband, close the dart; if you want to make a curved waistband, refer to the explanation on page 42.

NB: in the middle of the front of the waistband, leave a margin that is the same width as the fly, plus 1 cm (0.39") (for example, 4 cm / 1.57" + 1 cm / 0.39"); you might find it easier to draw the front of the waistband with the same width as the waist of the jeans, including the fly (2).

Cut along the markings drawn in chalk, then sew guide stitches on all sides of the jeans, with the patterns still pinned onto the fabric (3 - 4).

3

4

Once you have sewn the guide stitches, detach the patterns from the fabric, cut open the guide stitches and proceed to make the front side pockets for the jeans, as explained in the chapter on classic office trousers (5).

Jeans feature special "rib stitching" - that well-known visible seam: for this, you will need to buy special thread for denim (6) from a haberdashery. Keep in mind that most sewing machines do not support this thread if threaded through the needle.

So, in order to sew correctly with this type of thread, you only need to wrap it around the lower bobbin on the machine and thread the needle with normal yarn. To get the effect, therefore, you have to sew on the wrong side of the fabric. Alternatively, you can thread the sewing machine with a normal polyester yarn doubled up, but the result will not quite be the same. Now prepare the patch pockets for the back of the jeans.

5

6

PATCH POCKETS

Once you have pinned the paper pattern to the fabric, cut along the seam allowances (7) and sew guide stitches (8 -9). Then finish off all the edges of the pockets with a zig-zag stitch or with the cut-and-sew-machine. Turn the pocket flaps over to the wrong side of the fabric (for example, 2 cm / 0.78"), then make a double visible seam using the thread for denim (10). Still using the same thread, if you want to

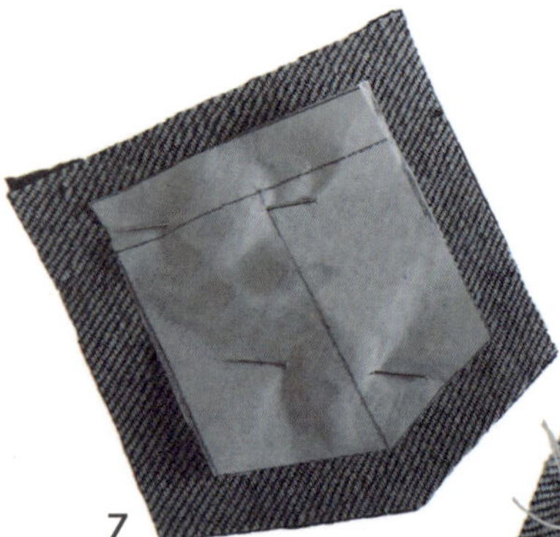

7

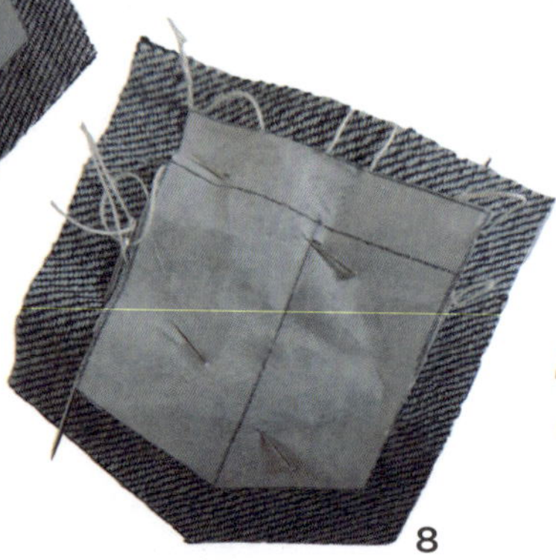

8

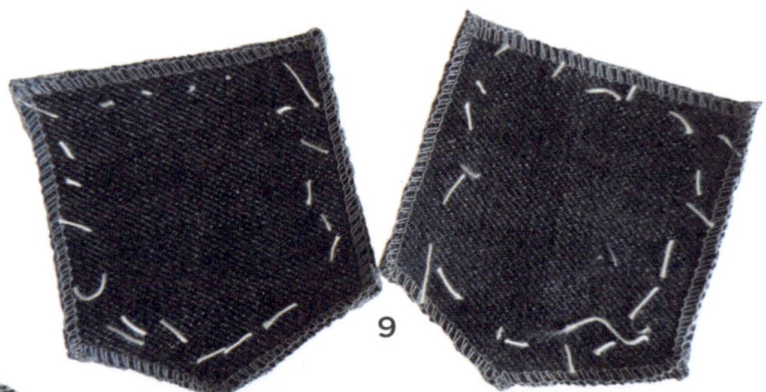

9

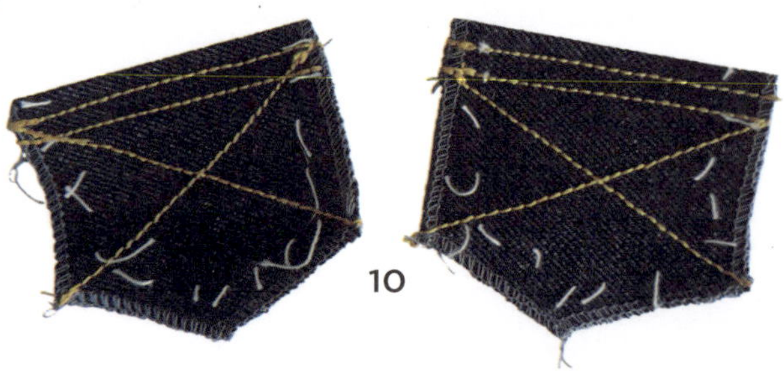

10

11

12

make fancy seams on the pockets, then fold the edges towards the wrong side of the fabric. Pin the pockets to the backs of the jeans in the desired position (11), then sew tacking stitches before sewing the seam with the special denim thread (12). Finish off all parts of the jeans with the cut-and-sew-machine or with zig-zag stitch (13).

Put the two pieces that make up the lower part of the back together so that they overlap from right to left (14). Do the same thing with the two pieces that make up the upper part of the back. Once you have

13

14

15

16

pinned the overlapping sections, sew tacking stitches for greater accuracy when you sew the double seam along the edges, using the thread for denim (15 - 16).

Always use the special thread to sew the overlapped parts together and for any sections with double stitching (17 - 18).

Now put the back and front pieces together, with the edges of the back parts overlapping the edges of the front parts along the sides. Pin the pieces together (19). For greater accuracy, sew tacking stitches and then sew a double seam using the special thread for denim (20). This procedure can also be done for the inside leg seams as an alternative to the hip seams.

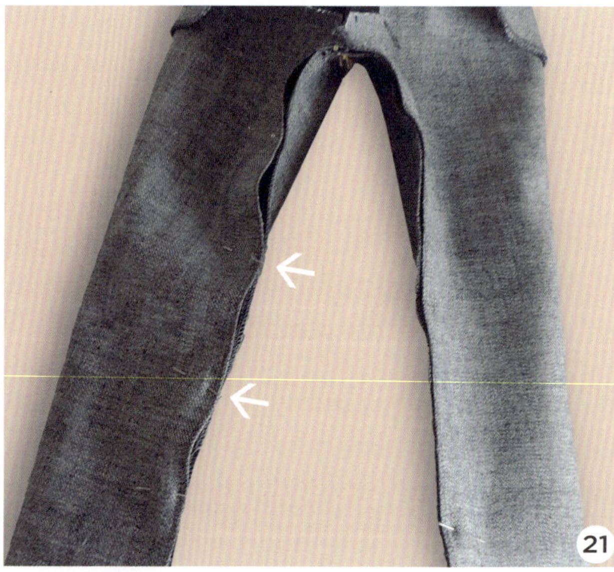

Pin together the edges of the inside leg of both the front and back (21), so that the right side of the fabric remains inside the jeans, then sew tacking stitches before sewing a linear seam with normal thread (22).

Turn the jeans inside out, so that the right side of the fabric is now on the outside, to attach the zip to the fly.

You will need a special zip that is suitable for denim jeans (23). Position the zip on the left flap of the fly first; then fold the denim back, so that the fold lines up with the teeth of the zip (24). Sew the zip on using the special foot (25). Fold the right flap of denim over the zip and pin it so that its inner edges are still pinned onto the right strip of fabric on the zip (26). Sew tacking stitches and then sew one or two visible seams, using the special thread for denim, obtaining the typical seam that is seen front and centre on jeans.

Prepare and attach the waistband, as explained on page 42 (27-28); sew a double seam on the upper part of the waistband using the thread typically used on denim jeans (29). Sew the hem using the sewing machine, as explained on page 49. Finally, attach two press studs on the waistband to complete the closure.

PATTERN FOR SKINNY-FIT ELASTICATED TROUSERS

When drawing the pattern for elasticated trousers, start by drawing the basic trouser pattern. There is no need to cut out the darts, since elasticated fabric stretches easily over the figure. You will also need to adjust the measurement of the width around the knee line and on the bottoms of the trousers, according to your measurements. To get a better understanding, look at the diagrams shown below.

Front

- A7_A8 = 1/4 of waist circumference.
- A12_A13 = 1/4 of knee circumference.
- A12_A14 same as A12_A13.
- A10_A15 = 1/4 of ankle circumference;
- A10_A16 same as A10_A15.

Back

- A9_A8 = 1/4 of waist circumference.
- A13_A14 = 1/4 of knee circumference + 1 cm (0.39").
- A13_A15 same as A13_A14.
- A11_A16 = 1/4 of ankle circumference + 1 cm (0.39").
- A11_A17 same as A11_A16.

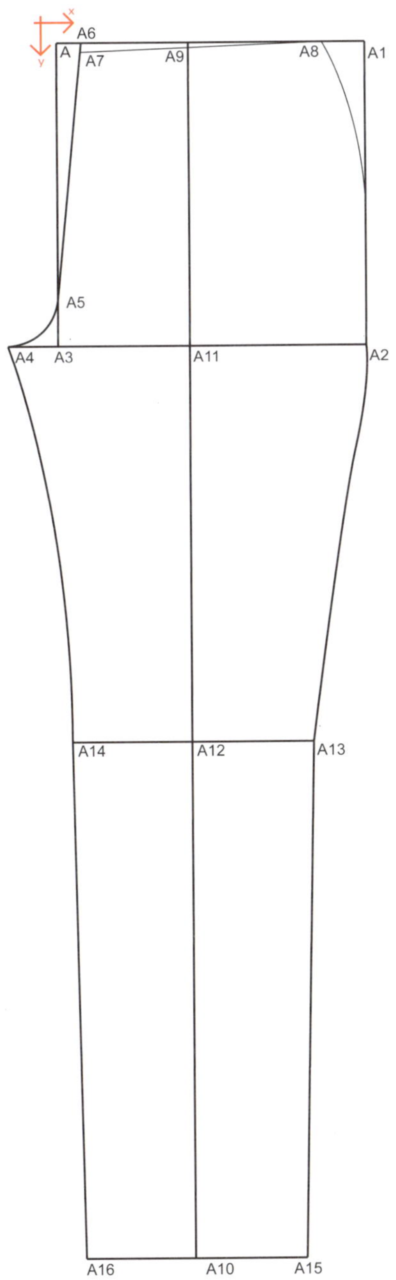

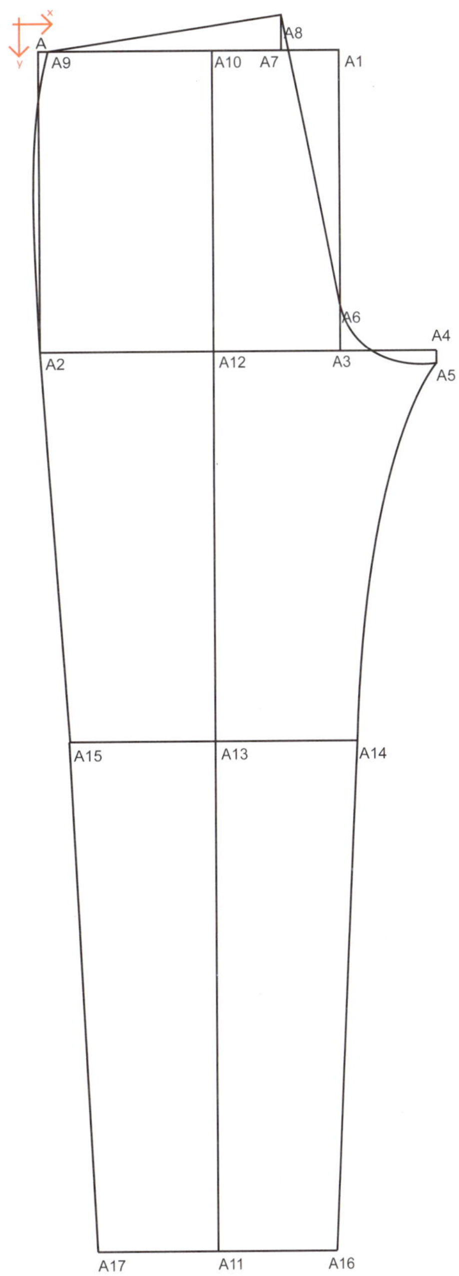

LOW-WAIST TROUSERS

All the trousers covered in this book so far have been high-waisted, however there are also some trousers with low-waists, which are usually sporty and casual designs.

Just like for the skirt, in order to lower the waist on a pair of high-waisted trousers, start by drawing the basic trouser design, then proceed as explained below.

Front

- A7_A21 the amount you want to lower the waist by (for example, 5 cm / 1.96").
- A8_A22 same as A7_A21.
- Draw a line between A21_A22.
- Using a pencil crayon, colour in the paper pattern to identify the various sections.

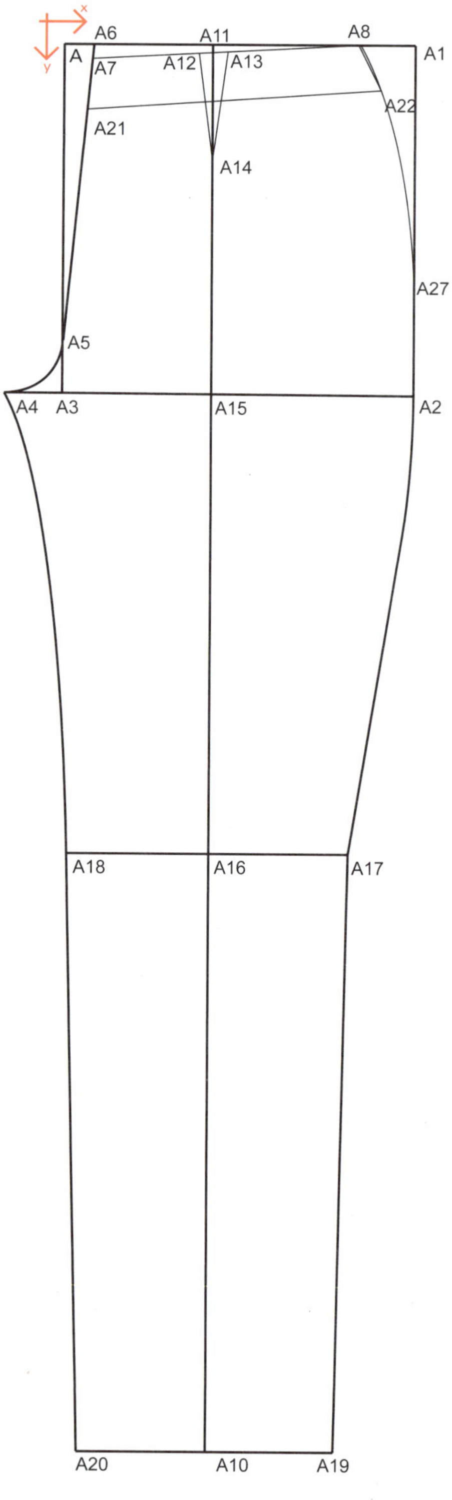

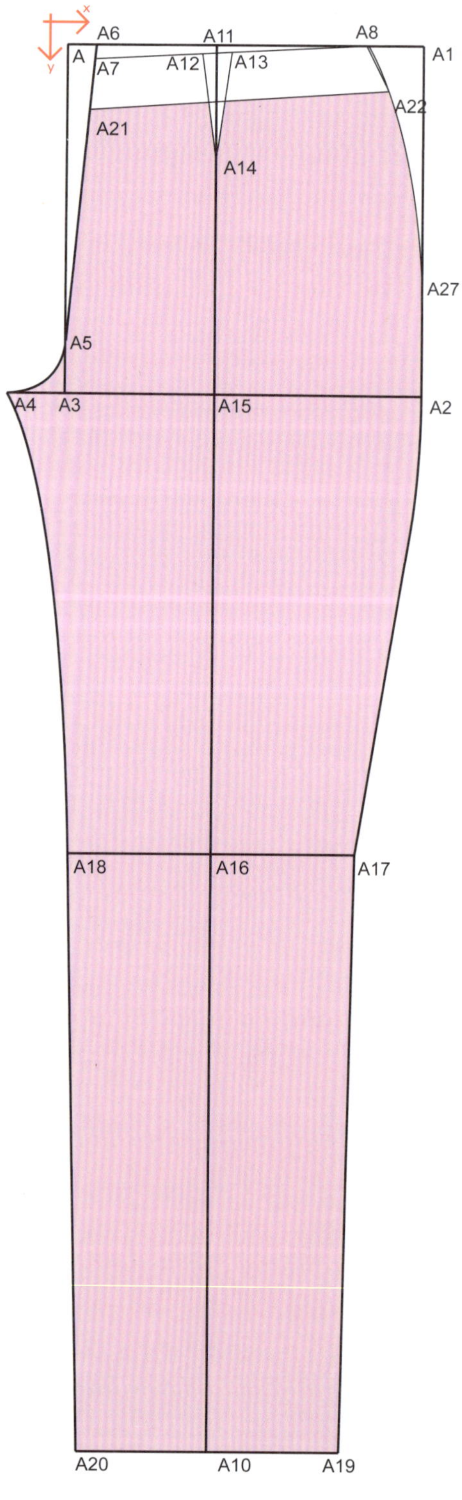

Back

- A9_A22 the amount you want to lower the waist by (for example, 5 cm / 1.96").
- A8_A23 same as A9_A22.
- Draw a line between A22_A23.
- Using a pencil crayon, colour in the paper pattern to identify the various sections.

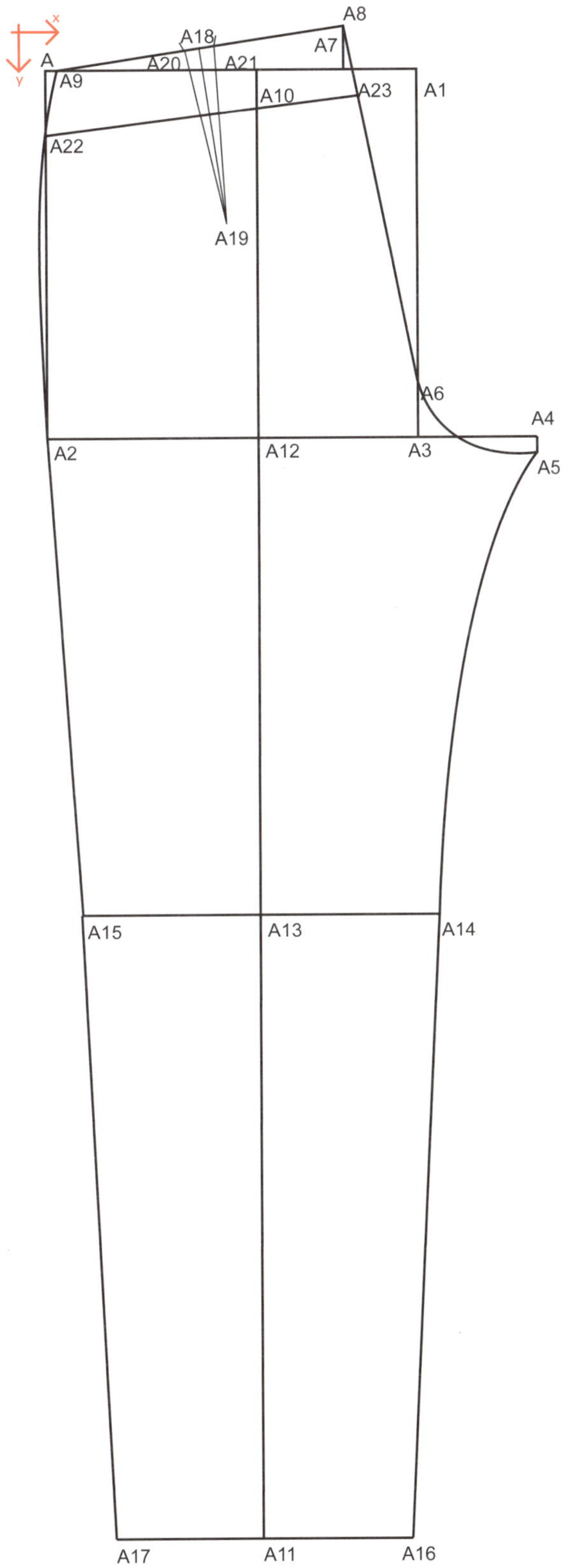

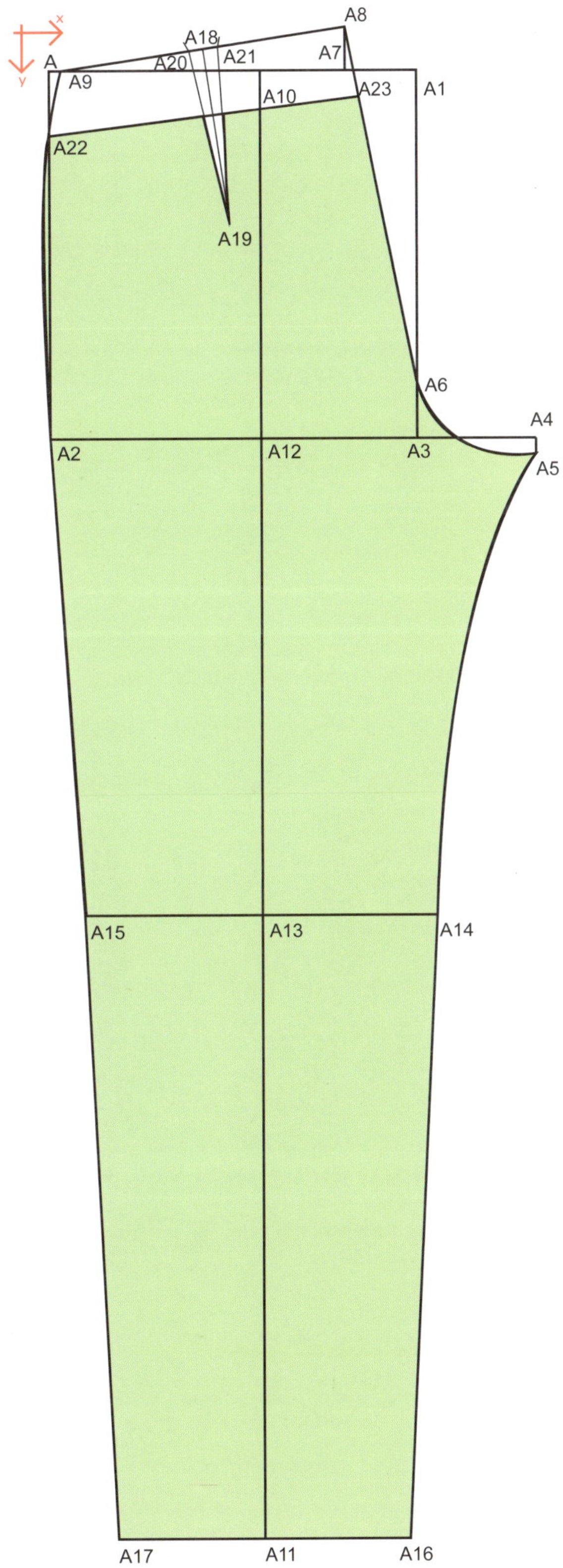

PROMOPRESS FASHION COLLECTION

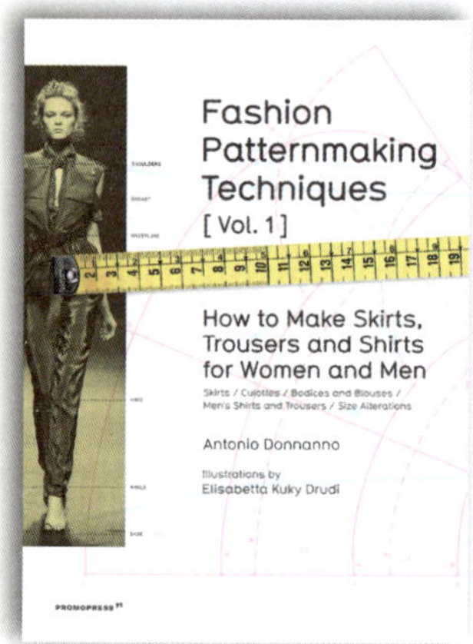

FASHION PATTERNMAKING TECHNIQUES [VOL. 1]

How to Make Skirts, Trousers and Shirts for Women and Men

Antonio Donnanno. Illustrations by Elisabetta Kuky Drudi

978-84-15967-09-5
210 x 297 mm. 256 pp.

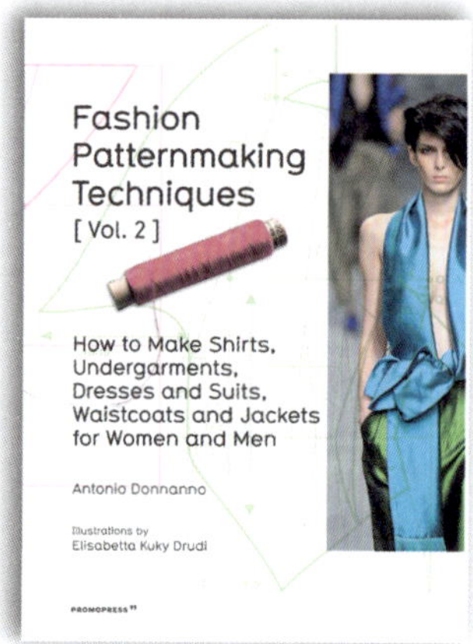

FASHION PATTERNMAKING TECHNIQUES [VOL. 2]

How to Make Skirts, Undergarments, Dresses and Suits, Waistcoats and Jackets for Women and Men

Antonio Donnanno. Illustrations by Elisabetta Kuky Drudi

978-84-15967-68-2
210 x 297 mm. 256 pp.

FASHION PATTERNMAKING TECHNIQUES [VOL. 3]

How to Make Jackets, Coats and Cloaks for Women and Men

Antonio Donnanno. Illustrations by Elisabetta Kuky Drudi

978-84-16504-18-3
210 x 297 mm. 176 pp.

FASHION PATTERNMAKING TECHNIQUES FOR CHILDREN'S CLOTHING

Dresses, Shirts, Bodysuits, Trousers, Shorts, Jackets and Coats

Antonio Donnanno. Illustrations by Claudia Ausonia Palazio

978-84-16851-14-0
210 x 297 mm. 232 pp.

FASHION PATTERNMAKING TECHNIQUES HAUTE COUTURE [VOL. 1]

Haute Couture Models, Draping Techniques, Decorations

Antonio Donnanno

978-84-16504-66-4
210 x 297 mm. 256 pp.

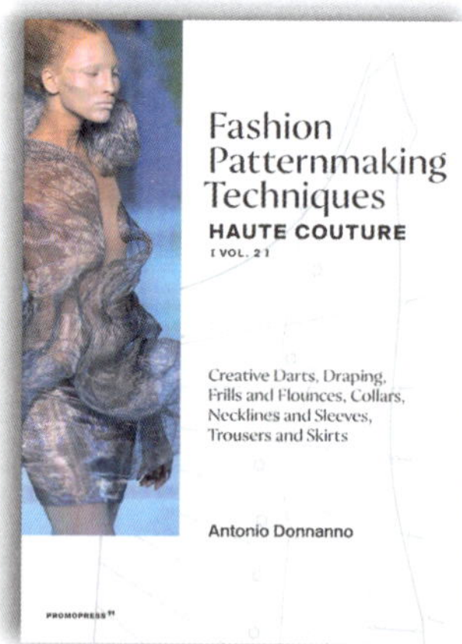

FASHION PATTERNMAKING TECHNIQUES HAUTE COUTURE [VOL. 2]

Creative Darts, Draping, Frills and Flounces, Collars, Necklines and Sleeves, Trousers and Shirts

Antonio Donnanno

978-84-17412-38-8
210 x 297 mm. 200 pp.

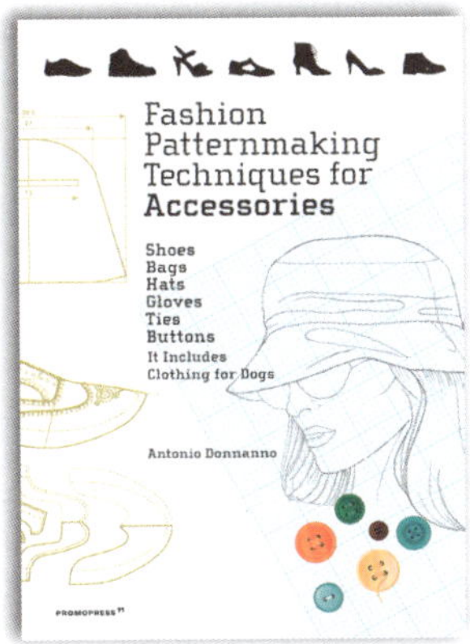

FASHION PATTERNMAKING TECHNIQUES FOR ACCESSORIES
Shoes, Bags, Hats, Gloves, Ties, Buttons. It Includes Clothing for Dogs
Antonio Donnanno

978-84-16851-61-4
210 x 297 mm. 240 pp.

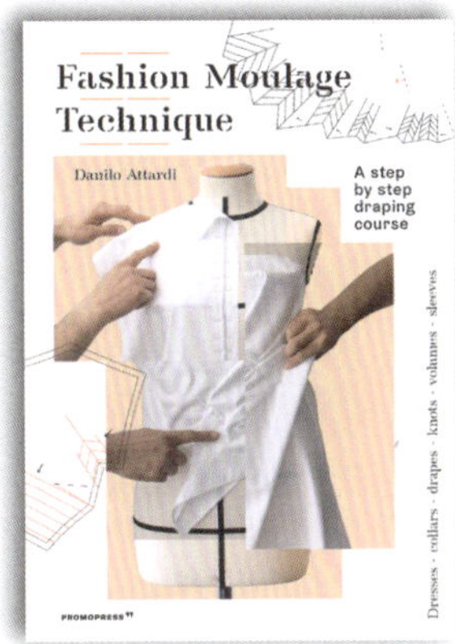

FASHION MOULAGE TECHNIQUE
A Step by Step Draping Course
Danilo Attardi

978-84-17412-12-8
195 x 285 mm. 192 pp.

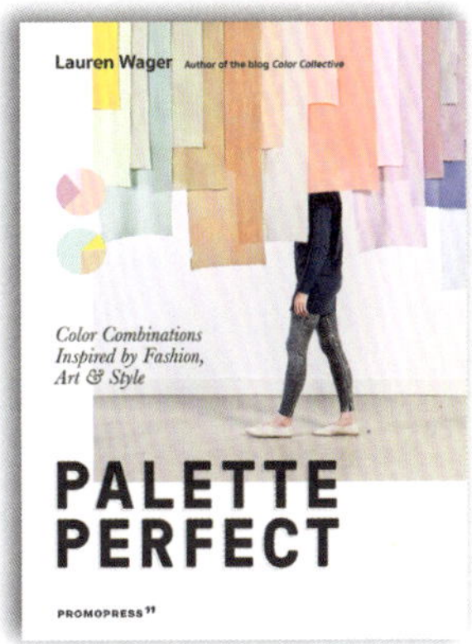

PALETTE PERFECT
Color Combinations Inspired by Fashion, Art & Style
Lauren Wager

978-84-15967-90-3
148 x 210 mm. 304 pp.

FASHION ILLUSTRATION & DESIGN
Methods & Techniques for Achieving Professional Results
Manuela Brambatti

978-84-16851-06-5
215 x 300 mm. 240 pp.

FASHION ILLUSTRATION & DESIGN ACCESSORIES
Shoes, Bags, Hats, Belts, Gloves and Glasses
Manuela Brambatti and Fabio Menconi

978-84-17412-64-7
210 x 297 mm. 264 pp.

FASHION DRAWING COURSE
From Human Figure to Fashion Illustration
Juan Baeza

978-84-15967-06-4
210 x 297mm. 208 pp.

FASHION DETAILS
4,000 Drawings
Elisabetta Kuky Drudi

978-84-17412-68-5
195 x 285 mm. 384 pp.

Second Edition in 2020

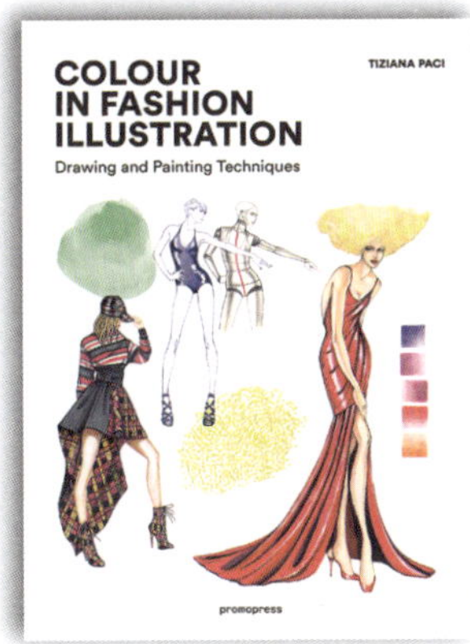

COLOUR IN FASHION ILLUSTRATION
Drawing and Painting Techniques
Tiziana Paci

978-84-16851-59-1
215 x 287 mm. 320 pp.

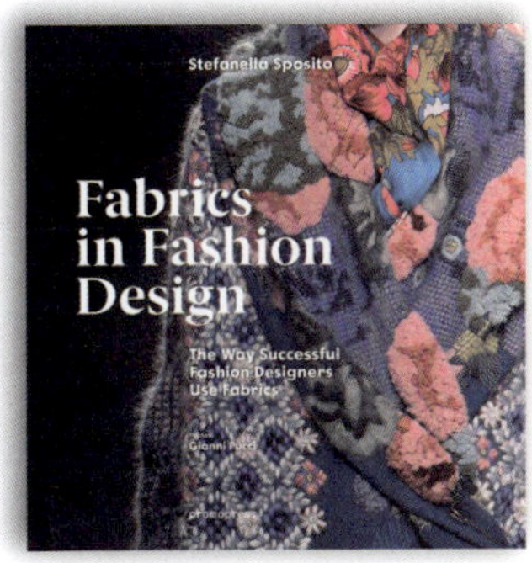

FABRICS IN FASHION DESIGN
The Way Successful Fashion Designers Use Fabrics
Stefanella Sposito. Photos by Gianni Pucci

978-84-16851-28-7
225 x 235 mm. 336 pp.